The Firide
to Exchnds
and Ind Funds

PEARSON

At Pearson, we believe in learning – all kinds of learning for all kinds of people. Whether it's at home, in the classroom or in the workplace, learning is the key to improving our life chances.

That's why we're working with leading authors to bring you the latest thinking and the best practices, so you can get better at the things that are important to you. You can learn on the page or on the move, and with content that's always crafted to help you understand quickly and apply what you've learned.

If you want to upgrade your personal skills or accelerate your career, become a more effective leader or more powerful communicator, discover new opportunities or simply find more inspiration, we can help you make progress in your work and life.

Pearson is the world's leading learning company. Our portfolio includes the Financial Times, Penguin, Dorling Kindersley, and our educational business, Pearson International.

Every day our work helps learning flourish, and wherever learning flourishes, so do people.

To learn more please visit us at: www.pearson.com/uk

The Financial Times Guide to Exchange Traded Funds and Index Funds

How to Use Tracker Funds in Your Investment Portfolio

Second edition

David Stevenson

PEARSON

Harlow, England • London • New York • Boston • San Francisco • Toronto • Sydney • Auckland • Singapore • Hong Kong
Tokyo • Seoul • Taipei • New Delhi • Cape Town • São Paulo • Mexico City • Madrid • Amsterdam • Munich • Paris • Milan

PEARSON EDUCATION LIMITED

Edinburgh Gate
Harlow CM20 2JE
Tel: +44 (0)1279 623623
Fax: +44 (0)1279 431059
Website: www.pearson.com/uk

First published in Great Britain in 2010
Second edition 2012

© Pearson Education Limited 2010, 2012

The right of David Stevenson to be identified as author of this work has been asserted by him in accordance with the Copyright, Designs and Patents Act 1988.

Pearson Education is not responsible for the content of third-party internet sites.

ISBN: 978-0-273-76940-8

British Library Cataloguing-in-Publication Data
A catalogue record for this book is available from the British Library

Library of Congress Cataloging-in-Publication Data
A catalog record for this book is available from the Library of Congress

All rights reserved. No part of this publication may be reproduced, stored in a retrieval system, or transmitted in any form or by any means, electronic, mechanical, photocopying, recording or otherwise, without either the prior written permission of the publisher or a licence permitting restricted copying in the United Kingdom issued by the Copyright Licensing Agency Ltd, Saffron House, 6–10 Kirby Street, London EC1N 8TS.
This book may not be lent, resold, hired out or otherwise disposed of by way of trade in any form of binding or cover other than that in which it is published, without the prior consent of the Publishers.

The Financial Times. With a worldwide network of highly respected journalists, *The Financial Times* provides global business news, insightful opinion and expert analysis of business, finance and politics. With over 500 journalists reporting from 50 countries worldwide, our in-depth coverage of international news is objectively reported and analysed from an independent, global perspective. To find out more, visit www.ft.com/pearsonoffer.

10 9 8 7 6 5 4
18

Typeset in 9pt Stone Serif by 30
Printed and bound in Great Britain by Ashford Colour Press Ltd, Gosport, Hampshire

About the author

David Stevenson is a columnist for the *Financial Times Weekend* edition, and authors the *Adventurous Investor* section where he writes about everything from investing in Mongolia through to using ETFs in your portfolio. He's also a columnist for the *Investors Chronicle* (based around his SIPP) and before that was a columnist for *Citywire*. David writes extensively about ETFs for the *Financial Times* and has developed a series of Master Portfolios that make use of index tracking funds for the *Investors Chronicle*. He is the author of *Investing for Income* and *Smarter Stock Picking*, both published by FT Publishing.

Contents

About the author / v
Acknowledgements / xi
Foreword by Matthew Vincent / xv

1 Introduction / 1
Welcome to the revolution – Investing 2.0 / Why asset class investing will change the way we invest / The believers / The fall and decline of the active fund manager / Don't trust the manager / Active fund management costs more / CMH – the Costs Matter Hypothesis / The remorseless rise of the indexers / Why you need to use index tracking funds in your portfolio and how this book can help you / Building your portfolio / Full circle

2 A quick primer on the theory – or how we got here / 19
Taking a random walk on the wild side / Efficient markets, rational actors? / The critics / More risk, greater returns / The rise of fundamentals-based index investing / The efficient markets purists' counter attack / A middle way – the reality of relatively efficient markets / Building the perfect index

3 Structuring the revolution / 44
Building the perfect index – the FTSE 100? / Putting it all together in an index fund / Capturing the index / The rise of ETFs / Defining ETFs / The European alternative: synthetic replication / An ETF in action / Stock lending: smoothing out returns? / Phenomenal growth worldwide / The future / Understand what you invest in!

4 Investing in commodities using index funds / 116
How to invest using index tracking funds / Spot prices v the futures index / The main commodity index providers / Composite or not? / The different types of returns on offer from ETCs / The risks of investing in commodities

5 The fiddly detail – risks, caveats and the indices / 138
A growing market / Choosing an ETF / Why might passive be suitable? / Why use ETFs instead of index funds? / Funds, notes, commodities or products? / How does the fund track? / How safe is my tracker? / Investment cost is a key factor / In summary

6 The new fundamental indexing revolution / 153

The rise of the fundamentalists / What are the choices? / Understand what you are buying into with fundamental trackers / Fundamental indexing: an insider's perspective / What is wrong with conventional indexing? / Is there a better way to index? / Book value / Profit and loss / Dividends / Single-measure or blended, historic or forecast data / The runners and riders / Dimensional Fund Advisors / Wisdom Tree / Research Affiliates / Fundamental Tracker Investment Management / Why fundamental funds?

7 On portfolios / 186

Introduction / What's the meaning of life? / Why invest? / A passive portfolio – why it matters? / Risk / Asset allocation / More on fixed interest / What about equity diversification? / Timing your investment in the markets / Rebalancing / Conclusion

8 Big theme investing and index funds / 209

The business cycle / As themes go by … / Waves not bubbles / 'It's better to travel than arrive': momentum investing works / Diversify / Globalisation / International diversification works, too / The big themes of the next decades? / Create your own themes

9 Active portfolios using ETFs / 223

Technical analysis and ETFs / Using technical analysis to determine price entry / Using technical analysis to determine stops / Using technical analysis to determine price targets / Using technical analysis for currency, bond and commodity ETFs / Six golden rules

10 Putting it all together / 238

Q1: To rebalance or not to rebalance? Should I constantly rebalance my portfolio? / Q2: The consensus seems to be to buy and hold over the long term. Does that mean I should never attempt to time the market? / Q3: I'm worried by the volatility of equities. Are shares really worth the extra risk? / Q4: Should I only use index tracking funds to build my portfolio? / Q5: How do I actually build a portfolio? Should I keep it simple? / Keeping it really, really simple and lazy / How's your lifecycle? / The all-in-one fund / Using trackers as part of a wider investment process for advisers / Summary

11 The master portfolios / 285

1 The Global Growth Portfolio / 2 The Low Risk Portfolio / 3 The Income Portfolio / The other master portfolios / 4 The Mid Risk Portfolio / 5 The Adventurous Portfolio / What do I do next? Where do the Essential 25 fit in? / Simple, lazy portfolios from *PortfolioReview*

Appendix: The Essential 25 / 325
FTSE 100 – UK Equities / Featured ETFs / Featured unit trusts / FTSE All Share / FTSE 250 – UK Mid Caps / FTSE All Stocks Gilt / FTSE Small Cap / FTSE World exc UK / DJ EuroStoxx 50 – European Shares / Money Market Funds / MSCI Emerging Markets / Japan – TOPIX, MSCI Japan and Nikkei 225 / DJ-UBS Agriculture / FTSE UK Dividend Plus / Comments / S&P Global Water / Global Property – FTSE NAREIT Developed Markets (Global) Property Index Series / China – HSCEI and MSCI / S&P Global Infrastructure Index / MSCI Latin America / MSCI World Islamic Index / S&P Global Forestry and Timber / S&P Global Clean Energy / S&P 500 / S&P Select Frontier Markets / Brent Oil / Gold / iBoxx Sterling Corporate Bonds

References / 459

Index / 467

Acknowledgements

Over the last few months ETFs and index tracking funds have become something of an obsession, encouraging in me something of the anorak – many a dinner has started with 'I bet you didn't know there's an ETF that tracks . . . .'. Fill in the missing exotic asset class or market and then imagine the pained look on the face of the person opposite me. Precisely because of this anorak-like behaviour I think it's important I acknowledge the patience and support of my editor at the FT, Matthew Vincent, who was also kind enough to write the Foreword for this book. I sense that a curry or two might be in order as part payment for his support!

I'd also like to thank Pearson Education's Chris Cudmore, who was very patient with me – we first discussed this proposal a great many moons ago and Chris has always been enormously positive in steering this project away from the inside of my head into hard copy.

The various contributors to this book also deserve a huge vote of thanks. James Norton at Evolve Financial Planning has been on the receiving end of much of that obsessive lunchtime chatter about ETFs, as has Fundamental's Rob Davies, although both I suspect are as equally fascinated by index funds as I am. Much the same could be said for Dan Norman of TCF who's a real treasure trove of information and analysis on ETFs. Dr Stephen Barber from stockbrokers Selftrade manages to keep a slightly more discreet distance from we ETF obsessives, rightly recommending a broader look at the investment universe, and again I owe many thanks, as I do to Stockcube's Mark Glowrey and Tarquin Coe.

Finally I'd also like to thank my old friend Dr Mike Mason, who has had the patience and fortitude to feign an interest in this book even though it's absolutely not about anything Green or world saving. And most importantly of all to Vanessa and the mob, Rebecca and Zac plus Jake and Harvey. Oh yes, and Mum!

Publisher's acknowledgements

We are grateful to the following for permission to reproduce copyright material:

Figures

Figure 2.1 from www.dartmouth.edu/~kfrench; Figures page 325, page 331, page 335, page 338, page 346, page 351, page 356, page 364, page 376, page 379, page 382, page 391, page 397, page 400, page 404, page 409, page 414, page 419, page 423, page 428, page 437, page 443, page 448, page 451, 3.1, 3.9, 6.1, 6.2, 10.2, 11.1 from David Stevenson; Figure 3.12 from State Street Global Advisors; Figure 5.1 from *Bank of England Financial Stability Report (June): Section 3 Risks to UK banks from the international financial system*, Bank of England (2010) page 41, Chart B; Figure 6.3 from *S&P Global Strategies Quantitative Analysis 1st Quarter 2010 report*, Standard and Poor's (2010) page 10; Figures 7.1, 7.2, 7.3, 7.4 from Evolve Financial Planning; Figures 9.1, 9.2, 9.3, 9.4, 9.5, 9.6, 9.7, 9.8, 9.9, 9.10 from www.investorsintelligence.com, Stockcube plc; Figure 10.1 from *Yes, You Can Supercharge Your Portfolio! Six Steps for Investing Success in the 21st Century*, New Beginnings Press (Stein, B. and DeMuth, P. 2008); Figure 10.3 from Idzorek, Tom, Lifetime Asset Allocations: Methodologies for Target Maturity Funds, 11/02/2008, Ibbotson Associates Research Report (http://corporate.morningstar.com/us/documents/Indexes/TgtMaturityMeth.pdf)

Tables

Tables 3.2, 3.3, 3.4, 3.5, 3.6 from Vanguard, https://personal.vanguard.com/us/funds/snapshot?FundId=0040, © The Vanguard Group, Inc., used with permission; Tables 3.20, 3.22, 3.23 adapted from http://www.direxionshares.com/etfs; Table 3.24 adapted from http://www.etfsecurities.com/; Table 4.1 from *Facts and Fantasies about Commodity Futures*, Yale ICF Working Paper No. 04-20 (Gorton, Gary B. and Rouwenhorst, K. Geert) Table 2; Tables 4.7, 4.8 from www.efficientfrontier.com; Table 6.5 from Vanguard, www.vanguard.co.uk, © The Vanguard Group, Inc., used with permission; Tables 6.6, 6.7 from http://themunrofund.com/; Table 7.1 after *Barclays Equity Gilt Study*, Barclays Capital (2011); Tables 7.2, 7.3, 7.4, 7.5 from Evolve Financial Planning; Tables 7.2, 7.3, 7.4, 7.5 adapted from Evolve Financial Planning; Table 9.1 from www.investorsintelligence.com, Stockcube plc; Table 10.3 from *The Active-Passive Debate: Bear Market Performance*, Vanguard Investment Counseling & Research (Philips, Christopher B. 2009) Figure 1, https://institutional.vanguard.com/iwe/pdf/ICRIBM.pdf, © The Vanguard Group, Inc., used with permission; Tables

10.4, 10.5, 10.6 from www.kirkreport.com/resources/lazyportfolios.html; Table on page 317 from *Inflation hedging for long-term investors*, IMF Working Paper WP 09/90 (Attié, Alexander P. and Roache, Shaun K. 2009) Table 2; Table on page 319 from *Inflation hedging for long-term investors*, IMF Working Paper WP 09/90 (Attié, Alexander P. and Roache, Shaun K. 2009) Table 4.

Text

Extract on page 11 from 'The Relentless Rules of Humble Arithmetic', *Financial Analysts Journal*, Nov/Dec (Bogle, John 2005), Copyright 2005, CFA Institute. Reproduced and republished from *Financial Analysts Journal* with permission from CFA Institute. All rights reserved.; Extract on page 121 adapted from www.efficientfrontier.com.

In some instances we have been unable to trace the owners of copyright material, and we would appreciate any information that would enable us to do so.

Foreword

Shortly after 4pm on 11 May 1997, Garry Kasparov further furrowed his customarily furrowed brow. He then shook his head in a rare display of apparent disbelief. He desultorily played bishop takes rook on e7. Seconds later, he rose from his chair, stretched out his arms, and strode away from the table. The world chess champion had resigned in the decisive sixth game of his challenge match against IBM's super computer, Deep Blue. For the first time, man had lost to machine.

To chess players, and to programmers in the field of artificial intelligence, this was a seismic event. To chess-playing investors, however, it was arguably to be expected – because, in the field of investment management, computer-run index tracking funds had been outperforming humans for years.

In a study of the returns from UK equity unit trusts and open-ended investment companies (OEICs) between April 1975 and December 2002, Keith Cuthbertson, Dirk Nitzsche and Niall O'Sullivan of London's Cass Business School found that only 2 percent of these actively managed funds outperformed their benchmark indices. Nor is this a peculiarly UK failing. Over the years, similar academic research has come to a similar conclusion: both the average US and UK fund manager consistently fails to beat a comparable benchmark index.

So it is no surprise that index-tracking exchange traded funds (ETFs) – for which computer models, rather than fallible humans, select stocks to sample or replicate index performance – are now a major growth industry. In the US, ETF manager Vanguard has conducted its own research to support its business model. It found that only 'a small percentage – 7 percent – of actively managed balanced funds have been able to consistently outperform their policy benchmarks'. It now manages approximately $1 trillion of investors' money and – with only an IT department rather than legions of fund managers to pay – it charges these investors an average of just 0.2 percent a year. These facts are not unconnected. Market performance, and market forces, will out.

Vanguard launched its first index trackers for UK investors – as conventional funds rather than ETFs – in the summer of 2009, with the lowest charges ever seen in this country: 0.15 percent for a fund replicating FTSE All-Share performance. It promised ETF versions to follow. Competition between fund managers soon escalated.

Weeks later, HSBC slashed the fees across its seven-strong UK-based index tracking range to 0.25 percent, having previously charged between 1 and 0.5 percent. Then, in August, it launched its first European ETF tracking the FTSE 100 index with a total expense ratio (TER) of 0.35 percent. HSBC's rationale was simple: research conducted by its Global Asset Management arm found that 95 percent of financial advisers would either 'significantly or moderately increase' their exposure to index tracking funds over the coming three years. With ETFs charging less, and paying advisers no commission, there is almost literally nothing in it for them. Evidently, though, there is a lot in these ETFs for their clients.

So this book on the use of ETFs in private investors' portfolios could not be better timed. Having read the early drafts, I can assure readers that it is far more than a technical exercise in cheerleading for Deep Blue and its ETF-managing computer progeny. Its author is a self-confessed technophile – although, as the commissioning editor of his Adventurous Investor column in the *Financial Times Weekend Money* section, I am yet to discover any evidence of a mastery of the 'spell-check' function on his own PC. What I have discovered in this book, however, and in his weekly columns, is an insightful and balanced view on the pros and cons of index tracking for long-term investors.

Clear explanations and examples abound: of the failings of actively managed funds even in bear markets, where human intervention should win out (a majority of active managers outperformed the market in just three of six US bear markets and in two of five European bear markets), but also of the failings of some index trackers and ETFs, where tracking error and less competitive charges make them serial losers (one non-ETF tracker underperformed the FTSE All-Share index by an average 2.4 percent a year). This is not a black and white analysis.

Where this book truly excels, however, is in its non-technical demonstration of the use of ETFs for diversifying your portfolio. With just a handful of ETFs, bought at low cost through an execution-only stockbroker, a private investor can gain the lowest-cost exposure to all major asset classes and thereby reduce the risk – and improve the returns – from any portfolio. With ETFs tracking fundamental indices – collections of shares selected by the strength of company fundamentals rather than their size or expensiveness – a private investor can even hope to outperform benchmarks by a small margin.

When you come to realise, as I did in the course of reading, that it's your choice of asset class rather than your fund manager's choice of shares that makes the most difference to performance – accounting for 94 percent of the variability in a portfolio's total return, against just 4 percent – you understand the value of ETFs. And when the numbers are as clear-cut as they are in this book, you don't need a super computer to do the maths. Checkmate.

Matthew Vincent
Editor, *FT Money*
2 September 2009

1

Introduction

'It's amazing how difficult it is for a man to understand something if he's paid a small fortune not to understand it.'

John Bogle paraphrasing Upton Sinclair

'Money often costs too much.'

Ralph Waldo Emerson

Welcome to the revolution – Investing 2.0

Ask yourself how you invest.

In 2001 I did just that – I looked at my long list of then failing investments and asked myself what I was really investing in. Two obvious 'facts on the ground' sprang up at me as I scanned the sorry list of assets – I had invested first in individual stocks, lots of them, and then second, funds, the vast majority of which were conventional unit trusts. In fact I had lots and lots of those funds and to judge by their performance, my strategy was not terribly successful, although to be fair not many investors were having a good time in 2001.

The important bit is that this list of assets comprised my future pension pot and so I repeated that question: what exactly was the strategy here? My initial conclusion seemed to be that I liked buying cheap stocks and investing in good fund managers.

Neither of these 'strategies' was or is a bad idea – buying distressed, cheap bargain stocks has in the past produced some extraordinary results and backing very successful managers like Bill Miller in the US and Neil Woodford in the UK has been a good idea. But I started to worry that maybe I was taking too much risk.

What would happen if those individual, distressed stocks really did blow up and the share price collapsed? Maybe they would issue three profits warnings in a row and then proceed to implode in value? What would happen if anything untoward happened to the fund managers?

A reliance on stock selection, star fund managers and the even more suspect practice of attempting to time the market convinced me, as a private investor, that something was amiss. I was taking too much risk with not enough potential return.

I am prepared to argue that what is true for me is true for other investors. Dr Stephen Barber of Selftrade – and author of a later chapter – suggests that for most of the time his investors tend to trade in individual stocks and star funds. But is this too much of a risk? Do we all think that we are better at investing than we think we are?

When you look at the US market, it is interesting to see what the Americans do. Investors do buy individual stocks, like me, and they did chase star fund managers, but they also increasingly use another investment approach that involves two very simple ideas: buying individual shares is suspect and that you need to be invested in either a whole sector or a market. For the US investors the best way to buy this 'diversification' across sectors and markets is not via a fund actively managed by someone famous like Bill Miller but through a fund that tracks a particular sector/market/asset. The thinking behind what we would call asset class investing was and is simple, namely that because virtually every theme, sector, market, even investment strategy is bound to be tracked somewhere by an index – the index provision business has been a very successful place to be over the past decade – it should be relatively easy to set up a fund that tracks that index.

The idea is brilliantly simple. De-risk your portfolio by avoiding individual stocks and fund managers and buy only the big theme or asset class by tracking it in a fund.

It is also hugely disruptive for the established way of doing things – it is an investing revolution that does away with two of the hallowed core principles of modern investing (individual stock selection and hiring fund managers actively to manage your funds) and replaces them with a simpler, more transparent, cheap concept involving a fund that tracks an index. As we will discover in this book, that revolution – I like to call it Investing 2.0

– is sweeping the US markets and is about to make its impact felt here in Europe as well.

What follows in this book is not a complicated story, although some of the underlying theory is a little tricky in places. The structures that have emerged out of this theory are also not that complicated as innovations go. However, it is fair to say that index tracking can, on first appearance, look confusing if only because of the use of hundreds of difficult-to-understand acronyms. Cut through the acronyms and you will discover that this asset class investing is simply about tracking key markets, sectors and themes by using a fund that mirrors the underlying index.

Of course, it gets a lot more complicated the more you understand how you should use these funds in a reasoned and cautious way – that is why I have written this book – but the bottom line, at least in my view, is simple: namely that index trackers really are the single best innovation in the past 50 years for private investors. Sadly, until very recently the revolution I have just begun to outline looked like it was going to remain a Stateside phenomenon; over here, in the UK, by contrast, nothing much seemed to be happening. A few tracker unit trusts had been launched and the iShares fund group (owned at the time by Barclays) had just started issuing the listed tracker funds (called exchange traded funds or ETFs), but by and large investing was still based on active fund management and rampant stock picking and tipping.

Fast-forward to 2012 – and everything seems to be changing. An amazing explosion of new investment products has kickstarted the slightly moribund fund industry – there are now hundreds and hundreds of index tracking funds here in the UK and even independent financial advisers (IFAs) and private investors are making the switch. The asset class investing revolution is now an important part of investment strategies in the UK and European markets.

Why asset class investing will change the way we invest

This revolution may sound enormously exciting but it will amount to nothing unless it helps to change the behaviour of investors – both private and institutional – and provides real benefits for all. Luckily the evidence is that this new world of investing is going to change everything – index or tracker products are slowly gaining market traction and although most small investors probably do not know what an ETF is, more and more experienced investors with bigger portfolios are beginning to build them into the core of their portfolios.

In a survey in 2008 for the European Asset Allocation Summit, more than 100 top institutions were asked to forecast the big trends in investing over the next year (2009). The results were mildly illuminating as there were various comments about equities and commodities on the rebound. But the interesting statistic was that the key product they were nearly all going to buy more of was something called exchange traded funds – stock market listed index funds structured tracking a key index.

Advisers, be they IFAs or wealth advisory managers, are also beginning to recommend these products. This is prompted in part by an increasing recognition that the salad days of investment advising (and high fees) could soon be over and that advisers might actually have to specialise in providing investment advice rather than just sell insurance policies or pensions. Investors of all kinds are beginning to ask awkward questions – why are you, my adviser, making big fees from commissions on actively managed funds but failing to deliver superior outperformance (called alpha in the trade)?

A whole series of changes in behaviour is under way in the business of investment – that is what this book is partly about, detailing the revolution and how you can use it to your advantage.

Inside we will encounter a number of core principles that are repeated again and again. We will show you why index tracking funds are transparent and cheap, and detail the huge choice of markets and assets on offer. Index tracking funds allow you to take a more strategic view of your investments and help build a diversified portfolio. They also cut through the variability of active fund management and give you the returns from holding the asset class. And they tend to produce better returns than most active fund managers.

That last statement is absolutely crucial. Index funds may be cheaper, they may be more transparent and they may help foster wide diversification within a portfolio, but the reason that so many American investors and institutions buy into them is because they deliver better results than traditional forms of fund management and stock picking.

The believers

As with all innovations, index tracking funds have sparked a large amount of controversy. Many active fund managers hate the whole concept of passively managed asset class investing, while many advisers do not feel inclined to recommend something that does not make them any money in trail commission.

On the other side of the debate it has to be conceded that fans of index funds have a certain, almost religious tone to their declarations in which there is a battle of faiths between the new schools, the indexers, versus the established school, the orthodoxy, represented by your mainstream fund manager who actively manages a portfolio.

Fans of indexing invite further comparison with evangelicals by having a slightly embattled tone to their declarations, invoking images of a titanic struggle against a very powerful and rich adversary in the shape of the conventional investment business. But the almost messianic zeal of the believers in Investing 2.0 should not hide the fact that there is a real battle going on and that an uncomfortable fact sits at the heart of this investing revolution.

Do funds actively managed by avowed stock pickers – the preferred route into investing for the vast majority of investors – actually deliver the goods? Is the 'norm' actually a bad idea, built upon very shaky foundations?

The most important fact in favour of indexing focuses on hard statistical analysis. This huge wealth of data has been developed by a collection of fairly sceptical academic economists who have been scouring the data sets on fund returns for the past 40 years. It is their research into the supposed benefits of active fund management that has chipped away at the legitimacy of the active fund management community and helped build the foundations for a new approach to investing called asset class investing.

The fall and decline of the active fund manager

There are a relatively small number of people who actively manage their own portfolios by investing directly in individual shares; until very recently, the vast majority of investors (private and institutional) used funds actively run by a manager. This fund manager would probably belong to one of the big asset management groups. In the US and UK, for instance, about 70 percent of institutional funds are actively managed and this rises to over 90 percent for retail funds. Put it another way – of the 14,304 mutual funds currently trading in the US, 13,796 of them are actively managed.

Clearly the fund management industry is convinced that using a fund manager to actively manage is essential and that it delivers the 'goods' in terms of returns. The only niggly problem is that the statistics, as mined by professional economists, do not add up. In fact, academic economists have been scrutinising the performance of active fund managers for decades now, with the first crucial paper produced by Michael Jensen dating back to 1968.[1]

Although some controversy still rumbles on, the majority of studies now conclude that actively managed funds on average underperform their passively managed counterparts. Study after study has revealed a huge discrepancy between actively and passively managed (i.e. index tracking) funds. This huge weight of evidence was nicely summed up by Rex Sinquefield, boss of Dimensional Fund Advisors, an index tracking investment firm. 'Researchers uncovered considerable evidence that past prices were of little benefit in forecasting future prices in ways that would earn excess profits; that fundamental data was too quickly reflected in prices to allow such data to be used for beat-the-market purposes; and, most importantly for us, that professional money managers could simply not outperform markets in any meaningful sense.'

Sinquefield's words summarise well some of the key observations from the research world: that the past is not much use in forecasting the future, that by and large prices set by the market are sensible and 'efficient', and that it is devilishly difficult for money managers to use that past data or those largely efficient markets and make any extra return. If he had made reference to Michael Jensen's paper he might also have noted when managers do outperform the market, they do so largely by taking on extra risk. And that is exactly what most private investors do not realise they are doing when they think they are buying a nice, safe, diversified actively managed fund.

As well as Sinquefield's view, there is now a long list of studies showing that hiring a fund manager is not always the right thing to do. I've detailed some of them below.

Gruber in 1996, for example, found that over the period 1985–94 the average mutual fund underperformed the passive market index by about 65 basis points per year.[2] Carhart in 1997 confirmed that net returns are negatively correlated with expense levels, i.e. that the more actively managed a fund, the higher the expenses and the lower the returns.[3] Carhart also discovered that the more actively a mutual fund manager trades, the lower is the fund's net return to investors. The University of Chicago professor also studied all the mutual funds that existed any time between 1961 and 1993 and found that, on average, actively managed funds underperformed their index by 1.8 percent per year.

In yet another study of equity mutual funds, Elton *et al.* examined all funds that existed over the period 1965–84 – a total of 143 funds.[4] These funds were then compared to a set of index funds – big stocks, small stocks and fixed income – that most closely corresponded to the actual investment choices made by the mutual funds. The result: on average those actively managed funds underperformed the index funds by a whopping 159 basis points a year. Not a single fund generated positive performance that was statistically significant.

It is also worth noting the first major study of bond market performance, by Blake, Elton and Gruber, in which they examined 361 bond funds starting in 1977, comparing various active bond fund management strategies with a simple 'buy the index' idea.[5] The authors found that active funds on average underperformed the index tracking strategies by 85 basis points a year.

Carhart returned to the fray with what is regarded as the definitive study, which looked at a total of 1,892 funds that existed any time between 1961 and 1993. After adjusting for the common factors in returns, an equal-weighted portfolio of the funds underperformed by 1.8 percent per year.

This research has even found support in journalistic circles – an article in *The Wall Street Journal* reported that the average mutual fund underperformed its risk-adjusted benchmark by 140 basis points (1.4 percent) a year.[6]

For many years this research focused on the work of American academics, but in the 1990s the British economists started examining the subject. One of the first was Dr Jonathan Fletcher in what was a fairly seminal paper called 'An examination of UK unit trust performance within the Arbitrage Pricing Theory framework'.[7]

Dr Fletcher's paper looked at a sample of 101 British unit trusts within something called the Arbitrage Pricing Theory framework and then looked at performance data. His conclusion was that 'there appears to be little relationship between performance and the investment objective, size and expenses of the trusts. Also portfolio strategies using past trust performance to rank the trusts fail to generate significant abnormal returns relative to two different benchmark portfolios'.[8]

The bottom line? Active fund management didn't seem to work. More research at the start of the twenty-first century continued to examine statistics, such as the Elton *et al.* study mentioned earlier.[9]

Another, much more recent paper by Keith Cuthbertson, Dirk Nitzsche and Niall O'Sullivan looks at another key aspect of active fund management: do active fund managers consistently outperform or do they eventually revert to mean, while still charging their relatively higher fees? Their conclusion is that 'only around 2 percent of all funds truly outperform their benchmarks. ... For different investment styles, this pattern of very few genuine winner funds is repeated for all companies, small companies and equity income funds. ... the majority (around 75–85 percent) of UK mutual funds neither underperform nor outperform their benchmarks.'[10]

Don't trust the manager

The message from this long list of studies (and there are many, many more) seems to be clear: the 'beat-the-market' efforts of professional fund managers achieve the exact opposite, namely they increase risk, increase cost and reduce returns. In almost any leading developed world asset class, the only consistently superior performer is the market itself.

As one analyst at Dimensional summed it up: 'Almost no one would wager millions of dollars on the flip of a coin, no matter how fair the flip. Similarly, it does not make sense to wager large sums of money on an active manager whose performance is erratic at best, when an index fund closely tracks the performance target. For any year, the return for an equity fund can be predicted only to be within the S&P 500 return –7.5 percent, approximately equal to the standard deviation of S&P 500 returns. Even though drift is random, the volatility of active manager drift is almost half as large as the volatility of the stock market.'[11]

It is also worth noting one additional set of observations – that even the best active fund managers are not consistent, i.e. they have good years but also lots of bad years which can destroy your wealth. A key US study looked at the most successful fund managers in a five-year period, starting in 1989; it then looked at their performance in the next five-year period starting in 1994. Looking at international fund managers, for instance, in 1989, their five-year results were 20.6 percent per annum, yet in the five years starting in 1994 that performance had dropped to a dreadful 9.37 percent per annum. Another fascinating study – by Vanguard, a fund management group big into indexing funds – looked to see whether excellent past performance was predictive of great, or even above-average, future performance. Its research showed that even if one's strategy was to buy the top 20 equity funds from the previous year, there is almost no chance they will be in the top 20 again and about a 40 percent chance that they will be worse than the average fund in the subsequent year.

So there is a consensus among academics: active fund managers are not good at consistently, over long periods of time, beating the benchmark index. In fact, they are so bad at it, most of the time you would be better off finding a vehicle – an index tracking fund, for instance – that simply tracks the index.

Active fund management costs more

However, any analysis of why active fund managers are not always a good idea has to recognise the work of a small band of eminent economists who have spent much of the past 20 years examining the costs of active fund management. In a paper called 'The Cost of Active Investing', the economist Kenneth French compares the fees, expenses and trading costs paid on actively managed funds and then compares them with an estimate of what would be paid if everyone invested in a vehicle that could track the benchmark index. 'Averaging over 1980 to 2006 I find investors spend 0.67 percent of the aggregate value of the market each year searching for superior returns. Society's capitalised cost of price discovery is at least 10 percent of the current market cap. Under reasonable assumptions, the typical investor would increase his average annual return by 67 basis points over the 1980–2006 period if he switched to a passive market portfolio.' He adds ominously: 'This estimate is conservative.'[12]

This paper is a hugely compelling tour de force of the pitfalls of active fund management and is worth sticking with a bit longer in this run-through of the pitfalls of active fund management. French examines overtrading via turnover measures – his hypothesis is that active fund managers trade too often and as trading costs money these expenses sap returns. According to French: 'Market turnover is above 110 percent in the 1920s. It reaches a high of 143 percent in 1928, then plunges with the market to 52 percent in 1932. By 1938 it is below 20 percent. In light of recent experience, it is perhaps surprising that annual turnover remains close to or below 20 percent from 1938 to 1975. Turnover rises fairly steadily over the next three decades, however, from 20 percent in 1975 and 59 percent in 1990, to an impressive 173 percent in 2006 and 215 percent in 2007.'[13]

French concludes that the cost of active investing was $7.0 billion in 1980, $30.5 billion in 1993 and $101.8 billion in 2006. Thus, in 2006 investors searching for superior returns in the US stock market 'consume more than $330 in resources for every man, woman and child in the United States'. And just in case you thought that your average actively managed retail fund manager was bad enough, pity the poor hedge fund investor: 'The value-weight average fee on US equity-related hedge fund assets in 2007 is 4.63

percent and the average fund of fund fee is 1.85 percent. Since fund of fund investors must pay both their own funds' fees and the fees of the underlying hedge funds, the typical fund of fund investor does not break even in 2007 unless US equity-related hedge funds generate average abnormal returns of 6.48 percent. There are $458.6 billion invested in hedge funds at the beginning of 2007, so even if we ignore the other costs they incur, hedge funds must take $29.7 billion in abnormal profits from other US equity investors for their fund of fund clients to break even.'[14]

CMH – the Costs Matter Hypothesis

The job of translating all this wealth of academic analysis has fallen to a small number of dedicated Investing 2.0 evangelicals in the US. The most prominent of these is John Bogle, a master at explaining what is wrong with active fund management and why passively tracking an index (maybe via his firm's funds) is the right way to go. He also argues that the costs of active fund management are destroying the wealth of America, as detailed by French's paper above.

Perhaps his most powerful attack came at the 60th Anniversary Conference of the *Financial Analysts Journal* in February 2005 at Pasadena, California.[15] His message to the gathered audience of US academics was that costs matter. He developed his own thesis to describe it: the Costs Matter Hypothesis, a companion theory to the Efficient Markets Theory which we will encounter in the next chapter. His research was focused on 'gross return in the financial markets, minus the costs of financial intermediation (advisers, brokers and fund managers) equals the net return actually delivered to investors'. Echoing some of French's work, Bogle discovered that during 2004:

- revenues of investment bankers and brokers came to an estimated $220 billion;
- direct mutual fund costs came to about $70 billion;
- pension management fees amounted to $15 billion, annuity commissions to $15 billion;
- hedge fund fees came to about $25 billion;
- fees paid to personal financial advisers totalled maybe another $5 billion;
- the grand total was 'approximately $350 billion, all directly deducted from the returns that the financial markets generated for investors before those croupiers' costs were deducted'. He also estimated that in 1985 these costs were a 'mere' $50 billion.

The big problem, according to Bogle, was that all these escalating costs did not actually deliver the goods. 'Let's look at the record,' he demanded. 'Over the past 20 years, a simple, low-cost, no-load stock market index fund delivered an annual return of 12.8 percent – just a hair short of the 13.0 percent return of the market itself. During the same period the average equity mutual fund delivered a return of just 10.0 percent, a shortfall to the index fund of 2.8 percentage points per year, and less than 80 percent of the market's return. Compounded over that period, each $1 invested in the index fund grew by $10.12 – the *magic* of compounding *returns* – while each $1 in the average fund grew by just $5.73, not 80 percent of the market's return but a shrivelled-up 57 percent – a victim of the *tyranny* of compounding *costs*. And that's before taxes.'[16]

Bogle then implored investors to focus on another measure of returns – asset-weighted returns, i.e. the actual returns of funds based on the flow of funds. This is a crucial concept – by and large investors *increase* their payments into investment plans while markets are booming and *decrease* them during a bear market (falling markets) – they do not always invest in a linear, fixed, regular amount.

'The *asset-weighted* returns of mutual funds – quite easy to calculate by examining each fund's quarterly cash flows – lag the standard *time-weighted* returns by fully 3.7 percentage points per year,' claims Bogle. 'Adding that shortfall to the 2.8 percentage point annual lag of time-weighted returns of the average equity fund relative to the 500 index fund over the past two decades, the *asset-weighted* returns of the average equity fund stockholder fell a total of 6.5 percentage points *per year* behind the index fund.'[17]

Using his own 'humble arithmetic', Bogle then spelled out what effect these extra costs might have on future returns. 'If the stock market is kind enough to favour us with a total return of 8 percent per year over that period,' Bogle argued, 'and if annual mutual fund costs are held to $2\frac{1}{2}$ percent, the return of the fund investor will average $5\frac{1}{2}$ percent. By the end of the long period, a cost-free investment at 8 percent would carry an initial $1,000 investment to a final value of $148,800. However, the $5\frac{1}{2}$ percent net return for the investor would increase his cumulative wealth by only $31,500. In effect, the amount paid over to the financial system, also compounded, would come to $116,300.'[18]

Bogle's work has been taken one step further by a rather less well-known American analyst, Geoff Considine, who runs a small research firm called Quantext Inc – among many endeavours, Considine's team helps to build simple, easy-to-use portfolios for a low-cost American broking service called

FolioFN. In a remarkable paper entitled 'The Humble Arithmetic of Portfolio Management', Considine takes Bogle's analysis and builds on it, adding other real-world costs that sap returns for the average private investor.

Looking at stock market returns between 1983 and 2003, Considine suggests the S&P 500 market returned an average annual return of 13 percent, from which private investors had to deduct 'average fund lag', which includes poor management and high expenses of 3 percent per annum, plus bad timing by investors (they invested when markets were close to their peak and withdrew money when they were at the bottom), which costs 3.7 percent, and finally the net effect of inflation, which was around 3 percent per annum. The final real return was just 3.3 percent per annum. The average index fund would yield just under 9.8 percent per annum by contrast.

But Considine is alive to another more important reality about most private investors – we diversify! We rarely shove all our money into just one market or just one fund – we tend to spread it out over different funds, which in academic theory is actually a good idea, as we will soon discover. Considine looks at a typical 60 percent equities/40 percent bonds return over the same period and estimates that annual returns were actually closer to 7.8 percent per annum. Deduct the 'fund lag' – this time just 1.5 percent because bond managers tend to be more efficient and charge less in fees – bad timing of 3 percent and inflation of 3 percent, and hey presto, the average real return is just 0.3 percent per annum. Opt for a financial adviser who uses index tracking funds (and charges a 1 percent annual fee), does not market time (sticks with long-term buy-and-hold strategies) and that same portfolio of 60 percent equities and 40 percent bonds could yield a real return of 3.5 percent per annum. Considine's bottom line? Index tracking works, but it works even better if you diversify.

The remorseless rise of the indexers

This detour into academic research on active fund managers and their fees is not just an exercise in showing how many academic papers it is possible to read. Rather this academic research is the bedrock of a new way of looking at investing. If stock picking by fund managers is largely pointless and counterproductive and it costs us all a lot of money, why bother? If you can receive better returns by finding a vehicle that invests in the benchmark used by these star managers – something like the FTSE 100, for instance – why not use this approach as the basis for building a new kind of portfolio that is full of different asset classes and markets, all via index tracking vehicles of various forms and guises?

A few years ago I made the leap – I dumped all my actively managed funds and started investing in index tracking vehicles, in my case these exchange traded funds. I have not entirely given up stock picking – I cannot quite resist the bug – but index tracking funds now sit at the heart of my portfolio. And my enthusiasm for ETFs is not unusual or idiosyncratic: as the hard statistics suggest, index funds are not just becoming *part* of the mainstream in American investing – in some niche markets, like commodities for instance, they are *the mainstream*. Index tracking funds, and especially ETFs, are now the main component of many US institutions' investing strategy.

The hard data on this global triumph, especially through the use of ETFs, comes from outfits such as iShares, once part of Barclays and now part of the giant fund management group Blackrock. According to iShares, as of the end of November 2011 there were globally more than 4,200 different index tracking products globally with assets under management of over $1.5 trillion – a grand total of over 700 new funds and products launched over the previous 12 months.

One of the most interesting statistics centres on the use of ETFs by institutions and advisers – in 1997 just 109 advisers used ETFs, now that number has grown to 1,564. That massive increase in demand has prompted the ETF providers to launch all manner of specialised, niche funds tracking everything from Vietnam equities through to forestry product companies.

Here in the UK, for instance, iShares offers 17 different European index tracking funds, 17 emerging markets trackers, 5 property funds, 4 infrastructure funds, 5 green funds (including a forestry fund and one that invests in the water sector), 3 funds that follow indices that screen according to Islamic criteria, and 33 fixed interest funds including 4 inflation linked gilt trackers, 15 conventional government fixed interest securities trackers and 10 corporate bond funds. And that is just one major provider in the UK – rivals including Lyxor, Deutsche DBX, Powershares and ETF Securities (a specialist in commodity funds) offer an equally wide range of index tracking funds.

The above is just for ETFs – these are not the only structures and vehicles launching unprecedented choice. Later in this book we will look at differing products, all built around the simple idea of tracking an index. Other funds and investment vehicles include:

- traditional mutual fund trackers, or unit trust trackers as they are known in the UK;
- trackers that are built around structured derivatives and go under the title of listed structured products or exchange traded notes (ETNs) in the US or certificates in Europe;

- traditional structured products that track an index;
- commodity trackers packaged as exchange traded commodities or ETCs;
- swaps used by big institutions where a counterparty guarantees to pay out the return of an index.

Within these structures different types of 'tracking' have also emerged. With index tracking funds you can:

- short a market using inverse trackers that give greater returns as markets or assets fall;
- leverage up returns, giving investors more than the increase in the underlying index;
- track a portfolio of different indices or asset classes in one fund;
- within specialised markets like commodities even track futures prices, with durations ranging from one month to one year.

The innovation is staggering but there is one big constant – the choice is huge. If your aim is to build a diversified portfolio of assets and markets, your first choice is probably to use trackers as the building blocks.

Why you need to use index tracking funds in your portfolio and how this book can help you

Most opening chapters to books on investment consist of a quick exposition of what lies ahead – a roadmap for the reader. We have started our journey in a slightly more unusual manner by diving straight into one of the most difficult debates in modern economics – I make no apologies for this because it is crucial that readers understand that using indexing and tracking funds is about a very different type of investing.

Nearly all the best investment strategies are based on simple-to-understand principles. Value investors, for instance, have stayed hugely influential because of the elegant theories and suggestions first articulated by Ben Graham in the 1930s. Graham does still have huge relevance, but markets have developed and investing has become a much more popular affair, with every nook and cranny now exploited by countless clever investors, strategies or hedge funds. In this new world Graham's thinking still resonates in some respects, but markets have become much more transparent and efficient. That forces investors to think in fresh and challenging ways and that's where the new world of asset class investing using trackers comes in – it is also making a huge impact because of its basic, easy-to-understand principles. If one could reduce the huge complexity of thinking and research into just a few slogans, they would probably be these:

> Active fund managers don't deliver the returns we all need
>
> Everyone needs to diversify cheaply, efficiently and with minimum hassle
>
> The easiest way to diversify is through index tracking funds
>
> Trackers are cheap and do the job

That last slogan is not, truth be told, the most revolutionary or the most challenging, but it does sum up the simple cost effectiveness and flexibility of trackers. As we will discover in this book, trackers have countless, day-to-day advantages over actively managed funds or even individual shares. A bigger list of these common-place virtues might include the following:

- They can be easily purchased, cleared and held in a brokerage or custodial account – they are liquid.
- Investors can go long or short using new forms of tracker index funds.
- Most listed tracker funds are lendable and marginable.
- They are transparent and offer investors a clear understanding of the underlying portfolios on a daily basis – exchange listed funds can be traded in real time with continuous pricing.
- They can be used in a strategic way to increase market exposure to key trades and market views as well as part of a core portfolio.
- They are cheap and effective at tracking key markets and asset classes – according to research from iShares the average total expense ratio (TER) for equity-based ETFs in Europe is 46 basis points or 0.46 percent per annum compared with 191 bps (1.91 percent) for the average actively managed equity fund.
- There is a huge choice of funds available, offering massive diversification benefits for an investor looking to diversify their portfolio.
- They can be used in a tactical sense – by day traders or even money market managers looking to access money market instruments or gilts and bonds.

We toyed around with turning all these advantages into a later chapter on its own, but rather than fill an entire chapter with these virtually self-evident advantages, this book attempts to dig a little deeper and flesh out the argument of why you need to use index tracking funds. By the time you've finished reading it, hopefully you will be able to understand the thinking behind trackers and index funds, comprehend the different structures (including their weaknesses and strengths) and work out how to use them on an everyday basis within a sensibly diversified portfolio.

That narrative 'arc' or journey – constructed to help you build a better portfolio – starts in the next chapter, where we take a step backwards and look first at the theory that spawned all these index tracking vehicles and this new style of asset class investing. 'A quick primer in the theory' spins through an elegant theoretical construct called the Efficient Markets Hypothesis and looks at the challengers to this new orthodoxy – in particular we focus on the academics who have been digging away at the inefficiencies of markets and what that tells us about winning future strategies. We will also take a look at precisely what an index is – looking at our own FTSE 100 – and how indexes are actually constructed.

In Chapter 3 we take that journey in the development of the thinking behind index funds right up to the current day, looking at the sheer variety of funds and structures, running through all the different types of index tracking funds you might encounter as you build your portfolio. We make no apologies for the fact that in this journey you will encounter a blizzard of acronyms and jargon, but stick with it, because the diversity of products and structures offers enormous advantages.

In Chapter 4 we take a slight detour and delve into the world of commodity index tracking funds – this most alternative of asset classes has boomed in recent years as new fund structures have emerged that allow investors to invest in everything from carbon credits to coffee, by going long or short. This commodities boom has spawned a whole new sub-culture of funds and investors, complete with its own peculiar language.

We return to the mainstream of index tracking funds in Chapter 5, written by the indexing experts at TCF, Dan Norman and James Cottee. Dan and James are on the front line of investing in ETFs as they use all manner of tracker funds within their various risk based portfolios. That means they need to run a proper due diligence process, looking in detail at the index tracking funds they use. In this chapter Dan and James share some of their insights, looking at all the different structures. The chapter picks out some issues to watch out for, examines risks inherent in complex subjects like counterparty risk and asks some probing questions about the construction of indices.

Chapter 6 picks up on some debates first encountered in Chapter 2 and takes us on a quick detour into the world of fundamental index funds in the company of fund manager Rob Davies, from the Munro fund, who runs his own dividend-weighted unit trust. He reminds us of the academic work that provides the foundation for this growing niche and tests out whether funds that use measures like dividends or book value really do provide extra returns.

Building your portfolio

By Chapter 7 we are ready to get into the nitty gritty of how you might use index funds in your portfolio. James Norton, a financial planner and investment director at Evolve Financial Planning, kicks off our investigation of how to build the better portfolio by examining why asset allocation is so important and why you might need something called a glidepath for future success.

In Chapter 8 Dr Stephen Barber of stockbrokers Selftrade looks at how you might juggle different investing styles and themes in a portfolio – how you might, for instance, juggle momentum investing with emerging markets or even alternative assets.

By and large most investors using index funds use a fairly conventional buy-and-hold, long-term investing approach, but a small band of hardy souls – chief among them Mark Glowrey from research firm Investors Intelligence – adopts a much more aggressive approach. In Chapter 9 Glowrey and Tarquin Coe examine how you might use ETFs by overlaying technical analysis to construct a portfolio that is much more short term focused and tactical.

In Chapter 10 we start to look at what asset class investing might mean for private investors. We look at some common issues and challenges encountered when trying to build a portfolio – should you rebalance frequently and should you use only index tracking funds? Are equities really such a good idea in volatile markets? How much do you need to diversify? All these questions and more will be tackled in this penultimate chapter.

In the final chapter we put some flesh on these bones and detail a set of model portfolios built on key indices or markets. These model portfolios are not the very best or most optimised portfolios, but they are easy to build and should provide you with the outline or backbone of a portfolio that should last over the long term. Whether they make you any money we cannot predict – they are not tips! Markets are volatile and mostly fairly random creatures, but by using some of the principles outlined in this book you should at least have a well thought through portfolio, full of cheap and efficient trackers that will do most of the heavy lifting for you.

The very last section of the book is our Essential 25, which is not some music hit parade but a look at the key 25 markets or indices you should seriously consider buying exposure to. With each of the Top 25 we will detail the index, how it is built, past returns and risks and examine the funds available to track this index.

Full circle

One last observation: what am I doing with my portfolio all these years on since that epiphany back in 2001? It is jam packed full of ETFs and index tracking funds, but I have not entirely kicked the active management habit or the stock-picking addiction. I use a core of trackers – ETFs – but I still layer it with some cheap stocks and I still use very specialist managers in niche markets where I sense that trackers might prove difficult (a discussion we'll have in the next chapter when we examine the limits of efficient markets).

My personal bottom line? Index tracking ETFs work for me but I do not use them exclusively. I still think other approaches have some validity. Are index tracking funds the answer to all our investing problems? Of course not, but they are still the best way of capturing key trends and markets in a cheap, efficient and diversified manner. Ignore them at your peril!

2

A quick primer on the theory – or how we got here

'An "efficient" market is defined as a market where there are large numbers of rational, profit-maximizers actively competing with each trying to predict future market values of individual securities, and where important current information is almost freely available to all participants.'

Eugene Fama[1]

'There is an old joke, widely told among economists, about an economist strolling down the street with a companion when they come upon a $100 bill lying on the ground. As the companion reaches down to pick it up, the economist says "Don't bother – if it were a real $100 bill, someone would have already picked it up".'

Andrew Lo and Craig MacKinlay[2]

Step back in time to the era of progressive rock, Marc Bolan and the slow but steady collapse of Western capitalism at the hands of wayward unions and the British miners in particular. In 1973 American writer and academic Burton Malkiel wrote *A Random Walk Down Wall Street*, a book that is now rightly regarded as an investment classic. The Random Walk thesis and its more developed sibling, the Efficient Markets Hypothesis (EMH to the uninitiated), are both crucial to an understanding of modern investment theory.

At their core sits a simple proposition that suggests that the past movement or direction of the price of a stock or overall market cannot be used to predict its future movement. Put simply, these theories argue that both logic and available evidence suggest that markets by and large get it right when it comes to pricing a share or a market, that you as an investor cannot beat that outcome most of the time and that the best, cheapest and most efficient thing to do is to follow the market by copying it via an index fund. If this quick summary suffices as an explanation, you should probably skip this chapter and start to examine the structures on offer.

As we will discover in this brief saunter around the most hotly contested bit of the investment economics war zone, this theory – EMH – has huge ramifications for all investors, suggesting as it does that attempting to stock pick is no worse than betting on the horses. More importantly, this theory and its various spin-offs have played a crucial part in the development of the index/tracker fund revolution.

But there are some nagging doubts – common sense suggests that buying cheap shares is a great idea and that when markets are booming, popular momentum stocks are the place to be. If so, you are asking all the right questions – not everyone in the investment economics wonderland has entirely bought into the efficient markets grand narrative, and if these renegades are right there is an awful lot of money to be made at the margins, mining the inefficiencies of a market that is clearly not perfect.

It is a hugely compelling debate and features some of the modern masters of academic finance – great names like Burton Malkiel and Eugene Fama, who in turn draw on slightly less well-known but influential figures such as French mathematician Louis Bachelier and English statistician Maurice Kendall.

This roll call of economic greats starts though with the genesis of a painfully simple idea, namely that of the random walk.

Taking a random walk on the wild side

Although the story that unfolds in the next few pages largely belongs to the current generation of award-winning American economists – notably Burton Malkiel and Eugene Fama – the development of the Efficient Markets Hypothesis has its roots in the work of a number of earlier, leading theoreticians and investment researchers, all puzzled by the seemingly 'random' distribution of prices in a very liquid market like the stock market. The first attempt to sketch an outline of what became known as the random walk of share prices came from a French mathematician, Louis Bachelier, who penned a dissertation called 'The Theory of Speculation' in 1900.

Bachelier deserves a book all by himself – he is one of those classic mathematicians whose work was initially rejected by the mainstream but was eventually revealed to be decades ahead of its time. Bachelier also has the disadvantage that he outlined the precepts of Brownian random motion not in 'trendy' physics – five years ahead of Einstein's celebrated study of the phenomenon – but in the dreary world of finance, a subject of much distaste to many bourgeois, capitalist-hating French intellectuals. His view is summed up in one key observation, namely that 'there is no useful information contained in historical price movements of securities', although his more pungent observation that 'the mathematical expectation of the speculator is zero' is possibly more relevant to modern investors endlessly chasing elusive profits from hot tips. Just in case the lay reader was in any doubt as to Bachelier's view of speculators, the opening paragraph of his 1900 dissertation nails its colours firmly to the mast, stating that 'past, present and even discounted future events are reflected in market price, but often show no apparent relation to price changes'.

In these simple words Bachelier outlined the foundation stone of modern investment economics – in his view share prices change unpredictably based on the result of unexpected information appearing in the market. Many observers have taken this simple idea and suggested that his theory requires that share price changes move randomly for no rational reason. Bachelier, by contrast, maintained that it is not the changes in share prices that are random but the news that influences that pricing that is random. In essence news is unpredictable – that is its definition after all, it is new(s)– and so investors behave rationally by reacting to this unpredictable news. The unpredictable prompts the eminently predictable!

Bachelier's work lay largely dormant and unnoticed for many decades until the work of another theoretician came to prominence, that of Maurice Kendall, one of those wonderfully talented statisticians that Britain seems to excel at. A genuine polymath – much of his most influential work derives from his spell as head of the World Fertility Survey – Kendall turned his attentions in 1953 to the long-term distribution of returns from shares as well as the price of cotton and wheat, across 19 different indices or markets. Elroy Dimson and Massoud Mussavian, in their review of the rise of the EMH, note that Kendall and his team of researchers were by now using relatively advanced computer processing technology to study long series of price returns.[3] Kendall's assumption was that this new technology could 'analyse an economic time series by extracting from it a long-term movement, or trend, for separate study and then scrutinising the residual portion for short-term oscillatory movements and random fluctuations' (Kendall, 1953).[4] According to Dimson and Mussavian, when 'Kendall examined 22

UK stock and commodity price series, however, the results surprised him. Looking at what statisticians call serial correlations – repeated analysis of the relationships between a series of outcomes – Kendall concluded that 'this series looks like a wandering one, almost as if once a week the Demon of Chance drew a random number from a symmetrical population of fixed dispersion and added it to the current price to determine the next week's price ... The data behave almost like wandering series'.

In 1959 American astrophysicist M. F. Maury Osborne drew upon Kendall's observations and outlined a hypothesis that share prices follow a geometric Brownian motion – it is also worth noting that Osborne worked in detail on the study of risk and extremely unlikely events and was the first to identify what later became known as fat tail risk or events, i.e. big financial crashes that are supposed to be very unlikely but in reality prove to be depressingly common and frequent.

One key insight from the Random Walk Theory made its mark, notably that because price movements will not follow any pattern or trend, you cannot use past price movements to predict future price movements – don't try to second guess the market because you will fail as randomness and reversion to mean will be your undoing! The logic of the random walk idea also suggests that if the flow of information is 'unimpeded', i.e. news channels do their job unhindered and information is immediately reflected in stock prices, then tomorrow's price change will reflect only tomorrow's news and will be independent of the price changes today.

In 1973 in his seminal book *A Random Walk Down Wall Street* Burton Malkiel famously summed up the idea that 'experts' cannot add any value to this random walk by suggesting that 'a blindfolded chimpanzee throwing darts at *The Wall Street Journal* could select a portfolio that would do as well as the experts'.[5] From these building blocks – suggesting that returns from shares are fundamentally random – all that was needed was a causal theory to explain the motives behind participants in this random market. Enter the Efficient Markets Hypothesis.

Many of the basics of this unifying theory came via a diehard fan of Bachelier's work, noted US economist Paul Samuelson. His 1965 paper began with the observation that 'in competitive markets there is a buyer for every seller. If one could be sure that a price would rise, it would have already risen'. According to Dimson and Mussavian, Samuelson asserted that 'arguments like this are used to deduce that competitive prices must display price changes . . . that perform a random walk with no predictable bias'. Samuelson explains that 'we would expect people in the market place, in pursuit of avid and intelligent self-interest, to take account of those elements of future events that in a probability sense may be discerned to be casting their shadows before them'.[6]

Samuelson's work started to lay out the conceptual building blocks of this new hypothesis of efficient markets. Although the maths that sit behind this theory are as elegant as they are sometimes impenetrable to the untrained eye, the Efficient Markets Hypothesis is not, in truth, a complicated concept to understand. At the core of the theory sits one key assertion – that an 'efficient market is one that quickly adjusts prices to reflect all available public information about the future prospects of an investment',[7] a familiar idea from the random walk thesis. When it comes to setting a price for a stock or a bond, potential buyers and sellers use the best information available to them. Add up all these individual approximations and estimations and you have the market price of a stock which is equivalent to the market's estimation of the 'fair' price.

Although no one academic completely developed the elegant framework that sits behind the EMH, one economist – a certain Eugene Fama – stands head and shoulders above the rest. If you feel so inclined you can easily download his seminal research paper from 1970, 'Efficient capital markets: a review of theory and empirical work'.[8]

In this relatively short work he outlines the key attributes of the EMH, including the idea that:

- 'the primary role of the capital market is allocation of the economy's capital stock';
- the market requires accurate signals to correctly allocate scarce resources, or as Burton Malkiel puts it in a later paper, 'when information arises, the news spreads very quickly and is incorporated into the prices of securities without delay. Thus, neither technical analysis, which is the study of past stock prices in an attempt to predict future prices, nor even fundamental analysis, which is the analysis of financial information such as company earnings, asset values, etc., to help investors select 'undervalued' stocks, would enable an investor to achieve returns greater than those that could be obtained by holding a randomly selected portfolio of individual stocks with comparable risk';[9]
- the outcome of this allocative framework is a market in which prices always fully reflect the available information, i.e. an efficient market;

- an 'efficient' market is thus defined as a market where there are large numbers of rational profit maximisers, actively competing, with each trying to predict future market values of individual securities, and where important current information is almost freely available to all participants;
- in an efficient market at any point in time the actual price of a security will be a good estimate of its intrinsic value;
- if a market is efficient, no information or analysis can be expected to result in outperformance of an appropriate index or benchmark.

Proof for this framework is now the subject of academic orthodoxy, but the early pioneers focused on two specific examples. The first was called 'event studies' – in essence how the market reacted to specific news-based events in the subsequent pricing of shares. Dimson and Mussavian, in their review of this new orthodoxy, reveal the conclusion reached by Fama and his team – that 'the market appears to anticipate the information, and most of the price adjustment is complete before the event is revealed to the market. When news is released, the remaining price adjustment takes place rapidly and accurately'. A study by Fama *et al.* (1969), in particular, demonstrates that prices reflect not only direct estimates of prospective performance by the sample companies but also information that requires more subtle interpretation.[10]

These studies nailed the first leg of the Efficient Markets Hypothesis – what later became known as the weak efficient market. Fama and his comrades then moved on to a tougher nut – surely insiders trading on their exclusive knowledge (their inside track) would be able to make extra returns. If Fama could prove that even this failed to produce extra profits consistently over time, then he could prove what became known as a strong form of efficient markets. This particular proof was not to come from Fama though – researchers around the world had been studying the returns of fund managers whose job it was to capture this inside track and make a quick buck with their funds. Dimson and Mussavian report on the key research from Michael Jensen in 1968 that analysed 115 fund managers' performance over the period 1955–64.[11] On a risk-adjusted basis, he finds that any advantage that the portfolio managers might have is consumed by fees and expenses. Even if investment management fees and loads are added back to performance measures, and returns are measured gross of management expenses (i.e. assuming research and other expenses were obtained free), Jensen concludes that *'on average the funds apparently were not quite successful enough in their trading activities to recoup even their brokerage expenses'.*[12]

With this research Fama had found his proof for not only a weak form of market efficiency but a strong one. A number of different forms of efficient markets were now presented to a sceptical world.

- A 'weak' efficient market claims all past market prices and data are fully reflected in securities prices. The bottom line? Don't bother trying to use clever systems to predict price movements as they will fail.
- 'Semistrong' argues that all publicly available information is fully reflected in the share price. This attacks the arguments of value investors by suggesting that fundamental analysis is misguided, i.e. that a share has an intrinsic value based on, say, its assets securities prices.
- The 'strong' form asserts that all information is fully reflected in a share's price. In other words, even insider information is of no use.

In essence, Fama's concept of the EMH suggests that because stock markets are vibrant, hugely liquid spaces, flooded with tens of thousands of intelligent, well-paid and well-educated investors seeking to make a return on the market by looking for a system or trying to find cheap shares, information becomes dispersed ever more quickly and efficiently and the pricing that results becomes ever more accurate and thus efficient.

Efficient markets, rational actors?

Crucially, although most commentators and the general public have assumed that this theory requires all market participants to be rational, EMH theoreticians have never believed this to be true. According to Fama, markets can be efficient even when a group of investors is almost completely irrational – all you need are more rational players like traders to exist who will make money by trading on or 'arbitraging away' those combined inefficiencies.

To understand this subtle distinction let's assume that a room full of schoolchildren is set the challenge to establish a market in a share certificate about which most of them know very little. They might all approach this irrationally, investing in each piece of paper their own behavioural biases and fantasies. Some unrealistic prices may appear based on the perceptions of the underlying value of these shares, but all an efficient market requires is one knowledgeable actor or trader in the room to effectively take advantage of the other players and establish a fair price or market clearing price. That arb, as they are called, might make a killing and some other children might feel deeply aggrieved – but an efficient price eventually emerges notwithstanding these problems and emotions.

Another key attribute mistakenly pinned on the EMH world view is that a share's price accurately represents the value of the underlying business based on certain key fundamentals like the profit rate or the assets on the balance sheet. Efficient market theorists make no such claim – the EMH simply suggests that the share price of a company represents only an aggregation of the probabilities of all future outcomes for the company, based on the best information available at the time, with all the market participants. To return to our room full of children, the price that is established is not a right one as such, i.e. an objective analysis of the value of the share, but simply the price based on the willingness to pay of participants in that room based on their own (frequently mistaken) perceptions of future value plus one key knowledgeable efficient market maker. As one commentator put it: 'EMH does not require a stock's price to reflect a company's future performance, just the best possible estimate or forecast of future performance that can be made with publicly available information. That estimate may still be grossly wrong without violating EMH.'

One last crucial clarification – in reality, markets are neither perfectly efficient nor perfectly inefficient. All markets are efficient to a certain extent, some more so than others. The key observation here is that where news/information flows are less efficient, the less efficient the market will be and the more likely it will be that discrepancies will emerge. A classic example of this phenomenon is in emerging markets space, in places like China or Russia. Crucial market information comes from insiders such as the company management, who do not always completely level with their wider shareholder base. Governments can also interfere with market processes, favour insiders or rivals and generally corrupt the information flows that a free market depends on. And not all these opaque markets are in the developing world – arguably the private equity space for one depends on varied information flows plus insider knowledge that cannot be efficiently and speedily recognised in the publicly listed share price. But – and here is the key observation – the bigger this market grows, and the more obvious these pricing inefficiencies are, the more professional traders will emerge who will arbitrage out or trade away these inefficiencies, making themselves a large amount of profit (note that EMH theorists recognise that arbitrage-based professionals can indeed make a profit via inefficiency) and deepening the pool of liquidity in the market, making it in turn more conventional and more efficient over time. The key conceptual point here is that as markets grow, they become more efficient and liquid, and as they mature those inefficiencies decline as more arbs emerge to make money out of the dwindling inefficiencies.

The critics

Many varied lines of attack against the EMH have emerged over the last few decades, some emanating from within the EMH school, others from outside schools based around classic value investing or behavioural economics influenced by modern cognitive pyschology. Some economists, mathematicians and market practitioners do not believe that man-made markets are inherently efficient, especially when there are good reasons for that inefficiency, including the slow diffusion of information, the undue power of some market participants (e.g. financial institutions) and the existence of apparently sophisticated professional investors. It is worth understanding the huge range of these critical voices because they have all helped shape various interesting and unorthodox indexing investment strategies – strategies that have in turn ended up in novel ETFs and tracker funds.

One of the earliest attacks on the EMH looked at the way that markets react to surprising news – this is perhaps the most visible flaw in the Efficient Market Hypothesis (called underreaction to new information by its observers). For example, news events such as surprise interest rate changes from central banks are not instantaneously taken account of in stock prices, but rather cause sustained movement of prices over periods ranging from hours to months. Recent work by Lo and MacKinlay (1999), for instance, finds that this phenomenon is clearly observable, leading them to reject the random walk thesis.[13] Even Malkiel himself, a great defender of the Efficient Markets Hypothesis in public debates, accepts that 'there does seem to be some momentum in short-run stock prices'. Malkiel also points to research from Lo, Mamaysky and Wang (2000), who find, through the use of sophisticated statistical techniques that can recognise patterns, that some of the stock-price signals used by 'technical analysts', such as 'head and shoulders' formations and 'double bottoms', may actually have some modest predictive power, i.e. that they can predict prices in the short term.[14]

You do not have to use technical analysis to understand the overall outline of this 'inefficient' phenomenon – investors see a share price rising and are drawn into the market in a kind of 'bandwagon effect'. Robert Shiller (2000) also described the late 1990s' stock market boom (or should we say bubble) as the result of psychological contagion leading to irrational exuberance.[15] Behaviouralist economists like James Montier, formerly at investment bank SocGen and now at fund management group GMO offer their own explanation for this short-run momentum – a tendency for investors to underreact to new information and distinguish statistical significance from economic significance. EMH enthusiasts certainly seem to accept that this phenomenon can exist, but Eugene Fama found that underreaction to information is about as common as overreaction and that 'post-event continuation of abnormal returns is as frequent as post-event reversals', i.e. the inefficiency can work both ways and is not a workable trading strategy. The killer rebuttal, though, to the whole 'momentum' as strategy argument is also the most obvious – once you have spotted the phenomenon and try to make a profit from it, the pattern begins to fade away, or as Malkiel puts it, 'many predictable patterns seem to disappear after they are published in the finance literature'.

Another take on the behavioural oddities of investors comes courtesy of those who observe a discrepancy between EMH and actual, real markets at their most extreme, where irrational behaviour becomes the norm, i.e. as a bubble starts to burst. Towards the end of a crash, markets go into free fall as participants extricate themselves from positions regardless of the unusually good value that those positions represent. Perhaps the most biting attack comes via something called the Grossman–Stiglitz paradox – if markets really are that efficient and everyone knows, no one will bother to beat the market and the market will begin to wither. In their 2001 Nobel Economics award 'for their analyses of markets with asymmetric information', Joseph Stiglitz and Sanford Grossman claimed that the very idea of efficient markets is inherently paradoxical – if a market was 'informationally efficient' (all relevant information was reflected in market prices), then no single agent would have sufficient incentive to acquire the information on which prices are based. Markets may as well be run by computers in the background, banishing all human experts to day jobs serving hamburgers at McDonald's!

These discrepancies and theoretical attacks are dwarfed, however, by a more thorough criticism of supposedly efficient markets which suggests that repeated patterns do in fact occur in markets that are clearly not efficient and that this ever present reality offers investors numerous opportunities to make a profit. The simplest way of understanding this is to look at the small number of investors who have outperformed the market over long periods of time, in a way which it is statistically unreasonable to attribute to good luck, including investment sages such as Warren Buffett, Peter Lynch, Bill Miller and Anthony Bolton, until recently head of the star fund at Fidelity. These investors' strategies are, to a large extent, based on identifying markets where prices do not accurately reflect the available information, in direct contradiction to the EMH which explicitly implies that no such opportunities exist.

Warren Buffett in particular has on several occasions stated that the EMH is not correct, maintaining that 'I'd be a bum on the street with a tin cup if the markets were always efficient' and that 'the professors who taught efficient market theory said that someone throwing darts at the stock tables could select a stock portfolio having prospects just as good as one selected by the brightest, most hard-working securities analyst. Observing correctly that the market was frequently efficient, they went on to conclude incorrectly that it was always efficient'. Some rigorous academic evidence for Buffett's contentions comes from a big Vanguard study on the importance of asset allocation and diversification in fund management.[16] The report mainly supports classic efficient market theories' suspicion of stock picking as an art form, but it does state that *'a small percentage – 7 percent – of actively managed balanced funds have been able to consistently outperform their policy benchmarks'*. A grand total of 7 percent may not sound much, but in a very diverse and well-populated market full of thousands of fund managers, that is actually an awful lot of successful fund managers with a great long-term track record. Either these fund managers are practising some mysterious form of market magic or the Efficient Markets Hypothesis has some pretty big holes in it.

More risk, greater returns

How do these star managers produce their super-sized returns? Many mainstream investment economists maintain that these star fund managers simply capitalise on a series of factors (as they are known) which contribute extra risk, and extra rewards, for those sophisticated enough to know where to look. This nuanced view accepts that you can make extra returns but only by taking on more risk, and that this extra risk is found only in certain places within the efficient market.

One of these additional forms of factor risk has been called the size risk by economists – this simply suggests that smaller companies grow faster than bigger companies and thus produce greater returns. Thus any strategy that focuses on small caps or even tiny micro-caps (sub £10 million in market cap) will produce exceptional returns over certain periods of time – even Burton Malkiel, in his study of the critiques of EMH, points to data since 1926 which suggests that small-company stocks in the United States have produced rates of return over one percentage point larger than the returns from large stocks (citing another study by Keim, 1983).[17]

Fama and French (1992) have also broken with some of their peers and backed this concept.[18] They examined data from 1963 to 1990 and divided all shares into deciles according to their size as measured by total capitalisation. The results, according to the two professors, showed a clear tendency for the deciles made up of portfolios of smaller stocks to generate higher average monthly returns than deciles made up of larger stocks. It is worth quickly noting one key caveat made by Malkiel, an erstwhile supporter of Fama and French's work except when it comes to the scale effect – he notes that 'from the mid-1980s through the decade of the 1990s, there has been no gain from holding smaller stocks. Thus, a researcher who examined the ten-year performance of today's small companies would be measuring the performance of those companies that survived – not the ones that failed'.

Another extra form of risk is sometimes called distress risk, although it is also known as the value premium. This is the risk of owning companies that the market perceives as being in some form of financial trouble. While none of us would choose to invest in a single company in potentially big trouble – that distress could be defined as a poor balance sheet or falling earnings or even loss – indices of 'value' stocks have historically offered very high returns precisely because most investors follow the crowd and target what are called growth companies, i.e. companies growing fast, that sport expensive share prices relative to their profits. From this simple observation – noted time and time again by analysts for 50 years – has emerged a whole new branch of the efficient markets school. This schism even has its own moniker – the fundamentalists – and a belief system that suggests that key measures of value (using key balance sheet and profit measures) are crucial to explaining why some shares do better than others.

The rise of fundamentals-based index investing

The hard work digging into the numbers that 'prove' the value premium comes from French and Fama. In 1997 French looked at data on the entire universe of US stocks for the period 1964–2000 (see Table 2.1). He found that small-cap stocks that were also good 'value' produced returns of 15.66 percent compared with 'poor value' (growth) small caps which gave just 10.15 percent. Likewise for larger companies that were good 'value' – they returned 14.28 percent compared with 11.49 percent for low-value peers. French and Fama's bottom line – take on extra risk and invest in both the size premium and the value effect and you can earn an additional 4–7 percent per year.

Table 2.1 Historical simulation results (in US dollars)

Time span	Index	Annual compound return	Annual standard deviation
1964–2000	Fama French US Large Value Index	14.28%	17.83%
	S&P 500 Index	11.90%	15.92%
	Fama/French US Large Growth Index	11.49%	18.65%
1964–2000	Fama/French US Small Value Index	15.66%	25.89%
	CRSP 6 – 10 Index	13.35%	25.52%
	Fama/French US Small Growth Index	10.15%	30.40%
1975–2000	Fama/French International Value Index	18.26%	20.61%
	International Small Company Index	18.07%	27.44%
	MSCI EAFE Index	13.69%	20.58%

Source: www.dartmouth.edu/~kfrench

Figure 2.1 presents an even more fascinating paradox – it establishes an inverse relationship between profitability and average share returns. The bottom line? Value stocks and small cap stocks that are less profitable than faster growing equivalent stocks produce greater share price returns. In effect this analysis suggests that efficient markets don't behave in quite the way economists first imagined.

As fundamental indexing fund management firm Dimensional puts it: 'Everything we have learned about expected returns in the equity markets can be summarized in three dimensions. The first is that stocks are riskier than bonds and have greater expected returns. Relative performance among stocks is largely driven by the two other dimensions: small/large and value/growth. Many economists believe small cap and value stocks outperform because the market rationally discounts their prices to reflect underlying risk. The lower prices give investors greater upside as compensation for bearing this risk.'[19]

Another variant on this idea of the value premium is to look at what some called cheap stocks, or bombed-out shares to you and I – shares that have crashed in price. A strong school of contrarian thinking suggests that buying these unpopular stocks can produce huge long-term outperformance for those willing to be patient, mainly because markets overreact in their punishment of certain shares and eventually the market is forced to admit the error of its ways by marking up prices. DeBondt and Thaler (1995), for example, argue that investors are subject to waves of optimism

Figure 2.1 Company size and financial strength annual data 1964–2000

Note: Earnings/assets through 1999 due to availability.
Source: www.dartmouth.edu/~kfrench

and pessimism which cause prices to crash below their fundamental value (the value of assets for instance) – give the market a few years and these prices revert to mean and reward the brave contrarian.[20] Looking at very long-term horizons they found that 'stocks which have underperformed the most over a three- to five-year period average the highest market-adjusted returns over the subsequent period, and vice versa'.

Dividend payouts also feature prominently in the arguments of value investors who attack the Efficient Markets Hypothesis on a number of fronts. Academics like Jeremy Siegel at Wharton Business School and James Montier at GMO, argue that buying high-yielding stocks cheaply makes analytical sense – Montier has produced evidence that close to 80 percent of medium-term returns from holding shares can be attributed to the actual dividend payout and the market's expectation of future higher dividend payouts.

But Fluck, Malkiel and Quandt (1997) discovered in their analysis that investors 'who simply purchase a portfolio of individual stocks with the highest dividend yields in the market will not earn a particularly high rate of return' – simply buying the highest yielders does not always produce abnormal returns.[21] Critics of this blind, buy-all high-yielders approach also like to point to 'Dogs of the Dow Strategy'. This US-based strategy involves buying the ten stocks in the Dow Jones Industrial Average with the highest dividend yields. Over many periods of time this strategy has produced some exceptional results, yet as soon as the strategy found its way into mutual funds, that premium mysteriously disappeared. Malkiel observes that 'such funds have generally underperformed the market averages during the 1995–99 period'.[22]

Yet another camp of fundamentals-based investors looks specifically to shares with low price–earnings multiples – that is where the stream of profits, expressed as earnings, is at a low multiple to the share price. In many studies these low price to earnings (PE) shares appear to provide higher rates of return than those shares with high PE ratios, i.e. where the share price is many more times greater than the low level of earnings. Nicholson (1960), Ball (1978) and Basu (1977) have all published papers looking at this particular market inefficiency and their results tend to confirm the view of the behaviouralist-inclined economists who think that investors tend to be overconfident of their ability to project high earnings growth and thus overpay for 'growth' stocks (for example, Kahneman and Riepe, 1998). Similar results have been shown for price/cash flow multiples, where cash flow is defined as earnings plus depreciation and amortisation (Hawawini and Keim, 1995).

This constant hum of research and debate has given shape to a whole new way of building indices – fundamentally weighted index funds mapped in detail by Rob Davies in Chapter 6 in this book. Its simple outline and form has been defined by Fama, now adviser to Dimensional: 'I agree that stock picking is gambling,' says Fama. 'I don't agree that the only legitimate indexing approach is holding the market portfolio.' Fama clearly articulates a view that simply 'buying the market' is itself buying a rather arbitrary portfolio of stocks. 'It gives a heavy weighting to financially healthy stocks and a light weighting to distressed stocks. Don't get me wrong: it's hard to fault a market index approach. But if there's more than one type of risk driving returns, it's possible for investors to use a wider range of strategies to gain greater expected returns – all within the bounds of indexing.'[23]

The efficient markets purists' counter attack

> *'I am convinced that Benjamin Graham (1965) was correct in suggesting that while the stock market in the short run may be a voting mechanism, in the long run it is a weighing mechanism. True value will win out in the end. And before the fact, there is no way in which investors can reliably exploit any anomalies or patterns that might exist. I am skeptical that any of the "predictable patterns" that have been documented in the literature were ever sufficiently robust so as to have created profitable investment opportunities and after they have been discovered and publicized, they will certainly not allow investors to earn excess returns.'*
>
> Burton Malkiel[24]

Academics supportive of the Efficient Markets Hypothesis in its purer forms do not dispute the weight of evidence that suggests some kind of value premium exists, especially if it is combined with the size risk. But as Burton Malkiel puts it, 'these findings do not necessarily imply inefficiency. They may simply indicate failure of the capital asset pricing model to capture all the dimensions of risk' – see the box on the CAPM on page 36. They also wonder aloud whether this observed past phenomenon is that relevant to current markets – according to Malkiel, Fama and French's own data suggests 'the period from the early 1960s through 1990 may have been a unique period in which value stocks rather consistently produced higher rates of return'. In other words, what worked in the past may not be relevant to current markets, and even if it does still exist, it is nigh on impossible to capture through any sensible investment policy.

Fluck, Malkiel and Quandt (1997) recognised that the price-reversal strategy mentioned above does seem to exist – over a 13-year period during the 1980s and early 1990s they simulated a strategy of buying stocks that had had particularly poor returns over the past three to five years.[25] According to Malkiel, his team found that 'stocks with very low returns over the past three to five years had higher returns in the next period, and that stocks with very high returns over the past three to five years had lower returns in the next period'. Crucially, though, they also found that 'returns in the next period were similar for both groups, so they could not confirm that a contrarian approach would yield higher-than-average returns. There was a statistically strong pattern of return reversal, but not one that implied inefficiency in the market that would enable investors to make excess returns', i.e. the phenomenon of means reversion might work but it would be very difficult to run it as a trading strategy.

This cynicism about the ability of investors to actually capture these inefficiencies received some support from a study by Schwert (2001), which pointed out that the investment firm of Dimensional Fund Advisors actually began a mutual fund that selected value stocks quantitatively according to the Fama and French (1993) criteria (the firm's academic consultant is Eugene Fama).[26] The abnormal return of such a portfolio (adjusting for beta, the capital asset pricing model measure of risk) was a negative 0.2 percent per month over the 1993–98 period, according to Schwert.

An exchange at a symposium about a decade ago between Robert Shiller, an economist who is sympathetic to the argument that stock prices are partially predictable but sceptical about market efficiency, and Richard Roll, an academic financial economist who is also a portfolio manager, beautifully demonstrates this debate about actually capturing these supposed inefficiencies (Roll and Shiller, 1992). After Shiller stressed the importance of inefficiencies in the pricing of stocks, Roll responded as follows:

> 'I have personally tried to invest money, my clients' money and my own, in every single anomaly and predictive device that academics have dreamed up. ... I have attempted to exploit the so-called year-end anomalies and a whole variety of strategies supposedly documented by academic research. And I have yet to make a nickel on any of these supposed market inefficiencies ... a true market inefficiency ought to be an exploitable opportunity. If there's nothing investors can exploit in a systematic way, time in and time out, then it's very hard to say that information is not being properly incorporated into stock prices.'[27]

The point here is that while many investment economists are willing to concede that there are some efficiencies, they doubt whether these form a pattern and that if they do persist, whether these patterns will self-destruct in the future, as so many have done once they have been observed. This almost philosophical notion that once a regular pattern has been observed, it ceases to exist by the very act of recognition and cognition is beautifully summed up in the following example from Burton Malkiel.

> 'Suppose there is a truly dependable and exploitable January effect, that the stock market – especially stocks of small companies – will generate extraordinary returns during the first five days of January. What will investors do? They will buy on the last day of December, and sell on January 5. But then investors find that the market rallied on the last day of December and so they will need to begin to buy on the next-to-last day of December; and because there is so much "profit taking" on January 5, investors will have to sell on January 4 to take advantage of this effect. Thus, to beat the gun, investors will have to be buying earlier and earlier in December and selling earlier and earlier in January so that eventually the pattern will self-destruct.'[28]

Some factors that produce extra risk and possible extra returns

Equity factors

Market	Stocks have higher expected returns than fixed income.
Size	Small company stocks have higher expected returns than large company stocks.
Price	Lower-priced 'value' stocks have higher expected returns than higher-priced 'growth' stocks.

Fixed income factors

Maturity	Longer-term instruments are riskier than shorter-term instruments.
Default	Instruments of lower credit quality are riskier than instruments of higher credit quality.

The single strongest argument made by efficient markets purists is, then, perhaps the simplest – if it is so obvious, why don't lots and lots of professional investors make super-sized profits as a result? Surely, this argument goes, professional fund managers should be busy trading away these inefficiencies and thus consistently beating the markets. The reality, as we discovered in the previous chapter, is that the vast majority of 'expert' fund managers singularly fail to capture these returns. Perhaps the best summary comes from Jack Tryenor, who wrote the following in the *Financial Analysts Journal* in 1981.

> 'I believe in a third view of market efficiency, which holds that the securities market will not always be either quick or accurate in processing new information. On the other hand, it is not easy to transform the resulting opportunities to trade profitably against the market consensus into superior portfolio performance. Unless the active investor understands what really goes on in the trading game, he can easily convert even superior research information into the kind of performance that will drive his clients to the poorhouse . . . why aren't more active investors consistently successful? The answer lies in the cost of trading.'

The Capital Asset Pricing Model (CAPM)

This is an economic model that describes the relationship between risk and return. It allows an investor to work out the rate of return on an asset like a share, if it is to be added to an already well-diversified portfolio, given a certain level of risk. The model is based around another deceptively simple idea, namely that higher returns are possible only if you take on higher risks. In essence it looks at risk, the expected rate of return and the equivalent return from something called a risk-free asset, like cash or bonds.

An equation sits at the heart of this model which looks something like this:

$E(R_i) = R_f + \beta_i(E(R_m) - R_f)$

Where:

- $E(R_i)$ is the expected return on the share or security
- R_f is the risk-free rate of return from something like bonds or cash
- β_i is the beta
- $(E(R_m)$ is the expected return of the market
- $(E(R_m) - R_f)$ is sometimes known as the market premium or risk premium (the difference between the expected market rate of return and the risk-free rate of return).

The CAPM assumes that investors:

- will be rationally risk averse;
- intend to maximise their utility or benefit;
- are price takers and do not influence prices by themselves;
- can lend and borrow as much as they like using the risk-free rate of interest;
- trade with shares and securities that can be sub-divided into small pieces;
- will not incur any transaction or taxation costs.

With the CAPM in hand, investors should be able to work out whether any share or asset class sits sensibly in their portfolios given their appropriate level of risk. They should also be able to construct a graph called the efficient frontier, which shows the very best mix of assets for a given level of risk and reward, i.e. an optimal portfolio that gives the lowest possible level of risk for its level of return.

Clearly a great many analysts do not subscribe to this model – many analysts like James Montier at GMO think that the assumption that investors will be rationally risk averse is ridiculous and ignores a large amount of evidence that suggests that investors are deeply behaviourally flawed and anything but rational. Many economists with a strong political economy bent also take issue with the idea that investors are simply price takers and do not influence prices by themselves, observing that any study of power in the market place would clearly reveal some substantial asymmetries.

A middle way – the reality of relatively efficient markets

Who are we to believe in this deeply charged debate? A strong case can be made for boiling down all this wealth of data and academic debate into six simple common-sense statements.

1. It's difficult to beat the market

You don't have to believe that all financial markets are completely 'perfect' to believe that most active fund management is a waste of money, most of the time. This is not to deny that some investors and some managers do not add value, some of the time. It is just a simple reality that most of the time, for most managers, you end up paying more for less. This fine balance should not also blind you to the reality that most investors – institutional and private – who use index-based strategies still make use of active fund managers for certain segments and markets.

2. Stock markets are mostly efficient but not always

Even within supposedly perfect markets there are imperfections. Buffett's observation is surely the important one, namely that while markets are mostly perfect, that is a long way from saying they are always perfect, all the time. Even the most ardent fans of perfect markets now accept that certain types of share – with certain risk profiles – can outperform the main market, much if not most of the time. This does not mean that this inefficiency and these market imperfections are easy to capture via some kind of index or fund or that in the future these imperfections will not correct themselves. Inefficiencies have a tendency to change over time and mutate and a rigid adherence to a fixed set of criteria in, say, a black box – an analytical computer-based system – full of variables might be a risky tactic if the markets do adapt and evolve.

3. It is possible to construct strategies that can deliver above-average returns … some of the time

Equally if a group of professional investors is nimble and fast and able to look into the 'nooks and crannies' of the supposedly efficient markets, it might be able to construct strategies that do capture above-average returns, although those returns might be at the expense of higher potential risk. We will be returning to this idea in Chapter 6 when Rob Davies looks at how the fundamental indexers construct their investment strategies (also see the box below on the new indexers).

4. Efficient stock markets do not necessarily behave rationally

The sensible investor recognises that in the debate between behavioural economists who use psychological insights and classical economists who have arrived at the Efficient Markets Hypothesis there is a sensible balance that needs to be struck – both are working towards the same goals from different directions. This is especially true at the macro level of national economies where it is clear that the behavioural insights of economists like Robert Shiller – his analysis of the pathology of booms and busts is deeply relevant – are hugely important in understanding why markets under- and overshoot in setting prices and valuations. It is clear that asset-backed markets like the stock market do not in the aggregate – in toto – behave that efficiently or even perfectly, thus requiring little or no regulation. To be fair to the EMH-based economists, they have never argued that efficient markets are 'perfect 'or that the markets ignore fundamentals-based valuation metrics, just that in aggregate the market is largely efficient. But investors ignore the wisdom of behavioural economists at their peril – their work may well give us causal explanations for market inefficiencies that might matter hugely in terms of our investment decisions.

5. For most investors copying an efficient market cheaply is a sensible long-term bet

The bigger the market, the more liquid it is, and the more liquid it is, the more likely it is to be relatively efficient. In these circumstances the key is to cut costs and be efficient when it comes to tracking these large, efficient markets – it means trying to copy the market most of the time, because most of the time the market is right, rather than trying to second guess it. The simplest way of doing this is to buy a fund that copies the market.

6. If you are going to copy the 'mind of the market', pick your index carefully

The best and most efficient way of copying 'the market' is to find an index that tells us the relative weights that the market attaches to its constituents, i.e. the shares in the market are weighted according to the price placed on those shares and then incorporated into an index. Crucially, not all market indices are created equally – some indices are based on very small and inefficient markets. By copying this kind of market you could be making a big mistake and opening yourself up to extra risk, whereas many markets are very large, very open and very transparent. These latter markets should be easier to track, replicate or copy using an index fund. The bottom line is that the best way to copy the 'mind of the market', as it is called, is to buy an index fund that tracks an index which in turns tracks the pricing decisions of the market.

Those myriad pricing decisions of the relatively efficient market translate through into a share, stock or security price and thus a market capitalisation (the value the market puts on the companies times the number of shares/stocks/securities issued). For most academic theorists the market capitalisation is the best measure of the market – this market cap figure isn't fair, or right, and it changes constantly, but it does represent the only true judgement of the market, namely the value placed on each and every company in the index. Add up all these market capitalisations and you have a total value for the market – an index simply takes this total market and then constructs a list of constituent shares where their percentage of the index is based on their market capitalisation. The key, then, is to buy this liquid and efficient market cheaply and efficiently. As we will discover in the next chapter, constructing an index is a deceptively simple idea, but the structures developed to capture those index returns have become increasingly complicated and varied over the last few decades.

Building the perfect index

In the next chapter we will explore how the rocket scientists and financial whiz-kids of Wall Street and now the City have taken on this challenge of building the perfect index fund. We will witness how a simple challenge from the big institutions – 'buy me the market' – has evolved into a wonderfully complex universe of new fund structures, strange acronyms and almost infinite choice.

Crucially, this explosion of innovation has brought markets ever closer to a vision of an ultimate diversified portfolio – if you want to track a major market or asset class, all you have to do is find an index that tracks that market efficiently and then track down an accompanying index fund. Suddenly the task of building a portfolio that comprises a diversified mix of assets becomes an awful lot easier. Also this profusion of new products and choice means that for those investors disenchanted with the traditional actively managed fund, a more efficient alternative is now on offer.

As we will discover in the next few chapters, though, there is still a big chasm between the theory we have discussed in this chapter and the reality on offer. Not all indices are created equally and investors need to be aware of the risks of investing in some types of index – they need to look in detail at the construction of the index and the risks involved. Crucially they might end up buying into an index tracking fund that apparently tracks an efficient market, efficiently, but in reality discover that tracking error, poor management, high costs and a multitude of other factors involved in the structure of the fund reduce efficiency and diminish returns. Over the next few chapters we will trace the evolution of the index tracking industry, look at the structures, warn about the pitfalls and then examine how you might start using these index funds in a diversified portfolio.

Do the right thing – track and diversify

> 'Tis the part of a wise man to keep himself today for tomorrow, and not venture all his eggs in one basket.'
>
> Miguel de Cervantes, Don Quixote de la Mancha, 1605
>
> 'Behold, the fool saith, "Put not all thine eggs in the one basket" – which is but a manner of saying, "Scatter your money and attention"; but the wise man saith, "Put all your eggs in the one basket and – WATCH that basket".'
>
> Mark Twain, Pudd'nhead Wilson, 1894
>
> 'A prominent magazine in 1926 recommended that a portfolio contain 25 percent sound bonds, 25 percent sound preferreds, 25 percent sound common stocks, and 25 percent speculative securities ... Until recently [1994], asset allocation was a pedestrian affair. Many institutional investors were advised to allocate 60 percent of their assets to stocks and 40 percent to fixed-income.'[29]
>
> Academic economists haven't spent all their time slamming active fund managers and constructing elegant efficient markets theories. They have also spent the last few decades building astonishingly sophisticated analytical frameworks about how to construct the perfect portfolio. At the heart of this work is a focus on diversification.
>
> We have already mentioned this widely abused word when discussing Geoff Considine's portfolios – many investors already intrinsically understand the concept of not putting all your eggs in one basket and practise a primitive form of diversification when it comes to building their portfolios.
>
> Academic economists have obviously taken the obvious and turned it into a much more noble form – modern portfolio theory. We are not going to bore you with a lengthy exposition of the ins and outs of this field, but suffice to say that most investors have three building blocks that comprise their total return:
>
> - the risk-free return – this is usually the rate of return you get from cash, although economists like to use terms like 'the rate that best neutralises your risks';
> - return from beta – technically speaking this is the return you get above the risk-free rate of return from holding an asset class like equities or a market. So if the risk-free rate of return is 2 percent and you buy a tracker for the FTSE All Share index that gives you 8 percent p.a., your beta is 6 percent;
> - return from alpha – this is the tricky one as it is the value added by a manager which is derived by the manager moving away from the beta.
>
> It is important to emphasise that even investors who concentrate on using tracking funds and thus cutting down on costs do make some use of actively managed funds – there are a great many specialised markets where trackers are of more dubious benefit compared with the diligent, research-focused active fund manager. When investors do trust an active fund manager they want to get the most extra added value from that expertise and that 'extra' added value is called alpha.

The key to understanding diversification is that lots of different kinds of markets and assets – bonds mixed with equities and, say, an alternative asset such as commodities – can give you lots of different betas and if you are lucky those different betas do not move as one, i.e. they are not correlated. Thus if equities go down, bonds might rise in value along with, say, commodities like gold – the key is that mixing up different betas might give you added benefits and improve returns.

In fact, economists are so smitten with the idea of diversification – some call it the diversification premium – that they suggest it is the one free lunch left in investing, although in recent years even that looks like it might now come at a rather hefty price, as we will discover. The prime mover in this field of optimising portfolios through beta was economist Harry Markowitz, who showed how you could combine different asset classes and betas without increasing risk. But it is later economists and analysts who have taken Markowitz's ideas and fleshed them out – Yale's fund manager David Swensen, for instance, has spent decades running hugely diversified portfolios investing in everything from forests through to private equity funds and hedge funds.

The key is that you can now juggle all these different betas in an accessible manner via index tracking funds. Swensen in particular has gone on the record and said that his hugely diversified portfolio is expected to return about 10.1 percent per year, with expected standard deviation of 11.8 percent per year, and that for most private investors the only sensible way of achieving that diversification is through index tracking funds. In an interview in the March/April 2009 issue of the Yale Alumni magazine Swensen proclaims: 'With all assets, I recommend that people invest in index funds because they're transparent, understandable, and low-cost … Almost everybody belongs on the passive end of the continuum. A very few belong on the active end. But the unfortunate fact is that an overwhelming number of investors find themselves betwixt and between. In that in-between place, people end up paying high fees, whether to a mutual fund or a stockbroker or another agent. And they end up with disappointing net returns.'

The killer piece of research, though, came in 1991, when three academics looked at what really contributes towards the performance of a portfolio. Brinson, Singer and Beebower looked at a fund manager's market-timing skills, their ability to pick shares or their ability to diversify assets.[30] They studied the largest 91 pension plans in the US over a 10-year period, with portfolio sizes reaching to $3 billion. Yet again the virtues of traditional active fund management were found to be wanting – the academics calculated that only 6 percent of total returns could be attributed to market timing and stock selection. A massive 94 percent could be explained by the careful use of diversification and the use of varying asset classes and markets over time. In fact, the study found that traditional active fund management skills like timing and stock picking produced negative returns over time after they had been adjusted for risk. The bottom line? Don't bother picking shares or trying to time the market, just allocate across different asset classes in an intelligent, diversified manner.

Another study, this time by consultants at research firm Ibbotson Associates in Chicago, looked at how including 'alternative' assets like commodities in a well-balanced portfolio could improve returns. They discovered that the average improvement in returns from these uncorrelated assets was worth 133 basis points per annum (1.33 percent per annum). They also found that 81.4 percent of the monthly variation in balanced return funds could be accounted for by asset allocation and active diversification. This analysis was backed up by eponymous fund management group Vanguard – big passive investors in the US – which has also studied the importance of active diversification or asset allocation. The firm found that 76.6 percent of the monthly variability of a fund's return around its average return depends on its asset-allocation policy.

By now you will be able to see that diversification can work wonders if done properly, especially if you are willing to stack up your portfolio with different types of asset classes. Geoff Considine has even gone so far as to put a number on the value of the diversification premium – between 2 percent and 2.5 percent per annum.

Traditionally, though, there has been a problem with trying to put this theory into everyday practice – although active fund managers have launched some funds that cover alternative asset classes, for instance, until recently there has not been an enormous diversity of asset classes with active fund managers. The analysis we have encountered above suggests a rather more exotic and rich diversity is needed – it is possible to do this with actively managed funds nowadays, but it is a lot easier to do with index tracker funds and especially easy if you are willing to use exchange traded funds, index tracking funds listed on the stock market.

3

Structuring the revolution

Not long ago I spent an entertaining afternoon talking to a focus group on investing. It was one of those amusing sessions organised by publishing companies to find out why so few people in the UK invest in shares.

The publishing director was concerned that the 'pool' of relatively active investors in the UK probably numbered only 500,000 and that that figure had not changed much in a decade. The publisher wanted to know why so many people think that houses are such a good investment compared with shares.

Shares do indeed provide greater returns over the very long term, but they do so with great volatility. In addition, most people do not actually pay themselves for the housing assets they buy – they have a mortgage, which means that their investment in housing assets is geared or on margin. Also, they live in their houses, not in their shares.

The focus group was hugely diverse, made up of people who had either actively invested in funds or shares or were thinking about it. My first set of questions was fairly general and included one about housing (bad) versus equities (good). But then I decided to see whether this group could grasp the logic behind EMH.

To my amazement, most of them understood that you cannot beat the system. Although they aspired, like all natural-born gamblers, to taking a flutter and beating that system (they all loved the idea of tips, of course), they were sufficiently cynical to know it's a mug's game and that it was largely bound to fail. That did not stop them thinking they could do it nevertheless, but it did mean they were arch realists.

When a 45-year-old working mum asked how they were supposed to make money in these stock markets if most fund managers did not actually produce the goods, I replied: 'Buy the market. Simply buy a fund that tracks a big index, like the FTSE 100 I suppose,' trying not to offer any advice while also sounding knowledgeable.

I followed up with this group a few months later and to my huge surprise discovered that out of the 12 in the room, 8 had done nothing at all, 2 had ignored the entire discussion and bought some dodgy unit trust offered by a high-street bank, and just 2 had bought a FTSE 100 tracker.

My point in recounting this story is that a great many of the central contentions of the efficient markets hypothesis when applied to stock markets are common sense, based on a kind of cold realism that we British specialise in, a brooding cynicism against all experts and a willingness to work with the system if it makes us a bit wealthier. The group mostly understood the central charges laid against the active fund management industry – although a few had ignored this realism in the subsequent months – but they were all at a loss to understand how to take advantage of their newly acquired insight.

Which is where the crucial insight into the index comes in – they realise that the odds are stacked against you beating the market, which implies that you may as well buy the market, and what better market to buy than an index you hear every day on the news channels. Buy the index. Buy the FTSE 100.

Add up all the wisdom of the random walk of markets, all the discussion of efficient markets and potential inefficiencies – and in the end its central invitation is to simply buy the market. That concept of 'buying the market' means that you buy an index you understand and think will deliver the right mix of returns alongside risk.

Building the perfect index – the FTSE 100?

By now you will begin to understand that the index you track really matters to the efficient markets theorists – track an imperfect index which is weighted improperly or does not truly represent the aggregate pricing decisions of the market on a daily, even real-time, basis and you are potentially opening yourself up to extra risk as well as to a host of inefficiencies that could cost you lots of money over time.

Luckily investors have a huge range of major markets to copy or track, with many of the key markets featuring an index that has become a part of everyday language. In the US, for instance, the level of the Dow Jones Industrial Average or the Standard & Poor's (S&P) is the subject of intense daily discussion on any number of major news programmes, while in the UK, all the major news organisations talk hourly about the current level of the FTSE 100 index of major London-listed blue chip shares.

These indices are not real as such – unlike the major exchanges which do exist in an electronic form, even if their trading floors have largely been consigned to the dustbin of history. In essence they are mathematical constructs, which are then marketed as brands to both institutional and private investors – they are a short-hand way of 'capturing' the changes in major markets. The number of these index 'brands' has increased exponentially in recent years with major providers like Dow Jones, MSCI, S&P and even the FTSE turning into research houses sporting every kind of niche index imaginable – want an index that tracks Islamic-compliant emerging markets stocks, then why not look at a niche index supplied by the likes of the FTSE (originally set up as a partnership between the Financial Times and the London Stock Exchange) or Dow Jones? The FTSE Group, for instance, calculates over 120,000 indices covering more than 77 countries and all major asset classes.

These global index brands – tracked by every kind of imaginable fund, actively managed or passively via an index fund – are usually built around one of those famous core indices that track a main market. In the UK the actual market-making bit is provided by the London Stock Exchange and the key indices are the FTSE 100 (known as the Footsie) and its related sibling, the FTSE All Share index, which comprises around 98 percent, by value, of all stocks listed on the London Stock Exchange. (Many very small listed companies based on market cap are not included in the FTSE All Share and thus this index is not one that features all listed companies and funds, despite the 'all' in its title.)

The FTSE 100 – some handy facts

- The FTSE 100 is a market-capitalisation weighted index representing the performance of the 100 largest UK-listed large cap or blue chip companies.
- All companies in the FTSE 100 must pass a test that looks at size in terms of market capitalisation and the availability or liquidity of their shares, i.e. only easy-to-purchase shares or investable shares are included. Constituents also need to have a full listing on the London Stock Exchange with a sterling or euro-dominated price on the SETS electronic trading system. Most constituents must by law include the abbreviation 'plc' at the end of their name, indicating their status as a publicly limited corporation.

- The index represents just over 80 percent of the entire market value of the various London-based stock exchanges.
- The index began on 3 January 1984 with a base level of 1,000; the highest value reached to date is 6950.6, on 30 December 1999.
- The FTSE 100 is calculated in real time and the level of the index is published every 15 seconds. Trading lasts from 08.00–16.29 (when the closing auction starts) and closing values are taken at 16.35.
- The constituents of the index are determined quarterly – the larger companies in the adjacent index, the FTSE 250, are pushed up or promoted to the FTSE 100 index if they pass the tests above and their market cap goes above a certain level.
- The weighting of shares in the index is a relatively simple exercise – the index is built around the market capitalisation of the constituent companies (all 100) so that the larger companies have a disproportionate impact on the value of the index, compared with a smaller (by market cap) company. So if HSBC, the bank, for instance, comprises 10 percent of the index and its shares rise by 10 percent, all things being equal with the other constituent companies, the index should rise by 1 percent. This 'methodology' is called the free-float methodology for constructing an index and the basic formula for any index is:

    Index level = (Price of stock* Number of shares)*Free float factor/Index divisor.

The **free float adjustment factor** represents the proportion of shares floated as a percentage of issued shares and then it is rounded up to the nearest multiple of 5 percent for calculation purposes. To find the free float capitalisation of a company, first find its market cap (number of outstanding shares * share price), then multiply its free float factor. The free float method, therefore, does not include restricted stocks, such as those held by company insiders.

At the back of this book we look at the 25 essential indices worth tracking, including the FTSE 100 and the FTSE All Share index. In each page we analyse the index, looking at its composition, past returns and pitfalls. We also suggest a range of index tracking funds that track this investment space.

To better understand how an index fund might try to capture the major moves of a major, very efficient market, let's focus on the Footsie. The box above lists some of the key characteristics of this hugely popular index as of December 2011, but in simple language the FTSE 100 has a number of key attributes at the time of writing, including:

1 There are, it goes without saying, 100 stocks in the list.
2 These are valued at a total of £1.54 trillion – that is £1,540,000 million.
3 The top 5 stocks are valued at a total of £486 billion.
4 The top 10 stocks are valued at £714 billion.
5 The bottom 50 stocks are valued at £189 billion.
6 Some companies in this list rose in value by more than 40 percent in a very volatile 2011; others dropped by more than 79 percent in the same year.

7 The top stock, Royal Dutch Shell, comprises 9.73 percent of the entire market cap while the bottom stock, financial services group Hargreaves Lansdown, comprises just over 0.13 percent of the entire market cap of the FTSE 100 – see Table 3.1.

Table 3.1 The FTSE constituents

Name	EPIC	FTSE 100 weighting %	Capital (£m)
Royal Dutch Shell PLC	RDSB	9.73	149980.0
Vodafone Goup PLC	VOD	5.74	88473.4
HSBC Holdings PLC	HSBA	5.68	87561.3
BP PLC	BP	5.66	87177.3
GlaxoSmithKline PLC	GSK	4.77	73488.1
British American Tobacco PLC	BATS	3.83	59040.1
BG Group PLC	BG.	2.97	45765.2
Rio Tinto PLC	RIO	2.57	45406.2
BHP Billiton PLC	BLT	2.48	39580.2
AstraZeneca PLC	AZN	2.31	38210.4
SABMiller PLC	SAB	2.24	35580.4
Diageo PLC	DGB	2.15	34448.5
Standard Chartered PLC	STAN	2.03	33067.6
Tesco PLC	TSCO	2.03	31348.9
Anglo American PLC	AAL	1.89	31213.1
Xstrata PLC	XTA	1.78	29048.1
Glencore International PLC	GLEN	1.77	27483.2
Unilever PLC	ULVR	1.56	27312.0
Imperial Tobacco Group PLC	IMT	1.5	24098.5
Reckitt Benckiser Group PLC	RB.	1.43	23168.5
National Grid PLC	NG.	1.42	21999.6
Barclays PLC	BARC	1.15	21831.6
Lloyds Banking Group PLC	LLOY	1.1	17655.9
International Power PLC	IPR	1.03	16891.8

Table 3.1 Continued

Name	EPIC	FTSE 100 weighting %	Capital (£m)
Prudential PLC	PRU	0.97	15911.4
Centrica PLC	CNA	0.97	15017.0
BT Group PLC	BT.A	0.88	14966.0
Rolls-Royce Group PLC	RR.	0.81	13583.1
Tullow Oil PLC	TLW	0.81	12528.9
British Sky Broadcasting Group PLC	BSY	0.81	12523.8
Shire PLC	SHP	0.8	12306.8
Royal Bank of Scotland Group (The) PLC	RBS	0.79	12165.5
Antofagasta PLC	ANTO	0.79	12106.3
SSE PLC	SSE	0.77	11804.7
Compass Group PLC	CPG	0.73	11256
Fresnillo PLC	FRES	0.71	11001.2
Pearson PLC	PSON	0.64	9901.5
CRH PLC	CRH	0.58	9008.8
BAE Systems PLC	BA.	0.58	9008.5
Associated British Foods PLC	ABF	0.57	8740.1
Aviva PLC	AV.	0.57	8715.2
Experian PLC	EXPN	0.55	8435.9
WPP Group PLC	WPP	0.54	8318.2
Morrison (Wm) Supermarkets PLC	MRW	0.53	8177
Eurasian Natural Resources Corporation PLC	ENRC	0.53	8112.8
ARM Holdings PLC	ARM	0.51	7830.1
Old Mutual PLC	OML	0.49	7523.9
Reed Elsevier PLC	REL	0.41	6278
Randgold Resources Ltd	RRS	0.4	6094.6
Legal & General Group PLC	LGEN	0.39	6018.8
Wolseley PLC	WOS	0.38	5929.6

Table 3.1 Continued

Name	EPIC	FTSE 100 weighting %	Capital (£m)
Kingfisher PLC	KGF	0.38	5816.0
Sainsbury (J) PLC	SBRY	0.36	5542.8
Smith & Nephew PLC	SN.	0.35	5414.0
Aggreko PLC	AGK	0.35	5338.5
Evraz PLC	EVR	0.34	5248.6
Burberry Group PLC	BRBY	0.34	5245.7
Petrofac Ltd	PFC	0.33	5011.0
Kazakhmys PLC	KAZ	0.32	4909.9
Land Securities Group PLC	LAND	0.32	4867.9
Marks & Spencer Group PLC	MKS	0.32	4867.1
Standard Life PLC	SL.	0.31	4775.6
Next PLC	NXT	0.3	4606.4
Carnival PLC	CCL	0.29	4540.9
Polymetal International PLC	POLY	0.28	4324.4
Weir Group PLC	WEIR	0.27	4152.9
United Utilities Group PLC	UU.	0.26	4073.8
British Land Co PLC	BLND	0.26	4035.7
Johnson Matthey PLC	JMAT	0.25	3905.0
Capita Group (The) PLC	CPI	0.25	3846.4
Sage Group (The) PLC	SGE	0.25	3804.2
G4S PLC	GFS	0.24	3731.2
Cairn Energy PLC	CNE	0.24	3728.7
RSA Insurance Group PLC	RSA	0.24	3685.7
Smiths Group PLC	SMIN	0.23	3536.8
Schroders PLC	SDR	0.23	3526.8
Severn Trent PLC	SVT	0.23	3518.6

Table 3.1 Continued

Name	EPIC	FTSE 100 weighting %	Capital (£m)
Resolution Ltd	RSL	0.22	3417.1
InterContinental Hotels Group PLC	IHG	0.21	3252.8
Tate & Lyle PLC	TATE	0.21	3219.3
Intertek Group PLC	ITRK	0.2	3107.1
Rexam PLC	REX	0.2	3068.5
Vedanta Resources PLC	VED	0.2	3025.5
AMEC PLC	AMEC	0.19	2998.4
GKN PLC	GKN	0.19	2856.2
Bunzl PLC	BNZL	0.18	2848.4
International Consolidated Airlines Group SA	IAG	0.18	2805.3
Meggitt PLC	MGGT	0.18	2732.5
Whitbread PLC	WTB	0.18	2726.4
Capital Shopping Centres Group PLC	CSCG	0.17	2601.7
Hammerson PLC	HMSO	0.16	2509.9
ITV PLC	ITV	0.16	2506.5
IMI PLC	IMI	0.16	2396.8
Serco Group PLC	SRP	0.15	2329.9
Man Group PLC	EMG	0.15	2328.8
Ashmore Group PLC	ASHM	0.15	2298.3
Essar Energy PLC	ESSR	0.15	2273.2
Admiral Group PLC	ADM	0.15	2251.6
ICAP PLC	IAP	0.14	2226.3
Hargreaves Lansdown PLC	HL.	0.13	2063.3
Total			**1,540,992**

Putting it all together in an index fund

To replicate this index, any tracker fund must try to copy it perfectly using its own basket or portfolio of shares. That means it must make sure that Royal Dutch Shell BP comprises 9.7 percent of the total value of the fund while the holding of Hargreaves Lansdown Invensys shares should be around 0.13 percent. Figure 3.1 shows the huge range of weightings necessary for such an index tracking fund.

This challenge of 'copying' the FTSE 100 introduces a number of hugely important issues:

- The composition of the fund – which in turn replicates the index – is *constantly changing*. Shares change in price on a daily basis and that change in relative weighting needs to be reflected in the index tracking fund if it is to faithfully replicate or copy the index.
- Some companies drop out of the index altogether every few months. That means not only that the weighting of stocks in the fund must be

Figure 3.1 FTSE 100 weighting

adjusted but the actual list of company holdings will also alter dramatically. In recent years resource companies (miners and oil outfits) as well as the banks have dominated the FTSE 100 index, at times accounting for more than 60 percent of the market capitalisation of the entire index. At the time of writing, these two sectors account for only less than 50 percent of the FTSE 100.

- With such a long list of possible constituents – 100 in this example – it is much easier if your index fund is very large. If you have an index fund that is worth £1,000 million (£1 billion), then that implies buying £1.4 million of shares in the smallest company in the list, Invensys (with 0.14 percent). Dealing costs are likely to be very low as a proportion of that purchase cost and the market makers (the institutions which buy and sell shares) will probably offer the fund managers a tiny spread between the bid and offer price. If, however, your total fund is valued at just £1 million, buying Invensys means buying £1,430 worth of shares. Proportionately that makes dealing costs much more expensive, and in addition you run the risk of getting caught out by high bid–offer spreads, i.e. the market makers might also add in a 1 percent or even 2 percent markup in the difference between the buying and selling price for relatively small deals.

The Vanguard definition of market cap-weighted indices

According to researchers at Vanguard:[1]

'Indices should reflect the market – or market portion – that they are intended to measure. They are therefore weighted according to market capitalization, where:

Market cap = Price per share * Number of shares outstanding.

Market cap-weighted indices reflect the consensus estimate of each company's value at any given moment. In any efficient market, new information – economic, financial, or company specific – affects the price of one or more securities and is reflected instantaneously in the index via the change in its market capitalization. Thus, a continuously updated market index gives an indication of how well a market is performing, and of the market's structural and risk characteristics at any given point in time. Since, according to capital market theory – specifically, the Capital Asset Pricing Model – current prices (and, hence, company values) are set based on current and expected events, cap-weighted indices represent the expected ... portfolio of securities in a given asset class. In addition, market-cap-weighted indices are continuously reweighted, and turnover is limited to changes in the constituents or in their shares outstanding due to corporate events such as share buybacks or issuances.'

Capturing the index

So much for the idea of capturing the index, but how do you go about building an index fund that does the job cheaply and effectively? To understand the inner workings – the mechanics – of such a fund you first have to understand the journey that brought us to the perfectly formed index fund.

This journey started many decades ago in the US. Many market professionals worked together in different organisations and stock markets to develop the first index funds, but one name towers above everyone else, John Bogle. Founder of giant US fund management firm Vanguard, Bogle is rightly regarded as one of the wisest men on Wall Street, whose open letters end up as op-ed pages on *The Wall Street Journal*.

Bogle graduated from Princeton University in 1951, boasting a thesis entitled: 'Mutual Funds can make no claims to superiority over the Market Averages'. His painstaking research showed that three-quarters of fund managers would not have earned more than an investor who had managed to invest across the index of America's 500 largest companies.

Clearly Bogle was already no great fan of active fund management and he spent the subsequent decades perfecting his idea of the perfect index tracking fund. Then, in 1974, his ambitious ideas began to take shape as he founded his own investment company, The Vanguard Group, now the second largest mutual fund company in the US. Curiously, the debut of his new concern closely followed the 1973 publication of *A Random Walk Down Wall Street* in which the Princeton economist Burton Malkiel called for the establishment of a low-cost fund that reflected the market index.[2] Bizarrely – given the timing – John Bogle later admitted that he had not actually read the book at the time, only catching up with it many years later. One of his first funds was a rather innocuous little fund called the First Index Investment Trust, which was started on 31 December 1975. According to one account of the start of this fund it was 'labelled Bogle's follies and regarded as un-American, because it sought to achieve the averages rather than insisting that Americans had to play to win'.[3] Another account of Vanguard's history noted the sour-puss reaction of one mutual fund executive who claimed that 'indexing is a sure path to mediocrity'.[4] By August 1976 this small fund had been relaunched with a snazzier name, the Vanguard 500 Index Fund, which in turn tracked a rather familiar index known as the Standard & Poor's 500 index (the S&P 500) – see Table 3.2.

Table 3.2 Performance of Vanguard 500 as of 31 January 2009 – average annual returns

	1 Year	3 Year	5 Year	10 Year	Since inception 31/08/1976
500 Index Fund Inv	–38.63%	–11.85%	–4.34%	–2.73%	9.70%
S&P 500 Index*	–38.63%	–11.78%	–4.24%	–2.65%	–

Source: from Vanguard, © The Vanguard Group, used with permission

The fund started with comparatively meagre assets of $11 million but at the time of writing has assets totalling a huge $74 billion. Even Bogle himself, now transformed into a titan of investing, seems to have been surprised by the success of the fund. Commenting on its success he noted, 'in the financial markets it is always wise to expect the unexpected' though it is very likely that few of his investors will be complaining about the returns from the fund. Annualised profits since inception have hit 9.70 percent p.a.

It is important to say that Bogle was not the only person experimenting in the index tracking space. John McQuown and David Booth at Wells Fargo and Rex Sinquefield at American National Bank in Chicago were all toying with similar funds, and in 1971 Wells Fargo established the first Standard & Poor's Composite Index Fund, with a minimum investment of $100,000. With such a high initial investment level, this proto-index fund was clearly aimed at institutions and not the private investors Bogle wanted to serve. Wells Fargo started with $5 million from its own pension fund, while Illinois Bell put in $5 million of its pension funds at the American National Bank version of the index fund. Within 30 years these institutional-side outfits had developed and been bought out by a hitherto unknown player in this space, Barclays Bank. The British investment bank had big plans to develop a strong global investment fund management business and reckoned that selling specialist funds that tracked an index was a potentially brilliant business to be in. How right they were.

So although the genesis of the index fund is hotly contested and does not really belong to any one person or institution, Vanguard's John Bogle has certainly made the biggest success of it. To describe the Vanguard 500 fund as the grand-daddy of modern mass-market index funds is possibly underestimating its impact – it is quite simply the biggest fund aimed at private investors in the US today. Tables 3.3 and 3.4 provide a quick snapshot of the fund as of the end of 2011.

Table 3.3 Equity characteristics of Vanguard fund as of 11/30/2011

	500 Index Fund Inv	S&P 500 Index
Number of stocks	504	500
Median market cap	$49.9 billion	$49.9 billion
Price/earnings ratio	14x	13.9x
Price/book ratio	2.1x	2.1x
Return on equity	20.7%	20.6%
Earnings growth rate	7.3%	7.3%
Foreign holdings	0.2%	–
Turnover rate (as of fiscal year end December)	4.8%	–
Fund total net assets	$101 billion	–
Share class total net assets	$27 billion	–
Total expense ratio	0.17% pa	

Source: from Vanguard, © The Vanguard Group, used with permission

Table 3.4 Equity sector diversification (figures in percent)

	500 Index Fund Inv as of 11/30/2011	500 Index Fund Inv as of 11/30/2010	S&P 500 Index as of 11/30/2011
Consumer discretionary	10.60	10.80	10.60
Consumer staples	11.40	11.00	11.40
Energy	12.50	11.80	12.50
Financials	13.40	15.30	13.40
Health care	11.60	11.10	11.60
Industrials	10.70	10.70	10.70
Information technology	19.40	19.20	19.40
Materials	3.60	3.60	3.60
Telecommunication services	3.10	3.10	3.10
Utilities	3.70	3.40	3.70

Source: from Vanguard, © The Vanguard Group, used with permission

This Vanguard fund tells you everything you need to know about the structure of a great index fund. It is big, it is cheap and it works brilliantly. Crucially, the fund does an amazing job of replicating or copying the index that it tracks. Its returns do not perfectly match those of the S&P 500 but they are very close – see Tables 3.5 and 3.6. Oddly enough, the fund has 504 stocks while the S&P has, of course, 500 stocks. But the composition of holding in the portfolio absolutely matches those in the index and the median market capitalisation of each underlying share is exactly the same, at $49 billion, with the average PE ratio being 14.

Table 3.5 Annualised returns from the Vanguard 500 index fund vs the S&P 500 index (figures in percent)

Average annual returns – updated monthly as of 11/30/2011

	1 Year	3 Year	5 Year	10 Year	Since inception 08/31/1976
500 Index Fund Inv	7.67	14.03	−0.26	2.80	10.36
S&P 500 Index	7.83	14.13	−0.18	2.91	—

Source: from Vanguard, © The Vanguard Group, used with permission

Table 3.6 Returns by year

Annual investment returns as of 12/31/2010

Year ended	Vanguard 500 Index Fund Investor Shares			S&P 500 Index
	Capital return	Income return	Total return	Total return
2010	12.81	2.11	14.91	15.06
2009	23.56	2.92	26.49	26.46
2008	−38.52	1.50	−37.02	−37.00
2007	3.49	1.89	5.39	5.49
2006	13.64	2.01	15.64	15.79
2005	2.94	1.84	4.77	4.91
2004	8.74	2.00	10.74	10.88
2003	26.52	1.98	28.50	28.68
2002	−23.36	1.22	−22.15	−22.10
2001	−13.11	1.08	−12.02	−11.89
2000	−9.95	0.90	−9.06	−9.10
1999	19.70	1.37	21.07	21.04
1998	27.00	1.61	28.62	28.58
1997	31.11	2.08	33.19	33.36
1996	20.53	2.35	22.88	22.96

Source: from Vanguard, © The Vanguard Group, used with permission

You will also notice from Tables 3.5 and 3.6 – they both detail annual returns – that there is never more than a 0.16 percent p.a. difference in returns between the fund and the index it tracks, i.e. its tracking error is very low. Remember that the tracking error is (nearly) always negative, i.e. the fund *underperforms* the underlying index and that is because the total expense ratio, which is the cost of managing the fund, is 0.17 percent p.a. That cost is, in fact, the primary reason for the tracking error – every year the investor must bear the burden of paying that 0.17 percent cost which in turn reduces fund returns. But that 0.17 percent is also probably a tiny price to pay for the tracking expertise. Most actively managed funds in the US, by contrast, charge more than 1 percent p.a. and deliver poorer returns than the Vanguard fund.

The new indexers

> The traditional model for index investing is based on holding a market cap or price value weighted portfolio of shares or stocks. The reality, even for big tracker funds, is that there are thousands of tiny stocks at the smaller end of the spectrum that are too costly to trade. Trackers tend to sample from these stocks, buying only some of the names until they have a portfolio that looks and hopefully behaves like that segment of the stock universe. This tiny 'long tail' of shares – lots of small companies, making up the list but not really mattering in terms of total market cap – can cause fund performance to deviate from the index, especially during small-stock-led bull markets. It also demonstrates that even pure indexers do not mimic the market exactly.
>
> The new indexers, led by Eugene Fama, start from a different place. As we noted in our earlier chapter looking at the theory behind trackers and the critics who have lined up to attack the new orthodoxy in academia, economists like Fama reckon that there are, in fact, three distinct risk factors in stock investing. Small company stocks expose investors to a completely different form of volatility, for instance they have unique risk–return characteristics. Each of these risk 'flavours' is unrelated to the others. Small stocks can do well when the overall market does poorly and value stocks can have dreadful returns when small stocks do well, and so on. According to new indexers like Fama, each of these risk factors has as much potential for increasing investment returns as wider market returns.
>
> Fama says: 'In the presence of more than one risk factor, the goal of indexing [now] switches from diversification across the available stocks to diversification across the available risk-return dimensions.'[5] To old-school indexers like John Bogle this all sounds a bit like taking a bet on sectors or themes – Bogle still believes that the overall market itself, what we call market risk, primarily determines performance and that small stocks and value stocks are not separate sources of risk and return.
>
> An even brasher new school of critics has emerged in recent years. These critics believe investors should dump the whole market cap weighting methodology, not alter and tilt its composition using the factors favoured by Fama.
>
> One school of radicals maintains that the best way to build an index is to equal weight every company in the index. In a paper entitled 'Are equal weighted indices better than market cap weighted indices?', Greg Burgess spells out this new line of thinking which has produced an entirely different form of index, something called the

Equally Weighted S&P 500.[6] The key insight here is to challenge the standard index structure which is biased towards a small number of very large companies. According to Burgess, the S&P EWI (Equal Weight Index) is a more 'neutral' version of the S&P 500 in that it offers higher exposure to small cap companies (and conversely lower exposure to really large cap companies), although it also has a higher turnover as a result of its quarterly rebalancing, and very different risk and sector profiles.

This radically different return and risk profile is a direct result of the very different small vs large cap exposure – an equally weighted index is bound to be biased towards smaller cap companies in the index as it gives them the same weighting as the huge, mega-caps. To use the earlier example of the FTSE 100, the smallest company on the list – Invensys – would theoretically comprise 1 percent of the total index weighting, as would the largest (by market cap), BP, which would also comprise just 1 percent. The index developers reckon that this new style of index might produce better returns but with a lower level of risk – index managers S&P also observe that 'historically when large companies have done well the S&P 500 has outperformed, and when smaller companies have done well the S&P EWI has outperformed'.

Burgess also points out that this new type of index is a trickier beast to track – it is reset quarterly and funds that track it end up with higher trading turnover, and that higher turnover tends to result in higher costs, which eat into returns. 'This means that the index's performance is difficult, but not impossible, to replicate with a low degree of tracking error,' suggests Burgess. Exchange traded fund provider Rydex does have an index fund that tries to replicate the performance of the S&P 500 Equal Weight Index, but its turnover rate is high – at 40 percent p.a.

But does this radical new way of constructing an index actually work, even if you can find a way to efficiently track it? In good years, i.e. bull markets, the Equal Weight Index does seem to produce better returns than the standard index, if only because of its relative weight towards smaller cap stocks. In distressed markets the Equal Weight Index does not seem to offer any great advantage, especially as investors flee smaller stocks for the safety of mega-caps.

Even more radical ideas about how to build an index are emerging from the asset management companies. These new approaches use some very different ideas about how to construct an index – some private banks in Europe, for instance, are pioneering an index built around a concept called minimum variance. This weights an index of stocks not by its market cap or its value-based fundamental measures but by each stock's volatility, i.e. low volatility stocks get a higher weighting.

Yet another approach comes from a brash new fund company called TOBAM, which has emerged out of the ashes of Lehmans. Its principals have come up with a radical new concept called anti-benchmarking. The methodology behind this new approach to indexing was outlined in a paper called 'Towards maximum diversification' in the *Journal of Portfolio Management* in autumn 2008 and was devised by two French quantitatively trained investment analysts, Yves Choueifaty and Yves Coignard.[7] They looked at the construction of traditional market cap weighted indices, such as the S&P 500, and questioned whether investors were taking on too much risk from lack of diversification and high levels of volatility. Their research acknowledged the reality that much of the S&P 500 or the FTSE 100 is closely correlated, thus providing low levels of diversification for those trying to build a balanced portfolio. For the TOBAM analysts, diversification is the crucial component of returns in a portfolio, so they set about finding a different way to construct an index of stocks. Their resulting anti-benchmark portfolios use an equation-based system to examine both correlation and volatility as the key components of any weighting system. In essence, their system looks for stocks with lower relative volatility and higher diversification.

Table 3.7, from a TOBAM publication in May 2008, shows what a typical basket of the top 10 stocks in the FTSE might look like in one of its anti-benchmark portfolios versus a traditional market cap weighting (used by the FTSE 100 and most trackers), a fundamental indexing strategy (used by the likes of Eugene Fama), an equal weight portfolio and a minimum variance portfolio. The TOBAM approach is not to overinvest in volatile stocks (it has low holdings of very volatile stocks like Barclays and Anglo American) but to weight its holdings towards shares that provide extra diversification because of their low correlation to the other stocks within the list, i.e. pharma companies like GlaxoSmithKline tend to move in a different way to a gaggle of bank stocks, providing investors with some extra diversification. Add up the lower volatility and higher diversification, and the TOBAM analysts believe you have a more diversified portfolio. In practical terms the resulting portfolios from the TOBAM and minimum variance approach look very different from more traditional indices – the top five banks comprise just 18 percent of this top 10 as opposed to 45 percent in a market cap weighted system, while Tesco is a staggering 27.90 percent of total holdings (compared with just 5.80 percent in a market weighted system).

Table 3.7 Example stock allocation system using TOBAM system (figures in percent)

Company name	Stock volatility	Market cap portfolio	Fundamental indexing portfolio	Equal weight portfolio	Minimum variance portfolio	Anti benchmark portfolio
HSBC	13.48	16.90	19.36	10	25.90	3.20
RBS Group	17.42	9.60	12.05	10	0	1.90
Barclays	22.24	7.40	8.04	10	0	5.00
HBOS	17.59	6.40	6.91	10	0	2.60
Lloyds TSB	16.13	5.10	5.72	10	9.70	10.30
Tesco	15.73	5.80	4.50	10	28.40	27.90
Anglo American	35.32	6.00	5.08	10	0	5.70
Royal Dutch Shell	16.04	17.90	17.47	10	20.50	18.70
GlaxoSmithKline	16.86	13.10	8.13	10	15.50	22.40
Vodafone Group	22.18	11.90	12.75	10	0	7.30

Source: www.tobam/ft

The rise of ETFs

Vanguard may have been at the forefront of this indexing revolution in the 1970s and 1980s but by the 1990s a new type of fund structure had emerged. To all intents and purposes this new creature – called an exchange traded fund (ETF) – was almost identical to the Vanguard range of index tracking mutual funds (Vanguard does not run index tracking funds only and has entered the ETF market aggressively in recent years). These new-fangled ETFs also track key markets via an index and they are cheap and easy to understand like the Vanguard 500 index fund, but there is one crucial difference – the ETFs are listed funds, bought and sold in real time, on the stock exchanges that they in turn track. The Vanguard funds by contrast are mutual funds, bought via an adviser with pricing based on an end-of-the-day review structure. While Vanguard funds may be loved by many American financial planners, ETFs are stock market creatures and it is no surprise that the creator of this fund structure was a stock market itself, namely the American Stock Exchange in New York.

The AMEX market had evolved from its origins quite literally on the kerb of Broad Street in New York. As it grew it became the home to the many smaller companies that were not quite big enough to get on the New York Stock Exchange (NYSE). But its very success in the small cap business soon caused it problems – rival markets started emerging that were much keener to let in even newer, even riskier, younger, untested, untried companies. In particular NASDAQ erupted on the scene and the love affair with tech start-ups blossomed with private investors. AMEX needed to innovate and stay ahead of the competition. By the late 1980s the gist of a new business idea began to take shape – why not combine AMEX's competitive edge with products like derivatives (options and other forms of futures) alongside more traditional closed-end funds? The initial idea was to get mutual funds to list or trade their shares on the exchange – the market even invited John Bogle to see whether his index fund could be traded like a share. Vanguard refused – the exchange traded platform would simply add to costs and Bogle's mission was to produce funds with the lowest cost possible.

Suddenly the clever futures-based rocket scientists working deep within the bowels of AMEX hit on an idea. Why not separate out the functions of fund management from the actual exchange trading – portfolios of stocks could be deposited with a trustee which could then be turned into a form of 'depositary receipt', an idea borrowed from the world of commodity trading where warehouse receipts were given to traders for hosting their products. That receipt, in turn, could be sub-divided into lots of little units that could then be traded on the exchange as 'equity securities'. These individual units would not be redeemable by the fund but could be reassembled into a full depositary receipt and redeemed by the trustee – a process of creation and redemption that was eventually to be turned into an art form.

The first of these new-style ETFs was born on 29 January 1993. It was called the Standard & Poor's depositary receipt – or SPDR for short, although an

'I' was soon added to the acronym to make SPIDER. This 'trust' tracked the popular S&P 500 index – also tracked by the Vanguard fund – and was built from scratch to appeal to institutional investors who wanted something cheap and easy to trade in.

American commentator Archie Richards notes that when the idea of the SPIDER was first presented to members of the Securities and Exchange Commission it was greeted with confusion and eventually took three years to get full approval.[8] The commissioners, Richards says, could not relate these new-fangled shares to anything else they had seen and eventually they classified these SPIDERs as something called a unit investment trust. These investment trusts were and are closed-end vehicles – a fixed amount is raised up front – and are listed on the exchange like any other share. But ETFs, unlike these traditional vehicles, changed in size and market capitalisation constantly via a creation and redemption process and were not managed on an active basis like most traditional investment trusts, i.e. they simply reflected the composition of the underlying index they tracked.

The structure used for the actual operation of the ETF was something called a depositary trust. The trustee of the SPIDER Trust ETF, for instance, is a bank called State Street, while the beneficial owners are the investors in the fund – both private and institutional. As Richards notes, this first ETF was as simple and effective as the first Vanguard fund: 'The trust, says the prospectus, is a pooled investment designed to closely track the price and yield performance of the S&P 500 Index. Tracking the S&P 500 worked for Vanguard, why not the SPIDERS.'[9] Crucially, this depositary structure allows for something called an undivided interest – every share purchased in the trust represents an infinitesimal holding in the underlying companies which are, in turn, held in the fund. So, every time you buy a SPIDER share, you buy into a basket of actual shares that track the composition of the S&P 500 and in turn you end up owning a tiny, tiny holding in not only the largest share in the index but also the smallest, and everything in between. Crucially, each share of the SPIDER contains one-tenth of the S&P index and trades at roughly one-tenth of the dollar-value level of the S&P 500.

This depositary structure – familiar to the SEC commissioners who had authorised it – allows a number of key advantages for both the issuer of the shares and the investors. A crucial change in the investment rules governing the US stock markets in 1990 had allowed for the creation of what were called SuperTrusts – funds that could operate like any share but also permit constant creation and redemption of new shares. This process is crucial to the inner workings of an ETF, as we will discover a little later, but in essence this simple process means that the SuperTrusts do not have to go through the palaver of shares placings and rights issues to create new stock – they can just operate a constant process of creation and redemption to make sure that the quoted share price is as close as possible to the underlying value of assets in the fund.

An even bigger advantage was that the trust structure let the SEC allow the short selling of ETFs. This meant that the SPIDER rapidly turned into a simple and cost-effective shorting instrument for investors looking to sell the S&P 500. This rapidly became a key feature of all ETFs – during the market meltdown, assets under ETF management doubled in a few weeks as shorters used ETFs as an instrument for hedging. Also, the depositary trust company structure of the SPIDERS meant that the managers did not have to keep track of individual shareholders, they only had to keep a book entry form at the trustees, substantially cutting down on costs. The Vanguard funds, by contrast, cannot be used as vehicles to short the markets and involve the fund managers in some fairly laborious administration and client management – they need to keep meticulous records of who owns each of the units within the fund.

This trust structure also endowed ETFs – or at least what we might call classic ETFs – with one last crucial advantage, namely management and custodial control of the fund. This structure is detailed in Table 3.8. The manager of the fund, State Street, is separate from the actual trust which is owned by its investors. This separation is crucial – modern-day variants of this SPIDER exchange traded fund structure, managed by outfits like Barclays, have retained a separation between your (tiny) bit of the overall fund and the various service providers to the fund, such as the investment manager, index providers, custodians, etc. If your manager goes bust, that theoretically does not have any effect on your investment as hopefully another manager will simply take control and carry on with the task of replicating the index.

Table 3.8 Parties involved in running an ETF

Investment manager	Day-to-day management of the fund
Index provider	Determines the index that is tracked by the fund
Data provider	Provides daily pricing for securities
Authorised participant	Creation and redemption of shares at primary market level
Custodian	Safe keeping and accounting of fund assets
Administrator	Processing subscription and redemption requests and other elements of fund administration
Registrar and transfer agent	Responsible for carrying out transfer agency and paying agency functions

Source: Barclays iShares

The SPIDER fund went on to be a huge long-term success – at the time of writing it is still the largest ETF on the market and accounts for about 16 percent of all assets in the ETF market – but for the first few years ETF trading was subdued as investors quietly came to terms with the new structure and the regulators grappled to understand the new product.

As the SPIDER ETFs slowly began to take off, rival forms (beset by a nasty case of acronymitis) also began to spring up. In Canada, for instance, the Toronto Stock Exchange had been trying out a similar structure called 'index participations' or TIPs, while in Philadelphia a short-lived variant of a futures contract emerged that allowed investors to track indices through something called index participation shares or IPS. In 1998 another variant called World Equity Benchmark Shares (WEBS) emerged, offering investors the chance to invest in single countries – Morgan Stanley's nation-specific indices were used as the index and the funds were managed by Barclays Global Investors, which had taken over Wells Fargo's fund management arm. By now the acronyms were exploding all over the place and another variant called DIAMONDS was launched – these were ETFs based on the Dow Jones index. The NASDAQ 100 Trust also emerged in 1999 – BNY's – and by 2000 ETFs were changing the face of modern investment. But despite the huge growth in both structures and dazzling acronyms, the basic idea that powers this innovation has remained relatively constant – buy the market efficiently and cheaply.

Defining ETFs

The American Stock Exchange defines an ETF as follows: '[They are] open-ended registered investment companies under the Investment Company Act of 1940, which have received certain exemptive relief from the SEC to allow secondary market trading in the ETF shares. ETFs are index-based products, in that each ETF holds a portfolio of securities that is intended to provide investment results that, before fees and expenses, generally correspond to the price and yield performance of the underlying benchmark index.'[10]

This long-winded and overly technical definition sums up ETFs very nicely. They are:

- an investment company
- that offers secondary market trading on the main exchanges, much like any other share;
- they are index based and are
- based on a portfolio of securities.

ETFs are in fact a mutant mix of the traditional investment trust – very familiar to British readers – and the open-ended mutual fund or unit trust. Like mutuals, ETFs represent a fractional ownership in an underlying portfolio of shares that tracks a specific index, but unlike mutual funds, individual investors do not purchase or redeem shares from the fund. Instead individuals buy and sell ETFs like ordinary shares on an exchange. Also, the price of the ETF varies on the basis of changes in the underlying portfolio and according to the changes in the market supply and demand for ETFs themselves.

How they work in detail

Let us assume that you are a large institution. You are managing a large pot of pension money for a local authority. This troublesome bunch of Northern municipal socialists has some rather old-fashioned ideas about keeping costs down and not trying anything too fancy by keeping it simple. They want a slice of the FTSE 100 – nice, boring companies paying a steady dividend.

In the 1980s, before the rise of ETFs, they could approach a big bank that operated something called portfolio trading to sell them a futures-based option that essentially gave them access to the FTSE 100 in one product. Alternatively they could, if they were large enough, just order their brokers to go out and buy all the constituents of the FTSE 100, in the right proportions. They would in essence have their own private ETF. But if they were really clever and were still doing this by the next decade, they could, in theory, take this ready-made basket of shares and pop along to a big ETF issuer like Barclays' iShares and swap that portfolio for a bunch of shares in the iShares FTSE 100 ETF. Barclays would then simply create more shares in its ETF and absorb the pension fund assets into its mutual fund.

Flash forward another year. The Northern pension fund types have noticed that their shares in the FTSE 100 ETF are behaving rather strangely. The year before they had swapped their basket of FTSE 100 shares for ETF shares, but they have now noticed that there is a difference between the market price of the ETF (for argument's sake, say £100) and the actual basket of assets in the fund (worth, say, £101). That discount to the underlying value or net asset value makes them a bit anxious, so they tell their City types to go to the ETF company and cash in their millions of shares for their 'bit' of the total fund, i.e. the basket of shares in the FTSE 100. Suddenly they have their old basket of FTSE 100 stocks back again and they have (hopefully) made a small profit because they have used their ETF shares (worth £100 per share) to buy £101 per share of assets.

Being really crafty types, this pension fund could carry on trading its assets back and forth with the ETF as the discount waxes and wanes, sometimes turning a discount into a premium – constantly making a bit of money on the side until the politicians in City Hall realise that the pension fund has in fact turned into what experts call an arb fund, making endless small profits from big trades. This rather ridiculous example – who would imagine boring pension funds involving themselves in risky activities normally reserved for hedge fund tyros? – demonstrates the very simple principles and processes that lurk in the engine room of an ETF.

The ETF manager or custodian decides that there is some money to be made setting up a fund that tracks a key index. They buy a basket of shares that tracks this index as faithfully as possible and then sell the shares to big institutions – and small investors alike – looking to buy exposure to that index. These shares have some important numbers pinned to them that indicate various levels of 'value':

1. The price to buy the shares – this is set by the market maker (a financial intermediary) and not the ETF manager.
2. The price to sell the shares – this is also set by the market maker, not the manager, and is usually less than the purchase price.
3. The net asset value (NAV) of the shares in the ETF. This is simply the total value of all the assets divided by the number of shares issued. This NAV should (hopefully) be very close to the market price above ... but not always.

Sometimes a difference emerges between the NAV and the market price – in traditional investment trusts, the investors just have to put up with this discount and hope that somebody important shouts loudly and the fund's managers work out a way of buying back the shares. In ETFs, by contrast, some very smart market players called authorised participants – also known as arbitrageurs or arbs – can exploit this difference as long as they have got enough money to buy a minimum 50,000 shares per deal. They can, like our pension fund, simply buy the same basket of shares and then present them to the ETF issuer and demand some ETF shares in return. If the ETF shares are trading at a discount to the NAV, that exchange – real shares in the index companies for shares in the ETF – might make them a quick profit. That profit is rarely the 1 percent difference experienced by our pension fund above – it is usually just a few basis points, but if you are dealing in millions of pounds of ETF shares, a few basis points every day can make your traders a lot of money.

The point of all this arbing and trading is that hopefully the efficient market in ETFs (remember that theoretical creature from the previous chapter) will constantly smooth out the premiums and discounts and keep the share price of the ETF close to the value of the underlying shares. That means when you buy your well-constructed, large FTSE 100 ETF you really are buying an almost perfect facsimile of the index, with no drag from any discounts to the NAV.

There is, of course, a more technical way of describing this chain of creation and redemption:

1. The market maker purchases a basket of shares, as specified by the ETF custodian, for cash.
2. This basket of securities is then exchanged with the ETF custodian for a set number of ETF units or shares (creation).
3. The market maker then has an inventory of ETF shares through which to satisfy market demand for buy/sell orders.
4. Redemption – this is simply the whole process in reverse, whereby a market maker will swap a defined number of ETF shares with the ETF custodian for the underlying basket of shares, which can then be sold for cash in the secondary market.

Figure 3.2 from the Global Index Research team at Deutsche Bank explains this process in even greater detail, looking both at the share creation process and the resulting ETF balance sheet. Crucially note that its description of the process of creation and redemption is based around a term called physical replication, i.e. the actual fund physically buys the shares in the index and then houses those shares within its fund structure. As we will see below this is the 'traditional' structure of an ETF, dominant in the US. (In Europe a different fund structure has emerged as a challenger based around something called synthetic replication. More on that in the next section!)

Returning to the basics of creation and redemption, the key point is that the price of this 'traditional' ETF is not entirely determined by market supply and demand, but rather the creation/redemption process. If the share price is above the net asset value, an arbitrageur can buy the index portfolio and sell the ETF short, thus making an instant profit. If the market price is below the NAV, they simply do the reverse, namely buy the ETF, and sell the index portfolio short. The net effect? As we have already discussed, the market price should be very, very close to the underlying net asset value of the basket of underlying stocks.

The Financial Times Guide to ETFs and Index Funds

Investment of €1,000 in an ETF tracking Euro Stoxx 50 — Physical

Share creation process – During Day 0

(1a) The investor pays €1,000 in cash to a broker and receives shares in exchange.
(1b) The investor gives an index slice (securities in kind) to the AP and received shares. This is less common than 1a.
(2a) The broker gives cash to the EFT in exchange for shares (delivery versus payment).
(2b) The AP gives index slice (securities in kind) to the ETF in exchange for shares (delivery versus payment).
(3a) The EFT will use the cash to purchase securities which closely, or fully, reflect the Euro Stoxx 50 index composition.
(3b) The EFT will receive an index slice (securities in kind) and will deposit those in its account with the fund's custodian.

Return enhancements – Day 1

– (4) The fund manager may elect to lend securities held by the ETF to a third party, in order to generate additional revenue.
– (5) The securities lending counterparty will post collateral in favour of the fund in order to mitigate credit risk resulting from the transaction.

ETF's Balance Sheet

	Day 0	Day 1
Assets		
ETF physical assets marked-to-market	€1,000	€1,000
Securities on loan	€0	€30
	€1,000	€1,050
Liabilities		
Fund shareholders' equity	€1,000	€1,000
Collaterall received – Sec lending	€0	€30
	€1,000	€1,050

* A 5% increase in the price of the Euro Stoxx 50 index has been assumed for this illustration.

ETF's Balance Sheet

– Investors hold shares which give them direct ownership to the fund's assets (as per balance sheet), which closely mirror the Euro Stoxx 50.
– Securities held by the ETF will be marked to market at the end of each day.
– The fund balance sheet will also include fee accruals and small cash balances, associated with fund running expenses.

Sampling: physically replicating an index entails purchasing a basket that mirrors or closely reflects the composition of a target benchmark. On certain occasions, a manager might decide to sample the composition of a certain index. The degree of sampling varies and will typically entail employing statistical techniques to derive the optimal sample to hold. Sampling is particularly popular with ETFs that track indices that have a very large number of constituents denominated in different currencies across countries or for omitting some constituents which are difficult to get hold of. Sampling is more commonly employed by ETFs that target emerging market benchmarks.

Figure 3.2 Physical replication and fund balance sheet

Source: Global Index Research Team, Deutsche Bank, www.etf.db.com

As you may have realised, this ETF is very different in design and operation from a traditional unit trust or mutual fund as it's called in the US. Table 3.9 is from the Global Index Research Team at Deutsche Bank and compares a typical ETF with its 'traditional' mutual fund cousin.

Table 3.9 ETFs and mutual funds: trading and valuation comparison

Trading and valuation comparison	ETF	*Mutual fund*
Similarities		
Who manages the fund's assets?	Fund Manager	
How is the fund's NAV determined?	Administrator/Fund accountant	
Who safeguards the fund's assets?	Fund custodian	
Applicable management fees	Total expense ratio	
Primary governing regulation	UCITS plus additional requirements by some local regulators	

Trading and valuation comparison	ETF	*Mutual fund*
Differences		
How can they be bought?	**Primary market:** authorised participants (APs), fund providers **Secondary market:** Brokers	**Primary market only:** fund providers, brokers
How often can they be traded?	Intra-day market price (on-exchange or OTC), set point in time, daily (some providers, at NAV)	Set point in time, typically daily, some less frequently depending on how often the fund is open for trading
Application trading fees	Brokerage fees	Distribution fees
Value at which they are traded?	Price intra-day, NAV end of day	NAV only, end of day or other interval
How is their price determined?	Supply and demand of shares traded	Not applicable, only NAV

Table 3.9 Continued

| Price bid-ask spread applicable | Yes, intra-day purchases and sales of shares subject to bid-ask spreads. APs need to hedge their risk for selling intra-day plus recover a profit margin | No |

Souce: Global Index Research Team, Deutsche Bank, www.etf.db.com

The European alternative: synthetic replication

In the US market ETFs are required to use the physical tracking structure explained above – the Securities and Exchange Commission mandates what is called physical replication for fund-based structures. In Europe the story is very different, as regulators have also allowed another form of tracking to exist alongside physical replication, which involves the use of options-based swap contracts. This alternative fund structure is called *synthetic replication* and is in some respects a much simpler structure, although critics allege that its reliance on IOUs issued by large investment banks opens investors up to unnecessary risks. Later in this chapter we'll explore these concerns in greater depth but it is worth exploring some of the challenges of traditional physical replication.

On paper, full replication essentially involves a fund manager working for an asset manager buying all the constituents of a major index, in exactly the right composition. Back in the real world the reality is a little different as most physically tracking funds boast a range of holdings that is not identical to the underlying index. For very liquid underlying markets, such as those companies in the FTSE 100, that difference in underlying holdings probably will not matter greatly but for more difficult to access markets that discrepancy could make a huge difference.

The chief concern for private investors is that the different holdings within the fund might generate returns that begin to diverge from those of the index. This is called *tracking error* and for some less liquid markets this can be a real challenge – high tracking errors eat into your returns. Traditional ETF companies have tried to narrow down this tracking error by using all manner of clever statistically-based methods such as sampling or optimisation – these methods can help reduce the discrepancy yet they rarely ever completely eliminate that tracking error. Step forward synthetic replication. This form of tracking is extensively used by outfits such as Lyxor and Deutsche db X-trackers although even a traditional physical replication specialist such as iShares has accepted the need for these options-based structures for a tiny number of its funds.

The idea behind a synthetic ETF is disarmingly simple. Rather than actually buy all the companies (or bonds) in the index, why not issue investors in the fund with what is in effect an IOU in which a major investment bank promises to pay out the total return on the index, i.e. the actual price returns plus any additional dividend-based income? The exact structure of this IOU varies, with two basic options, but the principle is the same – a bank issues what is called a total swap return (TSR) which guarantees to make the payment from the index. Swaps are widely used within the institutional world and amount to an options-based IOU involving a promise to pay a return. Institutions as varied as pension funds and hedge funds make extensive use of swaps.

Figure 3.3 from Lyxor demonstrates the exact structure of a swap-based, synthetic ETF. Lyxor makes extensive use of what is called an unfunded swap where the fund owns at least 90 percent of the value of its securities plus an

- Lyxor ETFs will, at all times, *invest more than 90% of a fund's assets in*:
    - Stocks for Equity ETFs and Commodities ETFs
    - European Government and Corporate Bonds for Fixed Income ETFs

- Each Lyxor ETF enters into an index swap agreement with a Counterparty* to exchange the performance of the fund holdings for the index performance

- The value of the swap will always represent *less than 10% of a fund's assets*

- The fund holdings are chosen following UCITS diversification requirements and to limit the overall cost of replication

ETFs Investing in basket of equities or bonds

Fund pays the performance of the basket to swap Counterparty

Swap Counterparty pays the performance of the index to the Fund

Swap Counterparty

*Counterparty is mainly Société Générale for most Swap Agreements with Lyxor ETFs

Figure 3.3 Structure of a swap-based, synthetic ETF

Source: Lyxor

additional 10 percent layer called the total return swap (TRS) exposure. Why 90 percent? European securities legislation stipulates that funds must have no more than 10 percent of their assets in any one share, bond or debt structure, lest the fund become too concentrated in a small number of holdings. Within an unfunded structure a bank trading desk issues the TRS exposure for anything between 0 percent and 10 percent of the value of the fund. The other 90 percent of the value of the fund comprises a range of securities offered up by the bank as collateral. Crucially these assets may not bear any relation to the actual assets being tracked in the index. You may for instance be tracking the FTSE 100 but the 90 percent or more of collateralised assets might comprise everything from Vietnamese equities through to European government bonds. But the collateral is directly owned by the fund and the valuation of those assets is managed by a fund custodian exactly as with any other mutual fund. Figures 3.4 to 3.6 outline this process in more detail. Figures 3.4 and 3.5 explain how Lyxor structures its ETFs while Figure 3.6 is from research by Deutsche db X-trackers and shows how redemption/creation works in practice on a daily basis using the unfunded (synthetic A) methodology.

- In line with UCITS III, the value of the swap cannot exceed 10% of Total Fund Assets
- The value of the swap, if positive, reflects the amount owed by the Swap Counterparty to the Fund
- Fund holdings will always represent more than 90% of Total Fund Assets and, as a result, the Counterparty Risk to the Swap Counterparty is limited to less than 10% of a Fund's NAV
- Fund holdings are segregated from the Swap Counterparty and held by the Fund Custodian
- No Securities or Asset Lending is implemented in any Lyxor ETF to limit overall Counterparty Risk

Index Swap (<10%)

Basket of Stocks or Bonds (≥90%)

ETF

Figure 3.4 Limited counterparty risk via a synthetic replication mechanism

Source: Lyxor

Structuring the revolution 73

The main alternative to the unfunded, synthetic structure is called a funded swap. This is arguably an even simpler structure to understand as it involves the ETF fund manager issuing a total return swap for the full 100 percent of the value of the fund. The backing for that IOU comes from collateral issued by the bank trading desk which will account for at least 100 percent of the value of the total return. In some cases this collateral backing actually amounts to more than 100 percent of the value of the liabilities to the fund,

Lyxor ETF Portfolio Construction & Index Replication (III)

Day 1:	Day 2:
Index level = GBP 100 → NAV = GBP 100 GBP 100 are invested in basket and fund enters into index swap with Counterparty → value of swap is 0 (or 0% of assets)	Index rises 5% & Basket remains flat = GBP 100 Index level = GBP 105 → NAV = GBP 105 → The exposure to the Counterparty under the swap is calculated as the <u>difference between the index and the basket performance</u> – GBP 5 (GBP 105 – GBP 100) or 4.76% of the NAV (GBP 5/GBP 105).

Day 3:	Day 4:
Index rises by GBP 2 to GBP 107, basket value rises by GBP 2 to GBP 102. NAV = GBP 105 + GBP 2 = GBP 107 to reflect new index level. → The exposure to the Counterparty under index swap would be GBP 107 (index) – GBP 102 (basket) – GBP 5, or 4.67% of the NAV (GBP 5/GBP 107).	Index rises to GBP 106 and the value of the basket falls back to GBP 100 → NAV of the ETF would be GBP 108. Counterparty Exposure via Swap is GBP 108 – GBP 100 – GBP 8, or 7.41% of the NAV (GBP 8/GBP 108). Lyxor will reduce the exposure or reset the swap to ensure we are below the max 10% Counterparty Risk UCITS III requirement. The reset involves a payment of GBP 8 from the Counterparty to the ETF and the proceeds are invested in the collateral basket. As a result the basket increases in value to GBP 108 and the value of the index is now GBP 108 resulting in 0 Counterparty risk (value of swap is 0).

Figure 3.5 Example of daily fund management* with index swap

Note: * Excluding TER and dividends (only for illustrative purposes)
Source: Lyxor

Investment of €1,000 in an ETF tracking Euro Stoxx 50	Synthetic A
Investor → 1	**Share creation process – during day 0**
Authorised participant (AP) → 2	1 The investor pays €1,000 in cash to the AP and receives shares in exchange. 2 The AP gives cash to the ETF in exchange for shares (delivery versus payment). 3 and 4 The EFT will give cash to the market/broker/TRS counterparty in exchange for securities.
ETF (holds securities) ⇄ 5/6 **TRS counterparty**	
↓3 ↑4	**ETF index exposure – end of day 0**
Market/broker/ total return swap (TRS) counterparty	5 The fund will pay the TRS counterparty the total return of the securities it holds. 6 The TRS counterparty pays the fund the return of the benchmark index, in this case Euro Stoxx 50. This flow might include index replication cost and performance enhancements (securities lending and tax enhancements).

Figure 3.6 How redemption/creation works in practice on a daily basis using the unfunded (synthetic A) methodology

Source: Global Index Research Team, Deutsche Bank, www.etf.db.com

i.e you the investor. Figure 3.7 from researchers at Deutsche demonstrates how this works on a daily basis.

The bottom line? Synthetic replication does introduce some very specific counterparty risks, risks which we will discuss later in this chapter. But the synthetic structure backed up by IOUs or swaps also has some major advantages, not least that tracking error should be drastically reduced if not eliminated. Synthetic structures can also be useful for emerging markets such as India where restrictions on foreign ownership of assets and repatriation of dividends can make a traditional physical replication approach tricky at best, and nightmarish at worst. Crucially, many swap-based synthetic funds provide tracking at a lower cost than their peers, even though in most cases that price advantage rarely amounts to much more than 10 basis points p.a. But that lower cost of running the fund and the massively reduced tracking error could amount to a sizeable advantage which outweighs concerns about counterparty risk.

Investment of €1,000 in an ETF tracking Euro Stoxx 50	Synthetic B
	Share creation process – during day 0
Investor → Authorised participant (AP) → ETF → Collateral ← TRS counterparty	1 The investor pays €1,000 in cash to the AP and receives shares in exchange. 2 The AP gives cash to the ETF in exchange for shares (delivery versus payment). 3 and 4 The EFT will give cash to the TRS counterparty and receive index performance daily in addition to collateral, typically in the form of a pledge or credit support annex (CSA) (5).
	ETF index exposure – end of day 0
	Note that the index exposure is achieved through the revaluation of the TRS at the end of each day.

Figure 3.7 How redemption/creation works in practice on a daily basis using the funded swap (synthetic B) methodology

Source: Global Index Research Team, Deutsche Bank, www.etf.db.com

An ETF in action

We have looked in great detail at the history of ETFs and their varying tracking structures (physical versus synthetic) but how does an ETF actually work in reality? Perhaps the best way of getting under the skin of these clever creatures is to look at one of the biggest and most successful funds in the UK, the iShares FTSE 100 index fund, with a ticker ISF. Like nearly all iShares funds, this physically tracks or 'replicates' the index, which in this case is the primary, London-based market for large, blue chip companies such as Royal Dutch Shell, BP or Vodafone. In this physically replicating fund, the managers attempt faithfully to buy all the companies within that index so that the fund almost exactly 'mirrors' the constituents of the blue chip index.

Table 3.10 gives you a quick snapshot of the key facts of this iShares ETF on one day at the end of December (28) 2011. Drill even deeper into this snapshot in time and we can see that the ETF was priced at £5.50 on Thursday 28 December 2011 with a bid–offer spread of less than one basis point, i.e less than 100th of 1 percent.

Table 3.10 Snapshot of the ETF

Holdings summary 28/12/2011	
Ticker	ISF
Total net assets £000	3,266,664
Price	£5.50
Number of holdings	103
Currency	GBP
Dividends	Paid quarterly
Total expense ratio	0.40%
Rebalance frequency	Quarterly for index
Dividend yield	3.31

In all there are 595,819,707 shares in issue with total net assets of £3,266,664,000, which equates to £5.48 4601 per share. The closing market value of the shares on 28 December 2011 was £5.50 a share, so there is also a tiny premium to the NAV. (See Table 3.11.)

And returns? In 2011, for instance, the underlying index returned –3.32 percent while the ETF fund returned 3.72 percent – that tracking error of 0.40 percent is almost entirely accounted for by the total expense ratio, which was 0.40 percent p.a. (See Table 3.12.)

The bottom line? The iShares fund largely does what it says on the tin – it tracks the FTSE 100 cheaply (it is not the cheapest as Lyxor has an ETF that charges just 0.30 percent), fairly accurately (the tracking error in a volatile 2011 was less than 0.50 percent p.a.) and with roughly the same holdings in proportion to the actual FTSE 100 Index.

Table 3.11 Top 20 holdings in iShares ETF vs the FTSE 100 Index

All holdings 28/12/11

% Weight	Security	ISIN	SEDOL	Price	Country	Sector
6.24	VODAFONE GROUP PLC ORD USD0.1143	GB00B16GWD56	B16GWD5	1.77	United Kingdom	Telecommunications
6.07	HSBC HOLDINGS PLC ORD USD0.5	GB0005405286	540528	4.87	United Kingdom	Financials
6.01	BP PLC ORD USD0.25	GB0007980591	798059	4.56	United Kingdom	Oil & Gas
5.94	ROYAL DUTCH SHELL PLC-A SHS ORD EUR0.07	GB00B03MLX29	B03MLX2	23.32	United Kingdom	Oil & Gas
5.21	GLAXOSMITHKLINE PLC ORD GBP0.25	GB0009252882	925288	14.65	United Kingdom	Health Care
4.56	ROYAL DUTCH SHELL PLC-B SHS ORD EUR0.07	GB00B03MM408	B03MM40	24.28	United Kingdom	Oil & Gas
4.21	BRITISH AMERICAN TOBACCO PLC ORD GBP0.25	GB0002875804	287580	30.58	United Kingdom	Consumer Goods
3.21	BG GROUP PLC ORD GBP0.1	GB0008762899	876289	13.61	United Kingdom	Oil & Gas
3.12	RIO TINTO PLC ORD GBP0.1	GB0007188757	718875	30.91	United Kingdom	Basic Materials
2.73	BHP BILLITON PLC ORD USD0.5	GB0000566504	56650	18.48	United Kingdom	Basic Materials

Table 3.12 Performance difference

Total returns after fees (capital and income)

Cumulative 28/12/11	iShares ETF %	Benchmark %
Year to date	–3.72	–3.32
One month	3.72	3.77
3 month	6.16	6.27
6 month	–3.13	–2.92
1 year	–5.46	–5.06
3 year	44.21	45.8
5 year	4.3	6.34
Since product inception	25.52	31.89

Annualised 28/12/11	iShares ETF %	Benchmark %
Since product inception	1.97	2.4

Stock lending: smoothing out returns?

The enterprising among you might have spotted an interesting opportunity for an outfit such as iShares – its funds track all the world's major markets and hold within them an amazing array of different company shares and bonds. These physical baskets of liquid assets represent a real opportunity for a sophisticated organisation like iShares and its parent BlackRock – why not lend out the share and bond certificates for limited periods of time to external organisations which might borrow them? The 'borrowers' are likely to be hedge funds or bank trading desks which might have a particular view on a company (bearish or bullish) and want to make a quick profit by speculating on stocks and bonds they do not actually own. The borrower of stocks and bonds in an iShares ETF portfolio will obviously have to pay a fee for the duration of the loan. They will also lodge 'collateral' in return which can amount to as much as 145 percent of the value of the loan in some isolated cases and more than 100 percent of the value of the loan in nearly all other cases. An outfit such as iShares openly discloses on its website how it manages its stock lending programme (look under the tab marked Securities Lending on each fund detail page): its FTSE 250 ETF for instance at the beginning of December 2011 had lent out 91 percent by value of the fund. Table 3.13 from iShares looks at a rather more typical fund – the FTSE 100 tracker. It shows that only 1.46 percent of the value of the fund had been loaned out in the 12 months up to 30 September 2011, with a maximum of just under 11 percent lent out at any one time. Where shares have been loaned out, iShares has demanded collateral amounting to an average of 112 percent of the loaned stock as backing.

Table 3.13 The FTSE 100 tracker

As of date	Fund name	Net returns to the fund	Average on loan	Maximum on loan	Average collateralisation
30/09/2011	iShares FTSE 100	0.01%	1.46%	10.96%	112.51%

English:

Net returns to the fund (%) is the net 12-month securities lending revenue to the fund divided by the average NAV of the fund over the same time period.

Average on-loan percentage (%) is calculated as the average value of loaned securities over the past 12 months divided by the average NAV of the fund over the same time period.

Maximum on-loan (%) is calculated as the maximum percentage of the total NAV lent on any single day over the past 12 months. The maximum on-loan percentage may increase or decrease over time.

Average collateralisation (%) is calculated as average daily ratio of collateral received on behalf of the fund to the value of securities loaned over the past 12 months.

The information in the file relates to securities obtained in the collateral basket under the securities lending programme for the fund in question. The information contained in this material is derived from proprietary and non-proprietary sources deemed by BlackRock to be reliable, is not necessarily all inclusive and is not guaranteed as to accuracy. Reliance upon information in this material is at the sole discretion of the reader. The primary risk in securities lending is that a borrower will default on their commitment to return lent securities while the value of the liquidated collateral does not exceed the cost of repurchasing the securities and the fund suffers a loss in respect of the short-fall.

Source: Based on data from iShares

iShare's investors can also download a spreadsheet that shows the collateral iShares has received in return. Table 3.14 looks at the collateral offered up by borrowers using shares from the FTSE 100 index. At the beginning of December that collateral in the FTSE 100 tracker consisted of shares in American tobacco group Philip Morris, giant consulting group Accenture and asset manager Invesco. The fact that none of these company names is very familiar to British investors is probably beside the point – average collateralisation is about 112 percent of the value of the shares loaned and custodians would want some diversified risk for lending out more speculative FTSE 100 large cap stocks. In return the fund has earned back over the last year 0.01 percent or 1 basis points in fees, 60 percent of which finds its way back into the fund via a lower TER.

Table 3.14 Stock lending activity for iShares FTSE 100 ETF

As of date	Security name	Security ISIN	Security country	Asset class	Security weight (%)
15/12/2011	PHILIP MORRIS INTERNATIONAL	US7181721090	United States	Equities	9.692
15/12/2011	ACCENTURE PLC-CL A	IE00B4BNMY34	United States	Equities	7.331
15/12/2011	MASTERCARD INC-CLASS A	US57636Q1040	United States	Equities	6.873
15/12/2011	INVESCO LTD	BMG491BT1088	United States	Equities	5.314
15/12/2011	STANLEY BLACK & DECKER INC	US8545021011	United States	Equities	4.006
15/12/2011	CBS CORP-CLASS B NON VOTING	US1248572026	United States	Equities	3.839
15/12/2011	OBRASCON HUARTE LAIN S.A.	ES0142090317	Spain	Equities	2.335
15/12/2011	FERROVIAL SA	ES0118900010	Spain	Equities	2.335
15/12/2011	ABERTIS INFRAESTRUCTURAS SA	ES0111845014	Spain	Equities	2.335
15/12/2011	SACYR VALLEHERMOSO SA	ES0182870214	Spain	Equities	2.335

Source: Based on data from iShares

Is there a risk? Yes, of course. If markets freeze up and borrowers start a scramble for liquidity, passive fund managers operating extensive stock lending programmes could find themselves in trouble, not least in liquidity terms as they try to unwind their collateral portfolios. But outfits like BlackRock are very careful about the collateral they accept in return for lending out their fund portfolios, and in many cases they make a deliberate effort to over-collateralise the risk exposure. The company regularly publishes data on its website that shows how much stock has been lent for each fund under its management as well as the accompanying collateral or backing offered up in return. Some iShares ETFs boasted no stock lending at all whereas the FTSE 250 index tracker was lent out to the average value of 92 percent of the fund. The iShares Japanese small cap fund was also greatly sought after by borrowers, with average stock lending at 73 percent. With both of these funds, collateral amounting to more than 100 percent of the borrowed value was offered up – in theory this stocks- and bonds-based backing could still decline by 10 percent in value and the fund would still be secure. The extreme concern must be that volatile markets impact massively on the value of that collateral. Stock lending is monitored on a daily basis but it is possible that sudden moves in value could happen so quickly that the fund custodians are unable to fully adjust the collateral backing, leaving investors in the fund at some potential for capital loss in extremis.

Phenomenal growth worldwide

The ETF revolution is now truly global. In almost every part of the developed world new ETF providers are springing up and ETFs are even threatening to invade the developing world with new launches in places as varied as Botswana and Taiwan.

Gauging just how successful this indexing revolution has become is fairly straightforward, as many of the leading issuers of ETFs such as iShares and Deutsche Bank (through its db X-trackers unit) closely monitor the market, attempting to spot key trends and generally keeping a watchful eye on liquidity on exchange.

At the end of June 2011, for instance, analysts at Deutsche estimated that the global index tracking industry had reached assets under management (AUM) of $1.4 trillion globally (see Figure 3.8), with 22 percent (€216.4 billion) concentrated in European listed funds. The Deutsche analysts also reckon that looking at the most recent 10-year period, over the past decade, the European ETF industry grew (measuring assets) by over 13-fold (13.2×),

Figure 3.8 Global ETF industry evolution

Source: Global Index Research Team, Deutsche Bank, www.etf.db.com

the US ETF market grew over six-fold (6.5×), while the Asian ETF market grew over two-fold (2.6×). These numbers represent extraordinary growth over the past decade – ETFs were virtually non-existent in Europe at the beginning of this new century and even in the US they were a tiny niche. Now ETFs are arguably the fastest growing part of the whole global asset management business (see Table 3.15).

Table 3.15 Global growth in ETFs

AUM	2003	2004	2005	2006	2007	2008	2009	2010	2011
US$	144	217	292	404	548	516	701	889	940
Growth rate		51%	34%	39%	36%	–6%	36%	27%	6%
Number of ETFs	117	151	200	343	602	698	771	896	1038
Europe (euro)	16.3	23.8	42	67	86	99	157	210	216
Growth rate		46%	77%	60%	28%	14%	59%	34%	3%
Number of ETFs	100	114	163	267	418	616	820	1076	1175
US ETF share	72%	75%	76%	75%	75%	73%	71%	71%	70%
Europe ETF share	10%	11%	13%	16%	17%	20%	23%	23%	23%

Source: Global Index Research Team, Deutsche Bank, www.etf.db.com

By the end of December 2011 the Deutsche analysts reckoned that there were over 3,210 exchange traded products (funds and notes) of some sort globally – of these, 2,823 were ETFs and 387 either ETCs or ETNs.

These top line numbers tell us that ETFs have now become mainstream globally, yet most investors will probably be far more interested in understanding what we are all collectively investing our money in, i.e which asset classes and markets are capturing these huge new inflows into ETFs. Table 3.16 from BlackRock along with the subsequent pie chart (see Figure 3.9) give us some idea of the key markets favoured by equity investors. Unsurprisingly equities of all shapes and sizes dominate the market although inflows into fixed income securities (bonds) as well as commodity funds have increased markedly over the past few years.

Turning to individual ETFs, Table 3.17 reminds us that the biggest funds are still American. All of the top 10 funds (based on assets under management) are US listed, with the State Street SPDR SPY tracker for the S&P 500 by far and away the largest index tracking fund on the planet with a market cap of $85 billion. One single US listed exchange traded fund has a bigger market

Table 3.16 What do exchange traded funds invest in?

Exposure as at November 2011 in US$ billion	AUM	Percentage market share	YTD change in assets under management (%)
Equity:	1067	69	0.4
North America	556	36	4.6
Emerging markets	204	13	−14.3
Europe	114	7	−5.8
Asia Pacific	79	5	−3.8
Global exc. US	66	4	3.2
Global equity	48	3	89
Fixed income	251	16	21.1
Commodities	196	13	5.7
Alternative	4	0	−1.2
Currency	8	1	27.8

Note: Data as at end of November 2011 or where updated data are not available, the most recent period available has been used.
Source: Based on data from BlackRock Investment Institute, Bloomberg

Developed equity	55.9%
Emerging markets equity	13.2%
Fixed income	16.30%
Commodities	12.70%
Others	1.90%

Figure 3.9 Percentage of AUM market share
Source: Based on data from BlackRock Investment Institute, Bloomberg

cap than some developing countries' entire gross domestic product (GDP)! According to BlackRock the global top 10 ETFs 'span a number of asset classes with the largest concentration in United States broad equity products (four products), emerging markets (two products), fixed income (two products) and one product each in gold and EAFE equity'.

Table 3.17 Top ETFs worldwide ranked by AUM: as at November 2011 in US$ million

ETF	Ticker	AUM$m
SPDR S&P 500	SPY	85,972
SPDR Gold Trust	GLD	73,003
Vanguard MSCI Emerging Markets ETF	VWO	44,654
iShares MSCI EAFE Index Fund	EFA	36,831
iShares MSCI Emerging Markets Index Fund	EEM	33,866
iShares S&P 500 Index fund	IVV	25,775
Powershares QQQ Trust	QQQ	24,124

Note: All top 10 ETFs are US listed.
Source: Based on data from BlackRock Investment Institute, Bloomberg

The European market

Yet this phenomenal growth in both the numbers of ETFs in issue and the assets under management should not hide the fact that ETFs and index tracking funds are still a small part of the overall, aggregate investment landscape in Europe and the US. According to Deutsche's research, 'ETFs were 2.8% of the mutual fund industry in Europe as of the end of Q1-2011. This represents an increase of 0.9%, as compared with September 2009 (1.9%)'. Crucially there is some evidence that European investors are less enthusiastic about using ETFs. According to the German bank's researchers ETFs are on average four times less popular in Europe than in the US. Crucially, if we look at the trading share of all daily activity taken by ETFs – this is defined as the percentage of ETF turnover versus cash equities turnover – ETFs account for around 30 percent of all activity in the US compared with just 7 percent in Europe. (See Figure 3.10.)

Crucially the European ETF market is increasingly dominated by synthetic ETFs. According to Deutsche's research team there are currently 411 ETFs using the traditional physical method of tracking an index compared with a much larger 764 ETFs that utilise synthetic replication, comprising 65

Figure 3.10 Reported on-exchange ETP turnover as a percentage of European equity market activity

Source: Global Index Research Team, Deutsche Bank, www.etf.db.com

percent of the European market. Researchers reckon that synthetic ETFs surpassed physically replicated ETFs back in 2007 (see Figure 3.11)!

And who are the key players in the fast-growing European market? Looking across the continent three companies dominate the market – iShares (now owned by US firm BlackRock), French-owned Lyxor and Deutsche Bank's db X-trackers unit. iShares is still the largest ETF issuer in Europe – as can be seen from Table 3.18 – but Deutsche DBX has been catching up fast with number two player Lyxor.

Figure 3.11 Historical split of physical/swap-based ETF turnover

Source: Global Index Research Team, Deutsche Bank, www.etf.db.com

Table 3.18 Major players in the European ETF market (all percentages)

ETF issuers	2006	2007	2008	2009	2010	2011	Gain/loss
iShares	48.7	45.1	38.1	37.6	35.7	36.3	−12
Deutsche db X-trackers	0	7.8	17.6	16.7	17.1	16.4	16.4
Lyxor	25.1	25.6	24.4	19.9	18.2	16.4	−8.7
Credit Suisse	5.3	3.8	4.3	4.2	5.5	5.7	0.4

Source: Deutsche Bank as of 24 June 2011, www.etf.db.com

The UK has not missed out on this exponential growth, although most of its increase has come only in the past few years. This late-adopter status is even more curious bearing in mind that the world's leading ETF issuer – with 45 percent of the worldwide market for ETFs and the leading player in the US – was originally a British company. Step forward iShares. To describe it as a powerhouse of the ETF industry is to sell it short – it is still by far and away the most prolific issuer of ETFs on either side of the Atlantic. Yet despite this huge international success, its UK presence has until recently been fairly subdued.

iShares waited until April 2000 to launch its first three ETFs, one based on the FTSE 100, one on the DJ Stoxx 50 and one on the DJ Euro Stoxx 50. In December 2000 it launched just one more fund, this time based on the FTSEurofirst 80, followed by another two between 2001 and 2002. In 2003 there were three more funds and in 2004 the number swelled to another six. The biggest growth in the UK market was in 2007 and 2008. iShares now has well over 100 different funds on the London market and is still the biggest provider in the tracker space by far. Every year iShares issues more and more funds – usually in two cycles, one around late spring and the other in late autumn – and investors should confidently expect it to add to its existing range. One note of caution about iShares: its focus until recently has been on serving the institutional market and it has not really bothered to develop products aimed exclusively at private investors, although that is changing fast as it now targets IFAs and wealth advisers. The iShares UK website (www.ishares.co.uk) is a model for the rest of the industry. This statistics-driven site is a goldmine of information and iShares, to its credit, has gone to extraordinary lengths to provide detailed information and transparency on all its listed funds.

To end this section Table 3.19 on the next page provides a summary of the available structures.

The future

This enormous global growth has been accompanied by an increasing number of new exchange traded structures. Some of these structures are particularly useful for private investors, allowing them to combine asset classes in one ETF or gear up returns. Much of the innovation within the ETF space has occurred within four very broad categories.

1 Exotic beta – these relate to tracking more complex/less understood markets, such as emerging markets, inflation, commodities, volatility and other relevant exposures. While these products are technically beta products, their level of complexity is higher than a standard passive product.

Table 3.19 Summary of structures

Structure	Listed on stock market, i.e. buy through a stockbroker	Full replication, i.e. full physical basket of underlying assets	Uses swaps (or other derivatives) to produce index return	Major counterparty risk	Could pay an income	Real-time dealing	Can a discount or premium emerge to NAV?	Any capital protection on offer?	Tax treatment	Stamp duty on purchase?
(Classic) exchange traded funds	Yes	Yes	No	No	Yes	Yes	Yes	No	CGT on capital gains income tax on income	No
Synthetic exchange traded funds	Yes	No – synthetic but total return should be same as underlying index	Yes	Yes	Yes	Yes	Yes	No	CGT on capital gains income tax on income	No
Unit trust or mutual fund index fund	No	Yes	No	No	Yes	No – daily only	No	No	CGT on capital gains income tax on income	Yes
Investment trust tracker	Yes	Yes	No	No	Yes	Yes	Yes	No	CGT on capital gains income tax on income	Yes
Certificate	Yes	No	Yes	Yes	No	Yes	No	Yes – in some cases	Only CGT	No
Exchange traded note (US only)	Yes	No	Yes	Yes	No	Yes	No	No	Only CGT	No
Listed structured products and investment trusts	Yes	No	Yes	Yes	No	Yes	No	Yes – in some cases	Only CGT	No

2 Beta plus – this consists of radically new funds such as leveraged or short index trackers where daily gains in an index both upwards and down are geared up within a fund. As we will discover in this section these leveraged and/or short products are classified as beta plus strategies as they have more risk due to the fact that leverage amplifies risk by multiplying exposure.

3 Semi-active – these products will typically track a diversified benchmark index; however, the weights of that index's constituents are not determined by market capitalisation. The weighting will often be determined by metrics which look at fundamental indicators (such as financial statement measures, for example gearing, profitability, capital return, etc.). According to one ETF analyst – at Deutsche Bank – 'substituting market capitalisation with fundamental measures constitutes an active decision as the index no longer gives market proportional representation'. We will explore these 'fundamental' index trackers in much greater detail in a later chapter.

4 Active funds – this is perhaps the most radical departure for the passive index tracking world, namely funds that track an index which is in fact a form of active management. These active passive funds are deeply distrusted by many passive aficionados such as John Bogle in the US as they are effectively just a traditional mutual fund wrapped up within an ETN or ETF that tracks an index designed by the fund manager. This category is still incredibly small and very few investors have actually switched into active passive funds.

Perhaps the fastest growing space within the index tracking industry is for those beta plus products, and especially geared or leveraged ETFs – these gear up your daily returns from tracking a major index, sometimes by a factor of four times returns. These innovative new structures are not without their critics though. Leveraged ETF products rebalance daily, which means that there is a gradual divergence from the long-term leverage performance of a target index due to compounding, which is especially evident during periods of high market volatility. Small, new issuers have dominated this space including outfits such as Direxion and Rydex. The first wave of funds offered investors *inverse* ETFs that made money from falling markets alongside geared ETFs that leveraged up returns in bull markets. Initially these were offered as simple 1:1 trackers, but as this niche has expanded fast that has quickly been extended to 2× bear (they go up when markets go down) and bull (they go up when markets go up) trackers. This market evolved again in 2009 with the launch by US provider Direxion of 3× bear and bull trackers on the major indices, including the Russell 1000 sub-index of energy companies and the MSCI Emerging Markets Index.

The full list of Direxion leveraged trackers is detailed in Table 3.20.

Table 3.20 List of US-based Direxion leveraged funds

US leveraged or short ETFs: Direxion	Ticker
Direxion Daily 10-Year Treasury Bear 3× Shares	TYO
Direxion Daily 10-Year Treasury Bull 3× Shares	TYD
Direxion Daily 2-Year Treasury Bear 3×	TWOZ
Direxion Daily 2-Year Treasury Bull 3×	TWOL
Direxion Daily 20+ Year Treasury Bear 1× Shares	TYBS
Direxion Daily 30-Year Treasury Bear 3× Shares	TMV
Direxion Daily 30-Year Treasury Bull 3× Shares	TMF
Direxion Daily 7-10 Year Treasury Bear 1× Shares	TYNS
Direxion Daily Agribusiness Bear 3× Shares	COWS
Direxion Daily Agribusiness Bull 3× Shares	COWL
Direxion Daily Basic Materials Bear 3× Shares	MATS
Direxion Daily Basic Materials Bull 3× Shares	MATL
Direxion Daily BRIC Bear 2× Shares	BRIS
Direxion Daily BRIC Bull 2× Shares	BRIL
Direxion Daily China 3× Bear Shares	YANG
Direxion Daily China 3× Bull Shares	YINN
Direxion Daily Developed Markets Bear 3× Shares	DPK
Direxion Daily Energy Bear 3× Shares	ERY
Direxion Daily Energy Bull 3× Shares	ERX
Direxion Daily Financial Bear 3× Shares	FAZ
Direxion Daily Financial Bull 3× Shares	FAS
Direxion Daily Gold Miners Bear 3× Shares	DUST
Direxion Daily Gold Miners Bull 3× Shares	NUGT
Direxion Daily Healthcare Bear 3× Shares	SICK
Direxion Daily Healthcare Bull 3× Shares	CURE
Direxion Daily India Bear 2× Shares	INDZ

Table 3.20 Continued

US leveraged or short ETFs : Direxion	Ticker
Direxion Daily India Bull 2× Shares	INDL
Direxion Daily Large Cap Bear 3× Shares	BGZ
Direxion Daily Latin America Bear 3× Shares	LHB
Direxion Daily Latin America Bull 3× Shares	LBJ
Direxion Daily Natural Gas Related Bear 2× Shares	GASX
Direxion Daily Natural Gas Related Bull 2× Shares	GASL
Direxion Daily Real Estate Bear 3× Shares	DRV
Direxion Daily Real Estate Bull 3× Shares	DRN
Direxion Daily Retail Bull 2× Shares	RETL
Direxion Daily Russia Bear 3× Shares	RUSS
Direxion Daily Russia Bull 3× Shares	RUSL
Direxion Daily Semiconductors Bear 3× Shares	SOXS
Direxion Daily Semiconductors Bull 3× Shares	SOXL
Direxion Daily Small Cap Bear 3× Shares	TZA
Direxion Daily Small Cap Bull 3× Shares	TNA
Direxion Daily Total Bond Market Bear 1× Shares	SAGG
Direxion Daily Total Market Bear 1× Shares	TOTS
Direxion Mid Cap Bear 3× Shares	MWN
Direxion Mid Cap Bull 3× Shares	MWJ
Direxionshares Developed Markets Bull 3× Shares	DZK
Direxionshares Emerging Markets Bear 3× Shares	EDZ
Direxionshares Emerging Markets Bull 3× Shares	EDC
Direxionshares Large Cap Bull 3× Shares	BGU
Direxionshares Technology Bear 3× Shares	TYP
Direxionshares Technology Bull 3× Shares	TYH

As already noted, these leveraged funds make their geared returns based on daily pricing – that means you should receive 3× the return of the underlying index on a daily basis. That gearing on both the downside and the upside means that these ETFs can become hugely volatile. It also means that they are not ideal for long-term investors looking to capture a major trend playing out on the markets.

To see how this can happen, Table 3.21 looks at one of the sets of Direxion ETFs, the energy shares that track the Russell 1000 index of mega-cap energy companies. Tables 3.22 and 3.23 detail the returns every day over March 2009 of the 3× bull and bear shares.

Over this one month the underlying index moved up by 11.3 percent in total (between 2 March and 31 March), which was clearly good news if you held the bull shares, which aim to pay out 3× the daily returns of the index. You thus might have expected the bull shares to go up by 34 percent, say, but in reality the bull shares went up only 29.87 percent – that lower return was because the underlying index had some bad days where the index lost over 4 percent, which in turn produced double-digit losses for the bull shares. Those losses eat into the capital sum and have a disproportionate effect on compound returns, yet on a daily basis the actual tracking error (the last column on the right) was remarkably low, at under 0.06 percent per day including expenses. Clearly, you would also expect the bear shares to have done badly and they did in fact fall back by more than 3× the monthly return, dropping more than 36 percent over the month, in part because of the compounding effect of big losses.

The point here is that daily returns mean daily returns and these hugely volatile ETFs will deliver some unusual returns over a long period if markets are very volatile. Do not expect an asset class that goes up over 50 percent in a year to produce a straight 150 percent gain in the bull shares if markets have yo-yo'd up and down over this year. Nevertheless the value of these products is obvious, especially for more active investors looking to gear up their returns from an asset class in either direction.

Unsurprisingly other ETF providers have jumped on board this broad trend. In the UK one of the major provider of bear trackers is Deutsche DBX with its popular FTSE 100 inverse tracker, while ETF Securities has also, since early 2008, been building up its leveraged and inverse/short-commodity trackers structured as exchange traded commodities. (Exchange Traded Products, or ETPs, is a broader term and includes both ETFs and ETCs.) The leveraged ETCs offer 2× the upside while the short ETCs offer 1× gains with every 1× move down in the index. ETF Securities has also issued a range of long/short foreign currency trackers and a small selection of main equity market leveraged products.

Not to be outdone Deutsche's db X-tracker unit has stepped up its exposure to the long/short and leveraged space within the past few years with a much larger range of leveraged equity market trackers. British bank RBS has also entered this fast-growing UK market with a small but growing range of funds that makes use of *monthly* returns to go long or short a market.

Table 3.21 Leveraged trackers – UK based

Deutsche db X-trackers short/leveraged funds – UK based	EPIC
db X-trackers – DJ Euro Stoxx 50® Double Short Daily ETF	XEDS
db X-trackers – DJ STOXX 600 Basic Resources Short Daily ETF	XBRS
db X-trackers – DJ STOXX 600 Industrial Goods Short Daily ETF	XIGS
db X-trackers – DJ STOXX 600 Insurance Short Daily ETF	XSIS
db X-trackers – DJ STOXX 600 Utilities Short Daily ETF	XS6S
db X-trackers – FTSE 100 Leveraged Daily ETF	XUL2
db X-trackers – S&P 500 2x Inverse Daily ETF	XT21
db X-trackers CAC 40 Short	XC4S
db X-trackers DJ Euro Stoxx 50 Short	XSSX
db X-trackers FTSE 100 Short ETF	XUKS
db X-trackers FTSE 100 Super Short Daily ETF	XULS
db X-trackers II UK Gilts Short Daily ETF	XUGS
db X-trackers LevDAX Daily ETF	XLDX
db X-trackers S&P 500 2x Leveraged Daily ETF	XSL2
db X-trackers S&P 500 Short	XSPS
db X-trackers ShortDAX	XSDX
db X-trackers ShortDAX 2x Daily ETF	XSD2
RBS Market Access EuroStoxx 50 Monthly Double Short Index ETF	REUS
RBS Market Access EuroStoxx 50 Monthly Leverage Index ETF	REUL
RBS Market Access LevDAX X2 Monthly Index ETF	RDEL
RBS Market Access Leveraged FTSE 100 Monthly Index ETF	RUKL
RBS Market Access Leveraged FTSE MIB Monthly Index ETF	RITL
RBS Market Access Short FTSE 100 Monthly Index ETF	RUKS
RBS Market Access Short FTSE MIB Monthly Index ETF	RITS
RBS Market Access ShortDAX x2 Monthly Index ETF	RDES

The full list of ETF Securities' leveraged and short ETCs is given in Table 3.24.

Table 3.22 Direxion energy bear 3x shares

Date	Index return RGUSEL	Index return	-3 return	Fees and expenses	Expected return	Expected NAV	ERY NAV	Daily return	Tracking difference
02-Mar-09	446.60	-6.686%	20.059%	-0.003%	20.056%	$60.83	$58.93	20.069%	0.013%
03-Mar-09	448.42	0.408%	-1.223%	-0.003%	-1.225%	$60.08	$58.21	-1.222%	0.003%
04-Mar-09	467.57	4.271%	-12.812%	-0.003%	-12.814%	$52.38	$50.74	-12.833%	-0.019%
05-Mar-09	445.30	-4.763%	14.289%	-0.003%	14.286%	$59.87	$57.98	14.269%	-0.017%
06-Mar-09	451.06	1.294%	-3.881%	-0.008%	-3.888%	$57.54	$55.68	-3.967%	-0.078%
09-Mar-09	453.37	0.512%	-1.536%	-0.003%	-1.539%	$56.65	$54.81	-1.563%	-0.023%
10-Mar-09	477.70	5.366%	-16.099%	-0.003%	-16.102%	$47.53	$45.99	-16.092%	0.010%
11-Mar-09	472.18	-1.156%	3.467%	-0.003%	3.464%	$49.18	$47.56	3.414%	-0.050%
12-Mar-09	486.17	2.963%	-8.889%	-0.003%	-8.891%	$44.81	$43.32	-8.915%	-0.024%
13-Mar-09	482.48	-0.759%	2.277%	-0.008%	2.269%	$45.82	$44.30	2.262%	-0.007%
16-Mar-09	486.32	0.796%	-2.388%	-0.003%	-2.390%	$44.73	$43.25	-2.370%	0.020%
17-Mar-09	503.14	3.459%	-10.376%	-0.003%	-10.379%	$40.09	$38.76	-10.382%	-0.003%
18-Mar-09	507.74	0.914%	-2.743%	-0.003%	-2.745%	$38.98	$37.70	-2.735%	0.011%
19-Mar-09	516.31	1.688%	-5.064%	-0.003%	-5.066%	$37.01	$35.79	-5.066%	0.000%
20-Mar-09	496.66	-3.806%	11.418%	-0.008%	11.410%	$41.23	$39.88	11.428%	0.018%
23-Mar-09	536.07	7.935%	-23.805%	-0.003%	-23.808%	$31.42	$30.39	-23.796%	0.011%
24-Mar-09	524.17	-2.220%	6.660%	-0.003%	6.657%	$33.51	$32.41	6.647%	-0.010%
25-Mar-09	526.88	0.517%	-1.551%	-0.003%	-1.554%	$32.99	$31.91	-1.543%	0.011%
26-Mar-09	532.41	1.050%	-3.149%	-0.003%	-3.151%	$31.95	$30.90	-3.165%	-0.014%
27-Mar-09	517.54	-2.793%	8.379%	-0.008%	8.371%	$34.62	$33.49	8.382%	0.011%
30-Mar-09	499.72	-3.443%	10.330%	-0.003%	10.327%	$38.20	$36.94	10.302%	-0.025%
31-Mar-09	497.18	-0.508%	1.525%	-0.003%	1.522%	$38.78	$37.50	1.516%	-0.006%
Change over month	11.33						-36.37		

Source: Direxion, www.direxionshares.com/etfs

Table 3.23 Direxion energy bull 3× shares

Date	Index return			Components of expected fund return			Fund return		
	RGUSEL	Index return	3 return	Fees and expenses	Expected return	Expected NAV	ERY NAV	Daily return	Tracking difference
02-Mar-09	446.60	−6.686%	−20.059%	−0.003%	−20.061%	$17.37	$17.71	−20.081%	−0.020%
03-Mar-09	448.42	0.408%	1.223%	−0.003%	1.220%	$17.58	$17.92	1.186%	−0.034%
04-Mar-09	467.57	4.271%	12.812%	−0.003%	12.809%	$19.83	$20.22	12.835%	0.026%
05-Mar-09	445.30	−4.763%	−14.289%	−0.003%	−14.291%	$17.00	$17.30	−14.441%	−0.150%
06-Mar-09	451.06	1.294%	3.881%	−0.008%	3.873%	$17.65	$17.98	3.931%	0.058%
09-Mar-09	453.37	0.512%	1.536%	−0.003%	1.534%	$17.92	$18.26	1.557%	0.023%
10-Mar-09	477.70	5.366%	16.099%	−0.003%	16.097%	$20.81	$21.20	16.101%	0.004%
11-Mar-09	472.18	−1.156%	−3.467%	−0.003%	−3.469%	$20.09	$20.47	−3.443%	0.026%
12-Mar-09	486.17	2.963%	8.889%	−0.003%	8.886%	$21.87	$22.30	8.940%	0.054%
13-Mar-09	482.48	−0.759%	−2.277%	−0.008%	−2.285%	$21.37	$21.79	−2.287%	−0.002%
16-Mar-09	486.32	0.796%	2.388%	−0.003%	2.385%	$21.88	$22.31	2.386%	0.001%
17-Mar-09	503.14	3.459%	10.376%	−0.003%	10.373%	$24.15	$24.62	10.354%	−0.019%
18-Mar-09	507.74	0.914%	2.743%	−0.003%	2.740%	$24.81	$25.30	2.762%	0.022%
19-Mar-09	516.31	1.688%	5.064%	−0.003%	5.061%	$26.07	$26.58	5.059%	−0.002%
20-Mar-09	496.66	−3.806%	−11.418%	−0.008%	−11.425%	$23.09	$23.54	−11.437%	−0.012%
23-Mar-09	536.07	7.935%	23.805%	−0.003%	23.802%	$28.59	$29.14	23.789%	−0.013%
24-Mar-09	524.17	−2.220%	−6.660%	−0.003%	−6.662%	$26.68	$27.14	−6.673%	−0.011%
25-Mar-09	526.88	0.517%	1.551%	−0.003%	1.548%	$27.10	$27.56	1.548%	−0.001%
26-Mar-09	532.41	1.050%	3.149%	−0.003%	3.146%	$27.95	$28.43	3.157%	0.011%
27-Mar-09	517.54	−2.793%	−8.379%	−0.008%	−8.387%	$25.61	$26.04	−8.407%	−0.020%
30-Mar-09	499.72	−3.443%	−10.330%	−0.003%	−10.332%	$22.96	$23.35	−10.330%	0.002%
31-Mar-09	497.18	−0.508%	−1.525%	−0.003%	−1.527%	$22.61	$23.00	−1.499%	0.028%
Change over month	11.32557						29.87013		

Source: Direxion, www.direxionshares.com/etfs

Table 3.24 ETF Securities' leveraged and short ETCs

ETF Securities' Long Short Funds – foreign currency

ETFS 3x Long AUD Short GBP	AUP3
ETFS 3x Long EUR Short GBP	EUP3
ETFS 3x Long JPY Short GBP	JPP3
ETFS 3x Long USD Short GBP	USP3
ETFS 3x Short AUD Long GBP	SAP3
ETFS 3x Short EUR Long GBP	SUP3
ETFS 3x Short JPY Long GBP	SYP3
ETFS 3x Short USD Long GBP	PUS3
ETFS Long AUD Short GBP	GBAU
ETFS Long AUD Short USD	AUDP
ETFS Long CAD Short GBP	GBCA
ETFS Long CAD Short USD	CADP
ETFS Long CHF Short GBP	GBCH
ETFS Long CHF Short USD	CHFP
ETFS Long CNY Short USD	LCNP
ETFS Long EUR Short GBP	GBUR
ETFS Long EUR Short USD	EURP
ETFS Long GBP Short USD	GBPP
ETFS Long INR Short USD	LINP
ETFS Long JPY Short GBP	GBJP
ETFS Long JPY Short USD	JPYP
ETFS Long NOK Short GBP	GBNO
ETFS Long NOK Short USD	NOKP
ETFS Long NZD Short GBP	GBNZ
ETFS Long NZD Short USD	NZDP
ETFS Long SEK Short GBP	GBSK
ETFS Long SEK Short USD	SEKP
ETFS Long USD Short GBP	GBUS
ETFS Short AUD Long GBP	AUGB

Table 3.24 Continued

ETF Securities' Long Short Funds – foreign currency	
ETFS Short AUD Long USD	SAUP
ETFS Short CAD Long GBP	CAGB
ETFS Short CAD Long USD	SCDP
ETFS Short CHF Long GBP	CHGB
ETFS Short CHF Long USD	SCHP
ETFS Short CNY Long USD	SCYP
ETFS Short EUR Long GBP	URGB
ETFS Short EUR Long USD	SEUP
ETFS Short GBP Long USD	USD2
ETFS Short INR Long USD	SINP
ETFS Short JPY Long GBP	JPGB
ETFS Short JPY Long USD	SJPP
ETFS Short NOK Long GBP	NOGB
ETFS Short NOK Long USD	SNOP
ETFS Short NZD Long GBP	NZGB
ETFS Short NZD Long USD	SNZP
ETFS Short SEK Long GBP	SKGB
ETFS Short SEK Long USD	SSEP
ETFS Short USD Long GBP	USGB
ETFS 3x Long AUD Short USD	LAU3
ETFS 3x Long EUR Short USD	LEU3
ETFS 3x Long GBP Short USD	LGB3
ETFS 3x Long JPY Short USD	LJP3
ETFS 3x Short AUD Long USD	SAU3
ETFS 3x Short EUR Long USD	SEU3
ETFS 3x Short GBP Long USD	SGB3
ETFS 3x Short JPY Long USD	SJP3

Table 3.24 Continued

ETF Securities' Long Short Funds on equities

ETFX Fund Company PLC ETFX DJ Euro Stoxx 50 Leveraged 2x Fund	LE2P
ETFX Fund Company PLC ETFX DAX 2x Long Fund	DL2P
ETFX Fund Company PLC ETFX DAX 2x Short Fund	DS2P
ETFX Fund Company PLC ETFX DJ Euro STOXX 50 Double Short 2x Fund	SE2P
ETFX Fund Company PLC ETFX FTSE 100 Leveraged 2x Fund	LUK2
ETFX Fund Company PLC ETFX FTSE 100 Super Short Strategy 2x Fund	SUK2
ETFX Russell 1000 US Large Cap Fund	RONP
ETFX Russell 2000 US Small Cap Fund	RTWP

ETF Securites' leveraged and short commodity-based trackers

ETFS Leveraged Agriculture DJ-AIGCI	LAGR
ETFS Leveraged All Commodities DJ-AIGCI	LALL
ETFS Leveraged Aluminium	LALU
ETFS Leveraged Cocoa	LCOC
ETFS Leveraged Coffee	LCFE
ETFS Leveraged Copper	LCOP
ETFS Leveraged Corn	LCOR
ETFS Leveraged Cotton	LCTO
ETFS Leveraged Crude Oil	LOIL
ETFS Leveraged Energy DJ-AIGCI	LNRG
ETFS Leveraged Ex-energy DJ-AIGCI	LNEY
ETFS Leveraged Gasoline	LGAS
ETFS Leveraged Gold	LBUL
ETFS Leveraged Grains DJ-AIGCI	LGRA
ETFS Leveraged Heating Oil	LHEA
ETFS Leveraged Industrial Metal DJ-AIGCI	LIME
ETFS Leveraged Lead	LLEA
ETFS Leveraged Lean Hogs	LLHO

Table 3.24 Continued

ETF Securites' leveraged and short commodity-based trackers

ETFS Leveraged Live Cattle	LLCT
ETFS Leveraged Livestock DJ-AIGCI	LLST
ETFS Leveraged Natural Gas	LNGA
ETFS Leveraged Nickel	LNIK
ETFS Leveraged Petroleum DJ-AIGCI	LPET
ETFS Leveraged Platinum	LPLA
ETFS Leveraged Precious Metals DJ-AIGCI	LPMT
ETFS Leveraged Silver	LSIL
ETFS Leveraged Softs Dj-aigci	LSFT
ETFS Leveraged Soybean Oil	LSYO
ETFS Leveraged Soybeans	LSOB
ETFS Leveraged Sugar	LSUG
ETFS Leveraged Tin	LTIM
ETFS Leveraged Wheat	LWEA
ETFS Leveraged Zinc	LZIC
ETFS Short Agriculture DJ-AIGCI	SAGR
ETFS Short All Commodities DJ-AIGCI	SALL
ETFS Short Aluminium	SALU
ETFS Short AUD Long USD	SAD
ETFS Short CAD Long USD	SCAD
ETFS Short CHF Long USD	SCHF
ETFS Short CNY Long USD	SCNY
ETFS Short Cocoa	SCOC
ETFS Short Coffee	SCFE
ETFS Short Copper	SCOP
ETFS Short Corn	SCOR
ETFS Short Cotton	SCTO
ETFS Short Crude Oil	SOIL
ETFS Short Energy DJ-AIGCI	SNRG

Table 3.24 Continued

ETF Securites' leveraged and short commodity-based trackers

ETFS Short EUR Long USD	SEUR
ETFS Short Ex-energy DJ-AIGCI	SNEY
ETFS Short Gasoline	SGAS
ETFS Short GBP Long USD	SGBP
ETFS Short Gold	SBUL
ETFS Short Grains DJ-AIGCI	SGRA
ETFS Short Heating Oil	SHEA
ETFS Short Industrial Metals DJ-AIGCI	SIME
ETFS Short INR Long USD	SINR
ETFS Short JPY Long USD	SJPY
ETFS Short Lead	SLEA
ETFS Short Lean Hogs	SLHO
ETFS Short Live Cattle	SLCT
ETFS Short Livestock DJ-AIGCI	SLST
ETFS Short Natural Gas	SNGA
ETFS Short Nickel	SNIK
ETFS Short NOK Long USD	SNOK
ETFS Short NZD Long USD	SNZD
ETFS Short Petroleum DJ-AIGCI	SPET
ETFS Short Platinum	SPLA
ETFS Short Precious Metals DJ-AIGCI	SPMT
ETFS Short SEK Long USD	SSEK
ETFS Short Silver	SSIL
ETFS Short Softs DJ-AIGCI	SSFT
ETFS Short Soybean Oil	SSYO
ETFS Short Soybeans	SSOB
ETFS Short Sugar	SSUG
ETFS Short Tin	STIM
ETFS Short Wheat	SWEA
ETFS Short Zinc	SZIC

iShares has not been left behind when it comes to new product ideas and has been developing a new platform consisting of *multi ETF portfolio funds*. These typically offer investors a portfolio of various asset classes comprised of iShare's own ETFs, all packaged into one fund appealing to everyone from low-risk to high-risk investors. We will look at these funds in more detail at the end of this book when we examine how investors can use ETFs to build their own portfolio. iShare's competitors (and especially Vanguard here in the UK) have also been developing their own takes on a one-size-fits-all approach, trying to develop a singular fund that could be used as the major building block of a portfolio, if not comprise the whole portfolio in one fund. Canadian firm Claymore (acquired by iShares in 2012), for instance, has licensed a small proprietary index (from Dorchester Capital Management) to offer a total market ETF that includes sub-indices that track everything from key US equity segments to bond markets. We will look at this new fund later in the book as well.

The greatest innovation has been felt in the commodity space. There were no ETFs tracking this huge and varied investment space until 2000 but since then the market has exploded, with new funds launching every month, tracking every conceivable part of the commodity business. Exchange traded commodities appeared in 2003 when ETF Securities listed the world's first exchange traded gold ETC in Sydney and London. There are now hundreds of funds on offer in the UK market and ETF Securities, in particular, has carved out a reputation for daring and innovative funds. In the next chapter we will look at this specialist niche in greater detail, examine the rationale for investing in this alternative asset category and look at the structures used to track the major indices.

Understand what you invest in!

In Chapter 5 David Norman and James Cottee from TCF Investments will drill a little deeper into the intricacies of how funds are structured, their tax treatment and what private investors need to watch out for. But hopefully our brisk description of the development of index funds and their evolution into ETFs should have alerted you to a number of likely challenges.

As we will see a little later in this chapter the indexing revolution has swept the world and has been translated into phenomenal growth worldwide both in the number of funds that track indices and the different types of index tracking structure. A veritable alphabet soup of acronyms has emerged, prompting enormous confusion on the part of most private investors. The vast majority of investors – private or institutional – do not really understand the difference between ETPs, ETFs, ETCs, ETNs, ETVs and ETIs, all of which are terms widely used in the industry to describe different index tracking structures.

That confusion has even turned into fear in recent months as the regulators have waded into the debate, highlighting the risks of some of the underlying fund structures. Authorities as varied as the Bank of England and the FSA in the UK through to the SEC in the US and the Financial Stability Board in Switzerland have highlighted the increasingly complicated structures that have become prevalent within the passive space.

In particular they have focused their attention on the growing number of investment banks which also operate index tracking subsidiaries. They are worried that these bank-owned asset managers structure their funds using what are in effect a number of IOUs (or swaps) issued by their trading desks to fund managers. As we have already discussed in this chapter these 'synthetic' index tracking funds as they are called offer investors access to exactly the same set of indices as any other passive fund, but their return is actually based around what is in effect a promise by the bank to make the final payout. There are many perfectly respectable reasons why this kind of structure might make sense for private investors, but the regulators have decided that these structures warrant further investigation and may even present systemic risks to the global financial system.

The regulators have also expressed concerns about trackers that use physical 'replication' or indexing – here the concern is not with the tracking as such but with an activity called stock lending. In the next section, we'll look at this highly profitable activity in greater detail but for now we can summarise stock lending as a heavily regulated and monitored process where the fund manager actually buys the underlying companies in an index (called physical tracking or replication) and then lends these stocks out to other third parties for a fee. This 'stock lending activity' can also be a power for good (generating fees that are mostly put back into the fund to cut costs) but regulators have expressed concern that the risk control procedures might not be strong enough in very volatile markets, leaving investors in trouble if the borrower of stock were to suddenly go bust.

This increasingly impassioned debate and regulatory probing has probably been a force for the good: it has forced the leading players to become very much more open about their practices and transparent about their reporting. Leading index tracking companies such as Vanguard, HSBC, Lyxor and iShares now offer unprecedented access to underlying data about their fund structures, all of which has thrown into sharp relief the rather paltry statistical reporting offered by many conventional active fund management companies.

But investors are still, nevertheless, confused by the rapid growth of this sector and no amount of transparency will overcome basic misunderstanding of a whole new way of investing. For readers navigating their way through this huge and constantly evolving new world, we have compiled a simple checklist of questions for private investors looking to invest in an index tracking fund. The key thing to bear in mind is that in nearly all of these questions there is no right or wrong answer – the issue is that you understand the risks inherent in each choice you are making.

Is it an exchange traded fund or a unit trust?

This is perhaps the most basic issue for many private investors. Most of the index tracking funds on offer are share-based funds that are 'listed' on an exchange, and thus the acronym used to describe them starts with an E, as in exchange. That means you have got to buy and sell through a stockbroker, who can deal in real time – although there will also be a bid–offer spread between the asking and selling price. Many investors do not have accounts with stockbrokers but use an adviser who might not even have access to a dealing platform. If this is the case they will probably use an index tracking unit trust fund or OEIC where the fund is structured in almost exactly the same way as an ETF but with dealing on a daily basis. Vanguard and Legal and General are especially strong in the unit trust space whereas iShares, Lyxor, Deutsche DBX and ETF Securities are more powerful in the exchange traded fund space. Unit trusts are a little less flexible in terms of dealing – you have to wait for a NAV value at the end of the day – but they can be an easy and cost-effective home for long-term savings.

What difference does the acronym make? A lot!

The profusion of acronyms used to describe index tracking structures listed on the stock market is nothing short of astounding. In the box below we explain the differences between the different fund and product structures in much more detail. The key point though is that nearly all the most popular structures for stock exchange listed funds come under the umbrella description of exchange traded products (ETPs), with the main difference being that between those products that are structured as funds – thus exchange traded funds or ETFs – and the rest. The rest includes exchange traded notes (ETNs), certificates and exchange traded commodities (ETCs). This last group of structures is a securitised derivative of one form or another where your risk is with the counterparty bank or financial institution issuing the options-backed security. That risk of dealing in complex underlying structures and taking on bank risk is compensated for by the ability to invest in difficult to access asset classes such as commodities where a traditional fund structure could not invest in only one asset. Funds by contrast have to have a diversified series of holdings – lots of individual company shares or bonds – and then structure the holdings within a clear fiduciary framework, with a custodian, a fund manager and a board of directors in the main holding company. Again there's no right or wrong here – ETNs for instance are probably the only way of accessing many alternative assets whereas most investors tend to invest in some form of fund like an ETF.

> **The acronym jungle**
>
> **ETP** – an exchange traded product, tracks a major index and includes ETFs and ETCs (see below). This is the general 'catch-all description'.
>
> **ETFs** – in the US these are fund structures that are traded on an exchange and behave like equities in a fund. American regulators only allow physical index tracking. In Europe ETFs also trade like shares, with the vast majority being UCITS III compliant (a regulatory framework for managing funds in Europe). In Europe both physical and synthetic index replication is allowed under the UCITS framework.
>
> **ETNs** – these are exchange trade notes and are in effect collateralised certificates, notes or instruments that track an index but there is no fund structure as such. The return from tracking the index comes from what is in effect an IOU from the issuer where a promise is made to pay the final return. That IOU is usually a form of unsecured senior debt.
>
> **ETCs** – exchange traded commodities. Single commodities cannot be traded within a simple UCITS III fund structure in Europe as the fund manager must have a range of diversified assets in the fund, i.e. lots of different company shares. Commodities can be tracked via certificates which offer investors a physical backing in actual assets or a synthetic debt instrument.
>
> **Unit trust** – the more mass-market variation of the index fund is called the mutual or unit trust. This structure is based on the big daddy of index funds, the Vanguard 500 fund. It is an open-ended vehicle that is priced daily and may issue new units on a daily basis if it so chooses as more and more investors buy in. These are typically run by large fund management groups like Vanguard in the US and Fidelity, Scottish Widows, Legal and General and HSBC in the UK. There should be no discrepancy between the underlying value of the units and the price quoted to your adviser or dealer and any dividends that come from holding the shares in the portfolio are distributed as a yield, paid on a regular interval, to unitholders.

Physical or synthetic tracking?

Many investors and advisers have taken the regulatory probe into synthetic ETFs as a negative sign, choosing only to invest in a fund that physically invests in the stocks (or bonds) of the underlying index that it's tracking. Yet that worry may sometimes be misplaced as synthetic tracking of an index can be enormously useful precisely because of its structure and design. As we have already discussed in this chapter, in a synthetic ETF the issuer still tracks a major index but that return is in effect a form of IOU. If we assume for argument's sake that an index is currently valued at 100, the issuer might offer up 'collateral' of stocks and bonds on its trading books for 90 percent or more of the value of that index return of 100. The remaining small portion of the return (100) is usually in a range between 10 and 0, and is made up of a swap or IOU by the bank. If the bank goes bust, that collateral should pay back well over 90p in the pound, and the maximum risk from the swap is 10p in the pound (and usually a good deal less).

Why offer this form of IOU or swap in the first place? In reality many indices are difficult to track because of regulatory issues, liquidity problems, tax issues and dividend payouts. That means that large differences can emerge between the return on the index and the return paid out by the fund. Synthetic ETFs get around this by promising to pay the total return – the banks' trading desks are left to hedge out all the other risks. That can smooth out the total returns at a relatively low cost in terms of the total expense ratio. Physical replicating funds, by contrast, invest in the actual companies or bonds in an index, with the fund holdings held by a separate custodian. Many investors find this simple holding structure and physical tracking of an index less difficult to understand and thus less risky.

Counterparty risk – how big a problem is it?

Exchange traded notes and certificates have an obvious risk – they are in effect an IOU by a large financial institution, a form of securitised derivative. The big US bank Lehman Brothers offered these derivatives – many as structured products or ETNs – and when it collapsed, many investors in these notes lost nearly everything. This reminds investors that bad things can happen and that banks can and do go bust, taking down all unsecured debt with them. But that risk can also be over-stated and can blind investors to opportunity. Two of the major ETF players in the UK are Lyxor and Deutsche DBX, owned in turn by national banking giants SG and Deutsche Bank. Both offer a huge range of funds, many at very low expense ratios. Investors who ignore the range of funds on offer from both providers must be concerned that the French and German governments would be willing to let these national champions go bust. It is absolutely possible this might happen, but on balance unlikely – and even if they did go bust, there is still an additional set of protections in place (including collateral) to shield the investor.

> Investors also need to remember that all listed products – funds, notes and certificates – are *not* covered by the financial compensation service, the FSCS. Invest in any ETP, regardless of the structure, at your own risk – the government will not bail you out!

Stock lending activity – how much goes on and who benefits?

Many exchange traded funds offer access to mainstream markets through index tracking funds at very low cost. The total expense ratio (TER) on most mainstream ETFs is usually well below 50 basis points or 0.5 percent p.a. – a full 1 percent or more less than an equivalent, actively managed fund. That lower cost in terms of the TER is helped by the fact that many physically replicated funds engage in stock lending. As we have already discovered in this chapter this stock lending is a perfectly acceptable practice – many actively managed funds also engage in securities lending – and involves the stocks and bonds in a portfolio being lent out to a third party. There is enormous potential for concern with this stock lending: what happens if the borrower of shares in the fund goes bust? How easy will it be to grab back and sell any collateral offered up by that borrower? Yet it is also important to note that this stock lending is carefully managed and monitored – you need to make your own decision if you are happy with the procedures and the collateral on offer. It is also worth noting that many of iShares' most popular funds such as its FTSE 100 tracker boast almost no major securities lending, while many of its competitors such as Vanguard and HSBC deliberately avoid all stock lending in the UK.

Liquidity – a potential curse

ETFs have become insanely popular in the USA, with trading volumes exploding in recent years. But that liquidity can also be a curse as markets stress or liquidity seizes up. Markets makers may choose to expand the bid–offer spread on lightly traded ETFs to unacceptable levels – these spikes in bid–offer spreads can also move around on an intra-day trading basis. These excessive bid–offer spreads also point to a bigger challenge – ETPs of all shapes and sizes may be emerging in Europe but that listing activity has not always translated through into actual 'action' on exchange. Many European ETFs for instance boast low average daily volume (ADV) figures and at times unattractive bid–ask spreads.

According to one study of trading in ETFs by State Street Advisors (a US-based firm with a substantial business in Europe) two factors explain this apparent lack of liquidity: 'market fragmentation through multiple ETF exchange listings (and sometimes multiple currency listings at each exchange) and the lack of trade reporting requirements'.[11]

This lack of liquidity has some very practical challenges for investors, both private and institutional, as their exchange of choice might not show the full picture of an ETF's on-exchange market from a spread and volume perspective. One of the key drivers behind this 'dark pool' of relatively unmonitored ETF trading is the existence of what are called over-the-counter (OTC) markets or 'off exchange' market places. Industry experts estimate that anywhere from 50–90 percent of ETF activity occurs OTC, which State Street reckons is another reason why looking at a fund's average daily volume as a gauge for liquidity is flawed.

Liquidity issues also show up in the difference between the asking and selling price – otherwise known as the bid–offer spread. In theory this should just be a difference of perhaps a few basis points, i.e. a few hundredths of a percentage point. But in many ETFs this is not the case and bid–offer spreads can shoot up to 1 percent or more – and the reasons for this widening of the spread are many and varied. The key participants are the market makers who buy and sell ETFs and other shares day in, day out. These are businesses which thrive on 'flow' of trade rather than the direction of a particular investment or share. ETFs can be especially difficult for these market makers as they have to hedge out their risk, i.e. make sure they do not lose money if the security shoots up in price while it is on their books. Multiple exchanges across Europe and the need to run incredibly quick trading systems also adds to their IT and implementation costs – all of this technology and know-how has to be paid for and that extra cost shows up in the bid–offer spread. The most important factor though is the extent of 'secondary market trading', i.e. the amount of shares traded 'on exchange' in a major stock market. In simple terms the greater the secondary market, the lower the spread – the growth of extensive OTC trading 'off exchange' in ETFs probably has a knock-on effect on spreads. Figure 3.15 from State Street shows the relationship between on-exchange activity and the bid–offer spread. It charts a typical ETF and shows how as daily trading volumes declined, the bid–offer spread increased very substantially to a high of 0.4 percent per trade.

Tax issues: is this ETF the most tax-efficient route for my investment?

Many investors are worried about some ETFs where the ultimate holding company appears to be based in Dublin, the Republic of Ireland. They worry that although Ireland is covered by EU fund rules, the structure of the fund could be looked upon as opaque and something of a tax dodge. In reality these offshore tax homes are a complicated way to deal with underlying fund administration problems based around tax on dividends and capital gains.

Figure 3.12 Relationship between on-exchange activity and the bid–offer spread

Source: State Street Global Advisors

Many ETFs for instance invest in foreign bonds and shares where the home government imposes a withholding tax. The US government for instance can grab as much as 30 percent of any income paid out on its domestic equities and bonds. These withholding taxes can be reclaimed in jurisdictions such as Ireland by the fund manager allowing the investor in the UK to receive their dividend income gross. But each fund and each asset class varies enormously and investors need to investigate the tax status of their passive fund.

Tracking errors – why has my fund returned less than the index over the past year?

Index tracking funds, by definition, invest in the constituents of an index. Many of these indices such as the FTSE 100 are very broad and deep with lots of liquidity whereas many lesser-known indices, especially those in the developing world, are much less 'efficient', i.e they might have lots of difficult to trade stocks. Tracking any index involves lots of technology and careful monitoring, especially as the index changes its composition, stock splits are announced and dividends paid out. All these challenges make complete 100 percent perfect replication of an index, especially via physical tracking, difficult though not impossible. A multitude of factors can work together to produce a noticeable difference between the return from the fund and the index return. This *tracking error*, as it's called, can be caused by a number of factors, including the following.

1 **Sampling error:** a fund may sample the universe tracked by the index rather than employ full replication. To understand this complex-sounding idea, compare an index tracking vehicle that tracks a big and easy-to-track market like the FTSE 100 with one that tracks the Chinese or Vietnamese markets, which both suffer from a number of regulatory 'issues' that include different classes of shares and government interference. It is incredibly simple to buy the basket of FTSE 100 shares cheaply and efficiently, whereas with some less efficient markets like these Asian ones errors can easily creep in. That forces index providers in these more 'difficult' markets to use a method called sampling, where they build a model that samples the spread of shares in a market but does not fully replicate it. This produces a portfolio that replicates the vast majority of the underlying index holdings, but sampling is simply never as strong as fully copying or replicating. What happens if your sampling model begins to produce errors?

2 **Regulatory requirements:** US investment company regulations state that a single company may account for no more than 25 percent of a fund's total assets. Thus, if a company makes up more than 25 percent of a market's index, that stock would be underweighted by the fund. To optimise a portfolio, the manager may increase weightings of other portfolio components or even go outside the index.

3 **Expenses:** even if a fund identically weights all the stocks in its benchmark, performance will be reduced by the expense ratio (i.e. net return equals gross return of index less expenses). This is what is called the expenses drag and it is a major factor in explaining why more expensive unit trust-based trackers produce bigger tracking errors after fees.

4 **Dividend payments:** one other factor that can result in tracking errors for some ETFs is dividend payments. An exchange traded fund typically pays out dividends received from the underlying shares it holds on a quarterly basis, but the underlying stocks pay dividends throughout the quarter. Therefore, these funds may hold cash for various time periods throughout the quarter, even though the underlying benchmark index is not composed of cash.

Add up all these factors and it is easy to see how tiny tracking errors of, say, 0.2 percent (typical of the Vanguard 500 index fund in the US) can turn into 2 percent tracking errors p.a. – over 5 or 10 years that could produce some radically different returns compared with the underlying index. Synthetic ETFs can help with the challenge of tracking error and it's worth noting that in more difficult to access markets such as India, even iShares, a vocal proponent of physical tracking, uses some form of synthetic structure to narrow the tracking error. Other leading players in the emerging markets space such as HSBC also make use of optimised tracking where they physically buy most of the constituents of an index but then use sampling to get close to the final return from an emerging markets index. This might reduce the tracking error but will not completely eliminate any discrepancies in returns.

What is in the index?

The structure of a fund matters enormously but arguably the biggest challenge is the composition of the index itself. What are you actually 'tracking' in the index? Is it a highly concentrated index comprising just a few top companies or is it genuinely diversified between lots and lots of different companies? Is it very sensitive to one sector such as mining or banks or is it diversified between sectors? Is it capturing changes in the local economy or changes in the valuations of large internationally diversified companies in the index? Are the top companies capped in the index or is it just an index of the top 30 companies? Again there is no right or wrong answer to these questions but if nothing else private investors need to know what they are tracking in an index and make sure they are happy with the risks.

Is the fund economic?

ETFs have grown enormously in numbers over the past decade, largely because they offer investors a cost-effective way of accessing major markets and asset classes. Yet that low cost should not blind investors to the reality that managing funds is not a charity – asset managers have to make a profit on each and every fund they run. And overall, market analysis suggests that asset managers do indeed make a great deal of money from index tracking funds and products. Deutsche Bank's main ETF analyst reckons that there is 'currently close to €2 billion of revenues to be had in the European ETF industry, annually, out of which up to €1.2 billion could be profits'.[12]

Those massive profits have served to attract a number of major players into the European ETF business, increasing competitiveness and generally lowering costs across the space. According to research from Deutsche, the European market is more competitively priced than its US peer, with TERs in almost every asset class and on every strategy type across the board. According to Deutsche's Cristos Costandinides – European Head of ETF research at Deutsche – 'on average, European ETFs are priced 38 percent below their US counterparts. The average cost of investing in an ETF (per annum) is 40 basis points in Europe and 55 basis points in the US'.[13]

In equity ETFs for instance the average physical tracking ETF charges around 0.45 percent p.a. as a total expense ratio while the average synthetic ETF charges even less at 0.43 percent – in the US the average is closer to 0.50 percent p.a. In fixed income (bonds) European ETFs are also cheaper, with the average ETF charging just 0.19 percent (physically tracked) or 0.17% (synthetic ETFs) compared with 0.27 percent in the US.

Table 3.25 ETF industry profitability estimate (percent)

Profit and loss estimate	Physical ETFs	Synthetic ETFs
Management fees	0.45	0.43
Securities lending	0.26	0.20
Other enhancements including tax optimisation	0.05	0.05
Trading P&L	0	0.35
Total revenues	0.75	1.03
Management costs	0.20	0.05
Collateral cost	0	0.20
Administration	0.05	0.05
Other expenses	0.02	0.02
Total costs	0.27	0.32
Net profit	0.48	0.71

Source: Global Index Research Team, Deutsche Bank

Yet these broad industry metrics should not fool private investors into thinking that every ETF or ETP is profitable. Far from it in fact: many exchange traded funds have assets under management of less than £10 million, with many, many more less than £50 million. At what point does it become uneconomic for the manager to run the fund? As the vast majority of passive funds charge less than 1 percent p.a., that implies that the asset manager is making not much more than £100,000 p.a. for managing a £10 million fund and £500,000 p.a. for a £50 million fund. Is that truly economic, once all the dealing costs and admin costs are accounted for? In the US many ETFs have been closing in recent months as asset managers decide that they are not happy soldiering on with small, uneconomic funds. Once a fund is closed down, the manager must sell the assets – sparking extra trading fees – and liquidity may start to dry up in the secondary market. In some extreme cases, managers have even been known to charge the full cost of business development to the fund, knocking as much as 20 percent off the net asset value post realisation. Large fund companies such as HSBC, iShares and Lyxor may be willing to run uneconomic funds for long periods of time as a loss leader but investors need to be careful that they do not end up with too much money in esoteric, lightly traded funds which are fundamentally uneconomic.

Is the fund distributing income or is it a total return structure?

Many investors choose to invest in an ETF for the income it produces via either bond coupon payments or dividends. Most funds choose to distribute this income to their fundholders but some ETFs and ETNs track what are called total return indices where the dividend from companies in the index is rolled up into the index price. This can be very advantageous because dividends might be taxable at source whereas a total return index, where the dividend is included, is only taxable as capital gains. But be aware that total return indices and their tracking funds will *not* pay out a dividend.

ETFs open up private investors to market risk

Exchange traded funds are diversified investment instruments that allow investors to access big themes and macro forces. That is a great idea as long as you understand the risks you are taking – you are opening up your portfolio to what is called market risk. The sector or the market your ETF is tracking may drop based on a variety of factors such as economic conditions and global events, investor sentiment and sector-specific factors. In a big sell-off, investors typically sell all shares regardless of structure – ETFs being very liquid may suffer disproportionately. Be honest, if you are panicking, what are you likely to sell first: an ETF share you can sell in real time via your broker or a unit trust fund where you have to wait until the end of the day to establish a proper pricing level?

Not all index trackers are cheap or low cost!

Investors also need to be careful of expensive ETFs and even more exotic indices. The reality is that not all ETFs are created equal. Market-leading ETFs may quote wonderfully low expense ratios in their marketing blurb, but a more detailed analysis of the US market reveals huge variations in costs. A study by the US-based American Association of Individual Investors (AAII) organisation was able to identify expense ratios for 281 of the 299 funds in the US market in 2006. Of these 281 funds, 35 had an expense ratio of between 0 percent and 0.22 percent, 130 between 0.21 percent and 0.5 percent, and 96 between 0.51 percent and 0.75 percent. Rather more alarmingly, 14 funds had expense ratios above 0.75 percent – that is an awfully high charge for what should be a simple exercise in tracking a major market.

British-based private investors need to take particular care with many – though not all – of the unit trust index trackers offered through IFAs and fund supermarkets. The horrible fact is that there is a 1.7 percentage point difference between the lowest and the highest unit trust tracker annual management charges in sectors like the FTSE All-Share or the FTSE 100. According to one respected adviser in the field, Patrick Connolly, research and investment manager at John Scott & Partners, that difference is inexcusable: 'We believe 0.5 percent is absolutely the most you should be paying for a tracker fund.' Another analyst, from Hargreaves Lansdown, a stockbroker cum IFA, put it even more succinctly: 'Tracker funds charging 1 percent are a rip-off in my view.'

Yet the list of high-charging tracker unit trusts in particular is lamentably long. Here is our roll call of dishonour: Axa UK Tracker, Credit Suisse FTSE 100 Tracker, DWS UK All-Share Equity Tracker, Eagle Star UK Index Tracker, Gartmore UK Tracker, Halifax's FTSE 100 and UK All-Share Trackers, Isis FTSE 100 Tracker, L&G UK Stock Market, Marks & Spencer UK 100 Companies, Norwich Union's tracker range Sovereign FTSE 100, St James's Place Tracker and Virgin UK Index Tracking.

Charges vary even more significantly on indices outside the UK market. For example, Allianz Dresdner charges 0.25 percent a year more for its Euro Index Tracker than it does for its UK offering. At the same time, HSBC has a range of fees going from 0.5 percent for its UK and Japan trackers to 1 percent for some of its other regional tracker funds. The bottom line is simple – never accept an index tracker costing more than 1 percent p.a., especially when there are plenty of good funds (identified in this book) that charge 0.5 percent p.a.

This shocking state of affairs reflects rather badly on UK-based index fund providers. In the US, by contrast, market leaders like Vanguard have priced their funds aggressively to undercut even ETF providers. Leading Vanguard funds are frequently priced at less than 0.2 percent p.a., and for major, large markets ETFs are rarely cheaper than their mutual fund rivals.

Vanguard is also quick to point out that its funds never trade at a discount (or premium) to net asset value and that its mutual funds are better suited to investors looking to make a regular (monthly) investment. 'Trading costs tend to make ETFs less suitable as investments for company-sponsored retirement plan accounts, because plan participants typically make frequent contributions. Unless the ETF's expense ratio advantage is substantial, transaction-oriented costs can quickly overwhelm the benefit of a lower expense.'[14] Just to confuse matters though, Vanguard has in recent years conceded that ETFs have some value and it now offers not only mutual funds but also ETFs.

ETPs: the need for greater transparency

Many experts within the index tracking industry recognise that investors need to be extra vigilant when it comes to using ETFs or products. One key concern articulated by many industry experts centres on the very structure of the asset management industry itself – is it truly a middleman or is it hopelessly compromised by its various revenue-generating options? Many critics are especially concerned by the growth of large asset management businesses issuing ETFs within large investment banks. As one report on the ETF industry pointed out: 'In truth, today, money management is performed both by asset managers, which are often part of banks, or by banks directly. The model of an independent fund manager providing services in exchange for a nominal fee, while still relevant, on most occasions is obsolete. Money managers are not middlemen any more, the information revolution is forcing them to transform. Money managers are now routinely involved in ancillary [to fund management] activities which result in additional significant revenues.'

In Europe, for instance, the top five issuers of synthetic ETFs are now bank controlled and account for 92 percent of the synthetically replicated ETF assets, while the top five physical replicators/asset managers control 90 percent of the physically replicated ETF assets. In reality Europe is now a battleground between European banks – largely operating synthetic ETFs – and big American-owned asset managers (iShares, Vanguard and State Street).

Ordinary, private investors sit in the middle of this very confusing – and profitable – industry, confused by the number of structures and even more worried by the growing wave of regulatory concern over ETF structuring. Many industry insiders think that these private investors would be better served by a more transparent approach to structuring – although no amount of bureaucratic interference should absolve investors from running their own detailed due diligence process, looking at some of the key issues highlighted in this chapter. Christos Costandinides at German Bank Deutsche is head of global ETF research and spends nearly all his time analysing ETP structures – many of which he thinks are less than transparent. In a widely read report in 2011, Christos made a number of suggestions for better reporting of ETPs – all listed below.

Suggestions for better ETF regulation and reporting, based on Deutsche Bank's ETF report on tracker/beta instruments

- Definition: what constitutes a tracker, as measured by return and risk characteristics (relative to its benchmark index). Distinguishing between active and passive products currently remains an 'industry practice' and no regulatory guidelines exist.

- Tracking effectiveness: presently, a beta [index tracking] fund can mis-track 10 percent of its stated benchmark index consistently and still be allowed to be called a tracker. This is possible as there is no requirement to publish tracking effectiveness statistics in a consistent manner across the mutual fund management industry.
- Replication techniques used: very few ETF providers utilising synthetic replication make specific details of the technique they follow publicly available. Similarly, for physical replication, a fund manager is free to sample at their discretion, often holding less than 70 percent of an index, without disclosing the practice. This elevates the risk for an investor to experience returns which are incompatible with their expectations and it has frequently happened in the past three years.
- Performance enhancement activities: disclosure of the so-called 'performance enhancement activities', including tax optimisation and securities lending, is currently not mandated. These ancillary investment activities carry risks and they should not be left at the fund manager's discretion to disclose.

Benchmarks

- Key information: benchmark index composition public disclosure is currently very poor. Some index providers refuse to disclose publicly a [fund's] benchmark constituents, their pricing and other relevant information. As a result, the investor cannot perform basic analysis in order to assess how well a beta fund tracks its index.
- Appropriateness: there is currently very little guidance governing the appropriateness of selecting and disclosing a benchmark. For example, there are occasions where mutual funds disclose an easy to beat benchmark [such as Libor] instead of a benchmark which reflects the risk in a portfolio. There needs to be stronger guidance in place on how appropriate is a benchmark for use when selling a fund.

Source: Deutche Bank Global Index Research by Christos Costandinides, July 2011, www.etf.db.com

4

Investing in commodities using index funds

A funny thing happened in the early part of the first decade of the twenty-first century – investing in commodities suddenly became sexy.

Anyone who remembers the wonderful John Landis film *Trading Places*, starring Eddie Murphy and Dan Akroyd as the hapless victims of a giant bet placed by some Wall Street titans, will also remember their subsequent encounters with the peculiar but high-powered business of pork belly futures trading. Commodities, you could reasonably surmise from the film, was a slightly obscure, rather niche business that was best left to specialists. Gold has always had its admirers and oil has been gaining traction in investing circles, but most investors remain firmly wedded to the great bonds:equities face-off.

At the turn of the century barely any commodity-based index funds existed worldwide. Then the wider investing world started becoming interested in the peculiar business of commodities trading. It is impossible to pin any one factor on what prompted the change, but as interest increased, commodity prices started soaring. Whether it was a booming global economy or possibly China, something seemed to have permanently changed. The legendary biking billionaire Jim Rogers caught the wave of euphoria perfectly in *Hot Commodities: How Anyone Can Invest Profitably in the World's Best Market*, a best-seller that clearly laid out the argument for a commodity super-cycle to beat all others, driven by a booming global population, China's industrialisation and a global economy operating at full capacity drawing down on limited reserves of key resources such as oil and coal.[1]

Small British exchange traded fund firm ETF Securities came to typify this incredible wave of investment euphoria. The management behind the small asset management firm launched the world's first listed index tracking fund called Gold Bullion Securities in Australia, followed in 2004 by a London-based sibling of the same name. In July 2005 it stepped up a gear and launched the world's first oil index tracking fund, ETFS Brent Oil, and by 2006 it had $2 billion in assets under management on the London Stock Exchange. By 2008 inflows into ETF Securities funds were totalling more than $170 million a week and the firm had over 50 different funds on five different exchanges. Flash forward yet another year, to the beginning of 2009, and the firm had over $9 billion under management in an astonishing 130 different index tracking funds. Suddenly mainstream British and American newspapers were writing about exchange traded commodities almost as much as mainstream bond ETFs – if not more.

A visitor from Mars might be tempted to ask at this point what was behind this huge success. Cynics were and are tempted to point to those rising prices – are commodities the classic momentum play involving shallow investors chasing the booming sectors until they crest, then fall, taking private investors' money with them? The statistics suggest otherwise. A wide range of commodities hit a peak in the early part of 2008 – oil crashed past $145 a barrel, for instance – yet by the end of the year most were on their back up as the global depression set in. Yet inflows into ETF Securities index funds have continued to grow – investment in gold exchange traded commodity funds set new records in 2009 and 2010.

A more subtle process seems to be at work – the mainstreaming in portfolio terms of commodities. You did not have to buy all the arguments surrounding a commodity super bull cycle to accept that resources have a role in a portfolio. Even hard-bitten, research-led outfits, like Ibbotson Associates, one of the world's leading consultancy firms, had concluded that commodities provided valuable diversification for investors of all shapes and sizes. In March 2006 the US bond giant Pimco commissioned the firm's researchers to look at commodities as part of a wider portfolio planning process. This research commission itself deserves some note. Pimco is a dedicated bonds house and for it to ask the world's leading investment research consultancy to look into the value of commodities in a portfolio is itself a testament to commodities mainstreaming.

But it was Ibbotson's conclusions that were even more revealing. The researchers discovered that magically adding some commodity index fund exposure to your portfolio appeared to add real diversification and spiced up returns. Looking at the period 1970–2004 the researchers found that this extra spice could be worth as much as an extra 133 basis points per annum to total returns. They concluded: 'We believe that commodities offer an inherent or natural return that is not conditional on skill.' The causes of this extra performance bonus were legion but none seemed to really matter. The researchers decided that commodities nearly always seemed to improve the risk/return characteristics of a portfolio, especially in inflationary times.

The Ibbotson research drew on an earlier, much more important paper that deserves a quick mention, 'Facts and Fantasies about Commodity Futures'. This 2005 paper by Gorton and Rouwenhorst looked at returns from commodities over the 45 years to 2005 and concluded that 'the average annualized return to a collateralized investment in commodity futures has been comparable to the return on the SP500 ... [and] ... outperformed corporate bonds'. These equity-like returns had been achieved with higher volatility, the authors concluded, and decade-long returns varied greatly (1970s great versus stocks, 1990s bad versus stocks), but crucially they discovered that 'over all horizons – except monthly – the equally-weighted commodity futures total return is negatively correlated with the return on the SP500 and long-term bonds. ... These findings suggest that Commodity Futures are effective in diversifying equity and bond portfolios'.[2] Even more importantly, the longer the holding period of the commodity index, the bigger the diversification benefit. They also investigated what provided this diversification and suggested two factors. 'First, commodity futures perform better in periods of unexpected inflation, when stock and bond returns generally disappoint. Second, commodity futures diversify the cyclical variation in stock and bond returns.'[3] See Table 4.1.

Table 4.1 Risk premium of commodity futures, stocks and bonds – annualised monthly returns 1959 to end 2004

	Commodity futures	Stocks	Bonds
Average	5.23	5.65	2.22
Standard deviation	12.10	14.85	8.47
Sharpe ratio	0.43	0.38	.26
% returns above 0%	55	57	54

Source: Yale ICF Working Paper No. 04-20, 'Facts and Fantasies about Commodity Futures', Table 2 (Gorton and Rouwenhorst, 2005)

Research findings from Gorton and Rouwenhorst on volatility in commodities and equities include the following:

- During the 5 percent of the months of worst performance of equity markets, when stocks fell on average by 8.98 percent per month, commodity futures experienced a positive return of 1.03 percent, which is slightly above the full sample average return of 0.89 percent per month.
- During the 1 percent of months of lowest performance of equity markets, when equities fell on average by 13.87 percent per month, commodity futures returned an average of 2.36 percent.

Commodities, the academics finished, provided one last supreme advantage: inflation proofing. They noted that commodity futures had 'outpaced local CPI inflation in the UK and Japan'. With conclusions like these, it is little surprise that both private and institutional investors have suddenly decided to jump on board the commodities super-cycle, pouring money into index tracking funds provided by ETF Securities.

How to invest using index tracking funds

ETF Securities is far from being the only provider of index tracking commodity funds. In the US Powershares is very active, as is the ELEMENTS ETN platform, while in London Lyxor has its own small range of broad commodity index ETFs, as do UBC and Deutsche db-X trackers, but it offers by far the biggest choice through its exchange traded commodities platform. Structures include:

- classic ETCs based on a major family of futures indices developed by Dow Jones and AIG;
- leveraged or geared upside ETCs based on the same index family but gearing up the upside;
- short or inverse ETCs that make money for investors even as a commodity falls in value;
- physical ETCs which are not based on an index as such but physically hold a commodity on behalf of an investor. They track the spot price of a commodity rather than the futures price of an index;
- futures ETCs which allow investors to track the 3- and 12-month futures price of a commodity.

This fearsome list of structures (each family of funds has dozens of specific commodities) should immediately alert investors to one crucial distinction:

what exactly is it that you are tracking? Are you tracking the spot price or the futures price of an index? This distinction is hugely important – many investors make no distinction between these two sets of prices, overlaying their judgements about the spot price (gold going up, oil going down) into the futures markets, which boast very different dynamics.

Spot prices v the futures index

When most ordinary investors think of commodities they think of the spot price that is quoted in the media, but in reality most professionals tend to ignore this as an investable idea except as the core component of something much more important – most commodity investors tend to use an index of some sort as the basis of their investment process and that index usually incorporates some form of futures contract.

Before diving into the slightly murky world of futures-based commodity indices it is worth mentioning that there are a small number of vehicles that do track actual spot commodity prices, in a fashion. On the London stock market both Close and BNP Paribas offer investment trusts (with tickers of EMB and CEO respectively) that structure a long-term investment (five years or more) around the final total returns of a combination of spot prices. These 'basket funds' usually mix and match energy-based commodities with hard commodities like metals and some agricultural prices also known as softs. The resulting basket is then offered to investors with a geared upside that ranges between 200 percent and 350 percent of any gains in the combination of spot prices.

This makes for easy-to-understand vehicles – which also offer some capital protection – but these structured investment trusts are not really representative of the mainstream of commodity investing. The ETCs and ETFs offered by ETF Securities (and Lyxor) tend to be based on broader indices that base their returns on futures-based contracts. In technical language this means that these commodity indices represent the total return of something called a non-leveraged (no loans involved) futures portfolio. Simply put, that means the full contract value of a futures contract – not just the margin requirement – nominally secures each position in the index. To understand how this might work, imagine a futures index for gold. Imagine that the spot price of each ounce is $1,900. Many producers of gold may want to make sure they have a good idea of the price their future production of gold will fetch and maybe even sell the rights to future production now in order to lock in prices. On the other side of this futures trade, buyers of gold like Indian jewellers might want to lock in a decent price in three months' time now. Thus you have two parties to a futures contract, namely the producer and the buyer. They might agree a price for 3 months in the future or even 12 months, or anything in between. To secure the purchase the gold buyer might pay an option price – they are, after all, simply buying a futures-based option on a commodity – and then deposit the rest of the final payment as a deposit in the form of Treasury bills. This way the buyer locks in the price and the seller receives their payment. Add up all these non-leveraged futures contracts and you have a futures index.

The returns from these futures-based commodity indices come in three different ways: the interest earned on that collateral deposited to secure the futures positions (typically you pay an advance as a deposit, based on collateralised Treasury bills on which you earn income), the return obtained from holding and trading futures themselves (based on moves in the underlying spot price) and something called the roll yield. To understand this crucial last term, let's go back to that example of gold with a spot price for delivery today of $1,900 per ounce. Let's assume that the supply of gold is low because stocks are down. Futures contracts might start trading at $1,895 a few weeks out and then fall to, say, $1,890 for two months. A smart investor could decide to buy these futures contracts and then sit around and wait for the due delivery date on the future. If nothing happens to the spot price, you would expect the futures price to move towards the spot price as delivery date approaches. This means you sell your fast-maturing futures contract (bought for $1,895) closer to $1,900 and then buy another futures contract for the $1,895 again. Over time this constant action of buying the cheaper short-term futures contract and rolling it as delivery approaches can produce a handy profit.

This roll yield is a crucial part of total index returns. These futures indices capture the 'roll' from one contract to another, selling the expiring contract and buying the new one. The next month's/quarter's contract frequently changes in price – if it costs more the market is in 'contango' and you lose out, while if it costs less the market is 'backwardated' and you make more money. The existence of contango indicates, among other things, that there are adequate supplies to be carried into future months. This roll yield is hugely important long-term and probably accounts for a large component of total long-term returns. To understand just how important the roll yield is, go to a US-based website and resource called HardAssetsInvestor.com. This is full of great comment and insight, but its research clearly shows up why that roll yield is so crucial. Table 4.2 shows a snapshot from the middle of 2008 of annualised roll yield looking one month out. The differences can be immense – lean hogs' annualised returns were –94 percent while heating oil was 44.96 percent. Get this roll yield wrong and you could end up destroying your investment.

Table 4.2 Annualised roll return from 2008 – based on next available month

Commodity	Annualised roll return %
Lean hogs	–94.52%
Feeder cattle	–30.63%
Cotton	–24%
Sugar	–14.9%
Corn	–12%
Gold	–1.94%
Natural gas	2.86%
Copper	3.50%
WTI crude oil	4.54%
Gas oil	16.4%
Heating oil	44.96%

Source: HardAssetsInvestor.com

HardAssetsInvestor has also done the long-term maths on which bit of the return profile really matters. According to data from the GSCI index series (more on that index below), the roll yield killed investors in the 2000s while in the 1980s the cash or interest income element was the biggest component of total returns (see Table 4.3).

Table 4.3 Annualised returns 1970–2005

Annualised	1970s	1980s	1990s	2000s*	2005
GSCI Spot Return	9.05%	–1.37%	–0.63%	12.39%	39.05%
GSCI Roll Yield	4.24%	2.44%	–0.53%	–3.45%	–12.55%
GSCI Cash Yield	6.67%	9.52%	5.11%	3.05%	3.24%

* January 1, 2000, through September 30, 2006
>GSCI Excess Return = Spot Return + Roll Yield
>>GSCI Total Return = Spot Return + Roll Yield + Cash Yield
Source: Van Eck Global Research, Bloomberg

And just in case you thought commodity markets had changed appreciably in the few years after this analysis, think again after looking at Table 4.4. Again this is from HardAssetsInvestor and it shows the annualised roll yield for a number of commodities in March 2011 (7 March to be precise). Notice the vast difference between those commodities showing a positive roll yield (especially oil) and those with a thumping negative roll yield (sugar).

Table 4.4 Commodity roll costs (all figures are percentages)

		Current annualised roll	Previous week's annualised roll	Past year average roll (not annualised)
Energy	WTI	13.34	24.18	1.40
	Brent	−0.82	−1.27	0.43
	HH Natural Gas	27.19	23.40	0.43
Precious metals	Gold	1.01	1.10	2.45
	Silver	0.76	0.35	0.10
	Platinum	−1.04	−0.39	0.28
	Palladium	1.68	2.92	0.25
Base metals	Copper	0.85	0.36	0.05
	Aluminium	4.72	4.61	0.40
	Zinc	4.03	4.14	0.39
	Lead	−1.36	−0.47	0.31
	Nickel	0.42	0.33	0.08
	Tin	0.27	0.30	0.05
Agricultural	Corn	5.75	7.49	2.47
	Wheat	26.29	28.49	4.01
	Soybeans	2.69	3.01	0.08
	Live cattle	10.74	19.59	0.89
	Lean hogs	243.92	210.11	3.01
Softs	Coffee C	−0.22	−4.92	0.86
	Cocoa	−6.32	−7.73	0.77
	Sugar #11	−63.86	−60.61	−4.06
	Cotton #2	−6.84	−28.24	−2.85

Source: http://www.hardassetsinvestor.com/weekly-commodity-reports/contango-report/2585-the-contango-report-brent-remains-in-backwardation.html

So, all in all, it's a bit confusing. Quite how you make your profit from investing in commodities varies over time and between these different components, but there is one crucial last point to understand – these three components of return all add up to the total return or TR. You will see this term bandied about a fair amount in the world of ETFs and ETCs and it means that all the income from holding the underlying index is rolled up into the total return and is not paid out separately to the investor, i.e. you do not receive that interest income from holding the T-bills as a collateral.

The main commodity index providers

If all these different and varying components to total returns from investing in futures indices have not completely foxed you, you are ready to face the next big challenge – which index to track. Sadly, there is no straightforward answer as there are a number of different index families that track a range of commodities in completely different ways (though they all track futures prices). Your exchange traded fund could track a number of futures indices, including the following.

The **S&P Goldman Sachs Commodity Index** is perhaps the most widely used index in the US and is what's called a 'production-weighted benchmark' of two-dozen commodities adjusted for liquidity. It is currently heavily weighted in energy products; 40 percent of the index's weight comprises crude oil futures. Agricultural and soft commodities, such as wheat and sugar, make up 11 percent, metals 6 percent and livestock 2.86 percent. Because the GSCI index is based around this notion of 'world production', the constituents can vary widely – the dominant energy sector, for instance, has varied over time from 44 percent through to 78 percent, making it very volatile indeed. This also makes SP/GSCI most susceptible to the effect of rotation between contango and backwardation in crude oil prices.

The **Dow Jones-UBS Commodity Index** is an equally popular series of indices and sits at the core of the ETF Securities range of funds. It is made up of 19 commodities weighted primarily for trading volume and secondarily based on global production, with index rules 'designed to dampen volatility' by setting floors and caps on component weights. Crucially the index has been set up so that no single commodity can comprise more than 15 percent of the index and no single sector can make up more than one-third of the benchmark's weight. By sectors, energy now carries the biggest weight of 33 percent, followed by industrial metals at 20 percent, precious metals at 10 percent, softs at 8.7 percent and grains at 18 percent. This index series is used by ETF Securities in the UK and the iPath range of ETNs in the US. DJ-AIGCI is the most evenly balanced across all five sectors, which means it captures much of the contango in livestock, agriculture and precious metals, without the luxury of having a larger presence in the energy sector where the backwardation is rife.

The **Deutsche Bank Liquid Commodity Index** consists of only six commodities, based around the most liquid (in trading terms) commodities in each sector. These are heating oil, light crude oil, wheat, aluminium, gold and corn. The index company claims that this narrow range of underlying commodities reduces the actual cost of roll and rebalancing. In practical terms it means that energy makes up 55 percent of DBLCI; agriculturals and metals equally split the remaining 45 percent. There is no exposure to livestock or softs in this index family. Crucially, the designers of this index – and the Powershares range of ETFs that tracks it – claim a unique 'roll strategy'. Rather than simply rolling expiring contracts to the next available month, DBLCI looks out as far as 13 months for the contract with the highest roll yield. Theoretically, the index developers claim, this should improve roll yields in both backwardated and contango-ed markets.

Lyxor, the UK ETF provider, has a small family of index funds that tracks a venerable and widely followed index called the **CRB Commodity Index**, started by the Commodity Research Bureau in 1981. This index is made up of 22 futures contracts combined into an 'All Commodities' grouping, with two major sub-divisions: raw industrials and foodstuffs. Metals make up 20 percent, energy carries a weight of 39 percent and soft commodities 39 percent.

Last but by no means least, many commodity purists rather like something called the **Rogers International Commodity Index**, which is by far and away the broadest and most international of all the indices. The RICI consists of 35 commodities, including such exotics as azuki beans, silk, rubber and wool. Energy comprises 44 percent of the index, agriculturals and softs 32 percent, metals 21 percent and livestock 3 percent. See Table 4.5.

Table 4.5 Commodity index comparison

Commodity	Measure	S&P GSCI	DJ-AIG Commodity index	Reuters Jefferies CRB	Rogers International Commodities Index (RICI)
ENERGY		74.28	35.1	39	44
WTI Crude Oil	$ barrel	39	14.6	23	21
Brent Crude Oil	$ barrel	14.02	0	0	14

Table 4.5 Continued

Commodity	Measure	S&P GSCI	DJ-AIG Commodity index	Reuters Jefferies CRB	Rogers International Commodities Index (RICI)
RBOB Gasoline	$ cents/gallon	4.06	3.95	5	3
Heating Oil	$ cents/gallon	5.22	4.47	6	1.8
Gasoil	$ metric ton	5.34	0	0	1.2
Natural Gas	$mmBtu	6.64	12.08	6	3
LIVESTOCK		4.16	8.5	7	3
Live Cattle	$ cents pound	2.49	5.43	6	2
Feeder Cattle	$ cents pound	0.44	0	0	0
Lean Hogs	$ cents pound	1.23	3.07	1	1
PRECIOUS METALS		2.58	10.2	7	7.1
Gold	$ troy oz	2.36	7.91	6	3
Silver	$ troy oz	0.22	2.29	1	2
Palladium	$ troy oz	0	0	0	0.3
Platinum	$ troy oz	0	0	0	1.8
INDUSTRIAL METALS		6.39	17.78	13	14
Aluminium	$ metric ton	2.59	7.27	6	4
Copper	$ metric ton	2.5	6.75	6	4
Lead	$ metric ton	0.34	0	0	2
Nickel	$ metric ton	0.49	1.63	1	1
Tin	$ metric ton	0	0	0	1
Zinc	$ metric ton	0.47	2.13	0	2
AGRICULTURE		12.58	28.43	34	31.9
Wheat	$ cents bushels	3.35	3.71	1	7
Kansas Wheat	$ cents bushels	0.82	0	0	0
Corn	$ cents bushels	3.45	6.2	6	4.75
Soybeans	$ cents bushels	2.09	6.67	6	3
Soybean Oil	$ cents pound	0	2.68	0	2
Soybean Meal	$ short ton	0	0	0	0.75
Cotton	$ cents pound	0.76	2.15	5	4.05

Table 4.5 Continued

Commodity	Measure	S&P GSCI	DJ-AIG Commodity index	Reuters Jefferies CRB	Rogers International Commodities Index (RICI)
Sugar	$ cents pound	1.22	4	5	2
Coffee	$ cents pound	0.64	3.12	5	2
Cocoa	$ metric ton	0.26		5	1
Orange Juice	$ cents pound			1	0.66
Rubber	JPY kilogram				1
Lumber	$ 1k board fleet			1	
Canola	CAD metric ton			0.67	
Rice	$ cwt				0.5
Oats	$ cents bushels			0.5	
Azuki Beans	JPY bag				0.5
Barley	CAD metric ton			0.27	
Greasy Wool	AUD kilogram				0.25
Data	1	10-Oct-08	30-Sep-08	31-Aug-08	12-Dec-07

Source: iShares

Composite or not?

If you are determined enough to have made your way through this maze of index families, you have probably ended up using the DJ-AIG group tracked by ETF Securities if you are based in the UK. You are now faced with one last choice, namely which bit of the index to track.

Many non-specialist investors look to commodities and ETCs in particular as a way to add a broad swathe of diversification to their equity- and bond-dominated portfolios. In reality they are not that bothered about which commodities they want to track, rather they want a 'composite' return. This composite idea is crucial to most private investors – they want to invest in a broad composite index that tracks all the commodities in a diversified manner, rather than pick out a favourite few.

But many specialist investors are suspicious of this broad-brush approach – they are aware that indices like the GSCI, for instance, are heavily biased towards energy-based products. This energy effect has been very significant over the last few years as the price of crude oil has doubled, dragging up heating oil and gas prices in its wake. But it makes many investors nervous about effectively betting their investment on geo-political risk, the proclivities of the Saudis and the huge debate raging over whether there is such a thing as peak oil. Some investors may want to buy exposure to commodities but want to exclude energy-related commodities – the index developers have anticipated this and developed a layering of sub-indices that groups commodities into energy and non-energy components. But composite indices drill down into even greater detail if you choose – some investors want to buy only hard commodities outside energy (say metals) while others want to invest in agricultural but not include wheat. These baskets tend to break down into four main sub-groups:

- energy commodities;
- agriculturals broken into softs and hards plus livestock;
- industrial metals including copper and nickel;
- precious metals.

Beyond these baskets of commodities you are into individual indices that track a specific commodity. These tend to be the territory of professional investors with specialist knowledge and are best avoided by most private investors.

The different types of returns on offer from ETCs

There is, sadly, one last important choice to make when it comes to finding the right commodity-based ETF and ETC for your portfolio: which fund structure do you want? In the early days of ETFs, investors were faced with a simple classic tracking proposition – a 1:1 return structure that made you money if the underlying futures index went up in value. Now you have much, much greater choice – you can, for instance, juice up returns by using short and leveraged ETCs.

These leveraged index funds, for instance, pay out two times the *daily* returns on the underlying futures index (before fees and adjustments) while short ETCs provide an exposure equal to minus one times (–1*) the daily percentage change in the 'Index'. Here's how these work: if the index falls by –1 percent in a day, a short ETC will hopefully increase by +1 percent in that day. If, by contrast, the index increases by 2 percent, the leveraged ETC makes a 4 percent gain (and vice versa if the index drops).

ETF Securities also offers yet another variation on the idea of tracking futures contracts – investors can specifically choose whether or not they want to track the 3-month and 12-month forward-based futures price of particular commodities. According to ETF Securities, these forward ETCs were launched because they 'have historically shown lower volatility, while the effects of contango and backwardation also vary between the existing Classic and Forward ETCs. The Forward ETCs provide investors with the opportunity to optimise returns by increasing exposure to backwardation or decreasing exposure to contango'.

Just to completely confuse private investors, they can also avoid the whole futures index-based business altogether and invest in the actual spot prices of precious metals like gold and platinum via a physical ETC. These give investors an actual share in a physical stockpile of precious metals (held in a bank deposit vault, of course) with the price based on the spot price, not the forward futures price.

The risks of investing in commodities

All these different fund structures, composite indices and varying components to total returns should alert private investors to one of the biggest risks of investing in commodities – the sheer variety of index and fund structures could end up confusing private investors and encourage them to invest in the wrong index and fund. You might, for instance, want to build some exposure to oil prices into your portfolio – each of the different composite indices offers very different levels of exposure to this commodity class and even within the broad sector of oil there are different sub-indices for West Texas and Brent Crude plus separate markets for heating and gas oil. These futures-based markets are also hugely affected by backwardation or contango and different ETC fund structures will also deliver different return profiles.

Investors also need to be aware of a much broader issue, namely that commodities as an asset class can be, like many equities, risky and volatile. To understand just how volatile these markets can be, look at Table 4.6 which shows performance from a broad range of commodities from 2007 through to the end of 2011. The overall picture is one of steady gains but with some very big exceptions: in particular notice many energy-based prices, with heating oil for instance up 66 percent in 2007 and then down 46 percent in 2008! By contrast some agricultural commodities over those five years have performed spectacularly badly, with cotton, for instance, suffering two very big price drops in the last five years.

Table 4.6 Commodities performance from 2007 through to 2011 (all figures are percentages)

Name of commodity	2011	2010	2009	2008	2007
Heating Oil Composite	14.02	16.7	48.8	−46.2	66.3
Diesel (NYH) Composite	13.36	18.3	46.4	−46.5	
Crude Oil (Brent) Composite	13.06	18.6	70.8	−51.9	66.6
Brent Oil Spot $	12.75	23.4	63.8		
Gold (LBM) £	11.4	31	15.1	39.2	33.7
Gold (LBM) $	10.88	26.3	27.6	2	34.3
Gold Composite	10.56	26.3	28	2.2	33.9
Gasoline (RBOB) Composite	9.52	15.2	90	−56.8	58.9
West Texas Intermediate Spot $	8.52	12.2	86.7		
Crude Oil (Light Sweet) Composite	8.02	12.2	75.5	−53.3	63.7
Coffee Composite	−6.56	70.6	26.8	−17.2	
Silver (LBM) £	−8.63	82.6	36.4	3.4	15.2
Silver (LBM) $	−8.95	76.1	51.1	−24.1	15.7
Silver Spot $ per oz	−9	74.4	52.7		
Silver Composite	−9.65	74.5	52	−23.9	15.6
Palladium Composite	−17.04	87.4	117.7	−48.7	16
Palladium (LBM) £	−19.58	96.7	95.5	−29.4	11.1
Palladium (LBM) $	−19.94	89.7	116	−48.1	11.5
Platinum (LBM) £	−20.56	20	43.9	−16.3	35.3
Platinum (LBM) $	−20.87	15.7	59.8	−38.7	35.9
Platinum Composite	−20.95	15.8	60.5	−38.4	36
Sugar (No. 11) Composite	−29.22	18.6	133	10.1	
Cocoa Composite	−31.37	−6.6	28.4	20.9	28.1
Cotton Composite	−35.28	85.6	56	−30.1	
Natural Gas Composite	−35.53	−20.8	−2.7	−23.6	24.6

Looking even further back in time, it is worth taking in the cautious prognostications of stock market historian William Bernstein, one of America's best investment thinkers. He looked closely at long-term commodity returns and did not like what he saw. You can read his analysis at **www.efficientfrontier.com** and see Table 4.7. His headlines included the following:

- Gold and silver 'both did exceptionally well in the high-inflation '70s when other traditional investments suffered, but have performed miserably during other market environments'. But the average annual return for gold since 1970 has been 'a modest 7.7 percent, below long-term government bonds and only modestly above the long-term inflation rate of 5.3 percent. ... Silver hasn't even managed to outpace inflation, with an average annual return of only 4.3 percent. ...These modest returns have been at the expense of massive volatility'. The best return for gold was a whopping 126.5 percent in 1979, while silver's return was even more glittering at 267.4 percent. However, the worst returns came just two years later in 1981 – a loss of 31.6 percent for gold and a loss of 46.4 percent for silver.

- Bernstein also looked at commodity spot prices for 23 different commodities, including cattle, pork bellies, cocoa, heating oil, gold, copper, orange juice, lumber and sugar. His conclusion? 'They haven't really performed as advertised: although their best years were in the '70s, the returns for the decade were only a few percentage points above inflation, and the long-term average has been considerably below inflation – the worst performer of all asset classes!'

Table 4.7 Long-term commodity returns

Annual returns	1970s	1980s	1990s	Average	Best	Worst
Gold	30.6	–2.4	–4.1	7.7	126.5 (1979)	–31.6 (1981)
Silver	28.3	–13.4	1.7	4.3	267.4 (1979)	–46.4 (1981)
REITs – NAREIT Index	4.8	12.5	14.1	10.5	48.9 (1976)	–31.6 (1981)
Commodities Spot Index	9.6	–1	0.5	3.1	57.7 (1973)	–46.4 (1981)
S&P 500	5.9	17.5	16.6	13	37.4 (1995)	–26.5 (1974)
Small Cap Stocks	11.5	15.8	16.5	14.4	57.4 (1976)	–31.9 (1973)

Table 4.7 Continued

Annual returns	1970s	1980s	1990s	Average	Best	Worst
Long Term Govt Bonds	5.5	12.6	10.7	9.5	40.4 (1982)	−7.8 (1994)
Treasury Bills	6.3	8.9	4.9	6.8	14.7 (1981)	2.9 (1993)
Inflation	7.4	5.1	3.3	5.3	na	Na

Source: William Bernstein, www.efficientfrontier.com

Table 4.8 tells another story. It shows summarised long-term returns from the broad CRB index dating back to the 1950s, compared with the FTSE 100 and the S&P 500. Between 1956 and the beginning of June 2008, the total return from the CRB TR index was 399 percent, compared with 2680 percent from the S&P 500 (in nominal terms). By comparison the FTSE has

Table 4.8 Summarised long-term returns from the broad CRB index

Summary	Correlation to CPI	Correlation to FTSE 100	Total return	Annualised average return
			%	% pa
FTSE 100				
S&P 500				
Reuters CRB Index (CCI)	0.781250713	0.386970964	399.95	6.96
CRB Spot Index	0.84	0.33	321.83	8.44
CRB Livestock Sub-index	0.85	0.31	351.40	7.35
CRB Fats & Oils Sub-index	0.66	0.22	306.41	6.87
CRB Foodstuffs Sub-index	0.74	0.19	306.41	6.87
CRB Raw Industrials Sub-index	0.87	0.37	286.24	8.44
CRB Textiles Sub-index	0.87	0.19	351.43	3.62
CRB Metals Sub-index	0.73	0.42	150.96	16.08

Source: based on data from www.efficientfrontier.com

returned a total of 374 percent since 1984. And within these returns, some commodities have clearly performed badly over the very long term – the CRB Metals Index over the entire period has returned only a total of 150 percent.

To be fair, this table also reminds us of two of the positives of investing in commodities – they are a great **inflation hedge** and they are also **relatively lowly correlated** with equities, thus offering investors some diversification within their portfolios. First, that inflation point – the telling number is the one which compares correlations between the CRB index and the US Consumer Prices Index (the CPI) – 0.78 percent for the broad index, which is statistically very significant, rising to 0.85 for livestock. These figures suggest that commodities could work wonders in stagflationary markets, with gold likely to do especially well. Investors also love the diversification benefits of commodities. Table 4.9 below is from Blue Sky Asset Management (now called InCapitalEurope) and compares a number of equity markets with key commodity classes. The statistics suggest that the diversification story is compelling, with wheat, oil and gold being particularly lowly correlated with the FTSE, for instance. But a slightly more disturbing picture emerges for other commodities – copper's correlation with the FTSE 100, for instance, has risen to 0.47 in recent years as more and more mining companies come to dominate the London Stock Exchange.

Blue Sky's research also points out that the three-month price relationship of wheat and gold as measured by something called the R2 factor is 0.26, a near doubling in recent years. The researchers conclude that 'this is also seen in the wheat/copper correlation (from 0.09 to 0.46) and the wheat/oil correlation (from 0.10 to 0.57). This highlights the recent investment trend of lumping commodity markets into one basket – they all go up and they all go down in tandem'.

It is also worth pointing out that as investor interest in the whole broad investment space snowballs, individual indices for specific commodities are beginning to move broadly in line with each other, even though they contain a very different mix of underlying constituents. According to 15-year data (to March 2008) from Barclays and 10-year data from Deutsche Bank, the three main broad 'composite' commodity indices tracked by index funds have an approximate 0.80 to 0.90 correlation based on their returns in the long run.

Table 4.9 Equity markets v key commodity classes

90 day/ 365 day	S&P 500	FTSE 100	Gold	Copper	CRB	Wheat	WTI oil	USD/ JPY	EUR/ CHF	VIX
S&P 500	1.00	0.62	−0.25	0.32	0.49	0.35	0.39	0.30	0.62	−0.80
FTSE 100	0.57	1.00	−0.26	0.50	0.57	0.47	0.41	0.34	0.33	−0.45
Gold	−0.02	0.03	1.00	−0.08	−0.03	−0.20	−0.12	−0.38	−0.22	0.25
Copper	0.27	0.55	0.27	1.00	0.62	0.34	0.38	0.32	0.08	−0.23
CRB	0.36	0.54	0.39	0.73	1.00	0.66	0.83	0.35	0.38	−0.40
Wheat	0.22	0.37	0.26	0.46	0.63	1.00	0.57	0.28	0.40	−0.23
WTI oil	0.30	0.42	0.29	0.53	0.82	0.45	1.00	0.35	0.39	−0.37
USD/ JPY	0.60	0.39	−0.13	0.21	0.23	0.09	0.24	1.00	0.16	−0.27
EUR/ CHF	0.60	0.37	0.03	0.16	0.27	0.14	0.27	0.52	1.00	−0.54
VIX	−0.83	−0.54	0.07	−0.25	−0.31	−0.23	−0.26	−0.56	−0.53	1.00

Source: Blue Sky Asset Management, 2008

Another big concern for analysts and advisers alike is that the commodity markets may have fundamentally changed in the last decade as investment levels have increased. Hedge funds and big fund management institutions have piled into the commodity markets, fundamentally changing them in quite possibly unknown ways. This evolution opens up some potentially very worrying issues about scale – take gold and the huge success of just one US-based ETF, the Street Tracks Gold Trust (GLD in the US). Launched just a few years ago it is already worth a staggering $63 billion and sits on 1,254 metric tons of the stuff, which is more than that held by the Bank of England and most other central banks. According to one report this one fund is buying up every year between 13 percent and 14 percent of annual mine supply and has more assets than the next five largest gold mutual funds combined. Such a huge concentration of physical ownership, especially by a legion of private investors through a fund, raises the possibility that a sudden loss of confidence in gold could spark a run, with the ETF selling huge quantities of gold overnight, causing prices to plummet even further.

Yet another concern raised by many portfolio managers is that commodities as a whole have become too dependent on that roll yield we encountered earlier on. Recent academic studies of long-term commodity returns by big commodity funds have shown that between 1959 and 2004 the annual return from changes in spot prices averaged just 3.47 percent. What happens if this one-way road to future profits suddenly switches and the futures markets turn back to contango? As William Bernstein points out, this new world could spell disaster for investors in ETCs and ETFs as the producers of commodities turn the tables and stop paying for this protection against inflation, i.e. stop using forward futures contracts. 'In a market whose major propelling force is the demand for insurance against inflation, those who supply it will demand a premium. Goodbye Keynesian normal backwardation, hello ... forwardation?'[4]

The ETC and why commodities make sense for private investors: an Interview with Nicholas Brooks, Head of Research at ETF Securities

Q: What do you think has powered the growth of ETCs? Is it still largely institutional?

I think the main reason there has been such strong demand for ETCs is that they have opened commodity investing to mainstream investors. Before ETCs were created, commodity investing was mostly dominated by a relatively small group of specialist investors. Because ETCs are listed on major stock exchanges, trade and settle like stocks and are highly liquid, they provide traditional fund managers, pension funds, private wealth managers and retail investors simple and direct access to an asset class previously difficult for them to gain exposure to. The bulk of the funds invested in ETCs are institutional, but there are signs of increasing retail activity as awareness of ETCs among the public has increased. Investors use ETCs for a variety of investment objectives. The largest flows tend to be long-term buy-and-hold investments by investors seeking to benefit from the diversification properties of commodities and to play long-term growth themes. Some are investing to hedge against inflation and currency risks and some are tactical investors using long, short, leveraged and different maturity ETCs to implement a variety of strategies.

Q: How do you actually structure your mainstream, classic ETCs?

We have three main types of ETCs. We have physically backed precious metal ETCs – gold, silver, platinum and palladium. These ETCs are 100 percent backed by physical bullion in vaults held by a custodian bank. We also have ETCs that track commodity indices based on commodity futures returns ranging from individual commodities such as sugar and copper to baskets tracking industrial metals, agriculture and other commodity sectors. These ETCs provide investors with long, short and leveraged exposures. All of these ETCs are 100 percent backed by collateral. The third group are our oil ETCs which track oil prices through different maturity oil futures contracts such as Brent 1mth, 1yr, 2yr, 3yr and similar for WTI oil futures. These ETCs are 100 percent backed by commodity contracts purchased from Shell.

Q: Why did you introduce later variants such as the forward ETCs and the physical ETCs?

The physically backed gold ETC was the first of the ETCs (and, incidentally, the world's first gold ETF) and silver, platinum and palladium naturally followed. Because most other commodities are difficult to invest in physically as they are difficult to store, are heterogeneous and decay, they are generally priced off commodities futures. ETF Securities therefore created the first exchange traded commodities to track futures returns, making it possible for investors to access commodity returns through securities traded on stock exchanges. Following the launch of the 'classic' ETCs that track near-dated commodity futures, forward ETCs were the next logical extension. Forward ETCs were created to provide a wider choice of investment options, giving investors the ability to gain exposure to either shorter-maturity or longer-maturity futures returns, depending on their views on the outlook for the shape of the futures curve.

Q: Back in the dark days of late 2008, you ran into controversy because of the implosion of American financial giant AIG. What happened and how did you react?

Because our ETCs based on the DJ-AIG index (not the physically backed or oil securities) were backed by swaps guaranteed by AIG, during the short period between AIG looking as if it might go bust and the US government stepping in to bail it out, many market makers were reluctant to take AIG risk on their books and there was a temporary reduction in liquidity in these ETCs. Recognising that the problem went well beyond AIG and was related to a general freezing up of financial markets globally as credit risk moved to centre stage for most investors, a decision was made to 100 percent back these ETCs with collateral (marked to market daily and held by a ring-fenced custodian) to ensure this liquidity problem would not occur again. Since then the ETCs have traded normally and volumes in a number of them are amongst the highest in Europe. The silver lining of this event is that these ETCs are now backed by one of the most robust structures in the industry. [Author note: AIG is now owned by the US government.]

Q: Do you think that commodities ETCs should sit in private investors' portfolios? Aren't they just too specialised, volatile and risky?

It depends very much on the investor's asset mix and investment goals. It is difficult to generalise about ETCs as there are ETCs that track broad commodity indices such as ETFS All Commodities or ETFS Precious Metals, which over the past ten years have had lower volatilities (and higher returns) than the S&P 500. There are other ETCs such as ETFS Copper or ETFS Wheat which historically have been more volatile in the same way that individual stock volatility is often more volatile than broader equity indices. Most studies indicate that adding the returns of a broad commodity index to a diversified portfolio of equities and bonds has improved the long-term risk-return profile of the portfolio. The main reason is that commodities have tended to have a low – even negative for some – correlation with equities and bonds, providing diversification benefits difficult to find in any other asset class. A number of endowments and large institutional investors have recognised and taken advantage of these characteristics, but until ETCs were created a few years ago, these strategies were not easily available to private investors. In addition, in the same way that private investors are able to take a view on a stock or equity sector, now they are able to implement strategic or tactical views on gold, oil, agriculture and nearly all key individual commodities and sectors.

Q: Do you think the commodities super-cycle, so beloved of Jim Rogers, is dead?

Commodity markets, like all financial markets, will always be affected by the cyclical swings of supply and demand. However, unlike other financial assets, supplies of commodities are finite and in some cases – such as oil – are in rapid structural decline. Extraction costs are rising, new discoveries are falling and existing fields and mines are being depleted. Technological innovation may be able to improve the efficiency of use of commodities and perhaps slow the rise in the cost of extraction, but ultimately commodities are finite in supply. Until the world's population stops growing and global per capita incomes stop rising, structural demand for commodities will continue to rise. Although the current economic slowdown is likely to be the largest since the Great Depression, structural demand from rapidly industrialising economies such as China and India is likely to remain extremely strong on at least a 10- to 20-year view. Given the size of their populations, the impact on final demand for commodities is likely to be extremely large. Because of natural supply constraints, higher commodity prices will likely be the key adjusting factor – both to force increased efficiency of their use and to stimulate new innovations to boost the productivity of their supply.

5

The fiddly detail – risks, caveats and the indices

Not all index tracking funds are created equally. Investors need to understand the nitty gritty of how index funds are actually constructed and then managed on a day-to-day basis. Pick the wrong fund, with the wrong structure, high fees and little disclosure and you could be buying into trouble. David Norman and James Cottee both work for a firm called TCF Investment (www.tcfinvestment.com) – a specialist in the art of building diversified portfolios using passive funds. In this chapter David and James pick up on some of the key ideas discussed in Chapter 3 about structures and discuss their own due diligence process for using ETFs and mutual index trackers.

This chapter looks at how investors might select a suitable ETF from the growing range of products. It looks at the risks and features of different product types and highlights the key factors that investors might use in their selection process. By definition every individual investor will be different, have different needs and risk tolerances/capacity – so different products will be suitable for different investors. This chapter is focused at retail investors – the person in the street – rather than the investment professional – though hopefully both will find the suggested process/steps for due diligence useful. It should also be remembered that all investing is risky – were it not so there would not be any excess return for undertaking the activity. Investors should always remember the simple truths of investing – keep it low cost, diversify and if you do not understand it (or it looks too good to be true) then do not invest in it!

A growing market

The European fund management industry is changing rapidly due to the growth of exchange traded funds (ETFs). These had a minimal presence seven years ago, but according to research by Deutsche Bank, at June 2011 there were 1,038 European ETFs with assets under management (AUM) of €216 billion.[1] This represents less than 3 percent of total funds under management, but around 14 percent of total fund inflows went to ETFs, in the first quarter of 2011.

There are a number of forces behind the rapid growth of ETFs. From the perspective of the customer, there is a far greater range of ETFs than traditional funds. They also tend to be lower cost and more convenient to deal than many retail index funds, and have considerably lower costs than the typical active fund.

From the perspective of the providers, though, the attraction of ETFs is financial. According to Deutsche Bank, an ETF business may have profit margins that are four times those of traditional fund management companies. This is surprising, given that the management fees are much lower than those of active managers. However, there are sources of income for ETFs other than the annual management charge.

Synthetic ETFs, which achieve replication by use of a total return swap, are particularly profitable and now account for more than half of the European ETF market. Investment banks are able to run an ETF business as an adjunct to their own balance sheet. Securities which cannot be profitably loaned can be used as the invested assets of synthetic ETFs, thereby reducing the bank's capital and generating extra income.

Synthetic ETFs are complicated products, though, which have embedded counterparty risk the nature of which might not be apparent to many retail customers. At times when the banking system is under stress, it is crucial to understand the nature of these products and the potential risks associated with them.

As well as ETFs, there are also a rapidly growing number of other exchange traded products (ETPs), such as exchange traded commodities (ETCs) and exchange traded notes (ETNs). These too have structures that can be more complicated than might appear at first glance, and again need careful analysis.

The market for ETFs and ETPs is dynamic, with many product launches each year as providers seek to grow their share of this rapidly expanding market.

The types of product and the indices they track is growing extremely quickly as some of the finest minds in the investment world unleash their full innovative power on capturing a share of this lucrative market. The downside of this is that there is sometimes overwhelming choice. Retail customers, who are free to buy any of the many complex ETFs that are listed, are faced with the many product complexities, and will hopefully benefit from this chapter's structured approach to sorting the wheat from the chaff.

Much of the innovation in the ETF industry has not, in fact, been particularly geared to retail customers. One target market has been wealth managers, for whom ETFs are a useful means of building client portfolios. Hedge funds have been another important customer for ETF providers. For example, there are many so-called exotic ETFs, such as leveraged and short products. These are launched with short-term traders in mind, but can be bought by any retail investor.

The Bank of England has expressed concern about the regulatory framework for synthetic ETFs. Apart from the risks to individual investors, the Bank believes that there are risks to the financial system as a whole from the rapid growth of the ETF market.

The European Securities and Markets Authority (ESMA) has stated that the current regulations on ETFs are inadequate and need to be upgraded.

One issue which is of particular concern is counterparty risk, which has been at the forefront of investors' minds since Lehman Brothers collapsed in 2008. If an investment bank with a synthetic (swap-based) ETF business were to fail, the ETF investors could lose out. Another potential problem is the sovereign debt crisis in the Eurozone. Current UCITS rules, which were formed in easier times, allow any OECD government bond to be held in a synthetic ETF as invested assets.

The ETF market, in our opinion, has grown ahead of proper regulation. There is also currently little proper research on passive products and ETFs in particular. Even professional financial advisers may not be properly equipped to offer advice on passive products, with many unaware of the differences between different types of ETP.

Choosing an ETF

With the ETF world rapidly changing, what is needed are some simple ways of navigating this complicated range of products. Perhaps the best way to do this is by using a checklist. TCF Investment uses ETFs and other passive funds in the construction of all its multi-asset portfolios. We employ a robust investment/screening process but at its core are the three key factors that any investment should display: suitability, safety and low cost.

What this means in the context of ETFs is broken down below. The following questions address the major issues about ETFs and should allow investors to be systematic in their approach. There is no way of making this process mechanical, as the matters of risk are subjective. Ultimately, it is for the investor to decide how to trade off cost and risk.

The key questions of suitability revolve around why a passive fund might fit an investor's needs, why then might an ETF be the right passive vehicle, what is the right benchmark to track and how does the ETF actually track?

Safety considerations concern counterparty risk – with the two main areas of concern being securities lending and swap-based ETFs (often called synthetic ETFs). The final screening area is cost – the total expense ratio (TER), the impact of any securities lending revenues and dealing costs.

While we highlight a series of questions to use for initial selection we also recommend on-going monitoring of any ETF portfolio using similar criteria.

Why might passive be suitable?

ETFs are primarily passive products (index funds) so it is first worth considering carefully why one might use index funds. The main reason is that over time they should outperform most active managers due to their lower costs. This important finding is often not understood by retail investors in the UK, who may not appreciate the effect that costs have on investment performance. Index funds have a rapidly growing share of the UK retail market, though, and are well established among institutional investors in the US.

The typical TER for an active retail fund is around 1.5 percent p.a. Dealing costs inside the fund can amount to another 0.5 percent to 1 percent p.a. of the fund's value (sometimes more if the manager is turning over the portfolio more frequently). Total costs for passive funds are much lower: TERs can be as low as 0.15 percent p.a. and internal turnover is minimal.

Whatever skill an active manager might have, the handicap of such extra costs is a difficult one to overcome consistently. Thus, picking active funds is generally a losing proposition. This key fact is not widely publicised by the fund management industry, which instead heavily promotes the idea of active fund management. The impression that is given is that there are in fact many skilful managers, who can consistently beat the market.

What happens in practice, though, is that the fund performance from active managers, whether stars or not, tends to disappoint. The reason is that very few managers who have achieved a good track record have done so through skill, as explained below.

In any given year around half of managers might outperform their benchmark index, in the same way that half of coin tosses are successfully guessed. (The ratio is actually lower after you take into account the fact that all funds have costs whereas an index benchmark will not – so on average less than half of managers will outperform.) But let us go with half for the purposes of demonstrating the point. Around half of these will outperform for a second year, and so on, until a few will have racked up several years of out-performance. There will always be managers who simply by luck will have achieved excellent track records – just as some people may throw a long series of heads when tossing a coin. Among them will, of course, be managers who have performed well due to skill, but experience shows that there are very few of them.

In spite of this, the fund management industry is still able to market active funds with high expenses.

This situation persists because there are two factors that make it hard for investors to evaluate performance records. The first is short-term variability versus long-term trends: the only way to compare active funds is over several years. It is only over time that differences in performance due to skill or costs will become apparent. But many investors do not have access to sufficient time data to investigate this.

The second issue is survivorship bias. In any league table, funds with poor performance are often closed or merged and their performance records vanish. The surviving funds therefore tend to be the better performers and so the average performance of the remaining active funds is biased upwards by 'survivorship bias'. This means the league tables do not always give a true picture of performance.

It can, therefore, be quite difficult to evaluate the merits of active management. There is, though, considerable academic research on the subject. The key findings can be summarised as follows.

- The average active manager will underperform the market due to fees and expenses.
- There are very few, if any, retail fund managers who can consistently outperform over the long term, after the effect of costs and expenses.
- Those managers who do outperform in any given year are far more likely to be lucky than skilful. There is very little, if any, relation between past and future performance.

For these reasons, we believe that it makes sense to use index funds for the majority of assets. One approach is to use index funds throughout a portfolio. Another is to use it them a core and use specialist funds for those niche asset classes where active managers may be more likely to add value or where indices are not yet developed.

Why use ETFs instead of index funds?

Once the decision has been taken to use index funds, the next question is whether to use traditional index mutual funds or ETFs. ETFs offer a number of advantages over traditional index funds:

- a much greater variety of funds, which cover all of the main asset classes and markets;
- live dealing during market hours;
- generally competitive TERs;
- negligible minimum deal size.

Some index funds are cheaper than ETFs, though. For example, the Vanguard FTSE UK Equity Index Fund has a TER of 0.15 percent, whereas those ETFs that track the FTSE All Share index have TERs of around 0.40 percent. The cheapest index funds usually require a substantial minimum investment size, or access through an investment platform (which will have its own separate charges). The impact of stamp duty costs also needs to be taken into account (sometimes appearing as a dilution levy on index mutual funds).

Another, albeit minor, difference between index funds and ETFs relates to securities lending. Index funds often have an indemnity from their securities lending agent, whereas those ETFs that lend securities do not generally have any indemnities against loss. More on this later.

A quick word on tax. There is potential pitfall for investors in ETFs, which is to fall foul of HMRC's rules on overseas funds. ETFs are, for tax reasons, domiciled abroad. This allows them to be traded on the London Stock

Exchange but escape stamp duty. HMRC has onerous rules, though, on the taxation of overseas funds, unless they qualify for UK distributing or UK reporting status. With traditional funds investors are unlikely to buy a fund that is intended for another market. There is nothing, though, to stop an investor from buying an ETF that is not intended for UK retail investors. Thus it is essential to check that an ETF has either UK distributing or UK reporting status.

Whether you choose an index mutual fund or an ETF the *most important determinant* of a fund's performance is its benchmark. For some asset classes there is an obvious benchmark, such as the S&P 500. For fixed income securities and commodities, there are many possible benchmarks and choosing the right one is critical. With regard to equity benchmarks, most benchmarks are market capitalisation weighted. The key issues are which securities are included, and what size of companies is included (e.g. those in the FTSE 100 or FTSE 350).

Fixed income benchmarks fall into three main categories – government bonds, corporate bonds and inflation linked bonds. The key issues for conventional bonds (i.e. not inflation linked) are maturity and credit risk. Bond indices will generally include bonds of a given maturity. The most useful measure of a bond fund's maturity is its duration or modified duration, which expresses its average life. Corporate bond indices will tend to measure bonds according to their credit rating. This information is usually available in a bond ETFs factsheet.

Commodities create a slight problem in that it is not possible for ETFs to track the performance of a single commodity, due to concentration rules (part of the rules for inclusion as a UCITS fund). There are products such as ETNs and ETCs that do this. There are, though, ETFs that track commodity indices. However, there are a few issues which need to be understood which relate to whether the fund is tracking commodities or commodity futures. There is a big difference between a commodity and a commodity future. Commodities are physical entities that need storing (e.g. oil, gold), whereas commodity futures are financial contracts (e.g. a three-month future).

The return from owning a physical commodity, such as oil, may be very different from owning the futures contract for the same commodity. A futures contract will generally trade at a premium or discount to the spot price of the commodity that reflects the costs of storage, interest rates and the immediate availability of the commodity. For example, if there were a sudden shortage of wheat due to a poor harvest, spot wheat might trade well above wheat futures contracts.

The major commodity indices are generally based on the returns from commodity futures rather than spot commodities. This makes it easier for investment banks to replicate their performance, as they can buy futures rather than hold physical commodities in warehouses.

The commodity index will consist of a basket of commodity futures, with maturities of a few months. They are continually 'rolled over' (expiring contracts are sold and further dated ones are purchased). The effect of rolling over the futures has a major effect on the return. When the futures curve is upward sloping (further dated months trading above nearer months), there is a negative return from rolling the future. The market is said to be 'in contango'. When near months trade above more distant months, the market is said to be 'in backwardation'.

Thus the return from commodity futures can be quite different from that of the underlying physical commodity. In the recent bull market of commodities, the returns from commodity futures were appreciably less than spot returns due to steep contango.

There is a further issue that needs to be understood. The return of a physical commodity, such as an ounce of gold, is a straightforward concept. It is simply the percentage change in the spot price over a given period. However, with futures, there is more than one way of calculating the return. Excess return is the difference in return from the future's position on a given amount of physical commodity. Whereas with total return calculations it is assumed that cash is held that could be used to pay for the physical commodity at expiry of the contract. The total return is the excess return on the futures and any interest earned on this cash.

As mentioned earlier, there is a wide range of so-called 'exotic' ETFs. These include leveraged and inverse products. These are not, in our opinion, sensible choices for long-term investors and should be avoided. One problem with them is that they do not perform as investors might expect. Due to daily rebalancing, the returns over a period are often appreciably different from what might be thought from the starting and end values of the underlying index. In the jargon the returns are 'path dependent'.

Funds, notes, commodities or products?

ETPs is a generic term which covers ETFs, ETCs and ETNs. All are traded on an exchange but are very different in structure. As their name suggests, ETFs are funds and regulated as such. The UCITS rules restrict what funds can do; certain investments cannot be packaged as ETFs. For example, single commodity products would breach concentration limits.

ETCs are debt securities which pay a return linked to the price of a given commodity. The commodity will usually be held in a vault with a custodian and thus the ETCs are backed by underlying assets. ETCs can be more convenient than holding a physical commodity directly. They can also be held in ISAs and thus shielded from capital gains tax.

ETNs are superficially similar to ETFs but are in fact unsecured bonds, which promise to pay a return based on an index, commodity or formula (as in a structured product). ETNs are typically issued by investment banks. While they trade on an exchange in the same way as ETFs, they typically offer investors much less protection in the event of a default.

Investors in such an ETN would rank alongside other unsecured creditors. Synthetic ETFs, in contrast, have much greater protection as they have invested assets which are held separately from the investment bank's assets. Only if there is a shortfall in the invested assets would investors be exposed to a failure of the swap counterparty. One could have a scenario where an investment bank failed, and its ETN notes were wiped out while the bank's ETF business remained unscathed.

Unlike ETFs, which have not had a failure, several ETNs backed by Lehman Brothers defaulted in the 2008 credit crisis. We would advise most non-professional investors to avoid ETNs.

How does the fund track?

ETFs are passive instruments and are intended to track the performance of an index. Over any given time period, though, an ETF will generally perform slightly differently to its benchmark. There are two reasons for this.

- the effect of costs and expenses;
- imperfect replication.

Costs and expenses will impose a steady drag on performance. Imperfect replication, on the other hand, will produce random differences in tracking. For long-term investors these are much less important than the effect of costs. There are two different ways to measure tracking, which capture these two sources of tracking error:

1 Tracking difference is the difference between the performance of a fund and its benchmark over a given period. Over time, the tracking difference of an index fund is largely determined by the effect of costs, as the effect of imperfect replication tends to cancel out.

2 Tracking error is the annualised deviation of daily tracking differences. This captures the effect of imperfect replication.

We suggest that investors compare the tracking error and tracking difference of an ETF with its peer group.

To summarise, ETFs are suitable for the typical investor and provide a straightforward means to access a wide range of asset classes. Costs are generally low, but some index funds may be a cheaper option. There are a few pitfalls with fixed income and commodity ETFs, as there is a far wider choice of benchmarks. We recommend avoiding so-called exotic ETFs for all but expert/professional investors. Tracking performance can be measured by tracking difference and tracking error. Unless tracking error is unacceptably high, which indicates a problem with the ETF, the most important factor will be costs.

How safe is my tracker?

The main areas of concern with regard to the safety of an ETF is connected with counterparty risk and thus this area is where most work is required. Different types of ETF have different risk profiles. In order to decide what is appropriate for an investor it is necessary to understand what risks are inherent in each type of ETF and eliminate from consideration any categories where the risk is unacceptable.

Counterparty risk can emerge from the activities of an ETF (which may engage in activities such as securities lending) or from the actual structure of the ETF which uses a swap contract, the performance of which depends on a counterparty. The counterparty risk in both cases may be mitigated by collateral.

Index funds and physically backed ETFs often engage in securities lending. The aim is to earn fee income by lending the stocks in the fund, which is split between the manager and the fund. By this means, some of the costs incurred by the fund can be defrayed.

The extent of securities lending and fees earned varies considerably by asset class. The markets where there is the greatest scope for lending are certain developing equity markets and some European equity markets. Lending rates in the UK and US are much lower.

In the 2008 crisis some traditional funds suffered sizeable losses on their securities lending activities. This was not due to the lending itself, but through the reinvestment of cash collateral into lower quality fixed income assets. Such practices were common in the US but not in the UK market.

The key variables for assessing securities lending are:

- the average amount on loan;
- the maximum amount on loan;
- the collateral quality;
- the percentage of fee income from securities lending paid to the fund.

It is for investors to decide whether they wish to hold ETFs (or index mutual funds) that engage in securities lending. iShares, the market leader in physically backed ETFs, uses securities lending extensively. State Street, which has the largest ETF by assets under management, does not carry out any lending as a matter of policy.

Investors should be aware that securities lending is not restricted to index funds and ETFs. Most pension funds, insurance funds and a large number of active funds also engage in this activity.

A swap-based ETF (often called a synthetic ETF) uses a total return swap that pays or receives the difference between the daily return of its invested assets and the ETF's benchmark. This is what makes it track. The ETF is thus exposed to counterparty risk, from the swap provider failing.

There are several models for synthetic ETFs. The original and most widely used is for the ETF to have a single swap counterparty that is part of the same investment bank that provides the ETFs. Another approach is to use multiple independent swap counterparties to diversify the risk. Firms whose main business is in physically backed ETFs use different arrangements and investors need to understand how the swap arrangements are structured (see Figure 5.1).

The traditional approach is for synthetic (swap-based) ETFs to invest in a collection of securities, which may have no relation to their benchmark, and a total return swap. The securities are known as the reference basket. Each day the swap earns the difference between the benchmark return and the return on the reference basket.

For example, if the benchmark return was 2 percent and the reference basket's return was 1 percent, then the payment due in the swap would be 1 percent. What is happening is that the swap is making good any shortfalls in performance from the reference basket.

Chart B Cash flows for a swap-based ETF

Figure 5.1 How the cash flows when investing in a typical swap-based ETF
Source: Bank of England

Any profits on the swap are usually not paid over daily but under UCITS rules must be done before they reach 10 percent of the ETF's NAV. Thus at any given moment the ETF could be owed 10 percent of its NAV by the swap counterparty. It is often implied by providers that this is the extent of any possible counterparty exposure. Potential losses, however, are much greater than 10 percent of NAV. In the event that the reference basket were to suddenly collapse in value, the amount owed on the swap would instantly rise and could reach 100 percent of NAV if the reference basket was wiped out. The ETF would then suddenly have counterparty exposure of 100 percent of NAV. Should the swap provider fail then the entire assets of the ETF could be lost.

This is not necessarily a realistic scenario, but the losses due to the failure of the swap counterparty are not limited to 10 percent of NAV. Another issue is that in the event that an ETF failed, it would be fully exposed to movements of the securities in the reference basket. Apart from the potential loss in value, the securities might prove illiquid, especially in the circumstances surrounding the default of an investment bank. The ETF might be unable to meet redemptions and be forced to suspend trading.

Another area for concern is the relationship between the ETF and the swap provider. In the traditional model, the swap provider and ETF manager belong to the same investment bank. This poses an obvious conflict as the investment bank has an interest in offloading lower quality assets for use in the reference basket, while the ETF manager would prefer only those of the highest quality.

What goes into an ETF reference basket may have more to do with the needs of the parent investment bank's balance sheet than the needs of the ETF. For example, UK equity ETFs may have reference baskets that contain no UK shares. European equity ETFs have had reference baskets that consist entirely of Japanese equities.

It is easy to see scenarios where failing assets are moved from the investment bank into the ETF. What happens in extreme situations is hard to say as there is no history to guide us.

In fairness to providers of synthetic ETFs, some 'over-collateralise'. That is, the swap provider in effect places excess investment assets in the ETF, which give some additional protection in the event of a default. And as concerns have been expressed by regulators and others, product providers have responded with far greater levels of transparency and this is to be welcomed.

Synthetic ETFs should also track better than those that use physical replication. The swap will provide the exact return of the index regardless of the performance of the reference basket.

With a swap-based ETF, then, the key issues are

- the nature of the invested assets;
- any over-collateralisation;
- potential conflicts of interest between the ETF manager and the swap provider;
- the credit rating of the swap provider.

By far the most important is the nature of the invested assets. If they replicate the benchmark, then there can be little problem (e.g. the top 100 UK stocks for a FTSE 100 tracker). On the other hand, if they are of poor quality and collapse in value (as might happen in the case of a sovereign debt default), then the ETF could be at serious risk.

So, what assets can a synthetic ETF hold in its reference basket? In the European market, almost all synthetic ETFs are UCITS. They have no special rules for ETFs and so any investment that qualifies for UCITS is permissible, subject to concentration limits being satisfied. There are no rules that relate to the benchmark of the ETF, and so a complete mismatch is possible.

These rules are far from restrictive. The maximum exposure to a single equity is 10 percent, but there is no restriction on equities of a particular type. Thus an ETF could have a reference basket that consists entirely of bank shares. Government debt from any OECD country is permissible and the maximum amount from any given country could be very high.

These rules were designed to cover the wide range of possible investments that a conventional fund might need to undertake, but are, in our opinion, extremely lax for the reference basket of an ETF. Individual ETF managers may have their own internal rules but these may still allow the seemingly absurd situations mentioned previously (Japanese equity collateral for a European tracker). They have no mention of maximum deviations between the reference basket and the ETF's benchmark, which is what we believe are required.

While investment banks continue with the traditional type of synthetic ETF, other providers have launched swap-based ETFs of a different kind.

Source, an ETF provider, uses a multiple counterparty model. This gives the manager freedom to exclude any swap counterparty if its credit quality was believed to have become unacceptable. Some providers which have traditionally offered only physically backed ETFs have launched swap-based products. These tend to have tougher rules on which assets can be held and use third-party swap providers.

The area of counterparty risk is complex and it is for the individual investor to decide whether to use synthetic ETFs. There is no straightforward means of measuring the extent of counterparty risk or what might happen in an extreme scenario. We recommend that investors decide on a limit to their holdings in swap-based ETFs and to individual providers. Diversification across products, ETF types and providers is surely the best approach. It is also important to monitor the credit rating and other indicators of credit quality, such as credit default swaps of the swap provider, on an on-going basis – just as depositors should monitor the credit worthiness of their banks, and structured product buyers their product providers.

Investment cost is a key factor

Whether you choose active or passive funds, costs matter. They are one of the few certainties in investment. For index funds and ETFs the main determinant of how well the fund tracks its benchmark is the fund's costs.

This will be approximately equal to the TER. This does not include internal dealing costs, but for a low turnover vehicle such as an index fund, these will be minimal.

Other key costs are dealing (spread and broking) charges. The importance of these will depend on the nature of the investor – buy and hold investors will be less interested, whereas active traders of index funds will be more concerned.

The effective cost of ownership of an ETF may be reduced by securities lending revenue. In the case of European equities and some developing markets, it may substantially reduce the drag from the TER. A simple measure of the effective cost of ownership is TER less revenues from securities lending.

In summary

The preceding list of topics gives a way of choosing ETFs systematically. The investor has only to answer a series of simple questions to cut the seemingly unmanageable jungle of ETFs down to size.

The key measures are:

- tracking error;
- tracking difference;
- credit rating (for synthetic ETFs);
- breakdown by asset class, strategy and provider.

Comparing the tracking error of an ETF with its peers is useful – any sudden changes might indicate a problem with the performance of the ETF itself or its price on the secondary market. In either case, it is a useful warning signal. For swap-based ETFs it is sensible to monitor the credit ratings and credit default swaps of the swap provider.

Whether you choose active funds, index funds or a combination, a sensible strategy is always to maintain limits for exposure to asset classes, strategies and providers – *don't put all your eggs in one basket*.

6

The new fundamental indexing revolution

Like all great revolutionary movements, the adherents of an indexing approach to investment have multiplied exponentially in numbers over recent years and that growth has been accompanied by an inevitable splintering into smaller groups with ever more detailed and considered doctrines. A vocal and hugely sophisticated group of analysts and fund managers has coalesced around a simple idea – that the traditional index is flawed in its design and that it needs to be rethought and linked back to a much older idea that suggests the only sensible investment idea is one that is based around the concept of good 'value'. Fund manager Rob Davies, from Fundamental Tracker Investment Management (FT/M), based in Glasgow, is one of these new-style indexers trying to combine the best of 'value' investing with the transparency and efficiency of index fund investing. In the second half of this chapter we will look in detail at his innovative approach to fundamental investing but before we hear from Davies, let us first understand the background to this fundamental indexing revolution.

The rise of the fundamentalists

The idea of using index tracking funds has suddenly become mainstream here in the UK and many investors now make extensive use of these lower-cost open ended unit trusts and exchange traded funds to 'buy the market', i.e track the leading companies in an index based on their market capitalisation.

Yet that enormous growth in demand for ETFs has left more than a few investors troubled by the implicit assumption that underlies the fund –

index tracking funds simply 'follow' the market and do not attempt to make any value judgements about what is good value or expensive. This passive or even 'dumb' form of investing does not use fund managers to actively control the risk profile of the companies within the portfolio but instead explicitly trusts the judgement or wisdom of the crowd, or in this case 'the investing herd'. That opens up passive investing, as it is called, to a powerful criticism: that as an investor in the fund you are essentially investing in whatever stocks are in vogue at that time.

This momentum bias comes about because popular shares increase in value at a relatively fast rate (in part because valuation multiples such as the PE ratio shoots up), pushing up the share price, and thus the market capitalisation – all of which means that the passive fund manager with an index tracker has to increase their weighting of the hot stock within the fund. Sometimes that momentum bias can lead to solid companies with relatively 'lowly' shares prices (as measured by their fundamentals) but great business franchises dropping out of an index tracking fund in favour of popular and expensive 'new' entrants to an index. Typically this momentum bias in indices such as the FTSE 100 means that lots of emerging markets companies in the oil or mining sector come into an index at the expense of more 'reliable' and 'trusted' domestic names whose share price cannot command the same (temporary) lofty valuations.

Rob Davies, founder and manager of the index tracking Munro fund (sold via Smith and Williamson on most fund platforms) cites one typical example from March 2009 when the FTSE 100 underwent another of its perennial re-weighting or rebalancing exercises: 'Out went Tate and Lyle with a price to book value of 1.37 and a PE ratio of 7.4,' says Davies, and in went mining giant 'Fresnillo which was trading at a price to book ratio of 5.1 and a PE ratio of 25. The fact that the Tate share price has slid from 400p to 250p while Fresnillo had soared from 100p to 434p in the few months prior to these changes confirms the view that indexes overpay for growth.'

Davies is a pioneering fund manager who believes that passively buying an index such as the FTSE 100 opens up investors to a particular and very significant risk – that you are potentially buying the wrong kind of stocks at exactly the wrong moment. Davies believes that a mainstream passive fund tends to buy more 'expensive', popular stocks at exactly the wrong price as the investment herd rushes into the shares, pushing up valuations and thus index weightings ... and then collapses in value as the bubble inevitably bursts!

In his view ordinary, passive funds tracking an index are automatically biased towards these 'expensive' shares and to demonstrate how this works Davies cites the following example:

> '*Assume the components of a stock index have aggregate earnings of £100 million and the whole market is valued on a PE ratio of 10. Therefore the total market is valued at £1,000 million. Assume also that half the stocks have an above average valuation of 11 so the other half must be valued at 9 times earnings. It follows therefore that the expensive half of the market is valued at £550 million and the cheap half at £450 million. Consequently any index tracker fund will have 55 percent of its assets in the expensive stocks and only 45 percent in the cheap stocks. We might not know which of the stocks are cheap and which are expensive. But we do know that cheap stocks outperform expensive stocks over time, yet the index fund is underweight in them*'.

The last statement from Davies is perhaps the most important – research by academics has demonstrated the power of a number of assumptions about investment returns but two stand head and shoulders above the rest. The first is that by and large actively managed funds do not deliver the promised returns and that in these circumstances investors are, on average, better off investing in a lower cost index tracking fund – this is the core argument in favour of passive funds. Yet many of these self-same academics who developed this thinking have also conceded that some types of shares have, in the past, beaten the 'buy the market' strategy. In a key paper, 'The cross-section of expected stock returns', two pioneering academics, Professors Eugene Fama and Kenneth French (founders of a leading index tracking fund management firm called Dimensional), suggested that 'value' shares and 'small cap' shares delivered superior returns, although much of those super-sized returns were a consequence of taking on extra risks.[1]

William Bernstein, a US-based investment writer, summed up the professors' conclusions thus: 'Size and value factors, because they were surrogates for risk, had positive returns. Therefore, value stocks should have higher returns than growth stocks, and small stocks, higher returns than large stocks; *small value stocks should have the highest returns of all*. The one place where the model "didn't work" was with small growth stocks, which empirically had much lower returns than expected, having the worst performance.'[2]

Enter the fundamentalists

This debate has given birth to a new movement based around the concept of the fundamental indexer: this still involves a fund tracking the constituents of an index yet there is one big difference, namely that the index itself 'weights' its holdings away from the most popular towards those stocks which are the best 'value'. Strip away the complex language and in effect you are buying into a value fund expressed through an index. This is proving increasingly popular, especially in the world of institutional and pension fund investing.

The new national NEST pension scheme for lower-paid workers has explicitly decided to explore fundamental funds within its new core range of low-cost pensions, and a growing number of mainstream public sector pension funds are also looking at tracking indices designed by one of the founders of fundamental indexing, Rob Arnott and his RAFI firm. Arnott, himself a financial analyst and founder of consulting firm Research Affiliates, has passionately defended the idea of fundamental index tracking, describing it as the 'third choice' between simple passive index tracking and investing in funds with an active fund manager. For Arnott, fundamental indexing is the new 'alternative beta', i.e a new way for investors to reap extra returns from investing the markets.

Arnott and his colleagues at Research Affiliates and RAFI reckon that old-style passive investing produces a number of dangerous biases within their portfolios, notably overweighting over-priced stocks, and underweighting under-priced stocks. These plain vanilla indices also 'fully participate in market speculation' and 'display substantial growth bias'.[3]

RAFI indices, by contrast – tracked by a number of ETFs in the UK and the US – attempt to track indices in a very different way. According to RAFI these indices are 're-designed to identify the fair value of each company and use fundamental variables that don't depend on the fluctuations of market valuation'. This new way of indexing 'may be less influenced by market bubbles' and will certainly seek 'to avoid overweighting overvalued stocks – a potential with market-cap-weighted indexes'.[4]

Crucially Arnott does not just base these conclusions on spurious marketing claims. He has spent the past decade meticulously researching the ideas behind fundamental indexing and tested them against past data. Arnott and his colleague Jason Hsu first published their conclusions in 2005 and demonstrated how their ideas:

> 'outperformed in US markets during a 43-year span ending December 2004, based on a simulation. That initial research was extended by Nomura Securities to cover the 23 developed markets in the FTSE Developed Index. ... The Fundamental Index approach generated excess returns over cap weighting in 21 of the 23 developed market applications over a 21-year period. The average outperformance in developed large company markets was 2.7%. With these results in hand, we concluded that an investor could achieve a return of 2–4% over cap-weighted indexes in developed markets, over a complete market cycle.'[5]

Arnott and his colleagues at Research Affiliates subsequently turned these academic theories into hard investing practice, via the RAFI index family developed in partnership with the FTSE index firm. This global range of indices has been in existence for well over five years and many of the key indices are now tracked by more than a dozen ETFs in the UK and the US.

Arnott and his team recently went back to these indices and tested their five-year record: 'Using live results [from their own indices], 19 of 23 countries added value via the Fundamental Index methodology. The average excess return per country has been 2.0. ... The FTSE RAFI US 1000 Index produced an excess return of 2.3 percent per annum.'[6] Tables 6.1 and 6.2 flesh out some of this analysis, looking first at individual country indices and then at the record of some of the (US) ETFs that have tracked the RAFI indices. In Table 6.2 these fund returns are then compared with returns from an equivalent mainstream index.

Table 6.1 Annualised returns since inception of FTSE RAFI indices in US$ between 30 November 2005 and 31 December 2010

Country	RAFI return (%)	MSCI return (%)	Value added (%)
Hong Kong	17.5	12.1	5.4
Germany	11.7	7.8	3.9
US	4.7	2.4	2.3
UK	2.8	3.2	−0.4
Ireland	−24.1	−19.2	−4.9

Table 6.2 US PowerShares ETFs: their record so far

ETF and equivalent index	Ticker of US ETF	Inception date of ETF	Percentage annualised return since inception
PowerShares FTSE RAFI US 1000	PRF	12/19/05	4.05
Russell 1000 index			2.46
PowerShares FTSE US 1500 Small – Mid Cap	PRFZ	9/20/06	6.77
Russell 2000			2.94
PowerShares FTSE RAFI Emerging Markets	PXH	9/27/07	1.57
MSCI EAFE Index			0.85
PowerShares FTSE RAFI Asia Pacific exc Japan	PAF	6/25/07	6.49
MSCI Pacific ex Japan Index			2.90

Source: Data correct at 31 December 2010.

Five years is not a long time in investing and in reality it is probably too early to draw any hard and fast conclusions from these numbers, but fundamental indexing does seem to add a small amount of extra value year in, year out, worth something between 1 and 2 percent per annum. Arnott concedes that the extra return is probably in part explained by a value tilt in the way that his index range is designed, although he also contends that the majority of the outperformance comes from 'contra trading against the fads, bubbles, crashes and constantly shifting expectations and speculations at work in the capital markets'.

Yet even Arnott would concede that his approach does not always work in every market, all the time – as investors here in the UK might note. Eagle-eyed readers will probably note that returns from the UK index in Table 6.1 have been much less impressive – in fact by their own statistics RAFI indices have failed to add value when compared to a simple FTSE 100 index tracker. Figure 6.1 shows returns from the Invesco PowerShares FTSE RAFI UK 100 ETF since the inception of the fund in late 2007. The thick line is the return from the FTSE 100 and the thin line is the ETF tracker – over some periods the RAFI tracker has outperformed the benchmark FTSE 100 index tracker, yet the record is patchy at best.

Figure 6.1 Returns from the Invesco PowerShares FTSE RAFI UK 100 ETF since inception

Figures 6.2 and 6.3 demonstrate an alternative approach to RAFI. Figure 6.2 shows returns for a relatively new unit trust from Vanguard called the FTSE UK Equity Income index which tracks an alternative version of the FTSE 350 based around the yield of companies. Details of the methodology used in the index are shown in Table 6.8.

The Vanguard fund does not mix and match different fundamental measures but gives primacy to one measure in particular – the dividend yield. The thinking here is based on the work of American academic (and friendly rival to Rob Arnott in the US) Professor Jeremy Siegel and his partners at fund management firm Wisdom Tree. This alternative camp of fundamental indexers believe that long-term success is all about focusing on companies that can afford to pay an above average yield that will hopefully keep rising over the long term. Each fund attempts to use a slightly different methodology, with some such as Rob Davies' Munro fund looking at the weight of dividend payouts while others such as the Vanguard fund as well as the iShares UK Dividend Plus ETF simply make use of a screen based on the absolute level of dividend yield. Another group of dividend indexers looks for an absolute commitment from companies to progressively increase their dividend payout over time. This progressive dividend idea has found shape

Figure 6.2 Returns from the Vanguard FTSE UK Equity Income index

[Figure 6.3: Line chart showing S&P 500 Dividend Aristocrats index vs S&P 500 from Mar-96 to Mar-10, with values ranging from $0 to $500.]

Figure 6.3 The S&P 500 Dividend Aristocrats index

Source: S&P Indices

in the Standard & Poor's Dividend Aristocrat family of indices which only include US companies that have increased their dividend year in year out for 20 or more years (10 in the European version). Figure 6.3 from S&P shows that the US version of its Aristocrats index has consistently added value over the past few decades.

What are the choices?

Investors looking to make the move to fundamental indexing of major markets still do not have a vast range of choices. The largest range of indices comes from RAFI and Rob Arnott and is tracked in the UK by the Invesco Powershares family of ETFs.

RAFI attempts to look at a combination of different fundamental indices and then 'mix' these measures together using its own internal formula. Crucially RAFI has started to extend its thinking away from the standard core equity markets in the UK and the US towards emerging markets – there is a RAFI EM from Powershares in the UK – and bonds. In the US Arnott has forcefully argued that existing bond indices, especially in the corporate space, are biased towards the most indebted companies, not the most financially prudent. This index bias towards excessive leverage opens up corporate bond investors to undue risk, Arnott reckons, and he has now started marketing a set of indices where the same mix of fundamental measures is applied to a company's bonds. This bond idea has found shape in two US-based ETFs from PowerShares – the Fundamental Investment Grade Corporate Bond Portfolio (Ticker PFIG) which invests in high-quality bonds, as well as a higher-risk, high yield alternative with the ticker PHB. According to RAFI this fundamental form of bond indexing would have generated more than 2 percent p.a. in added value for the 23-year period ended December 2009 in high yield bonds.

Investors looking to focus on dividends as an alternative form of indexing have traditionally focused their attention on either the iShares FTSE UK Dividend Plus ETF or the Munro fund managed by Rob Davies. The FTSE Dividend Plus index is a relatively unsophisticated mechanical screen of the FTSE 350 index which chooses to focus on the highest-yielding stocks based on forecasts whereas the Munro fund tends to be biased towards larger companies but with a bias towards the actual dividend payout. Over the past few years the Munro fund has outperformed the iShares ETF. The Vanguard UK Equity Income fund is a new entrant to the battle and has a strong, short-term record, a clear methodology, and lower costs – but it is still a young fund from an investment house that does not tend to have a strong belief in value orientated strategies. Investors looking for dividend weighted funds on a global basis might also want to take a closer look at the small number of European and world indices from either Dow Jones or Stoxx which look to invest in the very biggest companies with the highest yield. Both iShares and Deutsche db-X offer popular Euro Stoxx Select Dividend 30 ETFs which invest in the highest dividend paying eurozone stocks.

Last but by no means least, big US ETF firm State Street has entered the battle for dividend focused funds with two tracker funds – one that invests in the S&P US Dividend Aristocrats index (UK Ticker SPYD) and another which only invests in high-yielding emerging markets stocks, called the S&P Emerging Markets Dividend Opportunities Index fund, ticker EMDV.

Understand what you are buying into with fundamental trackers

Fundamental indexing in whatever shape or guise it takes opens investors up to a number of obvious risks. The first and perhaps most obvious worry is that your fund will have a value bias, i.e. it will probably be focused on stocks that many investors reckon are undervalued. That value bias can and does produce extra returns over certain timeframes but there are also many occasions when a value bias can massively underperform the wider market.

Many value-based investors have been caught short by momentum-driven markets and even world-renowned value types such as Warren Buffett or Jeremy Grantham at GMO have experienced long periods of underperformance as markets chase everything from dot-coms through Chinese start-ups, in the process ignoring 'value' stocks.

A focus on dividends also opens investors to some very specific risks. A simple strategy of only buying those companies with big yields and then weighting that index based on that yield might involve only buying companies the market regards as 'risky' – the risk here is that those dividends are unsustainable based on the balance sheet and that a very high yield will almost certainly be cut back in the future.

An obsession with dividends can also produce an overly concentrated portfolio with just a few sectors or companies dominating – in the middle of the last decade, for instance, banks dominated the dividend paying list and then summarily stopped paying. BP has also been a major source of dividends – again it stopped paying when the Gulf oil disaster struck. US critics of the Dividend Aristocrats index accept that a stated policy of only focusing on companies that constantly increase their dividend does introduce some discipline into the process but also worry that the dividend becomes almost sacrosanct, encouraging managers to lowball growth and only focus on cash flows, possibly to the detriment of the business over the long term.

On a practical level investors also need to understand that many fundamental indexing funds will not look terribly different from mainstream indexing alternatives. Table 6.3 shows the current weighting at the end of November of the FTSE 100 index.

Table 6.3 Actual FTSE 100 weightings

Name	FTSE 100 weighting
Royal Dutch Shell Plc	9.42
Vodafone Group Plc	5.79
HSBC Holdings Plc	5.74
BP Plc	5.73
GlaxoSmithKline Plc	4.65
British American Tobacco Plc	3.82
Rio Tinto Plc	3.19
BG Group Plc	3.01
BHP Billiton Plc	2.67
AstraZeneca Plc	2.50

Table 6.4 shows holdings within the RAFI UK 100 ETF – the holdings do not exactly mirror each other but the RAFI index is roughly tracking the same set of companies with similar holdings. In truth RAFI accepts that its indices will not look hugely different from a 'normal' index but it argues that its small weighting differences will add value cumulatively, over long periods of time.

Table 6.4 PSRU top holdings – FTSE 100 Holdings in RAFI Index

Weight (%)	Name
10.70	BP Plc
8.95	Vodafone Group Plc
7.08	HSBC Holdings Plc
5.89	Royal Dutch Shell Plc (CL A)
5.62	GlaxoSmithKline Plc
4.67	Royal Dutch Shell Plc (CL B)
3.13	AstraZeneca Plc
2.84	Tesco Plc
2.73	British American Tobacco Plc
2.20	Barclays Plc
2.09	BT Group Plc

Table 6.5 shows holdings in the Vanguard dividend focused UK Equity Income fund – the holdings here are radically different from those of the RAFI index, largely because of its explicit dividend focus. Yet this mix of shares looks very different from the Munro fund (see Table 6.6), which is also focused on the largest companies in the FTSE 350. In the Vanguard fund Imperial Tobacco accounts for over 5 percent whereas in the Munro fund it does not even make it into the top 10 of holdings. The difference is explained by the different methodologies for indexing – investors should investigate what they are buying into and understand the risks of each approach.

That focus on due diligence might encourage many mainstream investors to focus on the most transparent indices where there is no proprietal mixing of measures, just a small number of key measures (focused perhaps on the dividends paid) with a clear and open methodology. But beware – transparency is always welcome yet there is nearly always a trade-off between the obvious attractions of a simple, transparent strategy and the risk that that strategy might not work any more in ever changing markets!

Table 6.5 Vanguard UK Equity Income fund

Top holdings	Percentage
Imperial Tobacco	5.1
GSK	4.9
AstraZeneca	4.9
BT Group	4.8
Vodafone Group	4.8
National Grid	4.8
Centrica	4.7
BAT	4.7
HSBC	4.7
BP	4.6

Source: from Vanguard, www.vanguard.co.uk, © The Vanguard Group, used with permission

Table 6.6 Munro fund – portfolio breakdown

Largest holdings	Percentage
Vodafone Group	9.83
HSBC HLDGS	6.96
BP	5.60
BHP Billiton	5.60
Royal Dutch Shell	5.57
GlaxoSmithKline	5.10
Royal Dutch Shell	4.22
British American Tobacco	3.95
AstraZeneca Plc	3.11
Rio Tinto	2.32

Source: Munro fund

Fundamental indexing: an insider's perspective
By Rob Davies of the Munro fund

Fundamental indices are far from representing the mainstream at the moment – very few pension funds for instance have taken the leap into investing in an index that weights its constituents by measures such as the dividend or book value. But supporters of fundamental indexing are convinced that the tide is turning their way, slowly. One of the most passionate proponents of fundamental indexing in the UK is Rob Davies who is absolutely in the front line of this new movement of investors who believe that a traditional index such as the S&P 500 or the FTSE 100 is a deeply flawed exercise. In particular, Rob is convinced that dividends are hugely important for private investors. In the rest of this chapter he explains the background to fundamental indexing and explores how different investors have developed tracking funds to reflect the diversity of views.

What is wrong with conventional indexing?

Accepting the logic of index investing is a big step, but it is only the first one. The next step is to understand what you are actually tracking in an index. For most people that will amount to a choice between segments of the market usually based on size, such as the FTSE 100, the 250, or an all-encompassing single index such as the FTSE All Share, which captures nearly all the UK listed market. All these popular indices use a similar methodology and, until just a few years ago, there was no choice, as every index was based on capitalisation. That meant the weight of each stock in the fund was determined by its market capitalisation, with its total value determined by multiplying the share price by the number of shares outstanding.

For many academics this methodology for constructing an index simply reflects the underlying ideas of the EMH, namely that the share price of a company captures everything that is known about the business. That includes its balance sheet, business prospects and the quality of the management. The theory is that modern capital markets are so efficient that it is impossible for any individual to secure a sustainable, legal information advantage over their competitors. The fact that 80 percent of the market is still managed on an active basis by people who do not believe markets are efficient does not compromise the theory in the eyes of its academic adherents.

An equally important reason for using capitalisation as the mechanism for constructing a fund is that most, but not all, major stock exchange indices are based on the sum total of the value of the constituents. Basing a fund on the same principle as the index is a neat way of ensuring that the performance of the fund will never deviate too far from that of the index. There are exceptions, however. Both the Dow Jones Industrial Average and the S&P 500 are determined by a committee and can best be viewed as 'active' indices in contrast to the rules-based indices like the FTSE and the Russell. The old FT30 used a similar, committee-based, subjective approach.

Whatever the process, both rules-based and subjective indices have a growth bias. At first pass this looks illogical: why does a market cap-based index have a growth bias? The reason for this comes back to the issue of market capitalisation. Any company on the threshold of accession to the FTSE 100 will, by definition, be doing better than its peers. That means its valuation will be at a premium to its near neighbours, in other words it will be valued as a growth share. In contrast, the company that is about to be ejected will have fallen on hard times and its value will be discounted relative to its comparable companies. So companies joining an index will always be expensive and those leaving will always be cheap. The largest 100 companies in the FTSE All Share will not necessarily be the largest 100 by profits, book value, dividends or revenue, just price.

A real-life example of how this works in practice can be found in the March 2009 changes for the FTSE 100. Out went Tate and Lyle with a price to book value of 1.37 and a PE ratio of 7.4. It was replaced by Fresnillo, trading at a price to book ratio of 5.1 and a PE ratio of 25. The fact that the Tate share price had slid from 400p to 250p while Fresnillo had soared from 100p to 434p in the few months prior to these changes confirms the view that indices overpay for growth. Three years on and Tate is back in the FTSE 100 index at 680p. However, Fresnillo has done even better at 1538p although it is still more expensive on a PE of 19. Tate's PE remains low at 12.5.

But there is a problem with using just share prices to create a portfolio – they do not have a direct correlation to the value of the underlying asset, namely the company that the market is valuing. Instead they represent the opinions and views of all the market participants and that means they are subject to all the manias and fashions that dominate financial affairs. In the past few decades, those fashions have included technology, commodities, property and biotechnology. In previous centuries they have included railways, tulip bulbs and South Sea bubbles. Conversely, at the same time as one sector is fashionable, another one is out of favour. At some point or other these have included commodities, utilities and banks. What this means is that an investor buying into a conventional index fund will always have a larger position in sectors that are popular and a smaller position in unpopular sectors, irrespective of the relative valuation of those sectors. In practical terms this means that any capitalisation-weighted index is always overweight expensive shares and underweight cheap shares, as this little exercise will demonstrate.

Assume the components of a stock index have aggregate earnings of £100 million and the whole market is valued on a PE ratio of 10. Therefore the total market is valued at £1,000 million. Assume also that half the stocks have an above-average valuation of 11 so the other half must be valued at 9 times earnings. It follows, therefore, that the expensive half of the market is valued at £550 million and the cheap half at £450 million. Consequently any index tracker fund will have 55 percent of its assets in the expensive stocks and only 45 percent in the cheap stocks. We might not know which of the stocks are cheap and which are expensive, but we do know that cheap stocks outperform expensive stocks over time, yet the index fund is underweight in them. However, the situation is worse than that. Because the fund is overweight expensive shares it has a higher PE ratio than the market. In our example it actually has a PE ratio of 10.1, 1 percent more than the index itself. You might be buying £100 million worth of earnings, but doing it this way you are paying 1 percent more than the average. That is not good for long-term returns. The situation is even less attractive if there is a bigger discrepancy between the high and low valuations. If the market values the most expensive shares at 15 times earnings and the cheapest at 5 times, the average PE for the index fund becomes 12.5.

If that seems counter-intuitive this analogy might help. Imagine going shopping for apples and oranges. The apples are priced at 5p a pound and the oranges at 15p. A buyer, using the logic of a tracker, wanting equal amounts of the different fruits would buy one pound of apples for 5p and three pounds of oranges for 45p. He buys three times as many oranges because they are three times as valuable. So the shopper has spent 50p for four pounds of fruit at an average cost of 12.5p a pound. A more rational shopper would buy a pound of each for an average cost of 10p a pound.

Of course, no one really knows which shares are expensive and which are cheap at any given time. However, we do know two things:

- First, the market always overpays for growth. That is why value stocks outperform.
- Second, valuations always revert to the mean. Expensive earnings, like those of Vodafone in 2000, eventually become earnings that are priced in line with the market. That erodes returns for the investor.

Over time the index components will change as the popularity of a stock or sector waxes and wanes, yet starting a portfolio with an overweight position in an expensive sector and an underweight position in a cheap one is almost inevitably going to have a negative impact on returns in the long run. One of the oldest, and best, clichés in the money management business is that in the short term markets are voting machines but in the long run they are weighing machines. Conventional index funds are great at capturing the voting element of the stock market, yet what is needed is a way of weighing the market.

Is there a better way to index?

It is clear from this discussion that there is a potentially fundamental flaw in creating a portfolio based solely on capitalisation, i.e. share price alone. After all, in what other walk of life do we make purchase decisions solely on the basis of price? We do not, for instance, choose our mix of vegetables at the supermarket by buying most of whichever is the highest price on that day. Indeed, we do the opposite. Any special offers are snapped up, reducing our average cost per pound of vegetable. Cars are purchased on the basis of their size, reliability and performance, not just on price. Indeed, in every other avenue of commercial life we prefer to pay less for more. Supermarkets do not make buy-one-get-one-free offers without knowing what the reaction of shoppers is likely to be. Normally, when we spend our money we want some measure of what we are buying other than price. It might be the weight of a cauliflower, the top speed of a car or the number of springs in a bed. Why should we not do something similar when we buy shares? What we need is some fundamental measure of the value of a company.

A far-sighted investment manager called Robert Jones at Goldman Sachs is credited as being the first to ponder these issues back in 1990. He designed and ran a fund based around earnings, but the fund was closed down after it failed to beat the inhouse enhanced index fund. Since then the main proponents have been Rob Arnott of California-based Research Affiliates, (also known as RAFI), Jeremy Siegel of Wisdom Tree and ourselves at Fundamental Tracker. The main issue the two US-based analysts have had to address is which measure, or measures, they should use, as well as working out more mundane issues such as the frequency of rebalancing and whether to use historic or forecast data.

The attraction of a tracker fund is that it buys all the shares in a particular index. That reduces risks by ensuring that the fund holds all shares that might do well. Equally, it will hold ones that might do badly, thus dragging down the whole portfolio. So if we are going to design a mechanism that can be used across all stocks in the market we have to use some measure that is appropriate to a wide variety of companies and industries. Fortunately, there is no shortage of measures that can be used and ways in which they can be applied, though each has advantages and disadvantages.

One point to note is that all fundamental funds are blind to the data they use. This is in sharp contrast to active fund managers, who categorise companies by the sector they are in. Each sector will have its own valuation range to reflect the underlying nature of the business. That is why, for example, yields from utilities are always expected to be higher than yields from tech companies. The market is saying that dividends from tech companies are worth more than dividends from water or power companies. Fundamental funds say all dividends, book values, revenues and profits are equal. All index funds treat data in this agnostic way. But which measures should we focus on?

Book value

One traditional measure of value is the book value of the company, also sometimes known as net asset value. This is a pure accounting measure of the capital subscribed to create the company, the initial equity, less any debt, but including the profits it has retained over its life and minus the dividends paid out. This narrow definition can work for some industries such as those that develop a product or service over time and sell those profitably, but there are a number of necessary caveats. The financial accounts can become quite distorted where companies have made a lot of acquisitions as goodwill and write-offs have become significant. Periods of high inflation also have an impact by eroding the real value of debt and increasing the nominal value of tangible assets such as property or inventory. Companies working in natural resources that have made large discoveries of oil or other commodities are not able to include that additional value in the books. All they can do is record the cost of finding the deposits. Equally, a pharmaceutical company that develops a new drug can only charge the cost of discovery and development to its profit and loss account. As far as its book value is concerned, inventing a drug is just research and development expenditure. Other companies may have established important brand names, but it is hard to quantify their value and even harder to find a way to give that a value in the accounts. Without advertising, many brand names fall by the wayside. Finally, markets and tastes change so that what was valuable several years ago may be worthless now. Records and cassettes, for example, are no longer so much in demand when music can be digitally downloaded. Book value then has some merits as a measure, but it also has many drawbacks. Book value is usually seen as a key factor in selecting value stocks, so it is no surprise that it figures strongly in the approach used by leading US fund management firm Dimensional Fund Advisors (DFA). Research Affiliates also uses it as one of its four measures.

Profit and loss

The profit and loss (P&L) account is the traditional source of data for determining value. Starting at the top of the P&L statement many are attracted to the idea of using revenue as a measure because there is less scope for distortion. After all, it makes sense to assess a business on how much it sells. There is a problem with that, though, and it is summed up in this little ditty:

Revenue is vanity

Profit is reality

Cash is sanity

Quite often companies will chase business and then fail to make any money from it because the margins are too low. Unprofitable business has no value and giving it a weighting will lead to an index with a bias that does not reflect the real source of profits. In some industries even defining revenue is very difficult in a classic profit and loss sense, i.e. the banks spring to mind as an example. Other businesses are agency businesses, such as advertising where the scope for gaming the numbers can be considerable – they can move booked sales back and forth between accounting periods, especially if the contract is over a long period of time. It is also fair to say that some industries, such as retailing, will always have large revenue numbers relative to the size of the business in comparison to, say, a drug company. Commodity companies such as miners and the oil majors are particularly susceptible to wild gyrations in their top line as prices change. Finally, currency volatility can make a big impact on sales. Depending on whether the costs that are associated with those sales are in the same currency can make a huge difference to whether that volatility is beneficial or not. Notwithstanding these concerns, revenue is one of the four measures used by Research Affiliates as it is a very simple measure of a company's economic footprint.

Profits are a logical measure to base an index on – they could be the operating profit, profit before tax or net profit. The problem is that whichever level is chosen there is a high degree of subjectivity as to which items are included and which are excluded. A particular problem is the issue of exceptional items that can affect one year but reflect the accumulation of many years of business success or problems. In essence, the uncertainty here is that a great deal of the profit and loss statement has a discretionary element to it and that makes comparisons between companies difficult. The last decade has seen an unusually large number of seemingly profitable companies suddenly collapse, either through fraud or dramatic changes in their business conditions. In sum, profits have not always been what they seemed.

Many would argue that the cash flow statement is a better basis for comparison but again the issue of different standards is a key problem – what one company counts as capital expenditure another might include as operating costs. On top of that there are great differences in the nature of the cash flow between industries. A retailer, for example, will have a very different structure to its cash flow than, say, an oil company. Cash flow from a retailer may vary hugely over the course of the year as seasons change, but an oil company might be faced with years of exploration before it receives any cash. Moreover, cash flows for financial companies such as banks and insurance companies have a completely different nature to what might be called conventional companies. Using their data would distort any index based around them to a significant extent.

Dividends

There is, however, one measure that can be used across companies and has the great virtue of being independently verifiable. Dividends are the cash paid out by a company to its owners – the shareholders. That means it is a real transaction and can be confirmed by the recipients. Moreover, a dividend cheque from an oil company is just the same as a dividend cheque from a retailer, although usually larger! Nevertheless, there are cultural differences to the way companies view dividends. These are mostly between countries and usually derive from their tax treatment. Until quite recently the tax treatment of dividends in the US was quite adverse compared with stock options, so it therefore suited companies to issue fresh stock rather than cash, especially as issuing new stock diluted shareholders but did not impact the cash in the company. That was one reason why many US companies did not pay dividends. The other was a rather machismo reasoning that only mature companies paid them. It was argued that true growth companies reinvested cash to build the business. The tech bubble showed the fallacy of that argument.

The most important point about dividends is that in reality they account for virtually all the returns from equity investing. Active investors desperately seek capital gains, but study after study by the likes of Barclays, Credit Suisse and Société Générale on both sides of the Atlantic show the importance of reinvested dividend income and the growth of the dividend. Even over a short period of five years Société Générale showed that these two factors accounted for 80 percent of the return. Jeremy Siegel has calculated that the figure rises to 96 percent for US stocks over the 80 years from 1926 to 2006.[7] You ignore dividends at your peril. For these reasons all three fundamental fund processes use dividends either on their own or as part of a blend of measures.

A key argument of Rob Arnott at RAFI is that he aims to measure the economic footprint of a company rather than its financial one – that means key indicators such as number of employees, square footage of factory or retail space are all valid because they give an assessment of how significant a company is to the community. The problem is that comparing people on the sandwich production line at Compass with advertising executives at WPP will necessarily give a distorted comparison.

Single-measure or blended, historic or forecast data

With all these different measures the would-be fundamental tracker or index builder now has to make two decisions:

- Should you use a single measure in isolation or blend several of them?
- Are historic data the best to use or should you rely on future estimates or forecast data?

Using one fundamental measure like profits or earnings per share is obviously simpler and easier to comprehend, yet that measure may be unfavourable for some companies, or even exclude whole sub-sectors of the market. If, by contrast, a blend of measures is chosen, what proportion of each valuation metric, for instance, should be used? Would equal weighting be valid? Blending has the obvious advantage of not giving preference to any one particular measure that might favour, or disadvantage, one particular company or sector, but it does not avoid that second, equally daunting challenge, namely whether a series of blended measures is backward looking or forward facing in its use of data.

This second challenge – whether to use forward- or backward-looking data – is based on the reality that companies report full accounts twice a year, usually two or three months after the period end. That is the most accurate picture we are ever going to get of a company. Sadly, even when the companies report, we will be faced with the challenge of working out what some of those numbers actually mean. Terry Smith in his famous book *Accounting for Growth* pinpointed the many ways that companies can flatter the way they present themselves to the investing public.[8] Remember, too, that companies have a habit of restating figures when it suits them, so we should not treat everything in the accounts as gospel. Nevertheless, published accounts are the best we have to go on. But accounts published in, say, February tell us what happened to the company as far back as the January of the previous year. In stock market terms that is ancient history. These historic data are obviously going to be the most accurate but, in a rapidly changing world, how much value is there in knowing the precise amounts for a company from as much as 14 months ago? To get the hard data we really need we have to wait in effect for a whole 12 months, with an update every six months. That suggests the data in the index could be quite stale.

Would the fund not be better using forward-looking estimated data rather than accurate but historic data? Is it better to be roughly right about the future than precisely wrong about the past? Markets change and what was a market-leading product last year might be obsolete today. Having a factory geared up to produce CDs is not much use if everyone is downloading music from the internet. That plant may have cost £10 million to build, but it may not be worth that to a buyer today. Forecast data, though, is not without its problems, the key one being there is not much of it. Analysts tend to focus on only a few key measures like earnings and dividends. Not all will have reliable estimates for book value, or maybe even revenue. There is also the small matter of the reliability of those forecasts. That said, forecasts of fundamental measures do have the unique benefit of being able to incorporate expectations of the future on a real-time basis. Steadfastly holding to the historic book value of a company as a fundamental measure when its credit rating has changed from AAA to junk is clearly not satisfactory.

There are obvious attractions in using a blend of measures, namely that it smoothes out the numbers. Equally, there are some significant drawbacks, the most important being which ones do you use and how do you weight each parameter? The more subjectivity that is added by decisions such as these, the further the process moves away from being strictly fundamental. Research Affiliates is the only one to use a blended approach, while Wisdom Tree and Fundamental Tracker (my company) use single measures. Fundamental Tracker is the only one to use forecast data.

Having set out some of the issues related to data, we now need to consider the different research-based approaches to fundamental indexing offered by the big asset management firms.

The runners and riders

One of the first advocates of fundamental indices was Rob Arnott. He and his team at Research Affiliates use a blend of historic data to construct their indices. On the east coast of America the boffins at Wisdom Tree, by contrast, have opted to use two measures, dividends and earnings, but not in the same funds. In the UK there is only one fund using the fundamental tracker concept, the Munro fund (which I manage), and it uses forecast gross cash dividends – this approach uses dividend payouts, weighted by volume not price as they would in a conventional index yield fund like the FTSE Dividend Plus.

Table 6.7 details the unique approaches of the key fundamental tracker/index managers. Although they all use different measures and processes, not one of them has any use for the traditional share price way of constructing an index.

Table 6.7 Fundamental approaches

	Wisdom Tree	*RAFI*	*FTIM*
Measures	Cash dividends, earnings	Blend of revenue, earnings, dividends and book value	Gross cash dividends
Time	Current annualised	Five-year historic smoothed	One-year ahead
Rebalancing frequency	Annually	Annually	Monthly
Vehicle	ETF	ETF	OEIC

Source: Munro fund

A proper analysis of these different approaches is a long and detailed exercise and is beyond the scope of this chapter. Probably the most important factor to be considered is the benchmark the funds are compared with. ETFs are typically compared to the indices that were created for them so they can appear to be less risky, as measured by tracking error, than they are when measured against more familiar indices. A fund may appear to be doing very well against its own benchmark, but when compared with a traditional index it may appear as having a higher risk and a lower return. Ultimately, the test of any investment process must be whether it delivers better returns at lower risk than a conventional passive tracker.

Analysis of the data is also complicated somewhat by the profusion of funds that many of the fund providers have created, making it hard to choose one fund that is truly representative of each process. In the next section we take a brief look at each of the different index construction processes.

Dimensional Fund Advisors

One fund manager that does not quite fit into any conventional definition of fundamental indexing but is worth considering first is US firm Dimensional Fund Advisors (DFA). It does not describe itself as either a passive or an active fund manager – like some of the fundamental fund managers it has a clear and strong investment process but, unlike most of them, it has an overlay of subjectivity that makes it more akin to an active fund. Its aim is to outperform the index it is benchmarked against by taking positions that are biased to small-cap and value stocks. Its logic is based on the ground-breaking work by economists Eugene Fama and Kenneth French discussed in Chapter 2 – that small-cap and value stocks have an historic record of outperformance. DFA applies its process on a continuous basis so is not subject to the tyranny of being tied to only rebalancing a fund once a year. As we saw earlier, even when an index is rules based, such as the FTSE 100, it still has an inherent growth bias, so any process that promotes value will have a built-in advantage over an index that has an inherent growth bias.

DFA's unique approach is very different from that of the three main fundamental indexing outfits.

Wisdom Tree

Wisdom Tree builds indices based on earnings and dividends using the latest trailing 12-month data while rebalancing its run on an annual basis, on 30 November. That passive approach can have its flaws, as Chief Investment Officer Jeremy Schwarz admits. In 2008, for instance, Wisdom Tree was hostage to stale and out-of-date data, centred on rapidly changing dividend payouts and suffered dreadfully, as all value-biased funds did, when formerly reliable dividend payers cut payouts in response to extreme market conditions. Wisdom Tree is the brainchild of Jonathan Steinberg and started out as an indexing as opposed to fund management company. Steinberg kicked off with the concept of creating a blended index using market capitalisation and dividends and approached Professor Jeremy Siegel of Wharton to validate the exercise. Siegel, like many others, had realised the inherent flaws of cap-weighted indices during the dot-com bubble at the turn of the millennium. His regular surveys of long-term returns demonstrated the problems caused by cap weighting and in his 1994 publication reviewing capital market returns he acknowledged that other measures might be preferable.[9] That started him on the road towards the concept of using dividends to create an index. The triangle was closed when hedge fund manager Michael Steinberg joined and provided the financial backing to enable Wisdom Tree to launch its range of funds in June 2006.

Wisdom Tree creates indices for a very wide range of markets and sub-sectors. Some are based totally on dividends while some are based on earnings – in both cases annualised data are used. Its main funds are benchmarked against the S&P 500 index which, oddly, is a subjective index. This does present a slight inequality if only because a rules-based portfolio (Wisdom Tree's) is being measured against a subjective index like the S&P 500, whose composition is determined by a committee. In total Wisdom Tree runs 42 separate funds on fundamental indexing principles to track a variety of indices in and outside the US. All its funds are ETFs and in March 2009 it managed about $3.6 billion. Like many value-orientated strategies, it suffered in the 2008 bear market relative to the main indices, but the lags were not large. To address the issue of a value bias, Wisdom Tree has launched an earnings-weighted fund based on NASDAQ stocks which uses a more complex blend of measures.

Research Affiliates

Rob Arnott of Research Affiliates is probably the most high-profile advocate of fundamental indexing and his seminal 2005 paper, simply called 'Fundamental indexation', co-authored with Jason Hsu and Philip Moore, sets out the arguments very clearly. He uses an equally weighted blend of four measures to create the index. These measures are the trailing five-year smoothed data for revenue, book value, earnings and dividends. As with DFA and Wisdom Tree, the danger here is that the data can become very stale as the annual rebalancing approaches. Like many observers he watched the turn of the millennium tech bubble with alarm and resolved to find a better way to construct an index. He assembled a vast array of data stretching back to 1957 when the S&P 500 index was created. From this mass of data he and his team deduced that the most efficient construction – the process that gave the best return for the lowest risk – was an equally weighted blend of the revenue, profits, book value and dividends. His backtested time series starts in 1962, the first year on which five-year trailing (data from five years previous) can be assembled. This huge backtest showed clearly that Arnott's version of an index generated better returns than the S&P 500 index, with lower risk – although part of the reason for this relative success has, in my opinion, more to do with the construction of the S&P 500 index, which is subjective, than Arnott's fundamental index.

Arnott delves into even greater detail in his 2008 book, *The Fundamental Index: A Better Way to Invest*, co-written with Jason Hsu and John West.[10] In it he explores the growth bias of traditional market capitalisation-weighted indices and details the extensive backtesting work he and his team have done to prove that their fundamental indexation produces better returns with lower levels of risk. He also argues that the EMH is still a hugely important concept, but one that does not actually work in the real world any more.

Fundamental Tracker Investment Management

FTIM it is the only UK-based firm to offer a fund-based fundamental indexing approach through its Munro fund, which uses forecast gross cash dividends to create a portfolio benchmarked to the FTSE 350 index. It differs from the Wisdom Tree and RAFI approach in using forecast, not historic, data on the basis that it is better to be roughly right than precisely wrong – it uses the consensus forecasts from all the analysts sourced by Bloomberg for the financial year beyond the current one. Like its two US peers, FTIM uses the gross dividend the company will distribute, not the more commonly used per share figure – it weights dividends by volume not price as a conventional yield-based index fund would do. By rebalancing the model portfolio every month it is also able to continually adjust to the small changes that are made by analysts on an almost daily basis. Last but by no means least it assumes its key measure (the dividend) is all equal – in other words, the pound of dividend from an oil company is worth the same as a pound of dividend from a retailer. In conventional active management this is not the case.

The Munro Fund OEIC was launched in September 2007, just at the start of one of the worst bear markets in recent years, and in absolute terms the initial performance was poor as the stock market collapsed under the weight of the credit crunch. In relative terms – and that is what really counts for an index fund – it has delivered on its promise, namely better returns in its asset class relative to conventional index tracking funds.

> **The Munro fund – how it is managed**
>
> As this fund is run by the writer it might be fruitful to describe the mechanics of the process in detail. Each month we run the following process at the Munro fund:
>
> - The consensus forecast dividends per share, for one year ahead, for all the companies in the FTSE 350 are downloaded together with the issued share capital.
> - Adjustments are made where appropriate for changes in share capital for such things as rights issues or share buybacks.
> - The forecast dividend for each company is then multiplied by the expected number of shares to calculate the forecast gross cash payment, converted to sterling if needed. For a company such as Vodafone this can be as much as £4.5 billion while Marks and Spencer might be only £213 million. Individual contributions are then aggregated to get a total for the FTSE 350. In March 2009 this figure was £63 billion.
> - Finally, each company's contribution to the total is calculated as a percentage. So in one month, for instance, Vodafone's weight in the model portfolio might be 6.8 percent while Marks and Spencer's is 0.33 percent. These new weights are then applied to the portfolio. Normally this is done by using uninvested cash to top up underweight holdings to keep trading to a minimum.
> - Occasionally, where positions have become substantially overweight, the holding is trimmed back to bring it in line with the model. In essence the process keeps the fund aligned to the largest flows of cash, from dividends, into the market.

Why fundamental funds?

So, to conclude, the advantages of fundamental tracking/indexing over mainstream actively managed funds are numerous and easy to understand and include the following:

1. Defined process that eliminates subjectivity and human emotion.
2. That elimination of subjectivity reduces manpower, reducing costs and time to action changes.
3. Lower management fees improve returns to investors.
4. The defined process improves transparency for investors.
5. Most fundamental processes focus on dividends, the largest source of wealth creation in equity investing.
6. The process will not change even if the fund manager does – active fund managers suffer from high turnover so you never know who will be managing your money in five or 10 years' time.

The new fundamental indexing revolution

Fundamental funds also offer some substantial advantages over conventional index-based funds:

- They remove the growth bias – eliminating price from the construction process provides a better way of tracking the underlying earnings because it eliminates the popularity measure inherent in share prices.
- Fundamental index funds generally offer higher yields.
- Some fundamental fund managers offer more frequent rebalancing.

No one should expect any index fund to shoot the lights out – these funds are designed to give the returns of the index they are benchmarked to – but because they are process driven they are (hopefully) cheap to run and have lower management fees. Reducing costs has the same effect on the investor as higher returns, but without the risk. Most importantly, with index funds you are only paying for what is called beta – the returns of the market. With active funds you pay more for the pursuit of alpha (the ability of a manager or process to deliver more than the returns of the market) but often fail to get even that beta. Conventional index funds will never beat the index, indeed many lag behind the index by a considerable amount because of fees and the factors mentioned above. The advantage that fundamental funds offer is the ability to close the gap between the return of the fund and the return of the index. Indeed, one label now being used for them is Smart Beta, a fund that delivers just that little bit more than the index.

Perhaps the most profound thought on the logic behind using fundamental indexing comes from Arnott, who claims that the returns of fundamental funds are proportional to the square of the pricing errors of shares, i.e. the more that active investors try to beat the market by taking bigger and bigger bets, the easier it is for fundamental funds to beat the market.

Table 6.8 shows typical funds/indexes and their methodologies while Table 6.9 looks at the performance of existing fundamental trackers.

Table 6.8 Fundamental indices – details of each fund or index and its index methodology

Vanguard FTSE Equity Income index: seven-step process using FTSE 350 index	1 All stocks which are not forecast to pay dividends over the next 12 months are screened out (dividends exclude any non-regular or special distributions).
	2 All closed-end funds (including investment trusts and real estate investment trusts) are removed.

Table 6.8 Continued

	3 The remaining shares are ranked from highest to lowest by forecast annual dividend yield.
	4 The compilers begin building the UK Equity Income index by ranking it in order of the stocks that have the highest forecast annual dividend yield, until the total shares held in the index equal 50 percent of the float-adjusted market capitalisation of the available shares.
	5 Company diversification is automatic, as the number of shares in any organisation is restricted to a maximum of 5 percent of the total value of the index.
	6 Similarly, the maximum amount invested in any industry sector is restricted to a maximum of 25 percent of the total value of the index.
	7 The shares held in the index are reviewed semi-annually and, where required, changes are made (this is known as 'index reconstitution'). A stock will remain in the index until its forecast annual dividend yield is no longer in the top 55 percent of qualifying shares.
iShares EURO STOXX Total Market Value Large (IDJV) index	The EURO STOXX TMI Value Large index offers exposure to large cap eurozone value stocks, determined by the following six factors: projected price/earnings (PE) ratio, projected earnings growth, trailing PE ratio, trailing earnings growth, price/book (PB) ratio, and dividend yield.
iShares FTSE UK Dividend Plus (IUKD) index	The FTSE UK Dividend Plus index offers exposure to the 50 highest yielding UK stocks within the universe of the FTSE 350 index, excluding investment trusts. Stocks are selected and weighted by one-year forecast dividend yield.
ishares and Deutsche DBX Euro Stoxx Select Dividend 30 index	The EURO STOXX® Select Dividend 30 index offers exposure to the 30 highest dividend-paying eurozone stocks from each country out of the EURO STOXX® index. Only companies are included that have a non-negative historical five-year dividend-per-share growth rate and a dividend to earnings-per-share ratio of less than or equal to 60 percent. The index is weighted according to net dividend yield.

Table 6.8 Continued

iShares DJ Asia/Pacific Select Dividend 30 (IAPD) index	The Dow Jones Asia/Pacific Select Dividend 30 index offers exposure to the 30 highest dividend-paying stocks from developed countries in Asia/Pacific. Only companies are included that have a non-negative historical three-year dividend-per-share growth rate and an average dividend to earnings-per-share ratio of less than 85 percent. The index is weighted according to dividend yield.
STOXX® Global Select Dividend 100 ETF index	The STOXX® Global Select Dividend 100 index is calculated to measure the performance of the highest dividend paying stocks in America, Europe and Asia/Pacific. The index components are weighted by their indicated annual net dividend yield, and the largest dividend yielding companies have the highest weight in the index. The number of constituents is fixed and the cap factor guarantees the index diversification.
The Munro fund: 10-step process	1 **Update universe.** The fund managers download the current constituents of the FTSE 350 index and remove those companies classified as investment trusts. Removing these and companies that are not forecast to pay a dividend reduces the universe to about 300 companies.
	2 **Update shares outstanding and dividend forecasts.** From published data the managers extract the exact number of shares outstanding for each of the 300-odd companies and the most recent dividend forecasts using consensus estimates.
	3 **Adjust for foreign exchange.** A lot of companies report their accounts in currencies other than sterling, mostly in dollars. Using the prevailing exchange rates the fund managers translate those forecasts into sterling.
	4 **Adjust for share buyback plans.** If companies are expected to execute significant share buyback programmes the data for shares outstanding is adjusted.

Table 6.8 Continued

	5 **Calculate the forecast shares in issue.** Using this data the fund managers then calculate how many shares each company will have in issue for the next financial year.
	6 **Calculate dividend payments.** Using the dividend data and the share data the fund managers then calculate how much total cash each company will pay out as dividends in the next financial year.
	7 **Calculate a total dividend.** Using these data the fund then calculate a total dividend payout for the 300 or so companies in our universe.
	8 **Review data for consistency.**
	9 **Calculate a weight for each company.** Now that the fund managers know what each company is expected to pay out and what the total payout is we can calculate a weight for each company in the universe.
	10 **The process is then repeated every month.**
RAFI Indices: RAFI UK 100	The PowerShares FTSE RAFI UK 100 Fund is based on the FTSE RAFI UK 100 index. The index is designed to track the performance of the largest UK equities, selected based on the following four fundamental measures of firm size: book value, income, sales and dividends. The 100 equities with the highest fundamental strength are weighted by their fundamental scores.
	The fundamentally weighted portfolio is rebalanced and reconstituted annually.
S&P Emerging Markets Dividend index	**Criteria for index membership** The universe is drawn from all dividend-paying common stocks included in the S&P/IFCI and is narrowed down to an investable set of stocks based on the following criteria:
	■ Market capitalisation. Constituents in the index must have a minimum total market capitalisation of US$1 billion, with a minimum float-adjusted market cap of US$600 million for developed market stocks and US$300 million for emerging markets stocks.

Table 6.8 Continued

	▪ Value traded. Stocks must have three-month average daily value traded above the liquidity threshold of US$1 million, as of the rebalancing dates.
	▪ Exchange listing. Securities listed in emerging markets will be analysed to determine which listing offers higher liquidity. The stock with the higher liquidity is given preference in the final selection.
	Stability criteria
	▪ Earnings growth. Stocks must have a positive, three-year earnings growth. Existing index stocks will only be removed after failing this criterion for two consecutive rebalancing periods.
	▪ Profitability. Stocks must be profitable, as measured by positive earnings per share before extraordinary items, over the latest 12-month period, as of the reference date.
	Criteria for index additions
	All stocks in the selection universe are first sorted on the basis of annual dividend yield. The 100 highest yielding stocks from the index, subject to a 100 stock buffer for index constituents. No single country or sector can have more than a 25 percent weight in the index at each semi-annual rebalancing. Each stock in the index must have a minimum and maximum weight of 0.05 percent and 3 percent, respectively.
S&P Dividend Aristocrats index	To qualify for membership in the S&P 500 Dividend Aristocrats index, a stock must satisfy the following criteria:
	1. Be a member of the S&P 500 index
	2. Have increased dividends every year for at least 25 consecutive years
	3. Have a float adjusted market capitalisation of at least US$3 billion as of the rebalancing reference date.
	4. Have an average daily trading volume of at least US$5 million for the six months prior to the rebalancing reference date.

Table 6.9 Performance of existing fundamental trackers

	EPIC	Price	Correlation	Beta	Volatility
Benchmarks					
FTSE 100	UKX	0.71	1	0.99	1.21
FTSE All Share	ASX	1.02	0.99	0.93	1.13
UK-based fundamental trackers					
iShares FTSE UK Div Plus	IUKD	1.08	0.8	0.98	1.48
Smith & Williamson Munro A Acc Retail	WLSWAS		0.59	0.74	1.52
Vanguard FTSE UK Equity Income Index Inc	VVUKEI		0.88	0.74	1.02
PowerShares FTSE RAFI UK 100 Fund	PSRU	−0.27	0.7	1.02	1.76
Non-UK fundamental trackers					
db X-trackers DJ Euro Stoxx Select Div 30	XD3E	1.32	0.84	1.41	2.05
db X-trackers DJ Stoxx Gbl Select div 100	XGSD	1.11	0.69	1.05	1.85
iShares DJ Asia/Pacific Select Div	IAPD	0.67	0.76	1.07	1.71
iShares DJ Euro Stoxx Select	IDVY	0.85	0.62	1.18	2.32
iShares DJ Euro Stoxx Value	IDJV	0.1	0.87	1.29	1.79
PowerShares Dynamic US Mkt Fund	PSWC	0.76	0.7	0.88	1.54
PowerShares FTSE RAFI All World 3000 Fund	PSRW	0.69	0.76	1.1	1.76
PowerShares FTSE RAFI Asia Pacific Ex Japan Fund	PSRA	0.74	0.74	1.1	1.79
PowerShares FTSE RAFI Developed 1000 Fund	PSRD	0.76	0.77	0.99	1.56
PowerShares FTSE RAFI Emerging Markets Fund	PSRM	0.52	0.8	1.12	1.7
PowerShares FTSE RAFI EU Mid-small Fund	PSES	−0.24	0.77	0.97	1.53
PowerShares FTSE RAFI Europe Fund	PSRE	0.52	0.83	1.25	1.84
PowerShares FTSE RAFI US 1000 Fund	PSRF	1.05	0.75	1.03	1.67

Table 6.9 Continued

	2011 through to 31 October	2010	2009	2008
	RETURNS			
Benchmarks				
FTSE 100	−6	7.3	18.7	−30.9
FTSE All Share	−6.6	9.1	20.9	−32.4
UK-based fundamental trackers				
iShares FTSE UK Div Plus	−7.5	6.7	23.6	−48.2
Smith & Williamson Munro A Acc Retail	−1.9	8.2	22.9	−31.3
Vanguard FTSE UK Equity Income Index Inc	1.1	5.9		
PowerShares FTSE RAFI UK 100 Fund	−7.1	6.6	22.8	−35.1
Non-UK fundamental trackers				
db X-trackers DJ Euro Stoxx Select Div 30	−16.8	−7.1	16	−44
db X-trackers DJ Stoxx Gbl Select div 100	−6.7	8.4	22.3	−37.7
iShares DJ Asia/Pacific Select Div	−1.9	12	39.8	−40.2
iShares DJ Euro Stoxx Select	−15.1	−5.8	14.2	−44.2
iShares DJ Euro Stoxx Value	−13.5	−18.2	15	−33.2
PowerShares Dynamic US Mkt Fund	−6.7	18.2	4.9	−18.4
PowerShares FTSE RAFI All World 3000 Fund	−11.8	15	41.4	−47.7
PowerShares FTSE RAFI Asia Pacific Ex Japan Fund	−12.1	24	16.7	−36.3
PowerShares FTSE RAFI Developed 1000 Fund	−11.8	9.2	19.7	−24.2
PowerShares FTSE RAFI Emerging Markets Fund	−19.5	18.7	23.1	−37.3
PowerShares FTSE RAFI EU Mid-small Fund	−16.0	16.4	42.1	−35.9
PowerShares FTSE RAFI Europe Fund	−15.4		23.1	−30.3
PowerShares FTSE RAFI US 1000 Fund	−5.8	19.2	24.9	−23.1

7

On portfolios

James Norton is the Head of Investment at one of the most progressive financial planners in the UK, Evolve Financial Planning. A former stockbroker, like many he had an epiphany – he realised that endlessly chasing after hot tips and the next big small cap was an exercise in grand futility. Arguably it helped destroy his clients' wealth and encouraged investors to take a short-term view of financial planning and it absolutely wasn't making him a happy man. So he changed his entire way of working. He quit the prestigious London-based stockbrokers he worked for and the stockbroking game in general and decided to take a more holistic approach to money, investment and personal financial planning.

Two simple concepts sit at the core of his new approach. The first is to look at the individual and what they want out of their finances, especially via their portfolio or pension pot which involves asking some tough questions about the purpose of investment and a client's needs for the future.

The other idea is to take these planning ideas and then work them into a winning portfolio that makes extensive use of passive investment funds, bought at the lowest cost, with the greatest efficiency. To understand how this approach might work we asked James to outline in this chapter how he would go about building such a portfolio after asking some searching personal questions about why we invest.

James will then venture into the thorny issue of how to construct a portfolio – a diversified portfolio – where both risk and return are sensibly balanced. Along this journey we'll encounter the tricky issue of market timing (a subject we'll return to later in this book) and hold the fund management industry to account for its rampant abuse of marketing to sell us the latest hit thing! Not everyone in the investment business will agree with James's views but his belief in passive investing is slowly gaining traction among an elite band of financial planners.

Introduction

Car A has five doors, a two-litre petrol engine, a top speed of 140 miles per hour and goes from 0–60 in seven seconds. It has a history of reliability.

Car B has five doors, a two-litre petrol engine, a top speed of 160 miles per hour and goes from 0–60 in six seconds. It has a few more 'bells and whistles' than Car A and is seen as a more sporty/fashionable car. The make in question has a poor record of reliability.

Car B costs three times more than Car A. Which one would you buy?

This simple analogy reflects the fund management industry in the UK today. A typical investor can invest in a UK All Share Index fund with no up-front charge and an Annual Management Charge (AMC) of 0.5 percent while if they used fee-based financial planners that charge could be as little as 0.2 percent p.a. Most actively managed funds, on the other hand, charge either 1.5 percent or 1.75 percent p.a. and depending on how you access them, often carry a hefty initial charge, generally up to 5 percent, in addition. It is no surprise, therefore, that active funds have a history of underperformance and it is easy to see why so many fee-based advisers are recommending an index tracking approach to their clients.

What's the meaning of life?

Evolve Financial Planning makes extensive use of index funds in its approach to investment – index funds very much sit at the core of the process of building a client portfolio. But before we explore exactly how it goes about constructing such a portfolio using index funds, put this book down for one moment and ask yourself the following question: 'What is important to me about money?'

If you can't give a good answer to this simple question, then getting the right mix of investments is pure guesswork.

I've seen many clients in their late 50s and early 60s who have been working hard in jobs they don't like with the belief that in order to enjoy their retirement they would need a pot of money far larger than they in fact required. Sitting down and doing some simple financial planning, modelling income and expenditure, stress testing for inflation and investment 'shocks', many people are often surprised by how little money they need! Although we would never advise reaching your 'actuarial deadline' (a politically correct term for death!) with an empty wallet, most people have an unrealistic desire to reach this date with as much in the pot when they retire. It is human nature to want more than we need.

So, if you can help clients to understand not only how much they actually need as well as question what their money is for, I contend that it follows that their chances of financial success will be greatly improved. For many, the goal is to achieve what we call 'financial independence', i.e. to make enough money so they do not have to continue working. It may not actually mean they are going to retire, but they want the option of retirement. For others, who have already achieved this goal, capital protection or maintenance of financial independence is often more important. Nearly everyone will have secondary goals such as funding school or university costs for children, mitigating inheritance tax or increasing charitable giving. As financial planners, once we understand these goals we can help quantify them and really 'flesh out' the implications.

Take a couple in their mid-30s with a high income who are conscientious savers into their ISAs and pensions. They own their home but have a sizeable mortgage. They have two children aged five and seven. What might be important to them about money?

- financial security in the event of illness/death/redundancy;
- paying off their mortgage;
- buying a larger house;
- providing for their children's education;
- helping their children financially after university;
- making the most of their current investments;
- making the most of excess income;
- providing for a secure (early) retirement.

The death/illness scenarios could be addressed quickly and cheaply through insurance, allowing them to focus on other goals. If they want a bigger house and a private education for their children, unless their income is significant there is a distinct possibility that they will need to take a reasonably high degree of investment risk to have any chance of achieving early retirement. Perhaps the bigger house is not so important if it means working for an extra 5–10 years? As they are young they may be comfortable taking a relatively adventurous approach to investment.

Move this same couple forward 20 years to their mid-50s. What might be important to them about money now?

- financial security in the event of illness/death/redundancy;
- helping their children financially after university;
- making the most of their current investments;
- making the most of excess income;
- providing for a secure retirement.

The couple are now much closer to retirement. Their earnings potential is therefore greatly diminished. There is no turning back. Because of this they would probably be wise to reduce investment risk, particularly on pensions if they plan to convert their funds into an annuity. If they plan to use some form of income drawdown arrangement from their pensions, the fund choice decision will be different as the money will be invested for longer. By now the couple will have built up a sizeable ISA and collective fund portfolio in the knowledge that this will supplement their retirement income. The amount of risk they need to take on this portfolio will depend quite heavily on what sort of income they will draw from their pensions. It may be that the job of the investment portfolio is to provide protection in the event of high inflation and therefore a reasonable allocation to asset-backed investments such equity and property funds might still be appropriate.

Now let's move them forward a further 20 years, to their mid-70s. What might be important to them about money now?

- capital preservation;
- passing money to the next generations;
- reducing inheritance tax.

In their mid-70s the couple might be looking to downsize their home. They may find themselves in the fortunate position that they will never run out of money. The question they now need to ask themselves is whether there is really any point in investing for growth when any growth, and much of their capital, will get clobbered by 40 percent inheritance tax on their deaths. Given that one of their aims is to pass money to the next generation they might consider gifts, whether as outright gifts or via a trust. If gifts are via a trust, they may retain control over how the investments are managed. This then raises a question over what investment risk to take. The couple could decide that the investment really belongs to their children and grandchildren and therefore timescales for investment are much greater, meaning more scope for investment risk.

The process I'm trying to highlight here is what's called a lifecycle approach to investing, namely that the opportunities and threats change significantly at different stages of our lives and it is up to us to adapt our investment strategy accordingly.

Why invest?

This is really the most important question and is one that is often forgotten. Although many people think that investing is exciting, this is just down to clever marketing by fund groups. The reality is that if a portfolio is doing its job properly, it should be boring. Surprises are not good. So if you are not investing for excitement – and I would certainly recommend that you get your kicks elsewhere – why invest in the beginning?

Most people are not able to control their income completely. They work as hard as they can, fight for promotions and earn as much as possible. To some degree they may be able to control expenditure by eating out less, going on less expensive holidays and cutting back where possible. However, these simple tools may not be enough to achieve financial independence.

For many people, investing is therefore a necessity. If we put all of our excess income under a mattress, it would lose its real value year on year due to inflation. People often talk of wanting their money to 'work harder for them'. This is why we invest. Most people understand the concept that risk and reward go hand in hand and therefore in the long run if we take some risk we should be rewarded.

The figures in Table 7.1 are from the Barclays Equity Gilt Study 2011 and show simply why we invest in equities. The numbers speak for themselves. Equity returns have trounced those of cash and bonds over time.

Table 7.1 The value of £100 invested at the end of 1899 without reinvesting income

Asset class	Nominal (without taking account of inflation)	Real (taking account of inflation)
Equities	£12,655	£180
Gilts (government bonds)	£49	£1

Source: Barclays Capital

Despite the fact that equity returns have been so poor for the past 10 years, equities still come out on top by a substantial margin over the very long term. It is this additional return over cash and bonds that is the reason we invest and for many it will help fund the shortfall between earned income and lifetime expenditure. Without investment returns many of us would actually die in debt. The financial planning exercise helps us to understand the scale of this shortfall, if any, and can therefore assist us in determining an appropriate level of risk.

Good investing should be goals based and built around clear objectives. This is why investment advice must be personalised not through standardised portfolios built by big investment houses with names like 'LOW RISK', 'MEDIUM RISK' and 'HIGH RISK' or 'INCOME', 'BALANCED' and 'GROWTH'.

Having said all this there are many cases when investing simply does not make sense and any good adviser should point this out. If, for example, a higher-rate taxpayer has a mortgage with an interest rate of 6 percent, a gross, risk adjusted return of over 10 percent would be needed to beat paying down the mortgage. So, by paying down the mortgage early, this individual would be receiving a risk-free 'investment' return of 10 percent p.a. Now, of course, the stock market may outperform this, but certainly not without risk, so paying down debt may make more sense than investing.

A passive portfolio – why it matters?

Financial planning is about making the best use of money. Tax optimisation is a key part of this and can offer guaranteed returns on savings. The investment element is the big unknown but one thing we do know is that costs damage returns. Although much has been said about costs in this book already, it is worth reiterating it briefly at this point.

When we were experiencing high double-digit equity returns in the 1980s and early 1990s, few people questioned costs. When the stock market returned 10 percent to 20 percent a year, 1.5 percent p.a. in costs seemed immaterial. But with much more pedestrian returns, costs have taken on a new significance. Again, it is important to look back and ask why we invest when we all know it carries additional risk. What we are trying to capture is the equity risk premium. This is calculated as the difference in the expected return of the stock market and the risk free rate of return (this is usually taken as the return on government bonds). In other words, it is the additional return that investors seek for taking the additional risk. The equity risk premium changes over time, but a reasonable long-term estimate is 4 percent p.a.

So with an equity risk premium of 4 percent p.a. and the average active fund charging in excess of 1.5 percent p.a., 37.5 percent of the potential reward for investing in equities is being taken by the fund manager. This simply does not make sense.

Looking at it in pure monetary terms the impact of charges is staggering. Taking a 45-year period, which is a reasonable investment time horizon for most people (who might start saving at 20 and retire at 65), the charging structure has a huge impact. Assuming an index (or market) return of 7 percent p.a., £10,000 will be turned into £210,025 (before inflation). Using a portfolio of index trackers with annual charges of 0.5 percent this will reduce the return to £170,111 – so even using trackers a large part of the index return is eroded. However, taking the average AMC of an actively managed fund, the return would fall to £111,266. Finally, taking an annual charge of 2.5 percent which is not uncommon for many 'fund of fund' structures the return would be £72,482 with about 65 percent of the return eroded by charges. This is clearly illustrated in Figure 7.1.

Evolve sees fund management as a commodity service. Fund managers would raise their arms in horror at this as they try to justify their 'value add', but the fact is that more than half are likely to underperform the index in any one year. It is mathematically impossible for all funds to beat their benchmark, even though that is what all active funds aim to do!

Although the index approach will not deliver outperformance of an index, it should produce outperformance over the average actively managed fund.

Many people who adopt the passive route to investing have gone through some sort of conversion to get there, having invested actively for many

Figure 7.1 Impact of investment costs – gross of tax and inflation

years and realising that it has not worked. This is certainly the case of most of the contributors to this book! Stockbrokers, private bankers and fund managers by their nature must believe that they can do better than their peers and competitors. As a species, many behavioural physiologists have proved that by nature we all think we are better than average. However, we all know that in reality this cannot be the case.

Believing that active management does not work is not a reflection that we think analysts, brokers and fund managers are stupid. The reality is that a great many truly sophisticated brains work in 'the markets', so many in fact that achieving a competitive edge is nigh on impossible. If you accept that insider dealing rules are effective then all the market participants gain information at the same time. The next news that comes out must by definition be random. After all, that's what news is.

This is important to understand because when you accept that many of the brightest brains rarely beat the index with any consistency it is easier to accept that you will not. This helps with the discipline!

The aim of the rest of this chapter is therefore to look at the practicalities of running a portfolio using index funds. This ultimately comes down to two factors – investing with *a clear set of objectives* and, above all, *discipline*. Using index funds, in my opinion, requires the investor to understand the science behind this strategy and accept it is not an art form – it does not require constant fine tuning and matures best when it is left to do its own thing, which is to capture the market return. The temptation to make changes to a passive portfolio will generally be the result of external influences. Remember that changes increase cost, seldom add value and usually result in poor market timing decisions.

Risk

By now it should be clear that investing should *not* be about trying to get rich quick. It is seldom that easy. It is about knowing your objectives and building a portfolio that has the greatest chance of meeting returns consistent with those objectives. Assuming you have decided that some sort of investment is appropriate, where do you start with such a strategy?

At the very end of Chapter 2, we looked at the benefits of diversification, noting the research of Brinson, Singer and Beebower and the more recent research of Ibbotson – in this chapter we're going to take some of these basics and use them to look at the principles involved with constructing a portfolio.

The one decision that will have the greatest impact on portfolio returns for any individual is their allocation between fixed income and equities. Both in my previous role as a stockbroker (yes – in a former life I worked on the dark side!) and now as a financial planner the common response when I tell investors they are going to hold a sizeable allocation of fixed interest is that it is boring and adds no value to a portfolio. The first part of this statement is largely correct as fixed income should be boring, but it certainly adds value.

To understand this it is important to revisit the relationship between risk and return. As those figures from the Barclays Equity Gilt Study show, equities have trounced fixed interest over the past 100 or more years. Equities are the engine of long-term growth of any portfolio. They are the risk assets that are funding the large corporations to invest and grow. The equity holders of a company are the owners of the company – they are the ones who have put up the capital and are taking the risk.

However, this is not a free ride! Intuitively we all know that investing in the stock market involves risk. Most of the time the stock market just does its job, but it does sometimes make it to the front page of the newspapers. In early 2000 everyone was talking about how much they were making in tech stocks and how good they were at stock selection. With hindsight it is clear that the levels of euphoria were too high and it all ended in tears. Sadly now, well into the credit crunch the stock market is once again making the headlines, this time because it is making new lows.

Figure 7.2 shows the returns of the FTSE All Share from January 1956 to the end of 2010 – £1 invested at the start of this period was worth £540.50 by the end of the period. Importantly it shows the best return and worst return of the index over various timeframes. This is shown on a total return basis, and so includes the very important dividend income that delivers a crucial part of the return.

Figure 7.2 Best and worst returns FTSE All Share January 1956 to December 2010

Table 7.2 Annualised average rolling return using monthly data

	1 Year	3 Years	5 Years	10 Years	15 Years	20 Years
Average	14.53%	13.03%	12.83%	12.95%	13.64%	14.16%
Highest	151.41%	56.52%	36.06%	31.62%	27.71%	23.02%
Lowest	−55.84%	−26.21%	−10.58%	−0.68%	1.25%	6.94%

Source: FTSE, analysis by Evolve Financial Planning

The worst 12-month period for the FTSE All Share was a negative return of almost 56 percent in 1973. This was followed a couple of years later by the best one year return of 151 percent in 1975 (see Table 7.2). In other words, volatility is enormous with a difference between the best and worst return of over 200 percent. However, when the timeframe of investment is extended to 10 years the worst annual return is only just negative at −0.68 percent p.a. and the best is 31.62 percent p.a. The range has narrowed enormously – taking the analysis further to a 20-year period the difference between best and worst narrows even further.

This is absolutely crucial as it illustrates the fact that not only are risk and reward correlated, but also that the longer one invests, the lower the risk of loss. Given that investing is for the long term this is a significant advantage.

So what about fixed interest? Investing in fixed interest is a very different beast. Fixed interest securities is a term we use to describe government bonds or gilts and corporate bonds, which are the borrowings of a company. It is simply a different way for a company to raise finance. A bond will usually have a fixed term and pay out interest over this term at a pre-agreed rate. The owners of a fixed interest instrument do not own part of the company but their bonds will often be secured over some of its assets. If the company fails, then bondholders are paid out as well as ordinary shareholders. This is important to understand as it helps define the main characteristics of fixed interest holdings.

Figure 7.3 analyses the returns of one-year UK Treasury bills over the same period as the FTSE All Share in Figure 7.2. The difference is striking. First, £1 invested in 1956 only grew to £5,271. Not bad I hear you say, but after inflation is taken into account, it is only £2.60. Crucially, however, the fixed interest element has not lost money in any period and the volatility in returns is much lower. Over one year the worst return was 0.41 percent compared to best year of 16.83 percent. When the timeframe is extended to the best and worst 10-year rolling period, the picture is not much different, and for a 20-year rolling period the worst return was 5.41 percent p.a. and the best was 11.67 percent p.a. (see Table 7.3).

Figure 7.3 Best and worst returns UK T-bills January 1956 to December 2010

Table 7.3 Annualised average rolling return using monthly data

	1 Year	3 Years	5 Years	10 Years	15 Years	20 Years
Average	7.62%	7.79%	7.92%	8.30%	8.68%	9.05%
Highest	16.83%	15.09%	13.56%	12.27%	12.14%	11.67%
Lowest	0.41%	1.94%	3.24%	3.82%	4.64%	5.41%

Source: Datastream, analysis by Evolve Financial Planning

These figures help show that it is simply not right to say that equities are high risk and bonds low risk. While in essence this is true, time can change everything. In some respects over the long run when the volatility of equities is greatly reduced, bonds are actually a potentially higher risk asset class as they have less chance of protecting a portfolio against inflation.

Asset allocation

A portfolio invested entirely in the FTSE All Share is going to be suitable for very few individuals due to the risk profile highlighted above, so it is the combination of the different asset classes that counts – balancing some of the higher- and lower-risk assets. This is very simply demonstrated in Table 7.4.

This shows the performance of five portfolios of differing risk. The first portfolio only holds one-year Treasury bills. In other words it is the ultra-low-risk portfolio. Each portfolio thereafter picks up equity exposure (FTSE All Share) in increments of 25 percent until the final portfolio is invested entirely in equities.

Table 7.4 Portfolio returns and risk 1956 to 2010 – FTSE All Share and Treasury bills

Portfolio mix	Annualised return (%)	Growth of wealth	Annualised standard deviation (%)
0:100 (only bonds)	7.47	52.71	1.01
25:75	9.02	115.79	4.66
50:50 (mixed bonds and equities)	10.31	220.83	9.19
75:25	11.34	368.72	13.92
100:0 (only equities)	12.12	540.50	19.12

Source: Datastream and FTSE

As you would expect, as the equity exposure is increased so the average annual return increases. At the same time, so does risk. In Table 7.4 risk is shown as something called the standard deviation – this is a statistical measurement for how returns have varied over a given period. Simply put, a low standard deviation indicates a high consistency of returns and a high standard deviation indicates that returns are spread out over a large range of values – in other words higher risk.

As the equity weighting in the portfolio falls from 100 percent to 75 percent the return only falls slightly from 12.12 percent to 11.34 percent p.a., but there is a disproportionate fall in risk with standard deviation falling from 19.12 percent to 13.92 percent p.a. This is more clearly illustrated in Figure 7.4. Each of the portfolios is shown with risk along the *x*-axis and return on the *y*-axis. As the equity component of the portfolio increases, so does the return, resulting in a shift from bottom left to top right with an increase in risk. More importantly, the figure clearly shows that the correlation between risk and reward is not a straight line. There is a bulge in the line to the left. If the correlation was on a straight line basis one would expect the return of Portfolio 2 to be nearer 8.2 percent than the 9.0 percent that is actually the case. What this is showing is the free lunch in investment.

Figure 7.4 Returns and standard deviation of portfolios January 1956 to December 2010

Source: DataStream and FTSE

Diversification has rewarded the investor with an increased return that is not proportionate with the increase in risk.

When deciding on the most suitable mix of fixed interest and equities, it is therefore important to consider the time horizon, the average return that such a portfolio may deliver and also the best and worst returns you may experience.

More on fixed interest

Since equities – stocks and shares – are generally regarded as the main building blocks of a portfolio it is worth focusing on the chief alternative – fixed income securities or bonds. Most investors have a good knowledge of equity markets, but many would admit that they are on weaker ground when it comes to fixed interest stock.

By now it is relatively obvious that fixed interest stocks play a valuable role in reducing risk. They can also enhance yield for those looking for an income. But how do investors actually go about investing in fixed income securities like gilts (government bonds)? Fixed income securities, and especially corporate bonds, display a huge diversity of risk profiles, just as in equities. There are investment grade bonds, which are issued by large, reliable companies like McDonald's (the fast-food chain) that bizarrely have lower risk ratings than some government bonds. By complete contrast, there are also much riskier bonds issued by sub-prime entities – private equity deals, for instance, or small African countries – where the debt is regarded as very, very risky and each $100 of face value is actually priced at below $50 on the open market. Such bonds behave more like equities than gilts.

Unsurprisingly, the higher the risk profile, the higher the likely interest rate or yield. Traditionally that credit risk spread has also been true for time spans – if a government issues a 30-year gilt, it is likely that it will have to pay for the privilege of borrowing for a very long time as opposed to a two-year gilt. This last statement needs a qualification though – in some unusual periods, that yield spread inverts and we are presented with the odd spectacle of very long-dated gilts paying less than very short-dated gilts. Nevertheless the general principle holds true over the longer term – the riskier and longer dated the debt or bond, the higher the yield and the greater the spread between short-dated/low-risk and long-dated/high-risk.

As you have probably already guessed, two concepts are crucial to understanding this spread of yields – default risk and duration. It is pretty obvious by now that the lower the quality of the bond (in terms of risk) the greater the chance of default – the lowest risk comes from developed world sovereign debt with US government T-bills regarded as essentially risk free.

The concept of duration is also easy to grasp – as we've already noted, the greater the length of time that a bond is in issue, the greater the risk. Table 7.5 shows the returns of different maturity US bonds from 1964 to 2008 – as the maturity of the fixed interest instrument increases so does the return. The increased return between one- and five-year notes is modest but meaningful, but there is also a significant increase in risk. However, when the maturity of bonds is extended to 20 years, not only is there another jump in risk, but the increase in return is only marginal.

Table 7.5 Returns and standard deviation of different fixed interest maturities 1964–2008

	One-month Treasury bills	Six-month Treasury bills	One-year Treasury notes	Five-year Treasury notes	20-year government bonds
Annualised Compound Returns %	5.69	6.46	6.66	7.50	7.87
Annualised Standard Deviation %	1.34	1.71	2.32	6.24	11.1

Sources: Merrill Lynch and CRSP (Centre for Research in Security Prices, University of Chicago)

Some investors may be tempted to think that bonds are still risky (to a limited degree) and thus they may be tempted to invest more in the 'riskier' gilts, for instance – the problem is that this probably will not work as Table 7.5 on returns clearly tells us that additional risk (extra years, for instance) does not appear to be proportionately rewarded. Remember that fixed interest is included in a portfolio in order to reduce volatility and risk, not to increase it! The real risk element should be taken in equities and those seeking extra thrills should spend some of their budget on smaller companies and value stocks. The bottom line – fixed interest exposure should be concentrated in short-term, high-quality bonds. If they are globally diversified, that is even better.

What about equity diversification?

Once the split between the main building blocks of fixed income and equities has been decided, the next job is to think about the equity diversification. That aim is the same here, in other words to try to get the win–win of disproportionately increasing return compared to risk.

The example below shows the building blocks of a simple portfolio and how some basic diversification can be of benefit to all investors. All of the data for these portfolios is for the 21-year period 1988 to 2008 and it is designed to represent an 'average' risk portfolio with 40 percent in fixed income and 60 percent in equities.

The first portfolio is a plain vanilla portfolio. All the equities are in the FTSE All Share and the fixed interest is in a well-respected high-quality bond index.

Portfolio 1

Citigroup UK govt. bond index 1–30 years unhedged	40 percent
FTSE All Share	60 percent

This portfolio produces a respectable annualised return of 8.83 percent with a standard deviation of 9.58 percent.

The first change (which is not actually to do with equities at all!) is to switch the Citigroup UK government bond index for a globally diversified short-dated bond strategy, but keeping the equity/bond split exactly the same.

Portfolio 2

Global short-dated bond strategy	40 percent
FTSE All Share	60 percent

As we would expect the element of 'risk' actually falls as a consequence of this small change – risk as measured by standard deviation falls to 8.97 percent and the return shows a marginal increase to 9.20 percent. Making this sort of change is an absolute no-brainer!

The next change to look at is the impact of international diversification. We live in an increasingly globalised economy, but not all regions have the same growth rates or prospects. In this portfolio the UK equity exposure is reduced to allow exposure to international equities and more specialist emerging markets equities.

Portfolio 3

Global short-dated bond strategy	40 percent
FTSE All Share	25 percent
International companies	25 percent
Emerging markets	10 percent

The effect of this diversification is to increase the annualised compound return to 9.50 percent with an increase in risk to 9.41 percent. This is not such a no-brainer as the first change, because although the return has increased, risk has risen as well!

The final stage of building a portfolio is to further diversify some of the equity exposure to capture some of the small cap and value premium. To do this we need to look at some of the long-term sources of equity returns. A wealth of academic research from Fama and French has highlighted the fact that the long-term returns of smaller company shares and value companies have been much greater than the market as a whole.

A simple reminder, via some statistics, should remind the reader of what this shift towards small cap and value stocks can produce. From January 1956 £1.00 invested in the FTSE All Share index grew to £363 by the end of 2008. However, £1.00 invested in UK smaller companies grew to £1,664 and £1.00 invested in value companies ended up as £2,183. What is interesting is that research shows that these effects of small cap and value companies are repeated around the world. Although the risk/volatility of these asset classes is higher, the potential benefits of investing are obvious. So what is the effect of adding these to the portfolio? In the table below we have spread the UK equity exposure equally between the FTSE All Share and value and smaller company strategies.

Portfolio 4

Global short-dated bond strategy	40 percent
FTSE All Share	10 percent
MSCI World ex UK index	10 percent
Emerging markets	10 percent
UK value companies	7.5 percent
UK small companies	7.5 percent
International value companies	7.5 percent
International small cap companies	7.5 percent

The effect of this diversification is to increase the annual return of the portfolio to 9.91 percent p.a., with a modest increase in risk to 9.69 percent.

The results of these changes in the portfolio are summarised in this table.

	Annualised compound return %	Annualised standard deviation %
Portfolio 1	8.83	9.58
Portfolio 2	9.20	8.97
Portfolio 3	9.50	9.41
Portfolio 4	9.91	9.69

What this example has shown is that two basic portfolios with the same weighting in equities and fixed interest can have very different returns. By taking some simple measures, the annual return of Portfolio 4 was 1.08 percent higher than Portfolio 1 with almost no additional risk (only 0.11 percent). This may not sound like much, but over the 21-year period £100 invested in Portfolio 1 would be worth £591 compared to £727 for Portfolio 4. This is a difference in return of just under 25 percent and it was achieved through very basic diversification, the three main components of which were:

- globally diversified short-dated bonds;
- international and emerging markets exposure;
- smaller companies and value companies.

This chapter only has the space to look at some of the basics of diversification. The portfolio above is not recommended for anyone in particular, but is merely designed to illustrate some of the benefits of investing in these different asset classes. It is also worth noting the value and small cap stocks are international in nature and cross all major equity markets and we would also argue for the potential benefits of investing in areas such as private equity, hedge funds, commercial property and commodities, all of which may have diversification benefits. However, the simple conclusion still stands – the more you diversify, the better your returns, with less risk!

Timing your investment in the markets

In the last two chapters we'll return to the hugely thorny issue of how to construct a disciplined investing process and whether you should even attempt to 'time' your investments into the market. Should you simply invest a regular lump sum every month and then leave the investment alone or should you attempt to increase or decrease the amount you invest, based on varying market conditions?

One way of looking at this hugely important issue is to look at what the industry likes to call 'money-weighted returns'. When looking at, say, an individual unit trust, the money weighted return looks at when money is invested and withdrawn from the fund, and therefore shows the fuller picture of investor returns. This is different to the more commonly used 'time weighted returns' which simply calculate the difference in fund value between the start and end of a period without weighting those money flows – you'll only ever see time-weighted returns in marketing literature for funds, not money-weighted returns.

To illustrate this simple distinction, consider a fund that returns 80 percent in year one and loses 40 percent in year two. The time-weighted return of this fund is 3.92 percent p.a. This simply gives equal weighting to each year's return. In other words, a capital sum of £100,000 would be worth £180,000 at the end of year one and £108,000 at the end of year two, resulting in a compound return of 3.92 percent.

However, now look at the money-weighted return of two different investors. First, let's look at Tom, who is saving for retirement and has accumulated £150,000 in this fund. He is a long-term investor and is not making any additional investments or withdrawals. At the end of this two-year period his investment would be worth £162,000 representing a return of 3.92 percent p.a. which is the time-weighted or 'buy-and-hold' return.

Our second investor, Katie, is also saving for her retirement. However, she does not want to invest all of her money at once because she thinks that good investment opportunities will emerge over time – she wants to time her entry into and exit from the markets. Therefore she only invests £100,000 at the beginning of the investment period. After she sees that the fund has done really well she decides to make an additional contribution of £50,000 to her account. At the end of the period, her portfolio would be worth £138,000, representing a loss of –4.90 percent. The performance gap between the time-weighted return and the money-weighted return is –8.82 percent (–4.90 percent to 3.92 percent).

Although both investors have invested the same amount of £150,000 over the entire time period, Tom has achieved a superior investment outcome. This is due to the fact that Katie has made her additional investment when the fund was at its peak value and just before the negative returns. This is something that happens all too often to investors, both professional and retail, good examples being the recent dot-com bubble of the late 1990s or in the more recent property and commodities boom.

As far back as 1996, John Bogle, the founder of Vanguard, started lobbying fund companies to report money-weighted returns. This finally started in 2006 when Morningstar took up the mantle in the US. Sadly we still seem to be far from this in the UK.

So what do the real numbers tell us? Russel Kinnel, a director at Morningstar in the US, conducted research into the difference between funds' official returns and the returns earned by the typical investor – in other words the difference between time- and money-weighted returns. As Bogle had been arguing for 10 years, Kinnel states 'the best measure of a fund's quality (i.e. how much it makes for the typical investor) is actual money-weighted returns'.

The results of this research were staggering. The data showed that across the board the returns earned by investors were worse than officially stated returns. This was particularly noticeable in growth funds where average 10-year annualised money-weighted returns were 3.4 percent below the stated return. In many sectors, such as technology, the figures were much, much worse.

Until recently, there has been no significant research into money-weighted returns in the UK, but that changed with a recent paper – actually a thesis – called 'Are UK fund investors achieving fund rates of return?' by Lukas Schneider of Dimensional Fund Advisors. His conclusions are equally as damning as those of Morningstar – the data suggested that from 1992–2003 the annual return of the FTSE All Share was 8.99 percent. Looking at 266 funds which were active in this sector over the period, the average fund returned 6.93 percent. To those who buy index trackers this result may not be surprising – this difference is presumably largely due to costs. Estimating the total expense ratios of funds conservatively at around 1.6 percent, the difference is easily accounted for.

However, when money-weighted returns are looked at the picture gets even worse. The average fund investor received only 4.91 percent over the same period. To put this into context, if an individual invested £100,000 at the start of the period, the actual return of the index would have resulted in a sum of approximately £281,000 compared to only £178,000 from the money-weighted average of the funds examined. Remember, it is the latter figure that most investors are actually getting.

Schneider's research goes much deeper than simply looking at the overall market. He also splits the funds into categories for growth, value and smaller companies. This research showed that the performance gap was as much as 2.43 percent p.a. for smaller companies compared to 2.06 percent for growth stocks and a relatively modest 1.00 percent p.a. for the equity income sector. This suggests that investors may actually be better off capturing market returns in less aggressive sectors such as equity income.

These studies suggest that that niggling feeling many investors have that their returns are not as good as the marketing material tells them is correct. The reason? Poor market timing – investors have put too much money into funds at the wrong time and it's easy to understand when one looks at the advertising of the fund management houses. Most fund adverts detailing returns cover short periods – some as little as one month when performance may have been particularly impressive. Truth be told, even periods of, say, three or five years are not especially revealing in a true statistical sense – the manager might have done well but it is not really that meaningful, thus the fund managers' constant qualification that 'past performance is no guarantee to future performance'.

There is also a trend among fund managers to launch and promote 'hot' funds. There are no prizes for guessing which sector saw the most fund launches and largest fund flows in 1999 – technology – and which sector crashed in 2000 – technology. But fund houses and investors do not learn. Since then we have seen a boom and bust in both commercial property and commodities. It is important to remember that fund houses are remunerated on funds under management and therefore if they can gain critical mass for a fund in a very short timeframe, that is going to be very attractive to them. Investors must take responsibility for this, but the 'noise' created by the fund management industry does not help.

So what relevance does this discussion of market-weighted returns and hot funds have for anyone trying to build a portfolio? We simply do not think it makes sense to dip in and out of different sectors trying to time markets whether to increase exposure to commodities, property, infrastructure or indeed any other market sector. Some decisions will be right, some will be wrong, but each of them will have a cost.

In fact, we see this as one of the great problems of exchange traded funds. There is so much choice, and therefore the ability to slice and dice a portfolio – gaining exposure to the most minute market sectors – if not used wisely, can do more harm than good. The temptation is to listen to the noise – you have just read an article on private equity offering great returns so you call your stockbroker and pick up an ETF that specialises in this sector, or your partner on the golf course has just told you that Japanese small caps are the place to be, so you log on to your online share dealing account and pick up an ETF. Noise acts as a temptation and it is there all the time. We cannot escape from it. The money and business sections of the newspapers are full of insightful articles recommending all sorts of investments. This 'helpful' advice is best avoided. It removes the focus from the long-term investment programme.

So if we're not going to listen to the noise created by the media and the financial services industry, what should we listen to? Many passive managers opt for an alternative called regular rebalancing.

Rebalancing

Remember that word discipline? A large part of the discipline of the investment process is not twisting and turning with the prevailing opinion but an equally large element consists of realising that portfolios need some care and maintenance via a periodic rebalancing. The process behind this concept is best understood with an example.

Assume you have a £100,000 portfolio nominally split with 50 percent invested in global short-dated bonds and 50 percent in global equities. After a year if equities have risen by 20 percent and the fixed interest by 5 percent, then the equity component would have risen to £60,000 and the fixed interest to £52,500 for a total of £112,500. The equities now make up a little over 53.3 percent of the portfolio and the fixed interest 46.7 percent. Now there is no real harm in that, but if returns continue in that manner then after five years the equities would be worth two-thirds of the overall portfolio. Again, you may think that is fine – the portfolio is growing well and providing excellent returns.

However, think back to earlier in this chapter. Investing is not simply about making money – it is about achieving goals. While letting a 50:50 portfolio simply run is likely to deliver the best long-run returns (as equities should outperform the volatility reducing fixed interest), this is not what we think the investment and planning process is about. *Investing must be about managing risk.* When the stock market suddenly falls by 25 percent in one year the unbalanced portfolio is clearly going to suffer much more. Although it may still be worth more, the journey getting there has been much more volatile.

While there has been much academic research on the subject of rebalancing there seems to be little consensus as to the best way to do it. On the one extreme, David Swensen, the legendary manager of the Yale endowment fund, rebalances on a daily basis. He argues that frequent rebalancing activity allows investors to maintain a consistent risk profile. Others argue that portfolios should be allowed to run for two or three years before rebalancing, citing the often quoted 'the trend is your friend argument'. In other words, whatever direction the market is moving in at any time, it seems to have some momentum. Another solution is rebalancing on the basis of pre-defined tolerances, i.e when a particular asset class moves more than a pre-set amount then it is rebalanced back. In the penultimate chapter of this book, we'll look in detail at each of these strategies, plus a few novel ideas. However, a simple compromise which works for most people is to review the portfolio annually and if the portfolio has not moved sufficiently do not make any changes. Where movements are more material then go ahead and make the changes.

Conclusion

We all like to make money, but unless it has some sort of context it is meaningless. While it is wise for all of us to have a decent buffer to fall back on when times are tough, what is the point in having £1 million if you actually only require £750,000? Would it not be better to take less investment risk or even stop working a few years earlier than build up excess, unnecessary capital? In other words, investing should have a purpose and a clear set of objectives. Once that is done, a suitable investment strategy can be designed and implemented.

Hopefully this chapter will have helped demonstrate that investing is something for the long term and that there are some clear and logical rules that should be followed. This does not guarantee riches (because it will only deliver the market return), but it does help to avoid many of the pitfalls that both private and professional investors face. The marketing of active fund management is extremely good and investors are lured in by high potential returns. But it seldom delivers satisfaction to the end user in the long run. Remember that the more times your money is 'touched', the more the resulting charges will sap long-term returns.

My message is simply to build a sensible, long-term portfolio and stay disciplined. Concentrate on the aspects that you have control over such as tax, costs, the right level of risk and reward and the overall suitability of a portfolio to your circumstances. Do not get sucked in by clever marketing of active funds. Remember, it is ultimately the fund's investors who are paying for that marketing! Do not let it be you!

8

Big theme investing and index funds

The enthusiasm surrounding the development of index tracking funds should not blind us to the fact they are not an end in themselves – they are simply tools, cheap, efficient tools nevertheless, that aid us in building better portfolios.

The huge choice of index funds does provide us with one unique advantage, however – pretty much every big idea or theme that is prevalent in investment can be accessed by investing in some sort of index tracker, be it an ETF, an ETC or a structured product with a tracker in-built.

We should, rightly, be concerned with how index funds are constructed and why they might be a better structure, but a detailed examination of index funds should not ignore much more important debates about where growth will come from in the future and how and where are we going to make our positive returns. What are those big themes that will be reflected in our choice of index funds?

Dr Stephen Barber, Head of Research at Selftrade, one of the UK's biggest stockbroking firms, is ideally suited to help us answer these weighty questions. His focus is on providing ordinary private investors with reasoned investment ideas based on wider macro-economic and political trends. He is not really concerned with pinpointing any one ETF but with providing the 'brain food' that might prompt a closer examination of the range of emerging markets ETFs, for instance.

It is all very easy to get bogged down in the detail of individual investments. Just how far the Aroon Oscillator has moved or calculating the unlevered beta is all very interesting and should not be ignored. But it is not the little details that move markets or create trends. Investing historically is all about the big themes: political and economic change, industrial sector renewal, the rise and fall of national power and the like. It is about adjusting strategies to meet market conditions and not missing out on new growth areas. We all like themes, whether it is the property market or the dot-coms, to name two that have raged and burned and could rage again.

Investors need to ask the questions: which companies are prospering? What links their prospects? What developments across the world are affecting markets? Which are the sectors that will dominate the next decade?

Index tracking funds such as ETFs are ideal for big-theme investing. Low cost, accessible and transparent, they allow you to get in and out of regional and industrial sectors at the click of a mouse. And with such a wide range of underlyings, it is possible to build a portfolio of trends from the four corners of the world.

That is true for bull and bear markets – even in bull markets, a thriving sector will often be off-set by the downturn in another. Likewise, even in downturns, there will be countries and industries which catch the wave of the next big thing. Using index funds is the simplest way of buying exposure to these trends.

This chapter will look at how investors can profit from the big themes. It will look at a number of big questions – the business cycle, big themes of years gone by, advice on avoiding bubbles, the advantages of momentum investing, the importance of diversification, the impact of globalisation and the big investment trends of this young century.

The business cycle

The first port of call for the big-theme investor is the business cycle. Cycles mean that there are identifiable trends and in the economy that suggests that different sectors prosper and decline as the economy grows or contracts.

The pattern of growth, prosperity, contraction, recession and back to growth reflects the behaviour of actors in the economy and participants in the market. Think of the over-optimism as economies peak and the over-pessimism of the trough. The market cycle tends to run ahead of the business cycle, declining and recovering earlier. And within the market different sectors prosper and decline at different times, with financials associated with the growth phase and utilities doing better (relative at least) during contraction. Here we see the difference between cyclicals and non-cyclicals: the former produce products and services which are in demand when people feel financially comfortable (leisure, consumer electronics and the like), while the latter produce the necessities of life and include heating, food and health care. But the big investment themes are not about simply cyclical markets, they are about structural changes in the economy. The economic cycle is important in identifying environments most attractive to potential business growth, but it will not show the new trends that will outperform the herd. For that you need to look beyond the market and to what is going on in the world.

As themes go by ...

The big themes of the past are part of the fabric of our history, from the 'never had it so good' 1950s, to the flower power 1960s, the industrial strife of the 1970s, Thatcherism of the 1980s, dot-com mania of the 1990s and the globalisation of the new millennium.

In a broad sense, each decade tells a big-theme investment story and those who identified the story early enough have been able to profit by weighting their portfolios in favour of these trends. As the tectonic plates of state and economy shift, new sectors emerge as the pioneers of their age, forging ahead in profits and influence.

In the post-war 1950s, it was industry, the age of the car and consumer goods. In 1946 there were a mere 17,000 televisions in the US; by 1953 two thirds of US households owned a set. But it was car manufacturing that could be said to have driven the 1950s' Western economy as the middle classes burgeoned – real weekly earnings of US factory workers, for instance, increased by 50 percent during the decade and car ownership exploded. Reconstruction in Europe and mass affluence in the US drove the growth of technologies, automation, engineering and construction.

By the time The Beatles had their first number one, gross domestic product, trade and real incomes were higher than ever. The world yearned for the raw materials to fuel this affluence and the big theme was to be metals and other commodities. The oil crisis of the 1970s brought world growth to a shuddering halt and the big-theme investor of this sideburn-wearing decade would have been following oil. Black gold and its associated industry was one of the best-performing sectors as economies slowed. It was an asset class which responded well to rising inflation and crisis. So, too, did real gold, which as a store of wealth always prospers in economic downturn.

The 1980s were years of deregulation, laissez faire and privatisation. Thatcherism and Reaganomics meant that ordinary people invested in shares for the first time and good profits were to be made from the British government's sale of the 'family silver': utilities, telecoms and oil companies, once nationalised industries. Remember to Tell Sid ... (the privatisation of British Gas).

The dot-com rise of the 1990s lasted until 2001, resulting in a multitude of reckless investors eventually investing billions in internet companies based on a speculative whim. While many technology companies were solid, long-term, innovative businesses, the dot-com era was sustained by speculation which eventually spiralled downwards to bust. Like bubbles before it and since, the good companies were outnumbered by those which would never make the profits their multiples suggested. One US grocery company, Webvan, gained and lost $1.2 billion within 18 months. In order to make it to the top, companies had abandoned previous business plans and plunged all efforts and exceptional sums of money into creating brand awareness. Such was the dot-com euphoria, people were even reported to have quit their jobs with the intention of becoming full-time day traders. Wise hands with experience in the markets were already nodding their heads sagely and warning of the repeated existence of investment bubbles.

Waves not bubbles

A note of caution for big-theme investors is to ride the investment waves and not to get sucked into the bubbles. To explain how stock markets work, the great economist John Maynard Keynes developed what he called his *beauty contest* concept. Here he described a fictional newspaper competition whereby entrants had to pick the six most beautiful women from a page of photographs. Those who picked the six most popular would win a prize. 'Easy,' you say. So what would your strategy be? The more naïve (but well adjusted) might spend a pleasant afternoon selecting what they consider to be the prettiest faces. But the shrewd entrant would be more interested in what he thinks the majority think is pretty and would make a selection based on that view. And it doesn't end there. As Keynes puts it: 'We have reached the third degree where we devote our intelligences to anticipating what average opinion expects the average opinion to be.'[1]

What Keynes means is that, perhaps too often, investment decisions are not made dispassionately, based on the real merits of the instrument, but rather on what we think other people are doing. This creates bubbles: as a share or asset class does well, it attracts investors, which in turn pushes up the price. As investors pour funds into the stocks, even more investors sniff potential profits and buy into the ideas of their fellow investors, increasing confidence and valuations.

Economist Hyman Minsky had the idea that 'stability is unstable' and he had a point, even though many of his mainstream contemporaries take a different view. Minsky believed that during periods of economic stability investors increasingly take on more risk. As a result, we see an increase in debt and a willingness to buy increasingly expensive assets. Eventually investors rely on the value of their assets to finance their debt. And because of continued economic stability, these assets, on which debt is secured, become increasingly overpriced. The longer the period of stability, the easier the credit and the more overpriced the assets. As debts exceed investors' ability to repay from their revenues, this eventually causes a financial crisis. The bubble bursts. This will all sound very familiar to students of the 2008 sub-prime crisis in the US which led to a world banking crisis.

But don't think it is only the inexperienced that get sucked into these bubbles – professionals are just as vulnerable. Think of the fund manager who, fearful of underperforming, buys into the concept and sets up a voguish fund to tap the private investor markets with sexy billboard advertising. While history is littered with examples of bubbles, rarely do we notice when we are in one. There is always a reason that makes things 'different this time' and investors buy and buy more. The stock becomes more and more expensive until eventually someone blinks. With asset bubbles, someone always blinks eventually and then the bubble bursts.

Put another way, we might call it the *greater fool* theory of investing – the idea that you buy a financial instrument not because of a belief in its merits but rather because you think there is a greater fool than you who will buy it at a higher price. This, in a rather cynical view, is how markets can sometimes work. But big-theme investors can select sectors with real momentum – the key is to know the difference between a long-term trend and a short-term bubble.

'It's better to travel than arrive': momentum investing works

It is stating the obvious, but avoiding dangerous asset bubbles is easier said than done. However, momentum investing is one approach that has been shown to be hugely effective. Eschewing fundamental analysis, momentum investors not only identify sectors which have performed well but also identify durable trends. Although requiring steady nerves, in essence the process could not be simpler.

Examine the market for sectors which have performed badly over, say, a 12-month period and ignore them; instead look for those sectors which have performed well in price terms and start buying into them in a systematic way. Naturally, it is crucial to identify these trends towards the beginning of their run and then get out as they show signs of waning, always shifting funds into sectors of new momentum potential. It is a strategy that comes with great risks, both in terms of correctly identifying the trend and, just as crucially, timing investment and exit. There is also a broader market risk that a big drop in the stock markets might well cause chaos in popular, market-leading sectors.

The onset of a bear market can be particularly detrimental to momentum strategies which worked in nice, comfortable bull markets. But you don't have to focus just on price momentum – look at earnings momentum and revenue growth as well as relative strength. Using these measures, momentum investors can profit from big themes, especially in strong markets. But it is important to be disciplined and sell on any alert such as bad news.

The point about momentum investing is that not only can it work but focusing on the big themes gives the strategy added drive. This works both ways, helping to select the big trend but also as a way of running a portfolio where these themes can be identified independent of the screening. By analysing the market for new themes for inclusion in your portfolio, combined with this disciplined methodology, you can make investments work harder and deliver greater profits.

Mark Glowrey and Tarquin Coe from research firm StockCube look at this momentum-based approach in the next chapter. They will examine some key signals-based approaches to running a momentum-based portfolio.

Diversify

For those with weaker constitutions, building a diversified portfolio which gives exposure to the big themes could be a sensible strategy, as James Norton discussed in the previous chapter.

All investing is about the trade-off between risk and reward; you need to accept enough risk to achieve your desired returns but not so much that you stay awake at night worrying. Diversification is key to managing risk and it also means that you can gain access to numerous investment themes. Build a portfolio of diversified asset classes, allocating portions as you see fit.

One drawback of trend-picking is ensuring you do not pick the right theme but fail to select an instrument which benefits from this trend. Buying into an index or sector can help here, ensuring your portfolio has exposure to big themes without the need to pick the specific shares that might do well. This is a particularly useful tactic when investing beyond your home markets where specific research is more difficult to obtain.

Also be careful of fads – remember, at one point someone was telling investors that tulips were the future. Ask yourself why this is a big theme, where are future revenues coming from and what are the actual profits? Even if you can answer these questions, be careful not to pick the last trend, look to the next. Always relate these secular trends back to much bigger global shifts: does the theme work inside a broader narrative of globalisation? Themes that clash with these broader, almost 'tectonic' shifts are unlikely to have much shelf life.

Globalisation

Understanding this globalisation shift is a crucial part of understanding the success of any big themes-led strategy; understanding what makes globalisation tick is the easy part, the more difficult challenge centres on building it into your investment process.

As the world has grown smaller and communications have become faster, the interdependence between countries has meant big changes for business, governments and investors – cross-border capital flows are more frequent, plentiful and easier than ever before. Funds can move around the world at the push of a button, seeking the best available returns. Stock markets in one corner of the world react rapidly to market or economic changes happening in other countries as speedily as they react to more local events.

But these broad changes do not always develop in quite the way that most analysts first think. Take the once-fashionable notion of decoupling. This is, or should we say was, the belief that the economies and markets of the US-led West were becoming uncorrelated with those of the China-led East. As a consequence, we were once told, diversifying between these geographic sectors could protect against weakness in one or the other. The global economic downturn which began in 2008 put paid to that idea as markets around the world declined together – the bear market and subsequent recession showed just how interdependent and indeed synchronised economies and markets have become. But that does not mean that investors should avoid international investment.

International diversification works, too

Diversifying into overseas markets means that a portfolio can take advantage of the best the world has to offer and gain exposure to the growth stories being written every day in these disparate and exciting economies.

Bear in mind that the MSCI world index of developed markets weights the UK at under 10 percent, which means that a portfolio comprised only of FTSE securities is not properly diversified. Over recent years, the big growth areas of the world have been in China and other emerging markets. Portfolios exposed only to Britain would have missed out on these exciting prospects. While it is true that these markets have tended to be more volatile, this risk can be mitigated by drawing the asset classes into a diversified portfolio.

Effective diversification means building a portfolio of securities which is not positively correlated. While not always the case (as was evidenced following the 2008 credit crunch), one of the easiest ways to achieve this is by buying into the lower correlation existing between assets of different countries. Add to this mix hard assets such as commodities and property and over the long term the portfolio should not only perform as required but do so having managed risk effectively. Over the longer term, there will be times when equities and bonds underperform, but it is usually these periods that see a boom in real assets of oil, gold, land and metals. And such commodities are usually located in economies from across the globe.

Gone are the days when a portfolio would contain only stocks from home, but gone too are the days when gaining access to international markets was difficult and expensive. One of the great attractions of ETFs is the ability to buy into these markets, easily and cheaply. Building a globally diversified portfolio has never been simpler.

By building a portfolio of ETFs rather than using, say, traditional open-ended funds such as unit trusts and OEICs, investors are exchanging one type of diversification for another. Those who buy unit trusts are buying a readily diversified fund and paying for a fund manager to make investment decisions. But the ETF investor turns that logic on its head. First decide on your asset allocation and design this to meet your investment objectives and attitude to risk. Decide how much international and commodity exposure you want alongside bonds and domestic market. Draw up a simple pie chart where these asset classes are allocated in broad percentage terms. Then all you need to do is buy ETFs which track these markets in the appropriate quantity. You can adjust the allocation at any point and introduce new asset classes as you see fit. A big-theme investor would weight the portfolio towards the trends which embody the major stories of our time.

The big themes of the next decades?

It is all very well to have identified the big themes of the past, but just what are the big themes of the second decade of the twenty-first century? After all, investors want to be able to profit from the next big story, the next industry to boom, the consequences of economic change. Picking the next big theme is perhaps not as easy as it might seem, but there are some interesting candidates. For once the business pages of the newspapers are not necessarily the best place to look to find these themes. Take a look at international and domestic news for stories which represent changes in the way things are being done. Which new economies are emerging as the major players of the future? Which industries are they beginning to dominate? What are the major international institutions talking about? What are the trends in academic research? You could think about the businesses in which you, your friends and family work. What are the big changes that are affecting the business, from outsourcing to new customers to new products? Pretty soon you will get an idea of the big themes of our time. Here are a few thoughts.

Farmland and agriculture

The world population is not only growing but it is getting hungrier. It is estimated that the world's inhabitants will increase from six billion today to more than eight billion by 2,030. Over the same period it is anticipated that 3,050 kilocalories will be available per person per day compared with 2,800 today. This has already grown from 2,360 kilocalories back in the 1960s and can be attributed partly to rising consumption in developing countries. Asia, for instance, now consumes far more protein from livestock than it did a generation ago.

Statistics produced by the United Nations' Food and Agriculture Organisation show just how much meat consumption has increased over the past 25 years, in virtually every comparable country. The average American consumes around 130kg of meat each year, compared with around 115kg in 1980. But the comparison is starker in China with its population of 1.2 billion. In 1980 the average Chinese person ate around 15kg of meat per year; today it is almost three times that amount and growing annually. Meanwhile, if one were to examine world agricultural area per person, in 1960 it was almost two and a half times the size it is today – populations may be growing fast but the pool of useful land is not growing at anywhere near the same rate.

We also have to factor in climate change, which is making its impact felt on crop yields. It is also fuelling diversification into ethanol as a clean fuel, which means more land is required for growing crops. This rush to biofuels is one of the biggest pressures on farmland in the US and one of the biggest drivers of grain prices. One only has to look to Iowa, the country's biggest producer of ethanol, to see how demand has forced pasture values to rise. It is projected that in the next few years as much as a third of corn crops will be used to produce ethanol, even though it will account for less than 8 percent of annual US gasoline use.

Add to these trends both increasing urbanisation in the developing world and exurban sprawls in the developed world and one can begin to understand why so many analysts are bullish on land values.

Infrastructure

Every decade or so a whole new asset class emerges out of nowhere. Hedge funds, for instance, first hit the investment landscape in the 1990s, prompting a massive scramble into new funds by the first decade of the twenty-first century. Not long after, another innovative, headline-grabbing asset class emerged into investors' consciousness, namely infrastructure funds. These were built on the idea of investing in utility companies (long quoted on the markets) and new public–private partnerships and ventures to build roads or airports – all these 'secure' assets were and are regulated by the state and provided solid, dependable cash flow streams. Those secure income streams are crucial to anyone looking to protect their portfolios against the ravages of inflation and provide defence from volatile equity markets. Offering solid, durable and predictable returns, combining capital growth and reasonable income over the longer term, infrastructure can seem like the perfect investment sector. Remember that even in a recession infrastructure reaps returns from its underlying projects because children still drag themselves to school, the police still try to catch baddies, aircraft still need somewhere to land and we still fill up the roads with traffic. And these returns bear little relation to what is going on in the stock market.

Crucially, these projects can be found right across the world, in Europe and North America as well as the emerging economies of Brazil, China, India and elsewhere. Take China as one example. It is spending 10 percent of its gross domestic product on these infrastructure projects over the next decade. Elsewhere, it is estimated that a staggering $20,000 billion will be spent on infrastructure worldwide during the next decade. The Organisation of Economic Cooperation and Development (OECD) believes some $53 trillion of infrastructure spending is needed by 2030 simply to meet development goals. By any estimation, that is a massive pot of spending and, for big-theme investors, it represents plenty of solid, foreseeable returns. There are, of course, some inevitable caveats – we need a balanced picture. Infrastructure funds will usually suffer from underperformance during the early stages for the practical reason that funds take time to be invested into projects. Also, given the popularity of the sector, investors will rarely find a bargain. Its defensive nature can also be a drawback since it can result in more cash being raised than can find its way into viable road or rail projects, forcing the state to step in later to guarantee income streams. You can have too many roads and railways and power stations and they can lose money in certain circumstances – Victorian investors in the UK lost millions on rail projects and new canals.

Water

Old-fashioned H_2O may seem like an innocuous and rather dull theme for investing but that is perhaps because most people reading this book have constant access to a clean supply from the tap. We cannot, of course, live without water and it must therefore be considered as precious as any commodity. As a global sector it is already worth $400 billion a year in revenues. With wars already fought over natural resources, especially oil, it is not inconceivable that we will have wars fought over water in the next few decades.

The very same demographic factors affecting farmland are hitting water supplies. A growing population, many of whom lack access to safe drinking water, is increasing demand and global warming and environmental damage are reducing supply. It is this that is driving vast investment in water engineering projects across the world. Water is a big theme that is here to stay, not least because farmers use so much water in the production of cereal crops.

New energy and green investing

A fad it may well be but renewable energy is one of the big themes of our age and if ever there were a global sector that seemed to represent the future then it is surely this. The harsh realities of today's world should be foremost in investors' minds: peak oil, global warming, population growth and emerging economies mean that there is an increasing demand for carbon alternatives. And it is big business. Around $30 billion a year is being spent on developing renewables, representing something like a quarter of all investment in the energy industry.

Longer-term answers to reduce carbon emissions will lie in technology. We now know that companies which invest in technological alternatives and improvements are the companies which weather economic storms better. A lesson from the beleaguered Detroit car industry during the last economic downturn is that businesses which failed to invest in making their motors cleaner suffered the worst as demand fell off. In this new era of state intervention, funds provided by governments in Europe as well as the US have been linked to green technologies.

Nevertheless, investors should be balanced in their approach to this sector. It remains notoriously difficult to pick individual stocks and there remains the 'Betamax' risk – a new technology like Betamax tapes may be the best, most rational answer, but that doesn't mean that a rival technology with better resources and marketing might not win out in the end.

Going nuclear

For those not so socially conscious, nuclear power is seen as a realistic carbon alternative of the future, not least in Britain where the government has firmly thrown its lot behind it as the solution to the country's and the world's energy needs. For proponents of nuclear, it is a clean, plentiful alternative to carbon. But its detractors worry about massive expense, gallons of toxic waste and catastrophe.

Whatever the rights and wrongs of the debate, it is undeniable that it is going to be increasing demand for alternative power sources that will cater for a growing and more prosperous world population. It is the developing countries playing catch-up to the West which represent a major driver of energy demand. According to ETF Securities, it is the non-OECD countries which are experiencing the strongest energy demand growth, with these countries and China projected to represent the largest source of demand in absolute terms within a few years. There is considerable scope for change in the world's energy mix as coal and gas remain the most significant fuels for electricity generation, with nuclear representing around 16 percent.

Observers of the world today will find 439 operating nuclear reactors. A new nuclear programme in the US will see a further 32 reactors added to its current 104. Seven reactors are under construction in China and a fivefold increase is planned over the next decade. India is building six, Russia is building seven to add to the 32 it already operates, and four reactors are under construction in Europe, bringing the total to 154.

Nuclear energy will always be contentious and there are plenty of reasons for opposing its growth. But its progress appears somewhat unstoppable, playing a significant part in the energy mix for years to come, not to mention the billions of dollars being poured into its development across the world.

Create your own themes

If you are in search of the big themes, why not create your own? This is not as strange as it might sound. It is about searching for innovation and creating baskets of sectors which combined represent a trend. New brands could be one such talisman, bringing together globalisation, the growth of emerging markets and consumer behaviour. Brand trends from fashion to food are no longer localised in the metropolis of a single country but form part of the aspirations of the growing middle classes from Europe to India to China and the US. Successful brands are increasingly global, appealing to mass markets across the world.

A quite different consideration in today's brave new world is security. We have looked at how globalisation has meant interdependence between countries, greater communication between companies and more movement of people and goods across borders. As a big theme, this might include macro-level defence of countries, traditional aerospace and arms. But business also needs improved technology security against viruses and attack. It needs security against political instability and with pirates in the news, theft and hostage taking need to be tackled.

The perennial alternative asset class is commodities, seen time and time again as a theme of an era. They support other themes and trends, supplying industry with the necessary raw materials. Investors such as Jim Rogers believe that a commodities bull market is under way and will continue for years. While many disagree with the legendary investor, balanced portfolios can create commodity themes of these hard assets, raw material-rich economies and companies which invest in and produce such assets.

For those with a really creative eye, themes might be created around alternative assets such as rare coins, art, collectable wine, boats, stamps and the like. Alternative assets have their attractions in that they are fairly uncorrelated to equities (although demand is linked to prosperity), but the major drawback is that they produce no income. Creating alternative asset themes can be both profitable and fun. But if you are investing directly, it is probably important to buy things you like too because if you judge the market wrong, you're stuck with them. So you may as well own a painting you would hang on your wall. For the ETF investor, buy into sectors exposed to these asset classes. The theme could range from the assets themselves through to the storage, sale and dealing.

Exchange traded funds have opened up a world of big-theme investing for the ordinary investor. Building a thriving portfolio is about more than the technicalities of stock market movement. It is about viewing the world and creating investments which reflect the successes across the globe. With some creativity, the big themes can be rewarding and profitable.

9

Active portfolios using ETFs

Most investors who use ETFs are happy to stick with a buy-and-hold philosophy – they are using ETFs to access certain asset classes over the long term. But a sizeable minority of investors also use ETFs in a much more active sense – they invest in a particular asset class to take a short-term view on its direction. That decision to actively time the direction of a market or sector forces them to use some form of defined methodology – many use the direction of a share's market price in an attempt to gauge the 'momentum' of that stock. This methodology is commonly called technical analysis and is used by a great many investors to manage their ETF portfolios over the short term. Tarquin Coe and Mark Glowrey are analysts at Investors Intelligence, a research firm that specialises in using technical analysis as an aid to building a better ETF-based portfolio.

Technical analysis and ETFs

The beauty of technical analysis is that the discipline is applicable to all asset classes. Providing a liquid market exists and price data history can be obtained, technical analysis (TA) can be applied to identify the trend and extrapolate trading and investment strategies.

From the point of view of a technical analyst, ETFs are no different from any other tradable instrument. However, the variety of ETF issues available, particularly in the well-developed US market, opens up the possibility to trade indices, sectors, baskets, spreads and other activities previously accessible only by professional fund managers or proprietary traders.

Before we look at some of the applications of TA to ETFs, we should address the key tenets of this approach. The most important concept in technical analysis is that of objectivity. Charts have to be analysed in isolation, with no input from outside events such as fundamental news flow, as well as personal emotions.

Technical analysis itself is the study of past price and volume behaviour through charts to forecast future direction. A huge range of tools is available to the technical analyst, but even the simplest concepts can enhance the investor's judgement considerably. Indeed, it is fair to say that technical analysis, if done well, with discipline, is simple and straightforward.

In any trade, the three most important attributes are *entry*, *exit* and a *stop-loss*. Over the next few pages we will outline some simple TA tools that can be used to identify these points, including:

- using TA to determine price entry
    - support and resistance
    - momentum indicators
    - breadth indicators
    - industry analysis
    - relative strength;
- using TA to determine stops;
- using TA to determine price targets;
- using TA for currency, bond and commodity ETFs;
- six golden rules for trading with TA.

Using technical analysis to determine price entry

Support and resistance

The first step in analysing a chart is to study the long-term picture and identify major support and resistance levels. These levels reflect the battlegrounds between buyers and sellers. Although trendlines certainly exist, it is the horizontal levels that are more important as they are more readily identifiable and persist for many years.

It is good practice to limit the chart to two support levels and two levels of resistance. Each level should be based on a different timeframe, such as medium term and long term. Looking at the US-listed SPY (an S&P 500 index tracker) ETF chart in Figure 9.1, we can see long-term resistance at 153 formed off the 2000 highs. Long-term support sits at 80, formed off the 2003 lows.

Tests of support and resistance are rarely perfect and often a lot of noise occurs in and around these levels as bulls and bears battle for control. Note the behaviour at the 2007 high and at the test of support in 2008/09.

With support and resistance identified, the next step is to look at what we call the 'market internals' to determine whether a support level, or a breakthrough resistance, will hold.

Figure 9.1

Momentum indicators

One measure of the internals of the market can be gauged through momentum. A popular measure of momentum is the Relative Strength Index (RSI). RSI was developed by a technical analyst by the name of J. Welles Wilder and this indicator is detailed in many technical analysis books. One of the indicator's greatest strengths is its ability to highlight divergences – situations where uptrends and downtrends start to lose momentum.

Divergences are either bullish (at bottoms) or bearish (at tops). The SPDR Trust chart for the SPY in Figure 9.2 shows an example of bearish divergence. The 14-day RSI made a high in April 2007, followed by a lower high

Figure 9.2

in October 2007. That lower high by the indicator was a sign of waning momentum and was a warning sign that SPY was vulnerable to a downturn.

Other useful behaviour to watch for is oversold and overbought, indicated by below 20 and above 80 respectively.

Breadth indicators

Breadth is a measure of participation and is another valuable tool for measuring the internal health of the market. For instance, it may be common knowledge that a major index is moving up (or down), but what is behind this? Is the move caused by just a few stocks, or is participation being seen across the index's constituents? Breadth is a measure of this participation. For instance, an index showing a 60 percent breadth reading will have 60 percent of the constituent stocks displaying uptrends.

Investors Intelligence favours the bullish percentage technique for establishing the breadth of a sector or market index. This technique, which classifies stocks as 'bull' or 'bear' based on the trend displayed on their point and figure chart, was introduced in the 1960s.

Investors Intelligence uses many other breadth measures, such as percent 10-week moving average (stocks trading above the 10-week moving average), percent 30-week moving average (stocks trading above the 30-week moving average) and percent relative strength (stocks with outperforming trends). These breadth studies are applied by Investors Intelligence to the major indices across the world, from the NYSE to the FTSE.

The key point to consider when applying breadth studies is this: sustainable bull markets can be supported only by firm or rising breadth data. That means a healthy bull market will need to see breadth of support from constituent stocks in the 40–80 percent range. Weak or falling breadth, by contrast, will not support a rising market. Consider also extremes of breadth will indicate oversold/overbought conditions – often major turning points.

The same principles used for RSI studies can be used for breadth, namely bullish and bearish divergences and overbought/oversold readings. Note the bearish breadth divergence on the SPY chart in Figure 9.3 at the bull market top in October 2007.

Figure 9.3

Industry analysis

The principles outlined above are equally as effective when applied to the charts of industry groups/sectors and their corresponding ETFs. US investors are fortunate in this aspect, in as much that a wide range of sector-tracking ETFs is on offer. At present, the selection in the UK, and indeed Europe, is limited but rising fast.

For instance, the SPDR Energy (XLE) chart in Figure 9.4 shows breadth for the S&P Energy sector measured by the percentage of stocks in P&F bull trends. Extremes in the breadth are useful in timing tops and bottoms in the Energy ETF. Where over 90 percent of the constituents are in P&F up trends, the sector, and thus the related ETFs, is overbought, such as in May 2008. Likewise, when the reading is below 10 percent, the Energy ETF is oversold, as illustrated in October and November 2008.

Figure 9.4

Divergences in breadth indicators relative to the price chart can also provide great timing signals. On the chart, note the bullish divergence evident on the breadth indicator as the Energy ETF broke below the October 2008 low. That divergence occurred ahead of a 20 percent rally in the ETF.

In the deep US market, all the major sector ETFs can be analysed in this way and any moves in the underlying sector captured by the wide range of sector-specific ETFs available. This gives investors and traders an excellent opportunity to trade the powerful intra-market sector rotations that are so often seen in the financial markets.

The reason that these sector rotations are so important is this: professionally managed money rarely leaves the market. Instead, fund managers attempt to improve the performance of their funds by switching to higher beta sectors in upturns and back into defensive sectors (utilities, etc.) in market downturns.

For instance, at the time of writing this chapter (April 2009), the recovering US stock market has a fairly conventional distribution of sector strength, with the largest number of industry groups positioned within the neutral 40–60 percent area (see Table 9.1). However, we note that the defensive Electric Utilities (UTEL), Pharmaceuticals (DRUG), Food Beverages and Soaps (FOOD) have lagged. The recovering consumer cyclicals such as Restaurants (REST) have surged ahead and are now arguably overbought. This is a classic rally pattern.

Thus, the market is setting itself up for a defensive rotation. At present, the level of 'skewness' is fairly restrained, but the potential is certainly there. This potential is visible on the price charts of the SPDR Consumer Discretionary ETF (XLY) in Figure 9.5, looking overbought and up against the sideways resistance seen at $22–23.

Figure 9.5

Table 9.1 The US industry bell curve

								+REST
							+TRAN	+STEE
						+CHIN	+ASIA	+RETA
					-WALL	+GAMI	+BUIL	+META
				+UTGA	-MACH	+SOFT	+SEMI	+LATI
				+TELE	+EURO	+TEXT	+REAL	+AUTO
				+SAVI	+JAPA	+FORE	+FINA	+OILS
				+PROT	-INSU	+PREC	+CHEM	+AERO
				+MEDI	+HOUS	+ENER	+POLL	+OIL&
		+HEAL	+FOOD	+LEIS	+BUSI	+ELEC	-BANK	+COMP
+BIOM	+UTEL	+DRUG						
10%	20%	30%	40%	50%	60%	70%	80%	

Oversold – below 32%   Above 68% – Overbought </DIV< td>

                                                    Updated through Apr 21, 2009

Groups marked with a + are in an up column.
Groups marked with a – are in a down column.

By comparison, the rally in the Utilities sector looks much more restrained (see Figure 9.6). Similar chart patterns can be seen in the laggardly Biomedics and Pharmaceuticals sectors.

At times, these sector divergences can get quite extreme. As a rule of thumb, we would look to play divergences on the short side where the sector breadth has peaked and rolled over back through 80 percent. Conversely, rallies up through 30 percent on the BP chart should be viewed as a sign of interest moving back into the sector.

Figure 9.6

Relative strength

When using ETFs it is important to be invested in the areas that are outperforming. This can be achieved through analysing relative charts.

Relative charts typically come in two forms, P&F and line charts. Line charts offer more analytical scope, in that momentum and breadth studies can be applied. Support and resistance can be applied to both chart types. Some prefer one over the other, though it is largely down to personal preference and experimentation by the investor to see what they feel more comfortable with.

Figure 9.7 illustrates the relative performance of the SPDR Materials ETF against a broad benchmark, the S&P 500 equity index, plotted on a P&F chart. Observe how the chart bottomed in late 2000 (the S&P 500 did not bottom until 2002). The base was confirmed with a P&F breakout in February 2001. That relative buy signal lasted until September 2008 and if you had followed this chart, you would have outperformed the market substantially during that bull run.

Figure 9.7

Using technical analysis to determine stops

Just as much importance should be placed on the positioning of stops as determining a good entry price. Support and resistance levels, for longs and shorts respectively, are central to identifying a good stop loss. However, volatile trading often occurs in and around support and resistance levels for ETFs, so stops need to be flexible.

Flexibility can be gained through using stops where trading has to fall below or above a stop level for a number of sessions. A strategy used at Investors Intelligence is to use a setup where a position is closed out only following three consecutive end-of-day closes above or beneath a level (if triggered the position is closed out on the fourth day). For example, a trader sells the Diamond Trust Dow Jones Industrials ETF (DIA) at the start of October 2007 following the failed break above the July high (Figure 9.8). He then places a stop based on three consecutive closes above that July high (horizontal

Figure 9.8

line). Despite volatile trading for the next two weeks, the ETF fails to achieve three consecutive closes above the stop level and the position survives.

Using technical analysis to determine price targets

A number of methods are available to the ETF investor to determine price targets. More complex target determination can be calculated using something called Fibonacci extensions, but a very simple method called the 'measure rule' is just as effective. This technique is straightforward and involves taking the depth of a trading range and adding that to the point from where a break-out would occur (the support or resistance of a range). For example, using the 'measure rule' for the Currency Shares British Pound Sterling Trust (FXB) for the trading range of August through November 2006 (Figure 9.9), a price target was determined and then met in late January 2007.

Figure 9.9

Using technical analysis for currency, bond and commodity ETFs

The introduction of ETFs for commodities, fixed income, currencies and other non-equity asset classes has greatly increased the scope of investment possibilities for the man on the street. Technical analysis can be applied to all ETF areas and not just be limited to equity ETFs. The principles of charting are exactly the same.

Figure 9.10 illustrates the Deutsche Bank Liquid Commodity Index Tracking Fund (DBC). The writing was on the wall regarding the bubble in the first half of 2008. As the fund marched higher, the 14-day RSI was exhibiting bearish momentum divergence.

Figure 9.10

Six golden rules

We believe that technical analysis should be part of every investor's toolkit. Certainly, we would not dismiss the excellent work performed by many fundamental analysts, but in trading, as in life, timing is everything. TA is more likely to provide this timing input and is infinitely more useful in managing the subsequent trade in terms of fixed and trailing stops.

Hopefully, you will start applying some of the techniques we have summarised in this chapter to your own trading or portfolio management techniques. If so, the list below may help – these are our six golden rules for trading with TA.

1. *Trade the trend not the countertrend* – look at the long-term chart first to identify this long-term trend.
2. *Consider commonality and underlying index direction* – do not attempt to buck the general trend. The majority of your trades should be with-trend, not countertrend.
3. *Let the chart determine the tactics* – direction, time, expectations. Examine the instrument's historic price action.
4. *Consider volatility to determine trade size* – high volatility, smaller position, a similar point to (3) above. The market dictates the style and size of trade. This technique will allow you to use wider stop levels on more volatile instruments, helping the position to ride out the 'noise'.
5. *Protect unrealised gains with trailing technical stops* – avoid 'meaningless' financial stops (5 percent, 10 percent, etc.). Use identifiable technical levels such as prior support, etc.
6. *Have goals/targets* – but never get too greedy or too fearful by taking profits early.

10

Putting it all together

'I can calculate the motions of the heavenly bodies but not the movements of the stock market.'

Isaac Newton in the 1600s after he had been wiped out in a stock market crash

'Usually, you know a hot sector after the fact, not before.'

Marshall Blume, Finance Professor at the University of Pennsylvania's Wharton School

Portfolios, like stock markets, are very strange creatures indeed.

I constantly fret over the health of mine – it is my other child, that constantly causes me limitless grief and anxiety, interspersed with the odd moment of euphoria. What makes my behaviour towards my portfolio even more inexcusable is that I also constantly break all the rules advanced by behavioural investment gurus like James Montier (an analyst at fund management firm GMO and formerly chief strategist at SocGen) and constantly monitor my ragbag of investments. Montier claims this constant fussing over my pension pot is perhaps the greatest sin of modern portfolio management (and trust me when I say there are many, many other sins which he identifies). He contends that a smart investor structures their portfolio intelligently and then leaves it alone for weeks or even months on end, without constantly checking to see whether it is going up, down or sideways.

To be fair Montier does not suggest that you hide away, ignoring all that goes on around you, only that you intervene when it is obvious that significant events are occurring which have a direct effect on 'the life plan', i.e. global depressions, rampant inflation, government defaults.

If this all sounds a bit too good to be true, it is because it is. Montier is by background a value investor with a strong contrarian streak and like many of this creed he is used to taking a stand – based on many well-thought-through principles, it must be said – and then steadfastly sticking to this analysis through thick and thin. He is also benefiting from the mountain of research (courtesy of his leading position in the City) that suggests that certain approaches work over the long term and that most of the time markets revert to the mean – or mean reversion, as it is called.

For the rest of us life is considerably tougher, especially if we do not have access to Montier's constant stream of institutional information. Truth be told, we have probably not thought through the principles underlying our portfolios – they are largely opportunistic, built through bolt-on acquisitions and desperate forced sales – and we do not really look in detail at the very long-term evidence that suggests an alternative approach.

James Norton may well be right in his clarion call to diversification, outlined in Chapter 7, but for most of us managing a portfolio is about rather more mundane issues, including our tolerance of risk (which, of course, changes as we grow older), our individual financial goals (plentiful but not always realistic), our time horizon (are we saving for a specific point in the future?) and the growth (or otherwise) of our non-financial wealth. Any change in these very individual variables can have a major impact on our investing habits and no amount of academic evidence of what constitutes 'best practice' is likely to force us to change tack.

But once you have accepted that long-term saving through investment is a personal and idiosyncratic business, you can at least recognise that certain aspects of investing behaviour are dangerous and counterproductive and need to be understood and, hopefully, improved upon.

At this early stage in our discussion of portfolios it is probably worth reminding readers of the biggest and most dangerous behavioural bias – it is an absolute, incontrovertible truth that sits above and beyond all the other slightly murky debates that ooze around the tricky business of running a portfolio, and it is incredibly simple, namely that too many of us overtrade.

We have already made this point earlier in the book, but it is worth repeating yet again the sad reality that the more you trade in your portfolio, the lower your returns. And just in case you desired any more evidence for this, it is probably worth citing the work of behavioural finance professors at the University of California, Terry Odean and Brad M. Barber, who researched the portfolios of 66,400 investors at Merrill Lynch between 1991 and 1997.

The good professors concluded there were two very specific factors that reduced returns: lousy stock picking and transaction costs. In fact, the most active traders averaged 258 percent portfolio turnover annually and earned 7 percent less annually than buy-and-hold investors, who averaged 2 percent turnover. To keep repeating what should by now at least be an obvious truth, costs add up and eventually destroy your wealth. Assume you have a £50,000 savings pot (your portfolio) and that you expected an annual return of 8 percent. The results in Table 10.1 detail the cost of a seemingly small difference in the annual management charge of a fund. The data suggest that the difference of just 1 percent per annum in charges over 30 years results in a reduction of more than £100,000 in final returns.

Table 10.1 Annual management charge of a fund

Fees	5 years	10 years	20 years	30 years
0.5%	71,781	103,052	212,393	437,738
1%	70,128	98,358	193,484	380,613
1.5%	68,504	93,857	176,182	330,718

But although pretty much everyone in the world of investment accepts that overtrading and high costs kill long-term returns, the debate about many other aspects of running a portfolio is much murkier. Should you, for instance, constantly rebalance your portfolio to make sure it is not being pulled in different directions by varying returns from stock sectors and asset classes? If you do then decide to rebalance, how often should you do it, and how?

And what about trying to time the market? Is it an obviously daft idea that is bound to end in ruin or could you operate a simple system that saves you from much of the pain of bear markets? Should you just use index funds in a portfolio or should you instead use some active managed funds to add a little oomph to returns? Crucially, are index funds not potentially vulnerable to big momentum-based moves in the market? If you invest in a FTSE 100 index fund, will you not simply become a victim of over-reliance on sexy sectors like technology or banks which come crashing back down to earth as markets eventually wake up to the risks? Once all these really rather tricky questions have been answered, one last crucial issue remains: how do you actually go about building that perfect portfolio? Should it be complicated and full of lots of different, diversified index funds or should it be incredibly simple and easy to run? What would a model, diversified portfolio actually look like?

In this chapter we are going to build on the analysis first outlined by James Norton in Chapter 7 and try to guide you through the maze of portfolio construction and maintenance obstacles with the help of five simple questions, the answers to which should make your life considerably easier. The chapter then ends with a section by Julian Hince on using trackers as part of a wider investment process for advisers.

Q1: To rebalance or not to rebalance? Should I constantly rebalance my portfolio?

Many leading investment thinkers, including the eponymous John Bogle, reckon that the best way to survive turbulent markets is to adopt an almost Zen-like calm and never cut losses, and never rebalance. Mainstream experts take a middle course and suggest a limited form of (annual) rebalancing, while a few hardy radicals suggest a much more active approach. Who is right? Sadly, there is no definitively right or wrong answer, as we will discover – it all depends on your attitude to risk and how confident you feel about managing your portfolio.

To understand the challenge involved, let us imagine the portfolio of my good old Uncle Fred with his simple holding of three index funds tracking UK equities, UK bonds and gold (he is a cautious type). He invests £100 in each fund and within six months his equity investment has doubled, whereas his bonds have gone down by 5 percent and his gold holdings have dropped by 20 percent.

At the end of six months – an eventful six months it must be said – his portfolio looks something like this:

- UK equities £150,
- bonds £95,
- gold £80.

In total his portfolio is now worth £325, but equities account for 46 percent of total holdings against the original 33 percent allocation whereas gold has sunk to just under 25 percent. What should he do? Should he take his profits on equities and then reinvest in gold or stick with the asset mix?

Uncle Fred decides not to do anything until the end of this first year. By that point his equities have come down a little to £130, his bonds are back at £100 and his gold has rallied to £90, implying a total portfolio that is worth £320. Equities are still worth 40 percent of his portfolio but at least gold is back up to 28 percent of total holdings. Uncle Fred decides that he is now going to rebalance and sells some of his equity holdings (just over £23) and invests just over £16 back in gold and another £6 in bonds.

According to advisers Paul Merriman and Richard Buck, Uncle Fred was spot on – he managed his returns to control his risks. In a paper entitled 'One portfolio for life?', the US-based advisers suggest that although 'annual rebalancing is not absolutely necessary, if it's neglected, the portfolio's risk can start creeping up. To maintain the proper amount of risk, you should keep the portfolio within reasonable distance of its . . . target allocation. When the stock market is hot, as it was in the 1990s, the equity part of a balanced portfolio can quickly creep up'.[1]

To back up their conclusions the authors studied a hypothetical portfolio, without rebalancing, that began with a 60 percent holding in US equities and 40 percent in bonds at the start of 1990 to 2005. By the end of 1999, 78 percent of the portfolio was in equities and only 22 percent in bonds. Investors may have been very satisfied with the total returns, but Merriman and Buck remind us that 'that was just in time for the bear market of 2000 through 2002 to come along and teach unwary investors about the dangers of being over-exposed to equities. The portfolio that had never been rebalanced lost 22.2 percent of its value from the end of 1999 through 2002. But if that portfolio had been rebalanced every year, the loss was only 12.6 percent'.[2]

Merriman and Buck adhere strongly to the view that rebalancing on an annual basis is the right thing to do if only because it is so counterintuitive, forcing you to punish the winners to reward the losers. 'A more productive attitude is to think of rebalancing as a mechanical way to require investors to buy low and sell high,'[3] suggest the authors.

Merriman and Buck are not the only advocates of a regular rebalance. A recent study from US brokers Smith Barney concluded: 'Rebalancing also tends to reinforce one of the main benefits of portfolio diversification: the tendency of returns on different assets to offset each other over time. By remaining close to their target allocations, investors should be able to reduce portfolio volatility. This allows the magic of compound growth to work more quickly, boosting long-term returns.'[4]

Fund management group Vanguard has also weighed into this debate, looking at returns from both a rebalanced portfolio and one that is unbalanced. The conclusion: 'If a portfolio is never rebalanced, it will gradually drift from its target asset allocation to higher-return, higher-risk assets. Compared with the target allocation, the portfolio's expected return increases, as does its vulnerability to deviations from the return of the target asset allocation.'[5] The Vanguard bottom line? If you do not rebalance, you open yourself up to greater risk by becoming over-exposed to the fastest-growing, most risky asset classes.

To demonstrate what can happen if you ignore 'best practice', the Vanguard researchers looked at a very boring and standard split of 60 percent stocks and 40 percent bonds that was never rebalanced. According to the Vanguard study, 'Because stocks have historically outperformed bonds, the portfolio's asset allocation gradually drifts towards 90 percent stocks and 10 percent bonds',[6] i.e. your portfolio becomes too risky because the allocation of risky equities becomes dominant.

But not everyone in academia and commentator land agrees with this conventional annual rebalancing wisdom. David Jackson, author of the excellent online *ETF Investing Guide*, suggests that although annual rebalancing is a sensible risk-control mechanism, there may be a better alternative.

> 'Think about the multi-year outperformance of US technology stocks until 2000, for example. ... Imagine that you had divided your portfolio between only two asset classes – tech growth stocks and non-tech value stocks – and you frequently rebalanced the portfolio to maintain an equal weighting between the two. In that case, you would have limited your upside from the run-up in technology stocks, because you'd be constantly selling tech stocks too early to maintain your asset allocation. Instead, you should have rebalanced your portfolio only when it became heavily misaligned. That way, you would have benefited from the momentum run-up in technology stocks, but would have periodically corrected your portfolio to avoid a situation where 80 percent of your portfolio was in tech stocks that subsequently collapsed. For this reason, the correct question may not be "How often should I rebalance?" but rather "How far should I allow my asset classes to stray from their target allocations before I rebalance?". Rebalancing only when an asset class reaches 150 percent of the target allocation, for example, will perhaps result in a more tax efficient and more profitable portfolio.'[7]

US-based financial commentators Phil DeMuth and Ben Stein agree with Jackson's preference to use percentage-based tolerance limits, i.e. sell only when an asset reaches 150 percent of total holdings. DeMuth and Stein suggest that the rival idea of annual rebalancing is in fact a mug's game. They argue that the 'financial services industry loves to tout portfolio rebalancing as a value-adding strategy. The idea is that every year we should sell a little of that 12 months' winners and use them to buy the current losers so that we bring our portfolios back into alignment with their original specs. Although it can incur tax and transaction costs, rebalancing is promoted on the idea that it gets us into a righteous "sell high, buy low" discipline.'[8]

Rather than accept the conventional wisdom Stein and DeMuth put it to the test. They used a fairly standard 60/40 equities/bond split of assets in a portfolio and then looked at 10,000 (Monte Carlo) simulations involving complex, seven-asset-class portfolios. They 'experimented with several calendar-based strategies, rebalancing the portfolios monthly, annually, or never. We also looked at tolerance-based rebalancing approaches: rebalancing when the portfolio wandered 10, 15, and 20 percent from its original allocations'.[9]

The results of their simulations are shown in Figure 10.1, but the bottom line is simple to understand: although never rebalancing is hugely risky, annual rebalancing is also risky compared with an alternative strategy suggested by the authors.

Figure 10.1 Results of Stein and DeMuth's simulations

'The first thing that stands out,' they conclude, 'is that the more frequently we rebalance, the worse our returns. The next obvious point is that, as is commonly observed, rebalancing cuts our risks. What we'd hasten to add, however, is that it doesn't cut our risks efficiently. Specifically, the most frequently recommended ritual – annual rebalancing – puts our portfolio's returns risk profile below the efficient frontier.'[10]

The authors suggest an alternative approach, called a tolerance-based approach. This involves setting a barrier or tolerance level above which you force a rebalancing – in their analysis a 20 percent tolerance-based approach is suggested as the best compromise. How would this work for Uncle Fred and his portfolio? Suppose an asset class is 20 percent of his portfolio and it has a 20 percent rebalance band. Tolerance-based types like Stein and DeMuth would suggest rebalancing back to the original 20 percent mix only when the portfolio strays outside of a range of 16–24 percent, i.e. 20 percent of the original 20 percent allocation.

Academic turned portfolio software guru Gobind Daryanani, creator of the rules-based rebalancing software iRebal used by many US-based financial advisers, takes a similar view to Stein and DeMuth. He thinks it is wise to 'look frequently' for rebalancing opportunities by setting a tolerance band. He suggests that the problem with 'traditional' annual rebalancing ideas is that 'the dates chosen for rebalancing are arbitrary, and thus we cannot possibly expect to catch the juiciest buy-low/sell-high opportunities'.[11] Daryanani spells out what he thinks we should all do. We should:

- use wider rebalance bands [around 20 percent];
- evaluate portfolios biweekly;
- only rebalance asset classes that are out of balance – not classes that are in balance; and
- increase the number of uncorrelated classes used in portfolios.

He suggests that a 20 percent threshold monitored every second week is the optimal rebalancing strategy, producing a 'rebalancing benefit' of 55bps, or half a percent per annum. According to Daryanani, this kind of tolerance-based rebalancing is particularly important in volatile markets, otherwise 'you are likely to miss the rebalancing benefits during periods of short-term fluctuations'.[12]

Is there a widely accepted, undisputed bottom line? Should you rebalance annually or use tolerance limits? Or should you perhaps never rebalance at all? If anyone deserves the last word on this subject, it is probably John Bogle. He recently completed an analysis for *The New York Times* on the subject of rebalancing. Controversially, he is not convinced by most forms of rebalancing, annual or otherwise. According to a report on Bogle's blog: 'Fact: a 48 percent S&P 500, 16 percent small cap, 16 percent international, and 20 percent bond index, over the past 20 years, earned a 9.49 percent annual return without rebalancing and a 9.71 percent return if rebalanced annually. That's worth describing as "noise" and suggests that formulaic rebalancing with precision is not necessary. We also did an earlier study of all 25-year periods beginning in 1826 (!), using a 50/50 US stock/bond portfolio, and found that annual rebalancing won in 52 percent of the 179 periods. Also, it seems to me, noise. Interestingly, failing to rebalance never cost more than about 50 basis points, but when that failure added return, the gains were often in the 200–300 basis point range; i.e., doing nothing has lost small but it has won big.' Bogle's conclusion? 'Rebalancing is a personal choice, not a choice that statistics can validate. There's certainly nothing the matter with doing it (although I don't do it myself), but also no reason to slavishly worry about small changes in the equity ratio ... I should add that I see no circumstance under which rebalancing through an adviser charging 1 percent could possibly add value.'

Q2: The consensus seems to be to buy and hold over the long term. Does that mean I should never attempt to time the market?

The standard long-term advice from most equity enthusiasts, as well as nearly every fan of the EMH, is to run a buy-and-hold strategy, i.e. stick with shares through thick and thin and do not try to change your buying and selling behaviour based on market conditions. A host of both academic and broker research suggests that trying to work out the best time to 'buy the market' is difficult at best and disastrous at worst. For buy-and-hold enthusiasts the idea that private investors sitting at home watching their computer screens can somehow judge the direction of sophisticated global markets is frankly delusional. Researchers at the Schwab Center for Investment Research in the US have put some hard numbers on the cost of this curious behavioural vice of overconfidence.[13] It looked at three buy-and-hold investors who each received $2,000 annually for 20 years to invest in the markets, a grand total of $40,000. Two decades later here were the results:

- The Perfect Timer – $387,120. Strategy? The money is put into the market at the monthly low point every year.
- Treasury Bill (government gilt) Investor – $76,558. Strategy? Terrified of shares, the investor puts their money only into Treasury bills.
- Autopilot Investor – $362,185. Strategy? This investor automatically invests the money on the day received and then leaves it alone.

The Schwab study is just the tip of the research-based iceberg that suggests that poor market timing is incredibly costly. In 1998, academics at the University of Utah and Duke University reviewed 132 investment newsletter portfolios involving some form of market timing, over a period between 1983 and 1995.[14] The average return from these 'timed' portfolios was 12 percent with 11.9 percent volatility. An S&P portfolio with the same volatility returned 16.8 percent for the same period.

Embarrassingly the researchers suggested that the more famous the market timer, the worse the results. A newsletter called Granville Traders Portfolio lost 2.2 percent annually and the Elliot Wave Theorist Traders Newsletter portfolio was down 10.1 percent. The academics' withering analysis was backed up by investment research outfit the Hulbert Financial Digest, which also reviewed 25 newsletters with 32 portfolios and found that none of the newsletter timers beat the market. With a 10-year study ending 31 December 1997, market timers averaged from 5.84 percent to 16.9 percent, the average being 11.06 percent. However, the S&P 500 index earned 18.06 percent and the Wilshire 5000 value-weighted total return index returned 17.57 percent. Another 10-year study showed averages from 4.4 percent to 16.9 percent a year, with the average of 24 market timers at 10.9 percent. Even when adjusting for something called the risk–return average, these expert 'market timers' were still far below the average of the buy and hold.

US research firm Morningstar took a slightly different angle, looking at how investment risk declines as stocks and funds are held for longer periods of time, suggesting that buy and long-term hold is the only solution. The Morningstar researchers found that the best return on stocks for one year was +53.9 percent while the worst return was –43.3 percent. However, the best and worst returns over a 25-year period were less variable at +14.7 percent and +5.9 percent, i.e. the longer you decide to stay in the market, the lower your potential risk.[15]

Morningstar fund analyst Peter Di Teresa then grouped 4,880 domestic equity funds by turnover ratio and examined their performance over one year. These funds were, by and large, run by active fund managers who included market timing as one of their skill sets. 'In a bear market, the feeling is that the pros should at least be able to avoid the big disasters through trading,' said Di Teresa. First, he compared the performance of funds in the top third in terms of turnover ratio against the bottom third. The trigger-happy funds in the top third (1,626 funds) lost 10.5 percent over the year as of 2/28/2002, while the lowest third shed 6.3 percent. 'The effect of high turnover gets even more pronounced when you break things down further,' said Di Teresa. This time, he took the same group of domestic stock funds and broke them up evenly by turnover into five groups. Over the same time period, the highest turnover fund group (976 funds) finished down 11.5 percent for the year, while the lowest turnover group lost 5.8 percent. The presumption against attempting to time the market seems to hold true even for professional fund managers – the less you time your buys and sells, the less you trade and the higher the returns.

Just in case you thought it was only academics who suggest that market timing is for mugs, it is worth listening to the man who mightily influenced the great Sage of Omaha on the subject of market timing. Warren Buffett's great hero Benjamin Graham was one of the most famous timing sceptics, declaring in his book *The Intelligent Investor* that: 'We are sure that if [the investor] places his emphasis on timing, in the sense of forecasting, he will end up as a speculator and with a speculator's financial results.'[16]

But as is often the way with presumed investment orthodoxy, many investors beg to differ. The key to successful investing, these enthusiasts maintain, is not to keep moving in and out of the market but to work very irregular intervals when timing a big purchase or sell makes absolute sense. To use the jargon, this is not tactical market timing (constantly buying and selling to try to catch the high) but strategic market timing (timing the one key move every year, for instance).

Consider a report from US magazine *Business Week* in 2002. An MIT economist had calculated that someone who invested $1,000 in the S&P 500 or Treasury bills and correctly selected the right month to buy on a month-by-month basis since 1926 would have earned $14 trillion by 2002.

A rather more realistic analysis came from technical analysts at Birinyi Associates of Westport, Connecticut. They looked at market data and showed that investors who were out of the market during the five worst days each year do astronomically better than those who hold their stocks throughout each year. For example, in 2000, the S&P 500 stock index dropped 10 percent (not including dividends), but an investor who invested in the S&P on every day but the five worst days of 2000 made a profit of 9 percent. In 1998, being out of the market during the five worst days would have given you a return of 56 percent instead of 27 percent. Overall, a dollar invested in the S&P stocks in 1966 became $12 for the buy-and-hold investor (again, without dividends) but an incredible $987 for the investor who missed the five worst days each year. The only problem with these genius schemes is that it is relatively easy to spot the worst days with the benefit of hindsight but considerably more difficult on the day. A more sensible middle path lies in simply avoiding the excesses of the market, i.e. sell your stocks to control potential risks when valuations are too high or economic indicators suggest a recession.

Even a small but hardy band of academics has suggested that this strategic form of market timing might have some validity. Professors Hashem Pesaran and Allan Timmermann looked at simple systems to market time in a paper for *The Economic Journal*.[17] Using data sets from 1970 to 1993 their work suggested that without the benefit of hindsight, an investor could have correctly predicted the direction of the UK stock market roughly 60 percent of the time on a monthly basis. They suggested that when exploited in a market timing investment strategy, investors could have more than doubled their returns per unit of risk, even after accounting for transaction costs. The academics reckoned that using publicly available information, such as interest rates, money growth, oil prices and growth in industrial production, small degrees of predictability still remain and these could have been exploited by developing a relatively simple forecasting model that was incredibly simple to use.

In fact, a market timing strategy is conceptually fairly easy to understand. One strategy could be to stay invested when the market is up or flat and avoid the downturns. The strategic market timer develops signals to identify what condition a market is in. An overvalued market is called 'expensive', 'overbought' or 'overextended'. A normal market is 'fairly valued'. An undervalued market is 'cheap'. Timers use some form of mechanical model, using computer software to crunch numbers such as interest rates and investor sentiment – the timers are looking for signals that indicate a reversal of trend, overpriced markets or an early warning signal to switch from buy to sell or vice versa. Some will act immediately on that signal, while others will wait to see whether it is confirmed by subsequent trading days or weeks. Bizarrely, a huge number of private investors, who think they are buy-and-holders, are in fact using the most basic and least successful method of market timing, otherwise known as ICSIA or 'I can't stand it any more'. The markets are grim, so sell everything indiscriminately!

Hedge fund manager Hugh Hendry of hedge fund Eclectica is one of those who sides with the view that investors need to operate some form of simple market timing and dump the mantra of long-term buy-and-hold investing – simply sitting tight and waiting is going to make investors very poor over the next few decades in his view. He is one of the most successful hedge fund managers in the UK and even in the rough markets like that in 2008 had a good year – rather annoyingly for all those keen to predict the demise of hedge funds. In fact, his Eclectica fund registered a 49.8 percent return in October of 2008 alone while other active or hedge fund managers were bemoaning huge losses. His view is that markets are fundamentally too volatile to stick to buy-and-hold investing. 'The stock market could oscillate or go sideways for a period as long as 25 years,' suggests Hendry. 'We've got another 15 years of markets rising, falling and going sideways.'[18]

His pessimism on future returns is shared by a quick perusal of investment history. According to data from Chicago-based Ibbotson Associates, from

1926 to 1999, 90 percent of five-year periods were positive for stocks. That's the good news. The bad news is that those figures do not reveal long periods of pain in the stock market. After the 1929 crash, the Dow Jones Industrial Average took 25 years to regain its pre-crash levels. The Dow traded above 1,000 in 1968, but failed to close above that level again until 1984.

The key is the mismatch between long series data which suggest huge compound returns and shorter period data which suggest the potential for sustained low or even negative growth. Various studies of long-term data for the last hundred years suggest that shares do return a simple average gain of 7.2 percent p.a. but that is the very long term (100 years plus) and it is only an average. Most of us have to cope with finite life spans where we face a crucial 20-year window of opportunity to accumulate capital. Get the wrong 20 years and your buy-and-hold strategy is not such a winner. The evidence comes from the redoubtable US analyst and adviser John Mauldin (in a letter called 'While Rome Burns'),[19] who looked at 88 20-year periods and discovered that although most periods generated positive returns before dividends and transaction costs, half produced compounded returns of less than 4 percent, while less than 10 percent generated gains of more than 10 percent. Plenty generated negative long-term annualised returns!

If you want to understand this huge variance go to yahoo.com, where you can download the full data set of price returns for the Dow Jones Industrial Average since inception at the end of the 1890s. Take these data and then chart them, and you will see long periods of dreadful price returns. The trend overall is clear – up – but there is a huge amount of variation on the way. For example, if you invested in December 1905, you would have bought in at around 96 index points, but fast-forward 17 years to 1922 and the index is still at 98.17, having traded in a range between 55 and 118. Similarly, take the Wall Street crash. At the beginning of April 1929, the Dow was at 333.79, but it did not hit that level again until April 1954. More recently, the returns from 1965 to 1980 were equally dismal. Admittedly, these indices are stated on a price-return basis and do not incorporate dividends reinvested, but in reality, most of us do not actually reinvest our dividends.

Mauldin maintains that most of us are victims of our own 'glide path', i.e. we have to pick a 20-year buy-and-hold investment window. When we are young, we do not really save much (or at least I did not), so when we start saving in earnest, it is probably around our late 20s or early 30s. We therefore accept that we have 20–25 years in which we need to spice up our returns by investing in risky assets before we hit our 50s. Then we start winding back into safer assets such as bonds. However, if we pick the wrong

20–25-year glide path, we are in trouble unless we have been reinvesting those dividends diligently.

Mauldin, like Hendry, suggests that a simple buy and hold through thick and thin might be potentially calamitous. He suggests that investors need some form of signal that activates a switch from one asset class (defensive/ aggressive) to another. Such a strategic 'switching rule' was in fact advocated early on by John Maynard Keynes, who combined investment in real assets with switching between short-dated and long-dated securities based on movements in interest rates.

Is there a simple signal system that investors could operate without constantly moving back in and out of the market, incurring huge trading costs along the way? That is the question posed by Mebane Faber in the *Journal of Wealth Management*.[20] It is a compelling piece of analysis and suggests a system that is incredibly easy to implement. Faber is a wealth manager (and prolific contributor to the excellent seekingalpha.com website) and he has been trying to work out a simple way of protecting wealth by timing his equity investments. What he aspires to is a system that is simple to administer and clearly tells you when to buy and when to sell. His solution is the 200-day simple moving average, one of the most basic technical analysis indicators. It is worked out by adding up all the closing prices for the past 200 market days and dividing by 200.

According to Faber, the rule is to buy when the asset price or market shows a monthly price above the 200-day moving average and sell when it moves below. It is not really more complicated than that, although one implication is obvious: you will be spending a fair amount of time holding large parts of your portfolio in cash. To test his idea, Faber has run the data over the entire last century.

Faber's system does not really add much to total, accumulated returns – in fact, it underperforms the index marginally in roughly 40 percent of the years since 1900. But it massively cuts down on risk, the maximum loss and volatility. On average, Faber finds that you get roughly the same returns as the index but with less risk. (You get Faber's paper online at http://papers.ssrn.com/sol3/papers.cfm?abstract_id=962461.)

The bottom line? If you are willing to be bothered with rebalancing either annually or using a threshold, the evidence seems to suggest some advantage even if it only gives you some peace of mind that you are actively controlling risk. But equally, do not overestimate your capabilities in this regard and constantly time the markets. The odds are that frequent market timers will mostly fail.

Q3: I'm worried by the volatility of equities. Are shares really worth the extra risk?

Talk to most investment analysts and they advance the view that for most portfolios equities should sit at the core because they produce higher returns than bonds. But does the evidence actually support this broad, sweeping conclusion? Luckily the answer seems to be – yes – equities are worth the extra risk because they produce extra returns over the very long term. The key piece of evidence comes from a long-term study by strategists at Barclays Capital.[21] Their analysis suggests that over the 80 years from 1926 to 2005, the compound annual growth rate of return was 11.77 percent for the Small Cap Index of shares, 10.36 percent for the Large Cap Index, 5.50 percent for the Long-Term Government Bonds index, and just 3.70 percent for holding government bonds or T-bills. $1 invested in 1926 would have produced $18 if it had been invested in US Treasury bills and $2,661 if it had been invested in an equity-based large-cap index (and more than $7,300 with a small-cap index).

Part of the explanation for these stellar long-term returns is that equities are much, much riskier than other asset classes. Figure 10.2 shows the annual real returns of the S&P 500 index from 1872 to 2000. It clearly shows that although shares have produced some amazing returns, it is at the expense of very high volatility.

Q4: Should I only use index tracking funds to build my portfolio?

It is fairly obvious that we think that index funds should sit at the heart of any modern portfolio, but note the use of that term 'sit at the heart' – a sound portfolio is probably one that uses a core of well-diversified index funds around which circles a 'satellite' of slightly more unusual funds and shares that may involve some active fund management. That activity in the core may involve very inefficient markets where index trackers can be weak in both theory and practicality, i.e. the markets may be relatively inefficient and the resulting index funds could produce large tracking errors because of the difficulty of tracking these inefficient markets.

That acceptance of some role for actively managed funds, especially in imperfect markets, is in part motivated by the recognition that there are successful fund managers who do indisputably add value some of the time – they frequently work in those more inefficient bits of the market and they

Putting it all together 253

Figure 10.2 S&P 500 Composite Total Returns index 1872 to 2000 can produce excellent returns for a substantial period of time. US fund manager Bill Miller of Legg Mason, for instance, beat the S&P 500 for 15 straight years using a distinctive, value-influenced strategy. But even he has had some terrible recent years, which we think proves the broader point that even the best and most successful can lose their touch (their alpha) – in fact his recent performance has been so underwhelming that he has decided to quit mainstream fund management altogether!

Our general concern with active fund management is that most investors do not actually use the very best managers – they use below-average managers suggested to them by fund-wrap platforms and financial advisers motivated by news stories and commission kickbacks rather than true long-term excellence. If you had some magic ability to spot the successful managers, time and time again, we might concede that active fund management might be worth the greater risk most of the time. That is the promise of a band of experts called fund-of-fund managers – they claim that their constant focus on researching the best managers and switching between them produces huge long-term outperformance.

These fund-of-fund managers reckon that their risk-control mechanisms in picking the best fund managers more than make up for their higher fund charges. But their criticism of index funds goes even further – they think that index funds are fundamentally flawed in volatile and bear markets. They claim that index funds simply leave investors open to market risks. One of the most articulate critics is Jason Britton of T Bailey in the Midlands, a specialist fund-of-fund company. At the end of 2008 he produced research that suggested that sticking with index funds was 'crackers' in a bear market – or in fact any market.

The cornerstone of his highly critical analysis is a piece of research that looked at the average performance of FTSE All Share trackers in the UK and active fund managers over the 15 years between 1993 and the end of 2008. His conclusion? 'During this time, FTSE All-Share Index tracker funds have underperformed the Index by 24.7 percent on average, equivalent to 1.9 percent per annum. People investing for the long term (and after all, investment in equities should be for the long term) are being sold short here; having decided to replicate the market they would, on average, have found 24.7 percent of their returns missing over the last 15 years.'[22]

Britton's argument then turns to specifics and to one of the most successful (in funds under management at least) UK index trackers, marketed by Virgin Money – the Virgin UK Index Tracking Trust, launched in March 1995.

According to Britton this fund has underperformed the FTSE All Share index by an average 2.4 percent per annum. 'This accumulates to a total underperformance of 28.6 percent by the Virgin UK Index Tracking Trust since its launch,' he says.

The cause of this underperformance by the Virgin fund is, Britton alleges, a high tracking error and a relatively high cost of 1 percent per annum in management charges. Britton is spot on in his analysis of the Virgin fund, which is indeed expensive and not terrifically efficient at tracking the underlying index.

There are, by contrast, many other index tracking funds that do a similar job at half the cost and almost non-existent tracking error, a point that Britton glosses over. Britton then goes on to concede one key argument – that during the 2007 and 2008 bear market index trackers have actually caught up relative to the active fund managers. Britton suggests that the causes of this 'have included the very volatile markets (up or down by as much as 8 percent in a day) and the desperate selling of good stocks (which are more likely to be held by active managers) at any price by hedge funds in the face of their huge redemptions'.[23]

Britton's honesty is admirable because many active fund managers have over the last decade suggested the exact opposite – that index trackers do worse in a bad market because index trackers cannot make decisions about getting into and out of momentum-based sectors that are inherently risky. These critics maintain that by tracking popular indices like the FTSE 100, index tracking investors open themselves up to the peculiar biases that emerge in big markets. This extra risk can be better controlled by active fund managers who, allegedly, know a bubble when they see one and can avoid it by active stock selection.

The context to this broad charge that index trackers fail in bear markets is contained in a small paper from stockbrokers The Share Centre entitled 'The changing face of the FTSE', published at the back end of 2007.[24] This paper examined the composition of the hugely popular FTSE 100 index and how it changed over time – see Table 10.2. It is a remarkable table and demonstrates how the composition of the FTSE 100 has changed over the period from 1984, when the index kicked off, through to the middle of 2007, just before the markets crashed. The holding in banks tripled in size, as a percentage of total holdings, followed closely by investment in the giant pharmaceutical companies, which more than doubled as a holding. Utilities came from no holdings to 6 percent and retailers dropped back from 11 percent to 6 percent.

Table 10.2 The FTSE 100 index over time

	% share of the FTSE 100 index as at:	
Top sectors	*01/01/1984*	*05/04/2007*
Banking	6	22.8
Insurance	5.80	5.70
Mining	2	10.10
Oil and gas	15	17
Pharmaceuticals	4	9.7
Retailers	11	6
Technology	3	0.25
Telecoms	7	7.80
Tobacco	2.60	2.20
Travel and leisure	6	2.2
Utilities	0	6

Source: The Share Centre, http://www.share.com/shareholder/Q207/changingface.pdf

If we flash forward to the beginning of 2012, these figures would look very, very different. Financials – banks and insurance companies – have collapsed back to just 11 percent of holdings, oil and gas companies are up at 21 percent and the big mining companies have continued their remorseless rise to just under 12 percent of the total FTSE 100 index.[25]

What is extraordinary is that if you had bought the FTSE 100 tracker in spring 2008, you might not have thought there was anything wrong with having over 28 percent of your fund in financials. Sadly, the catastrophic demise of the British quoted banking sector would have crushed your portfolio, losing you over 40 percent in one year. The big problem, the critics maintain, is that big indices like the FTSE 100 become victims of style and fashion – they become weighted towards hugely risky sectors that shoot up in value and then shoot down again. One oft-repeated statistic is that at the height of the dot-com boom Cisco, the US networking company, comprised over 6 percent of the total value of the S&P 500. Now it is less than 1 percent. Successful share prices attract other investors to buy the shares, chasing up prices and making the successful companies a larger component of market-weighted indices. But that success is risky and investors in index tracking funds end up in effect buying momentum funds that chase the most dangerous stocks in an index. Introduce bear markets and momentum as a strategy collapses, taking your index trackers and your portfolio down with the market.

There is no particular way of denying this charge – market-cap indices obviously focus on the most successful companies. There are alternative ways of building indices that do not rely on market caps as a weighting system – we explored ideas like equally weighting an index in our section on alternative indices earlier in this book – but these are not regarded as mainstream by most analysts and are shunned by most investors. The reality is that if you accept that big markets are mostly efficient, then you must also accept the risk that goes with them.

More to the point, can active fund managers do a better job of controlling this style drift into momentum and thus control risk? Research from Vanguard in the US suggests otherwise. In a paper entitled 'The active passive debate: bear market performance',[26] analyst Christopher Philips looks at how active fund managers performed in bear markets using the Morningstar Direct database of equity mutual funds in the US and Europe. His results fit in with the general rule that active fund managers tend to underperform, even in bear markets:

> *'We observe that a majority of active managers outperformed the market in just 3 of 6 US bear markets and in 2 of 5 European bear markets. To be sure, in each bear market, funds existed that successfully outperformed the broad market. However, these results clearly indicate a lack of consistency with respect to the success of active funds in general.'*[27]

Philips looked in particular at the 2000–03 bear market and found that although 60 percent of all active funds outperformed the US stock market, only 23 percent of active funds outperformed the European stock market over the same period. His conclusion? Although some fund managers can outperform in a bear market, there is no real consistency overall – in some bear markets they do, but for most of the time, most managers do not. 'As a result, it should not be assumed that an indexed investor is at an immediate disadvantage during a bear market relative to an actively managed fund, despite the opportunity for the manager to add value,' says Philips.

Table 10.3 Performance of active funds during bear markets

US funds versus Dow Jones Wilshire 5000 index

Bear market – years of low or negative returns	Number of funds	% outperforming market benchmark
1973/74	110	43
1980/82	167	78
1987	291	57
1990	405	44
1998	1082	39
2000/03	1405	60

European and offshore funds versus MSCI Europe

1990	37	57
1992	81	33
1994	128	66
1998	378	39
2000/03	796	23

Source: from *The Active–Passive Debate: Bear Market Performance*, Vanguard Investment Counseling & Research, http://institutional.vanguard.com/iwe/pdf/ICRIBM.pdf © The Vanguard Group Inc., used with permission

But look closely enough at the Vanguard data in Table 10.3 and you will see two interesting themes – first, that in Europe as the number of funds grows, their success in beating the markets falls; in the US, by contrast, active fund managers seem to have been more successful and to have worked their way through the bear markets moderately successfully.

Is there any bottom line? Some active fund managers indisputably do add value some of the time and there is evidence to suggest that active fund managers in inefficient markets can add value for certain periods of time. Also if you find a good fund-of-fund manager who is talented at consistently picking the good managers of the future, stick with them. Their skill (or clairvoyance) will deliver you above-average returns, but ask yourself how they spot these funds in advance. And even if they have been successful in the past, will that winning streak/consistent analysis and research hold for the future as well? More to the point, if most active fund managers fail to beat the index, why should most active fund-of-fund managers do any better? Last but by no means least, be aware of the index you are tracking and understand the risks you are taking – many big indices can perform truly badly in a bear market as momentum-based stocks take a hit. Do not blithely assume that the bigger the index, the less risky it is. Use our Essential 25 section at the back of this book and look at what you might be tracking when you buy an index fund – when you understand those risks, make sure you find an index fund with a low tracking error and minimal charges. Remember that the average fund-of-fund manager charges more than 2.3 percent in costs for their expertise whereas most ETFs charge around 0.5 percent p.a. A superb fund-of-fund manager might deliver some extra value, but that extra 1.8 percent p.a. in lower fees via an ETF, for instance, adds up to a lot of money over the very long term.

Q5: How do I actually build a portfolio? Should I keep it simple?

To understand how you might go about building your own portfolio, it is probably a good time to mention the slightly odd world of portfolio theory. This hugely extensive and influential body of work was pioneered by economist Harry Markowitz. It isolates all the key elements of a well-diversified portfolio and then guides investors through an optimum portfolio construction process and how to build an efficient frontier. It is a hugely technical analysis which we are largely going to avoid in this chapter; instead we will simply repeat the following story. Professor Markowitz was asked at a conference in Chicago what he invested in. 'I should have computed co-variances of the asset classes and drawn an efficient frontier – instead I split my contributions 50/50 between bonds and equities,' he said. Just to ram the point home, it is also worth quoting the father of modern risk analysis in economics, Bill Sharpe, on the subject of how he builds his portfolio. 'I invest in various funds, large stocks, small stocks and international stocks.' Or Eugene Fama, the father of the index funds movement, asked by a publication called *Investment News* what he invested in, who replied by detailing a mixture of funds that invested in a very broad-based US index called the Wilshire 5000, plus a little in small-cap and international index funds and a little over a third in value-oriented stock indices and short-term bond funds. That is it.

Professor Fama, along with Professors Markowitz and Sharpe, did what so many people have done in the past, namely mix and match a small number of key asset classes, cheaply and efficiently. They could have made the exercise enormously efficient and endlessly optimised the mix of asset classes to build their own efficient frontier (which in turn defines the optimum efficient frontier), but they kept it simple and intuitive and mixed and matched a bit of equity and a bit of bonds. This consensus in favour of simple diversification is also in evidence when talking portfolios with most British investment academics. Most of these 'experts' stick to a simple, classic split, namely 60 percent equities (broad equity market indices)/40 percent in government bonds.

Keeping it really, really simple and lazy

In America the idea of keeping it simple has been adopted by a school of commentators which demands that we slow down our investment process, get simple, even lazy, and stick with simple long-term buy-and-hold portfolios made up of a small number of simple index funds.

These lazy portfolios are hugely popular in the US, especially with economists and market commentators like Paul Farrell, who has written a book on lazy investing and is a highly regarded commentator for the MarketWatch website. Like many in the US, he is convinced that constantly buying into the latest hot funds is a complete waste of time for private investors. 'Unless you're working full-time in the financial world,' Farrell suggests, 'you don't have the skills, tools, information, time or interest in playing the market, especially the bond market. And even if you do play the market, the odds are you'll lose because the more you trade, the less you earn; transaction costs and taxes kill returns.'[28]

You will probably recognise the principles embedded within his argument – simplicity and low cost. Farrell's answer is what he calls the lazy portfolio. Crucially, there is not just one portfolio. Farrell has asked a multitude of leading analysts and investment writers to build and then test their own simple, lazy portfolios.

Farrell's lazy portfolio proposition is built on four simple principles:

1 Use funds to capture the market not individual shares.
2 Use index tracking funds to track the market efficiently and cheaply.
3 Keep it simple, with most portfolios never comprising more than 10 individual funds.
4 Buy and hold – do not overtrade and overcomplicate. Stick with the portfolio for the very long term.

In our next chapter we will take these ideas and examine some simple, Lazy portfolios designed specifically for readers of this book and a publication of mine, *PortfolioReview*, available free online at www.portfolioreviewonline.com – these all fit into Farrell's template of keeping everything simple and easy to understand. Many of these lazy portfolios in the next chapter have been modelled on those developed by William Bernstein, author of a seminal book called *The Four Pillars of Investing*.[29] Bernstein is a physician, neurologist and financial adviser to high-net-worth individuals as well as a commentator for the US magazine *Smart Money*. He is a big fan of two very simple portfolios – his No-Brainer Basic portfolio of just four funds (built using cheap unit trust trackers from Vanguard) and his slightly more complicated No-Brainer Coward's portfolio (also built using cheap Vanguard funds).

William Bernstein's No-Brainer Basic portfolio

- 25% in the main S&P 500 index (Vanguard 500 index (VFINX))
- 25% in the main US Small Cap index (Vanguard Small Cap (NAESX) or (VTMSX))
- 25% in a diversified international index (Vanguard Total International (VGTSX) or (VTMGX))
- 25% in a US bond fund (Vanguard Total Bond (VBMFX) or (VBISX))

William Bernstein's No-Brainer Coward's portfolio

- 40% in Short Term Investment Grade funds (VFSTX)
- 15% in Total Stock Market (VTSMX)
- 10% in (US) Small Cap Value (VISVX)
- 10% in a Value index (VIVAX)
- 5% in Emerging markets stocks (VEIEX)
- 5% in European Stocks (VEURX)
- 5% in Pacific Stocks (VPACX)
- 5% in real estate trusts or a REIT index (VGSIX)
- 5% in Small Cap Value (NAESX) or (VTMSX)

Bernstein has been running the Coward's portfolio since February 2002 and it has produced an annualised return of 9.37 percent per annum (compared with 6.19 percent for the benchmark S&P index – see Table 10.4) and 11.35 percent over the past year (compared with 10.44 percent for the S&P 500), all via simple tracker funds that in total cost less than 0.4 percent p.a. in management fees.

Table 10.4 The Coward's portfolio v the S&P 500 index

Fund	1-year return	3-year annualised return	5-year annualised return
Coward's portfolio	14.70	11.35	9.37
S&P 500 index	15.79	10.44	6.19

Source: www.kirkreport.com/resources/lazyportfolios.html

Another compelling lazy portfolio comes from David Swensen, Chief Investment Officer of Yale University's endowment fund, which boasts a two-decade investment record of +16.1 percent per year returns, a track record that easily places him as one of the best managers of institutional money in the US. Here is his portfolio, again built using ultra-cheap tracker funds from Vanguard.

David Swensen's lazy portfolio

- 30% in Total Stock Market index (VTSMX)
- 20% in REIT index (VGSIX)
- 20% in Total International Stock (VGTSX) or (15% in VDMIX and 5% in VEIEX)
- 15% in Inflation Protected Securities (VIPSX)
- 15% in Short Term Treasury/Gilt index (VFISX)

As with Bernstein, this simplicity does not come at a cost in terms of returns – it beat the S&P 500 17.6 percent to 15.8 percent in 2008 and on a three- and five-year basis – see Table 10.5.

Table 10.5 Swensen's portfolio v the S&P 500 index

Fund	1-year return	3-year annualised return	5-year annualised return
Swensen portfolio	17.62%	13.55%	11.54%
S&P 500 index	15.79%	10.44%	6.19%

Source: www.kirkreport.com/resources/lazyportfolios.html

Farrell, Swensen and Bernstein are just three of the more famous exponents of the lazy portfolio – a US website called the Kirk Report at **www.kirkreport.com** has dedicated a whole section to this brilliantly simple idea, publishing a much longer list of simple, buy-and-hold portfolios. Some of the highlighted lazy portfolios on the Kirk Report site include the following:

American financial commentator and planner Paul Merriman's suggested portfolios

Paul's website at **www.fundadvice.com** is a great source of simple, easy-to-understand research – we will look at his analysis of rebalancing later in this chapter. His model portfolios are built around a much larger number of components than Farrell's – his risk-based portfolios include as many as 14 different index funds or ETFs. This more diversified approach is essential according to Merriman because building a lazy portfolio with just four indices is not enough – his research suggests that owning 10 asset classes increases your total return. See Table 10.6.

Table 10.6 Merriman model portfolios

Overall structure

	Aggressive	Moderate	Conservative
Equity	100%	60%	40%
Bond	0%	40%	60%

Individual portfolios

Fund name	Symbol	Aggressive	Moderate	Conservative
S&P Depositary Receipts (SPDR) S&P 500	(SPY)	11.25%	6.75%	4.50%
Vanguard Value VIPERs	(VTV)	11.25%	6.75%	4.50%
i-Shares Russell Micro Cap Index Value VIPERs	(IWC)	11.25%	6.75%	4.50%
Vanguard Small Cap	(VBR)	11.25%	6.75%	4.50%
Vanguard REIT Index ETF	(VNQ)	5.00%	3.00%	2.00%
i-Shares MSCI EAFE	(EFA)	9.00%	5.40%	3.60%
i-Shares MSCI EAFE Value index	(EFV)	9.00%	5.40%	3.60%
i-Shares MSCI EAFE Small Cap	(SCZ)	9.00%	5.40%	3.60%
Wisdom Tree Int'l Small Cap Div Fund	(DLS)	9.00%	5.40%	3.60%

Table 10.6 Continued

Individual portfolios

Fund name	Symbol	Aggressive	Moderate	Conservative
Vanguard Emerging Markets VIPERs	(VWO)	9.00%	5.40%	3.60%
i-Shares S&P World ex-US Property index	(WPS)	5.00%	3.00%	2.00%
i-Shares Lehman 1–3 yr	(SHY)	0.00%	12.00%	18.00%
i-Shares Lehman 7–10 yr	(IEF)	0.00%	20.00%	30.00%
i-Shares Lehman Treasury Inflation linked	(TIP)	0.00%	8.00%	12.00%

Source: www.kirkreport.com/resources/lazyportfolios.html

Ben Stein is another hugely successful US commentator and adviser, whose colourful career has included being a speechwriter to Richard Nixon and a Wall Street Journal commentator. According to Charles Kirk (of the Kirk Report), 'Ben is in favour of indexed-focused long-term investing and believes that you should focus your investments on dominant big picture themes to produce even greater returns. For example, Ben has made it clear that he thinks Americans would be smart to have exposure to the world's emerging markets.' Stein also suggests a portfolio for those in or approaching retirement, called his 2 ETF retirement portfolio. Kirk reports that according to Stein's research, 'this portfolio presents no risk and plenty of upside potential for those who live 30 years after retirement who withdraw 5 percent annually'.

Ben Stein's Long-Term Portfolio

- 30% in Fidelity Spartan Total Market index (FSTMX) or Total Stock Market ETF (VTI)
- 15% to 20% in iShares MSCI EAFE index (EFA)
- 10% in iShares MSCI Emerging Markets index (EEM) or Emerging Markets 50 ADR (ADRE)
- 10% in iShares Cohen & Steers Realty Majors (ICF)
- 10% in iShares Russell 2000 Value index (IWN)
- 15% in cash

Ben Stein's Retirement Portfolio

- 50% in StreetTracks Dow Jones Wilshire REIT ETF (RWR)
- 50% in iShares Dow Jones Select Dividend (DVY)

Kirk is also a fan of Jim Lowell's Sower's Growth Portfolio. Harvard-educated Lowell is editor of a number of US newsletters (Fidelity Investor and The ETF Trader at MarketWatch), author of investment books including *What Every Fidelity Investor Needs to Know*[30] and a partner at investment advisory firm Adviser Investments, a private money management firm advising on more than $1 billion, based in Newton, Massachusetts.

The Sower's Growth Portfolio

- 25% in iShares MSCI EAFE (EFA)
- 15% in iShares DJ US Total Market (IYY)
- 15% in Mid Cap SPDR Trust (MDY)
- 10% in Diamonds Trust (DIA)
- 10% in iShares Russell 2000 (IWM)
- 10% in iShares MSCI Emerging Markets (EEM)
- 7.5% in Fidelity NASDAQ Composite (ONEQ)
- 7.5% in Power Shares Dynamic Market (PWC)

The list of lazy portfolios could go on and on, and there are dozens of variations, many of them forming the centrepiece of hugely successful get-rich-quick finance books, so popular in the US. But it is worth mentioning just three more quick examples. The first of these alternative approaches is perhaps the very simplest. It is called the Couch Potato Portfolio, designed by Scott Burns, a financial columnist on the *Dallas Morning News*. Just two funds feature in his ultimate lazy portfolio:

1 50% Vanguard 500 index – tracks the S&P 500
2 50% Vanguard Total Bond Market index fund – tracks the Lehman Brothers Aggregate Bond index

Burns launched his Couch Potato Portfolio in 1991 but has backtested it to 1973 – according to Burns returns have averaged over 10 percent p.a. A slightly more complex variation sits at the centre of something called The Coffeehouse Portfolio, devised by Bill Schultheis, a former Saloman Smith Barney broker turned financial adviser. The portfolio sits at the heart of a hugely successful investing book stateside – called, unsurprisingly, *The Coffeehouse Investor*[31] – and is built around Schultheis's elegantly simple investing credo, which consists of the following rules:

- Diversify across different asset classes.
- Capture the entire return of each asset class – use index funds.
- Develop a long-term financial plan and start saving early.

As for the portfolio, Schultheis's advice is to keep it simple. Just six Vanguard funds should do the job long term:

- Vanguard S&P 500
- Vanguard Large Cap Value
- Vanguard Small Cap index
- Vanguard Small Cap value
- Vanguard International
- Vanguard REIT Stock index

According to Schultheis his Coffeehouse portfolio has averaged an 11.42 percent annual return.

Last but by no means least, it is worth mentioning one worthy contender for the Keep It Simple Lazy Portfolio Challenge – it comes from US savings and investment magazine *Kiplinger*. The Kiplinger Keep It Simple Portfolio features just four investing ideas based on major indices:

1 25 percent large-cap stocks.
2 25 percent foreign stock funds – in particular the Vanguard European Stock Market index or the Vanguard Total International Stock Market index.
3 25 percent small-cap funds. Russell 2000 or the S&P 600 BARRA Small Cap Value index.
4 25 percent domestic bond.

How much is enough? What does good diversification look like?

> All these elegantly simple lazy portfolios may make some readers deeply nervous – simplicity may sound like an admirable principle but surely a commonsense definition of diversification suggests that we should use more than just a couple of funds to spread risk? Surely the Couch Potato approach of just two index tracking funds, for instance, is dangerously undiversified. In defence of Scott Burns and his Couch Potatoes he would argue that his chosen indices – the S&P 500, for instance – are already hugely diversified, containing the vast majority of the US equity market assets.

In Chapter 7 James Norton outlined how increasing the diversity of holdings within a portfolio can bring tangible benefits in both returns and the control of risk. An even more detailed analysis of what actually constitutes a diversified portfolio was attempted in the US by analysts Paul Merriman and colleague Richard Buck in September 2005 when they tried to resolve the struggle of how to go about building 'one portfolio for life'. Using the Dimensional Fund Advisors' database, their research department looked at returns between 1955 and 2004, a 50-year period that included lots of bear, bull and sideways tracking markets.

Merriman and Buck looked at three potential portfolios:

- S&P 500 tracker.
- Another variant invested 60 percent in the S&P 500 index and 40 percent in five-year Treasury notes. This is very easy for any investor to replicate.
- Another 60/40 split made up of 40 percent Treasury bills and 60 percent equity but this time the equity was split four ways between US-based large-cap stocks, large-cap value stocks, small-cap stocks and small-cap value stocks.

According to Merriman and Buck's analysis, the 'all-equity S&P 500 Index portfolio had an annualized return of 10.9 percent over that 50-year period' while the '60/40 version's annualized return was 9.6 percent'. Surely the average private investor would have always plumped for this all-equity version? Merriman and Buck are not so sure – though the 60/40 equities/bond mix returned less than the pure equities approach, it did so with a much lower level of risk. 'Statistically, you could say the 60/40 portfolio reduced return by 12 percent while reducing risk by 42 percent,' say Merriman and Buck. 'Or you could say the 60/40 portfolio provided 88 percent of the return with only 58 percent of the risk.'

The best performer by far, though, came in the shape of the third mixture, the 60/40 portfolio with greater equity diversification. 'Over the 50 years in our study,' Merriman and Buck report, 'this diversified 60/40 portfolio produced a return of 11.4 percent, with a maximum drawdown of 25 percent. Compared with the all-equity portfolio, this diversified mix raised the return by an extra 0.5 percentage point while it reduced the risk by 44 percent.' That 0.5 percent per annum difference may not seem so great, but the authors remind us that over 50 years $100 invested at 10.9 percent would grow to $17,643. The same $100 invested at 11.4 percent would grow to $22,093, a difference of $4,450, or an increase of 25 percent! 'In dollar terms,' they add, 'that difference alone is equal to more than 44 times the entire original investment of $100.'

But what about going global? Merriman and Buck's original analysis looked only at US investments, but surely there must be some benefit from investing internationally as well? The authors agreed and subsequently looked at year-by-year returns from 1970 through to 2004 if an investor had stuck with the diversified option number three from earlier (no international stocks) or invested in an alternative strategy which consisted of a 60/40 percent equity split but with that equity portion split 50 percent into US-based stocks of varying sizes (large-cap stocks, large-cap value stocks, small-cap stocks and small-cap value stocks) and 50 percent international (split five ways this time to include large-cap stocks, large-cap value stocks, small-cap stocks, small-cap value stocks and stocks in emerging markets). The returns increased by more than 40-fold! The bottom line? The more you diversify internationally, the greater your potential returns.

Source: Based on Merriman, P. and Buck, R., available online at www.fundadvice.com/articles/market-timing/one-portfolio-for-life.html

How's your lifecycle?

A growing number of asset management houses in the UK and the US take a slightly different tack to the challenge of building a one-size-fits-all simple portfolio. Clearly the concept of designing a simple two- or four-fund structure made up of cheap underlying funds is probably beyond the ken of most expense-heavy marketing departments (with the obvious exception of Vanguard) – most big fund managers are instinctively much happier selling a highly skilled fund manager with their higher expense structure. But more than a few innovative fund managers have started to roll out an easy-to-understand investment idea built around an eminently simple idea – it is called lifecycle investing and it is the institutional equivalent to lazy portfolios.

Imagine you are 25 years old. You have just landed a job managing the night shift at a Sainsbury's superstore in south London and the world is your oyster. You are earning just enough money to put aside, say, £100 a month in a fund that you will stick with for the next 40 years of your working life, but for now you want lots and lots of growth in your underlying investments. That means you are willing to take on some risk – now – and the long-term data on returns suggest that the riskiest, most rewarding of the major asset classes are equities. Bonds, by contrast, are a bit boring and safe and although you are probably never going to lose more than 20 percent in any one year (that is called your maximum drawdown in the trade), equally you are never going to bag any huge tenbaggers that make your fortune. In summary, our 25-year-old thrusting young buck quite sensibly tells his adviser that his risk tolerance is high and that he wants to stack up on equity exposure and 'go for it' in terms of risk.

Flash forward 30 years. Our young buck is now a considerably older 55 year old who is just 10 years away from retirement (still with Sainsbury's, now owned by a Mongolian coal conglomerate!), working in Department 23 at Head Office examining Sigma Six Efficiency. He can just about put up with the boredom of the job because he knows that retirement is only 10 years away (although he has heard rumours that the retirement age might increase to 85 soon). That means capital preservation is all important. He absolutely cannot afford a 'drawdown' of something like 20 percent in one year – that means he takes a very negative view of equities and he is a big fan of bonds.

This transition I have described in both tolerance of risk and awareness of potential returns sits at the heart of lifecycle analysis. Over those 30 years (from 25 to 55), our private investor changes – both physically and in his tolerance of risk – and over time that translates into a big change in choice of assets. Early on he is sensibly interested in equities and probably no bonds, in his mid-40s he is probably making the shift away from equities into some bonds and by his mid-50s he is probably biased towards bonds. Curiously, once he gets to retirement at 65, the consensus on the 'correct' balance becomes a little muddier. On paper, retirees should be ultra cautious – they have to preserve their pension pot for a retirement that could last 30 or more years. But they also require an income to live on and the assets with the safest profile – bonds and especially government bonds or gilts – tend to pay the lowest yield. Also pensioners have to be cautious about another major risk – inflation. Sticking all your money in conventional bonds in high inflationary times might mean you preserve your nominal (before inflation) returns, but the real value after inflation could be diminishing rapidly. Some academics and economists maintain that pensioners should be willing to take on extra risk, to grow their income and to grow their capital sum in inflationary times. *Investors Chronicle* economist Chris Dillow has suggested that pensioners should not really be paranoid about preserving all their capital until death primarily because they cannot benefit from that wealth when they are six feet under. His strategy? Possibly consider taking on extra risk via equities, and especially those equities that pay a dividend, and reducing your bond exposure.

Regardless of this post-retirement debate, the simple process of constructing a mix of assets that can be used as the building blocks of a single portfolio and can change over time, has evolved into a complex research literature at whose heart sits something called the glidepath. Figure 10.3 is from consulting investment organisation Ibbotson Associates, a unit of Morningstar, Inc. in Chicago, but most other outfits' glidepaths look pretty similar. This glidepath starts with high-risk assets, transitions through a balanced approach in mid life and ends with a mixture of assets with a bias towards bonds later in life.

Every provider and analyst will have their own starting and ending points and relative combinations, but they all feature the exact same blended glidepath. The only substantive debate seems to be whether a very young person has some limited bond exposure and whether a retired person should have some equity exposure and at what level.

This blindingly simple analysis has evolved into something called a target date fund. This involves you sitting down, working out your planned retirement age (which will nearly always be massively wide of the mark, given changing longevity patterns) and then finding a fund that has the closest equivalent to that year, called a target date. Given that it is 2012 as this book is being written, if you are 30 now, you will probably be looking at retiring in 35 years' time, in which case your 'target date' is probably around 2047.

Figure 10.3 Generalised Ibbotson target maturity glidepath

Source: Ibbotson, http://corporate.morningstar.com/us/documents/Indexes/TgtmaturityMeth.pdf

The Ibbotson Associates research notes: 'Target maturity investment solutions should help investors through the investment phases of accumulation, transition, and retirement.'[32] A second variation on the same model can also be found, called target risk funds, which do not specify an actual year but take a measured risk approach, suggesting a transition from ultra high risk to ultra low risk and all shades of risk control in between. This new niche is growing fast – according to Ibbotson's research, at the end of 2007 there were approximately 38 registered target maturity fund families in the US representing 256 individual target maturity funds with assets under management of $178 billion. In 2008 two major UK providers, Fidelity and ABN Amro, also launched their own versions of the lifecycle approach and over the next few years investors can expect a plethora of new launches as asset managers wake up to the huge marketing opportunity.

Obviously this approach is not restricted to just index fund providers (although Vanguard is a major player both in the US and here in the UK) and active fund managers have been positively salivating at the prospect of tying their customers into a savings scheme for life. But the index funds approach is uniquely well suited to supply the funds that sit at the core of such an approach, if only because of the low cost of their products and their refusal to keep taking a chance on an active fund manager's luck or skill over many decades.

ETF providers have moved fairly aggressively into this space and one of the pioneers is US stockbroking firm TD Waterhouse, which has teamed up with ETF provider XShares to run a range of target-date lifecycle funds. The composition of each of the funds in its target-date ETFs is detailed in Table 10.7.

Table 10.7 XShares TD Waterhouse Lifecycle Funds

	Before retirement							Retirement		After retirement		
Years	35	30	25	20	15	10	5	0	5	10	15	20
Equity (%)	100	100	100	90	82.5	75	60	50	37.5	30	25	20
Fixed Income (%)	0	0	0	4	8.5	14	29	40	63.75	62	67.5	73
Real Estate (%)	0	0	0	6	9	11	11	10	8.75	8	7.5	7
Age	30	35	40	45	50	55	60	65	70	75	80	85
Portfolio	2040		2030	2025	2020	2015	2010	2005				

A slightly different approach to the same target-date concept has also been launched by the giant ETF provider iShares, which has brought out its own lifecycle ETFs. These index tracking funds are based on an underlying target-date index independently provided by Standard & Poor's and featuring very low expense ratios that range around 0.30 percent after fee waivers.

iShares has also brought out another variation on the same theme, not based on a target date but instead looking to tiered risk profiles or target risks, in this case ranging from aggressive (high risk) through to conservative (low risk), in all cases based around an S&P target risk approach with roughly the same fee structure. See Table 10.8.

Table 10.8 iShares asset class breakdown between four different asset allocation, risk-based funds (data as of 29 December 2011)

Aggressive Portfolio	
ISHARES S&P 500 INDEX FUND	39.35%
ISHARES S&P MIDCAP 400	22.76%
ISHARES MSCI EAFE INDEX FUND	13.97%
ISHARES S&P SMALLCAP 600	8.74%
ISHARES BARCLAYS AGG BOND FUND	5.65%
ISHARES BARCLAYS TIPS BOND	4.72%

Table 10.8 Continued

Aggressive Portfolio

ISHARES MSCI EMERGING MKT IN	2.62%
ISHARES IBOXX H/Y CORPORATE BOND	2.11%
CASH or COLLATERAL	0.68%
Total	100.62%

Conservative Portfolio

ISHARES BARCLAYS SHORT TREASUR	30.81%
ISHARES BARCLAYS AGG BOND FUND	25.99%
ISHARES BARCLAYS TIPS BOND	18.45%
ISHARES S&P 500 INDEX FUND	13.02%
ISHARES IBOXX H/Y CORPORATE BOND	4.86%
ISHARES S&P MIDCAP 400	2.86%
ISHARES MSCI EAFE INDEX FUND	2.12%
ISHARES S&P SMALLCAP 600	1.00%
ISHARES MSCI EMERGING MKT IN	0.80%
CASHCOLLATERAL	0.25%
Total	100.17%

Growth Fund

ISHARES S&P 500 INDEX FUND	29.01%
ISHARES BARCLAYS AGG BOND FUND	19.23%
ISHARES S&P MIDCAP 400	10.63%
ISHARES BARCLAYS SHORT TREASUR	10.41%
ISHARES MSCI EAFE INDEX FUND	10.40%
ISHARES BARCLAYS TIPS BOND	10.23%
ISHARES S&P SMALLCAP 600	5.26%
ISHARES IBOXX H/Y CORPORATE BOND	3.05%
ISHARES MSCI EMERGING MKT IN	1.69%
CASHCOLLATERAL	0.50%
Total	100.42%

Table 10.8 Continued

Moderate Fund	
ISHARES BARCLAYS SHORT TREASUR	24.67%
ISHARES BARCLAYS AGG BOND FUND	23.37%
ISHARES S&P 500 INDEX FUND	17.78%
ISHARES BARCLAYS TIPS BOND	13.47%
ISHARES MSCI EAFE INDEX FUND	8.93%
ISHARES IBOXX H/Y CORPORATE BOND	4.02%
ISHARES S&P MIDCAP 400	3.94%
ISHARES S&P SMALLCAP 600	2.08%
ISHARES MSCI EMERGING MKT IN	1.66%
CASHCOLLATERAL	0.37%
Total	100.29%

Source: iShares

Here in the UK competition within the lifecycle space has also intensified in recent years, with a number of fund managers launching asset allocation or lifecycle funds. A number of independent asset managers have launched multi-asset portfolios based around differing levels of risk, with the major players being TCF, 7IM and Evercore Pan. All of these niche managers have started to carve out a reputation for their own distinctive approach but the biggest player by far has to be the giant US-based group Vanguard which has launched a range of lifecycle funds under the brand LifeStrategy – this range of funds varies the equity allocations based on your risk level.

Low-risk, conservative investors would probably be tempted to go for the 20 percent equity fund while very adventurous types might opt for the 100 percent equity fund. Table 10.9 contains all the differing allocations between the funds but readers' attention might be drawn to the very last row in the table that shows the underlying total expense ratio (TER) of each of these asset allocation funds. Not one of these funds charges more than 40 basis points in underlying fund costs although Vanguard does make a small initial charge for buying into the fund.

Table 10.9 Vanguard LifeStrategy fund range by asset allocation

	\multicolumn{5}{c}{*LifeStrategy fund range: allocations to Vanguard funds*}
	20%	*40%*	*60%*	*80%*	*100%*
UK Government Bond	34.5	29.4	19.4	9.4	0
UK Investment Grade Bond	23.4	17.5	11.5	5.5	0
UK Inflation Linked Gilt	21.6	12.3	8.2	4.1	0
FTSE Developed World exc UK Equity	11.6	23.1	34.4	34.7	36.0
FTSE UK Equity	7.2	14.7	21.4	28.7	31.9
Emerging Markets Stocks	1.7	3.0	5.1	6.7	8.9
US Equity	0	0	0	5.9	12.5
FTSE Developed Europe exc UK	0	0	0	2.7	5.7
Pacific Ex Japan Stock	0	0	0	1.2	2.7
Japan Stocks	0	0	0	1.1	2.3
	100	100	100	100	100
TER	0.29	0.3	0.31	0.32	0.33

Source: Vanguard, end December 2011 (www.vanguard.co.uk)

The all-in-one fund

Yet another take on the idea that simplicity – and low cost – is the best way forward for sinning, overtrading, overconfident investors comes in the novel idea that you might only ever need to buy one fund that tracks all the major moves in the market. This idea received its biggest boost in 2008 with the launch of a new index by small Texas-based company Dorchester Fund Management. According to the firm its 'CPMKTS' index or The Capital Markets index 'views the capital markets on a broader basis and therefore includes stocks, bonds and money market instruments'.[33] So instead of just one big major index for bonds, another for money market funds and yet another for shares, you can invest in a fund that tracks all these major markets via one index.

According to Dorchester:

> *'The index was created over the past nine years, with more than four terabytes of compressed historical data – including government statistics and market changes – collected over the past three years. An additional 530 million pieces of new information are integrated into the CPMKTS database each day... The data is organized and processed using our patent-pending, rules-based methods, to formulate the index. This selection process removes the subjectivity associated with some other indices and more accurately reflects the capital markets environment. It is designed to track the weighted average of more than 1 million securities.'*[34]

This is clearly an ambitious project – it is one index that captures the vast majority of the investable (US) universe, with everything from inflation-linked Treasury (government) bonds through to dodgy tech companies. As its developer (a University of Chicago alumni) Warren Schmalenberger puts it, with one index you can 'cover the entire efficient frontier' of all asset classes. Schmalenberger started work on his all-encompassing index in 1995. 'For the next 3.5 years, I devoted myself to building a construct for a true capital markets index.' The end result is an index that is built around four separate computer systems in Chicago and Houston, processing a total of about 3.5 billion different pieces of market information crunched every day in a single index that covers the 2,000 largest US stocks, over 2,000 short-term fixed income instruments as well as 5,600 investment-grade bonds. Its entire market cap at the end of 2008 was a staggering $31 trillion and covered 80 percent of all the value of the US capital markets, although it did not include municipal bonds, junk bonds and convertibles.

Schmalenberger's hard work has found its way into index tracking land via a newish ETF from Claymore, the Claymore US-1 Capital Markets Index ETF (AMEX: UEM). Sitting beside this uber ETF are two variants based on sub-indices – the Claymore US Capital Markets Bond ETF (AMEX: UBD) and the Claymore US Capital Markets Micro-Term Fixed Income ETF (AMEX: ULQ). One is focusing on micro-term fixed income markets, the other is just the master index's bond side.

Dorchester's new index is an extreme variant on a rather more popular pursuit – to design a single exchange traded fund that captures most of the market. Yet again fund management group Vanguard has been most assiduous in this pursuit. One of its most successful ETFs is the Total US Stock Market fund, which tracks an index from MSCI called the US Broad Market index which is itself an aggregation of the MSCI US Large Cap 300, Mid Cap

450, Small Cap 1750 and Micro Cap indices. According to the index designers at MSCI, 'this index represents approximately 99.5 percent of the capitalization of the US equity market and includes approximately 3,900 companies'.[35] So when you buy the Vanguard ETF you are effectively buying the 'mind of the US market' at an extraordinarily low tracking charge of just 0.7 percent.

Using trackers as part of a wider investment process for advisers

By Julian Hince

> More and more Independent Financial Advisers (IFAs) are choosing to use index tracking funds, with many drawn to the low cost of products like ETFs and their relative simplicity. But how should advisers construct an investment approach for a client built around index tracking funds? In this short section, Julian Hince, formerly with iShares, outlines a simple process for advisers – and even if you are not an adviser this is essential reading. In this book we have already encountered many of the ideas discussed in this section, but it is worth understanding the thinking that goes into a financial adviser's investment planning process as well as some of the more regulatory inspired constraints.
>
> With the explosion of interest in, and supply of, Exchange Traded Products, (ETPs), in recent years, it is worth taking a step back both to understand the case for investing in them, and also how they can be used as ideal building blocks in implementing a wide range of asset allocation strategies on behalf of clients.

Although choice is good, too much choice can be both intimidating and off-putting, often with the net result being no change in behaviour, and hence no real increase in choice. In context, this means that the 3,649 ETPs currently available globally may not be being considered for use in clients' portfolios.[36]

In fact, those advisers looking to operate under an 'independent' banner post-2012 will, ironically, have no choice but to consider ETFs on behalf of clients. In the FSA's Retail Distribution Review (RDR) consultation paper 09/18, released in June 2009, point 2.9 under 'The range of products an independent adviser should consider', states:

> 'However, to the extent that ETFs can be a cheap and transparent way to invest in a particular market, even under our current whole of market requirement, these products should be considered when deciding which products are suitable for a retail client.'[37]

With opportunities to invest via ETFs in markets as broad as MSCI World, Citigroup Global Government Bond, to as narrow as FTSE UK Gilts 0-5 and S&P Global Clean Energy, it is easy to see where the regulator is coming from as never has an investment vehicle lent itself as well to precise portfolio construction as ETFs.

Passive investing explained

However, before individual fund selection can take place it is worth exploring the role and objective of passive investing as the former can only be achieved with an understanding of the latter.

Passive investing refers to a buy-and-hold investment approach whereby an investor invests in accordance with a pre-determined strategy that does not entail any forecasting such as stock picking or any use of market timing. The objective is to achieve 'market' return at a minimum cost and avoid the adverse consequences of failing to correctly anticipate the future valuation of stocks or markets.

The case for passive investing is supported by the zero-sum game theory, the efficient market theory and the capital asset pricing model. The 'zero-sum game' states that, on average, all funds together can only deliver the return of the market in the long term. The average portfolio will usually earn the market return because it is difficult for the average active investor to consistently outperform. This difficulty is partly attributable to the efficient market theory, which proposes that market prices of stocks reflect the knowledge and expectations of both return and risk of all investors. It asserts that any change in return and risk expectations are instantaneously reflected in an index via a change in the market capitalisation of stocks, thus making it impossible to consistently beat the market. The capital asset pricing model proposes that since current prices and hence market capitalisations are based on expectations of future returns and risk, cap-weighted indices represent the combination of securities offering the best expected return for a market, given its risk characteristics. Hence a fund indexed to 'the market' is the only fund investors need.

In order to achieve 'market' return, an investor tracks a capital-weighted index. A capital-weighted index is a group of securities, designed to mirror the performance of a broad market or segment of the market, with weights proportionate to their market value. Passive investing uses quantitative risk-control techniques that seek to replicate a capital weighted index's return with a minimal expected tracking error. Innovation in the industry, such as ETFs and indices, has facilitated a range of passive investment strategies which use direct investment, index mutual funds, index-based ETFs or derivatives to achieve market return.

The asset allocation decision

An abundance of academic work has examined how much of the return and risk of a portfolio is driven by the long-term asset allocation. Three academics, Brinson, Hood and Beebower, who studied the performance of 91 large US pension plans between 1974 and 1983, analysed the impact of key decisions made by investment managers regarding long-term asset allocation (i.e. 60 percent in equities, 40 percent in bonds), stock picking and short-term tactical changes to the asset mix. The results concluded that 90 percent of return and risk in a given fund was determined by the long-term asset mix, with both stock picking and short-term tactical changes having a negligible impact.[38]

This research has been updated by well-respected academic researchers. For example, Roger Ibbotson, a Yale finance professor and chairman of Ibbotson Associates, and Paul Kaplan, chief economist at Ibbotson Associates, who examined pension return, also concluded that on average asset allocation explained more than 90 percent of the quarterly variation in a given portfolio's returns. They also considered how much of the difference between funds could be attributed to asset allocation policy. By comparing funds that were invested passively but with different asset allocations, they determined that 40 percent of all the inter-fund variation in performance was due to asset allocation.[39] In summary, then, based on the evidence of academic research, asset allocation is the unquestionable driver of portfolio performance supporting the case for the avoidance of active stock picking.

Passive and active investing used in combination

The rationale for investment across multiple asset classes is supported by the modern portfolio theory. This theory, which was developed by Professor Harry Markowitz,[40] states that overall portfolio risk is reduced and higher risk-adjusted return is attainable by allocating a portfolio's assets across imperfectly correlated assets classes or, in other words, assets which do not move in tandem with each other. Diversifying across a greater number of uncorrelated asset classes can further reduce volatility and protect against significant losses without necessarily having a negative impact on overall return. Combinations of assets that maximise the expected return for each level of risk can be selected. These portfolios are 'efficient' as it is not possible to achieve a higher expected return without taking on additional risk. The efficient frontier indicates the optimal mix of asset classes.

To achieve this optimal mix of assets, Burton Malkiel, author of *A Random Walk Down Wall Street*, recommended that investors take a core-satellite approach to investing. Both active and passive investing can be used in combination to construct core-satellite portfolios, where more expensive active strategies can complement and enhance passively managed market exposure. The core of index funds provides diversification, low volatility and allows efficient switching between classes as markets evolve, while the satellite portfolios consist of a range of uncorrelated active investments. The satellite portfolio, which Malkiel believes could constitute up to 20 percent of total assets, should be invested in low-cost expert managers focused on less efficient markets where there may be more opportunity to earn excess return and for which index investments do not exist. Although indexing has historically outperformed active management (see above), there are some active managers who have consistently outperformed in certain markets. A core-satellite approach may help to increase a portfolio's expected return while keeping the risk constant. This would bring the portfolio closer to the efficient frontier thereby attaining the best possible return for a particular risk tolerance. A sample core-satellite portfolio is shown in Figure 10.4.

Figure 10.4 Sample core-satellite portfolio

- S&P 500 index fund: 25.00%
- Lehman aggregate bond fund: 37.50%
- Actively managed high-yield bond fund: 12.50%
- Actively managed biotechnology fund: 12.50%
- Actively managed commodities fund: 12.50%
- (12.50%)

Further benefits of passive investing

Diversification across asset classes can reduce risk but can also reduce risk within asset classes. Stock specific risk is the risk inherent in investing in individual companies such as the management strategy or the capital structure. Index funds are generally more diversified than actively managed funds (except for index funds that track a small niche market or sector).The broad range of securities reduces the stock specific risk associated with specific stocks, removing a component of return volatility. Actively managed funds, on the other hand, tend to hold fewer securities which can lead to greater volatility in returns.

An index fund maintains its style consistency by tracking the characteristics of the index. An active manager may have a broad mandate which can allow the fund to change from a style perspective. For example, an active manager may change the distribution of assets across the market capitalisation spectrum in line with a short-term investment view. This can lead to style 'drift' which can also result in additional volatility.

The potential for greater tax efficiency is a feature more commonly associated with indexing than with active portfolio management. An index fund's distribution of capital gains is lower than an active fund, as selling only occurs when the composition of the index changes. This can enhance return as the majority of the investment compounds over time. ETFs use a strategy known as 'redemption in kind', a tax-efficient tool whereby the ETF manager can redeem ETF shares 'in kind' when necessary (i.e. when an investor sells). It permits the manager to deliver stocks rather than cash to meet redemptions and avoid realisation by the fund of capital gains on transactions.

A study done by John Shoven[41] compared the after-tax returns on one of the largest ETFs, the SPDR fund that holds the stocks in the Standard & Poor's 500 index, with the after-tax returns on large index funds. It was found that the after-tax returns differed by very little for the two types of funds. Results suggest that, going forward, ETFs that hold broad and diversified baskets of equity securities are likely to generate returns and tax burdens that are similar to those on low-cost equity index funds.

Implementation

It is with the growing understanding of the importance of asset allocation that ETFs lend themselves so well as implementation tools. For example, portfolio construction strategies that can be executed through the use of ETFs are:

- *Broad diversification* – you can get exposure to a variety of markets quickly and easily.

- *Core-satellite approach* – you can use them to build core holdings in your portfolio or 'satellite' exposure to certain areas.
- *Tactical short-term investing* – ETFs' ability to trade whenever you want enables you to take advantage of market movements.

Before any of the above strategies are implemented there are a number of financial planning considerations to be covered.

Financial planning

The introduction of the RDR is likely to act as a catalyst in fuelling the growth of ETFs: it is also a truism that ETFs are currently one of the only truly RDR compliant investment products. With no product commission payable, ETF client costs have always been, and will continue to be, agreed between adviser and client and this is a core tenet of the RDR.

Income and growth

With the search and demand for income showing no signs of slowing, it is important that financial planners understand the income treatment of and taxation status applied to ETFs. Whether income is distributed or forms part of a total return strategy depends largely on the ETF structure. Typically, physical ETFs can distribute income, although accumulation options are now available and due to the low-cost nature of ETFs, the client receives a higher percentage of the net income payable.

As swap ETF structures are total return (sometimes capital only) income, payments are therefore not distributed. This is a consideration worth noting depending on a client's circumstances, requirements and individual tax status.

Tax matters

Due to the offshore domicile status of ETFs, investors and their advisers need to be aware of the tax status of their chosen ETF. In December 2009, HMRC introduced the reporting fund regime for all offshore funds with UK investors. Replacing the UK distributor status regime, the conversion meant all ETFs domiciled outside the UK would have to apply for Reporting Fund Status (RFS) in order to be eligible for capital gains rather than income tax. For instance, this meant that funds under the UK distributor status regime were not able to offer accumulating shares; as the name suggests, at least 85 percent of the funds' income had to be distributed. Under the RFS this is no longer the case and accumulating share classes are now being offered in some cases alongside income producing shares.

There is a transitional period that stretches into 2012 for UK distributor funds to apply for RFS. Finally, on the whole most ETFs qualify as approved ISA and SIPP investment vehicles, although you must verify this.

Protection

As a result of their offshore domicile status, ETFs are not covered by the Financial Services Compensation Scheme (FSCS). A form of protection is provided, however, for those funds that apply/qualify, via UCITS legislation. This not only limits the counterparty risk the fund can be exposed to, to a maximum of 10 percent of the fund's assets, but also in that an appointed custodian will hold the fund's assets in segregated liability accounts, just as they do for other mutual funds such as OEICs and ICVCs.

How are ETFs being used?

It is difficult to get a completely accurate picture of how ETFs are currently being used by financial planners, but from the limited data that exist (via wrap platforms), it is clear that ETFs are being used mainly as core, buy and hold investments within client portfolios.

Excluding the inverse and leveraged exposures (not suitable for the retail market) the limited data correspond closely to that of the European usage of ETFs by exposure type as at end of February 2011 (see Table 10.10).

Table 10.10 Use of EFTs by exposure type (as at end February 2011)

Exposure	%
Fixed income	19
Country exposure Europe – equity	15.6
Emerging markets – equity	12.5
Regional exposure eurozone – equity	11.3
Commodities	9.3
Country exposure US – equity	6.9
International – equity	6.3
Regional exposure Europe – equity	4.7
European sector exposure – equity	4.2

Table 10.10 Continued

Exposure	%
Global exposure – equity	4.1
Style – equity	2.2
Inverse	0.9
Eurozone sector exposure – equity	0.9
Alternative	0.7
Leveraged inverse	0.6
Leveraged	0.5
Currency	0.1

Source: BlackRock iShares monthly research report, February 2011.

It could therefore be argued that investors are using ETFs in place of traditional active funds to help reduce the overall cost of investing to the client, reduce volatility and reduce the risk of the absence of alpha.

Access

When buying or selling ETFs, investors and their advisers can either:

- deal via an open architecture wrap platform; or
- via a brokerage service (e.g. Barclays Stockbrokers).

When transacting through a wrap it is important to understand how and when the trades are placed, and also the costs involved.

While it is true that a key differentiator of ETFs when compared to daily priced mutual funds is that they offer real time pricing/trading, in reality this is a function rarely required by financial planners operating in an advisory capacity.

Questions to ask a wrap provider are:

- Do you 'real time' price and trade?
- Do you aggregate trades and deal once a day?
- What are the ETF trading and platform costs?

Why are these points important? The simple answer is cost, as wrap providers levy a dealing charge, typically between £10 and £12, but this can be higher. For a regular saver, small lump sum or investment top-up, this additional cost may prove uneconomical, negating the lower cost advantage of investing in the ETF in the first place.

Alternatively, and an increasingly popular option, is that of daily aggregated dealing. That is, all trades for the same ETF are pooled, treated as one transaction and dealt at a specified time once a day. For example, if 100 trades in xyz ETF are traded together at a charge of £10 then the net cost per client is only £0.10.

Access to ETFs for financial planners is good, and will continue to improve as fund supermarkets adapt their propositions ahead of the RDR.

Summary

Demand, interest and use of passive investment funds by financial planners and advisers is on the increase. In the past 10 years, according to the Investment Management Association (IMA), passive assets have grown at an annual rate of 10 percent compared with a 6 percent growth of the overall assets of the top 500 asset managers.

The IMA has reported record net retail sales of tracker funds which have reached a 10-year high, with a total of £1.2 billion sold in 2010, almost trebling sales in 2009. Funds under management in trackers amounted to £33.5 billion at the end of 2010, marking a 20 percent increase on 2009. These figures do not include the UK sales of ETPs where assets increased 49.0 percent in 2010 to $93.4 billion, and the number of ETPs increased by 77.5 percent over the same period.[42]

Despite this growth, many industry figures believe the growth in passive funds is being held back because they do not pay commission, unlike actively managed funds. Commission payments on advised sales are due to be banned from the end of 2012 in the wake of the RDR.

In the US, according to State Street (the world's second-largest ETF provider), the single biggest driver of ETF sales through financial intermediaries has been the huge shift to fee-based advice. If this is the case then it is possible we could experience an increase in passive assets under management of approximately £105.47 billion, from the current £27.75 billion, which would represent 24 percent of the £554.9 billion of assets under management, according to the IMA.[43] Note these figures exclude ETPs which are a rapidly growing investment vehicle.

11

The master portfolios

The rapid development of ETFs ready made for a diversified portfolio – detailed in the last chapter – is an almost exclusively American phenomenon. The mainstream investment industry in the UK by contrast is built around trying to get you to buy the latest 'best idea', be it a fund, an investment strategy or a new business concept that can be floated on the stock market. The idea that investors might crave a one-size-fits-all portfolio approach – with low costs to boot – has so far largely translated itself into expensive and largely failing absolute returns funds or slightly more successful balanced/managed equity funds that might, if you are lucky, include some form of bond exposure. It seems that here in the UK, although the idea of diversification has started to take root – more and more fund managers are offering diversified, actively managed multi-asset funds – no one has yet launched a cheap one-size-fits-all tracker portfolio available to the mass market.

This rather sorry state of affairs leaves you with a rather ambitious DIY project: build your own multi-asset index fund portfolio. The obvious answer to this conundrum is to consult a professional adviser – with luck they will have enough knowledge of the market and some understanding of the academic debates about sensible portfolio construction to develop a risk-adjusted personal approach. Sadly, most private investors are not quite so lucky – many independent financial advisers (IFAs) (although not all) are happier dealing with mainstream insurance-based financial products and farm out their asset-allocation analysis (the term used in the trade to describe portfolio construction) to bigger firms that rely on black-box software systems to produce 'model portfolios'. These portfolios may well do the job, but the principles behind them are rarely spelled out and openly debated.

Which is where this last chapter comes in – working with *Investors Chronicle* magazine, we have developed a series of master portfolios which you can easily construct using ETFs and tracker index funds. These simple, easy-to-understand portfolios (first published in the magazine at the beginning of 2009) are built around a set of open principles – some of them uncontroversial, others highly debatable, but all detailed and discussed in detail. Later on in this chapter we will also look at a set of very simple 'lazy' portfolios that can also be built. These model portfolios are exactly what they say they are, only models, and need to be adapted to suit your own principles and risk tolerance. If you accept that this 'model'-based approach has some validity, it is worth detailing some of the portfolio principles involved in building them.

It is asset class investing – the portfolios are based on asset classes and key markets, not individual shares or managers. This is an absolutely crucial first principle. Investors become obsessed by star managers, sexy sectors or cheap shares. They fixate very early on on identifying a hot share that might double, or a star manager who has a great winning streak. There is some validity to both exercises – there are good managers and some individual shares can make a great investment – but investors need to refocus much, if not most, of their attention on working out the broad asset classes and markets they want to be invested in. Do they want to focus exclusively on UK-based equities, probably with a blue-chip bias – the default position for most UK equity investors? Or do they want some foreign exposure or a small investment in bonds? The challenge is to work out the broad categories that will achieve your diversified return, not the much riskier reliance on individual fund managers or particular stocks and shares.

The portfolios are simple – they never comprise more than 15 and never fewer than three asset classes or markets. Remember Paul Merriman's analysis of what constitutes the optimum number of categories for true diversification? The consensus seems to be that at least three or four different broad asset classes is a minimum, with more asset classes generally regarded as a good thing. But there is also a sensible upper limit – you could end up having literally dozens of different asset classes, making your life virtually impossible as a result of all the portfolio monitoring and constant rejigging. For these *Investors Chronicle* model portfolios we have tried to cap the number of different asset classes at 15.

In an ideal world you would make the portfolios easy to operate on a day-to-day basis using ETFs. In the *Investors Chronicle* articles accompanying these portfolios we have been careful not to spell out any particular funds or managers – in this book we will be far more frank on whether an active fund manager or an ETF is a better idea. We would not entirely rule out actively managed funds in specialist sectors – private equity or emerging markets, for instance – but for very developed markets we would suggest buying the asset class exposure cheaply and efficiently through an index fund of some sort. The decision about which index to buy into is entirely dependent on the choice available, the expenses charged, the tracking error and the financial strength of the company running the fund.

The portfolios are based on a risk profile and/or stage in a lifecycle, i.e. low to high risk. There are five portfolios in all and they have been constructed using a very simple gradient, starting with low risk and ending up at global growth for equity investors. You could swap the risk-based titles around and use a target date approach and you would have the same portfolios. Lower risk are more likely to be useful for older investors keen to preserve capital while the higher risk portfolios are more likely to appeal to younger investors determined to shoot the lights out with potential rewards achieved through higher potential risk.

They are not optimised. Modern portfolio theory, and its application within large fund management firms and big investment banks, has spawned an alarmingly complex netherworld of fiendishly complex, dynamically allocated, multi-asset portfolios built by very clever people willing and able to crunch the data until it confesses. Every once in a while, a portfolio manager comes up with an alarmingly good mix of assets that could produce future bumper returns. This approach, usually involving some form of clever black-box analytics, is called the optimised approach and is great for building portfolios that are finely calibrated to balance risk and reward. Sadly, it is a far from ideal approach for ordinary private investors, who will probably have no idea what is going on inside the black-box quantitative model.

Our approach is to try to build something that is a 'best fit', is simple and can be easily understood. We have not built the mix of assets in each portfolio using backtesting; rather the starting point for this analysis was to analyse dozens of notional and actual portfolios published from around the world, including those from big British financial advisory firms, the *Financial Times's* own survey of wealth advisers plus academic analysis of big pension funds. In detail, this process involved the following steps:

1 The *Investors Chronicle* analysed lifecycle and glidepath studies as well as adviser-based, multi-asset class portfolios.
2 We analysed the mix of assets based on the criteria specified below and looked for average variables as well as median (most common) compositions.

3 We then applied the *Investors Chronicle's* own asset-allocation principles to alter the mix – detailed in the box below.
4 Finally, we looked at historic performance to understand past returns – but no alteration was made to the portfolio composition.

Armed with the aggregate data derived from this vast range of model portfolios, the *Investors Chronicle* then structured the actual building of each portfolio by a process of questions which produced trade-offs or ratios. This trade-off process consisted of a number of key questions:

- The first big question is exactly which risk profile you subscribe to – this suggests one of our five core portfolios.
- Based on this answer we then structure the first *layer* of components based on a trade-off between bonds and equities and what we call alternative assets, i.e. foreign exchange funds (forex), hedge funds, commodities. This established an overall balance between three very broad investment categories.
- We then focus on the equity index component of that three-fold structure and distinguish between *mainstream equities* (which is all developed and emerging markets stocks) and what we like to call '*equities – the rest*' which we define as real estate investment trusts (REITs), utilities and infrastructure funds. This latter group consists of actual equities – quoted on major exchanges – but they are tracking more unconventional markets.
- Within the first *mainstream equity* we then differentiate based on region, looking at the ratio between UK holdings and international holdings expressed as a ratio.
- Looking at the UK holdings, we then distinguish between a bias to the FTSE All Share index (the main UK index) or whether we differentiate markets based on the size of the company, i.e. small v mid v large cap.
- Within the international equities component we distinguish between developed world and emerging markets.
- After this equities-based layer we then move on to *bonds*. Within bonds we distinguish between government *all* – both index linked and conventional – and corporate bonds (only ever sterling based).
- Within government bonds we differentiate between conventional and index-linked gilts or government bonds.
- We finally move to the major category of investments called alternative assets and distinguish two separate investment niches, namely *commodities*, broadly defined using the Dow Jones AIG index (now owned by UBS), and what we call *other* alternative assets, such as hedge funds and forex.

This process – a series of questions which involves a trade-off that results in a ratio of different assets – is summarised in the box below.

The trade-offs or ratios

> Bonds vs equities vs Alt Assets
> Equities: Mainstream vs Rest ratio
> Equities: UK vs International ratio
> Int Equity: Dev vs EM
> UK Equity: ALL vs Size bias
> Bonds: Corps vs Govt
> Gilts: Conv vs Index L
> Alt Assets: Commodit vs Other Alts

Clearly this process is far from being neutral or judgement free. It is based on some key asset allocation principles. We have broken down these principles into two distinct categories – the blindingly obvious motherhood and apple pie observations followed by the more debatable loaded principles.

First, though, those motherhood and apple pie concepts. These are fairly widely agreed ideas that should not spark too much debate. The most obvious example is that all portfolios are a trade-off of risk and return. Essential to this is the concept of the glidepath over time (when it comes to pensions) where the balance between risky assets and less risky assets changes over time. Our overall view is that the better risky assets are equities rather than bonds, although it is also true to say that over certain periods of time bonds can actually produce higher returns. Nevertheless, it is still largely true that equities are higher-return, riskier assets than bonds, which by contrast are less risky but tend over the very long term to produce lower returns.

The next key concept (familiar from previous chapters) is that based on the mountain of academic evidence (Ibbotson *et al.*) a diversified portfolio is better than an undiversified portfolio, and that optimal diversification is probably achieved with a minimum of five to six asset classes. Crucially, the data also suggests that developed world markets are increasingly correlated and that no great advantage is gained most of the time by choosing to diversify within developed world markets, unless there is a convincing rationale that says otherwise, i.e. to target small caps or value stocks based on portfolio assumptions. This means that wherever possible it is probably best to look for the broadest index that captures developed markets, i.e. MSCI World for the developed world and FTSE All Share for the UK.

Last but by no means least, international diversification is crucial. Most UK investors are too focused on purely UK-based stocks and shares and funds. The reality of global capital markets suggests that investors seriously consider the importance of international diversification, particularly with reference to emerging and frontier markets.

Not many investors or analysts would disagree with most of these conclusions, but the next set of arguments is much more contentious. Below, we have listed our top ten loaded principles – a great many analysts would probably radically disagree with each and every one of them, but these principles were outlined in the *Investors Chronicle* articles which kicked off this series. You may choose to disagree with them yourself, but if you do accept the logic, we have detailed the inevitable investment idea that results from this principle, i.e. an overweight position in an asset class or market or an underweight position (less than the market would suggest).

1 Emerging markets will continue to power ahead and investors should have some bias if they are growth orientated. OVERWEIGHT emerging markets for mid- and high-risk portfolios.

2 Although inflation will be a short-term issue, there are heightened risks over the very long term. UNDERWEIGHT index-linked gilts near-term portfolios OVERWEIGHT over a longer time horizon.

3 Be cautious towards commodities. They are too volatile and frankly underanalysed in portfolio terms. UNDERWEIGHT commodities for mid to low risk.

4 There is too much UK equity bias among British investors and not enough developed world focus, i.e. not great enough understanding of the importance of indices like the MSCI World Index. OVERWEIGHT international developed equity markets for long-term or horizon portfolios.

5 Be very cautious when examining corporate bonds in the near term. They are much riskier than many investors think. UNDERWEIGHT all portfolios.

6 We generally like the investment space we have called equities rest – utilities, infrastructure and REITs. OVERWEIGHT equities rest for most portfolios.

7 Fundamental indexation is an interesting idea but for the vast majority of investors it is still a little risky if they do not fully understand what is actually involved with the stock-selection process. UNDERWEIGHT fundamental index for all but the adventurous portfolio.

8 Although there is a strong argument for equity income bias within developed world equities, we have chosen not to favour this over a straight UK FTSE All bias. UNDERWEIGHT UK equity income.

9. Within bonds it is probably not that good an idea to seek international diversification within either government or corporate themes. This view is largely based on accessibility – it is very difficult to find funds that track global bonds – and exchange rate risk, although more sophisticated investors might want to explore this as an option as new global bond ETFs launch. No international bond diversification currently.

10. Last but by no means least, none of these portfolios has any allocation for cash – these are invested portfolios, not portfolios based on market timing. Again this is a thorny issue, sure to generate much disagreement, but the question of market timing is crucial here. Our view is that for most investors, market timing is impossible to get right, so investors should not attempt it unless they work with a well-thought-through strategic valuation-based system or using a signal like the 200-day moving average as a buy/sell signal. Market timing can and does work for some investors – it requires the use of relatively sophisticated ideas, which we explored in the last chapter.

With these asset-allocation principles explained, let us understand how they translate into an actual portfolio. We will look at the most adventurous master portfolio of all, the Global Growth Portfolio, which is aimed at equity investors looking for some racy returns built around investing globally.

1 The Global Growth Portfolio

Target date:		2045
Asset class	*Target index*	
Devel Equity: UK (FTSE 100)	FTSE 100	9
Devel Equity: UK (FTSE ALL)	FTSE ALL	0
Devel Equity: World exc UK	MSCI WORLD exc UK	27
Devel Equity: Value Stocks UK	FTSE Div Plus or equity income fund	0
Devel Equity: Value Stocks Global	DJ Global Select Divid	0
Devel Equity: Mid Caps	FTSE 250	4.5
Devel Equity: Small Cap	FTSE Small Cap	4.5
Emerging Markets	MSCI EM	27
Global Infrastructure and Utilities	FTSE Util/S&P Glob Infra	9
REITS	EPRA/NAREIT Global	9

Asset class	Target index	
Corporate Bonds: Sterling	iBoxx Sterling Corporates	0
Government Bonds: Conventional	FTSE All Stocks Gilt	0
Government Bonds: Index Linked	Barclays UK Index Linked	0
Alts: Commodities	DJ-AIG Composite	6.5
Other Alts	Credit Suisse Tremont Hedge	3.5
Total		100

As the title says, this is very much a global equities-based portfolio, with a large percentage of its assets invested abroad, with nine different asset classes in all. Is it riskier than our low-risk portfolio for example? Absolutely, yes, but in the past this extra risk from investing in global equities would have produced extra returns for those willing to hold over the very long term and ride out any volatility. It boasts 9 percent in the UK large-cap market – via a FTSE 100 tracker – plus another 4.5 percent in mid caps and small caps. You will also see a chunky 27 percent in a global developed markets index – the entire world's leading markets excluding the UK – so that we can capture the big European, US and Japanese markets. The other big idea is the emerging markets investment space which comprises another 27 percent of assets. This is an unashamedly risky category that involves investing in countries like Brazil, Russia, India and China (collectively known as the BRIC countries) as well as the Gulf states and places like Vietnam.

Finally, you will see two groups of what are called alternative assets. The first is the 'equity rest', or the rest of the equity class outside mainstream companies. This rather strange moniker is meant to apply to things like real estate investment trusts in the commercial property sector and utilities and infrastructure companies. We have separated these off from core equity assets because they behave in a slightly different way, and in the case of utilities at least are viewed as slightly less risky.

The other big group of alternatives comprises a 6.5 percent investment in a commodity index fund, broadly defined into one big index (the Dow Jones AIG composite index) and not broken down into individual commodities, plus a small 3.5 percent investment in hedge funds.

Below you will see all these biases and weightings broken down into a simple form, with the actual trade-off percentages between different assets in the section below.

Portfolio name: GLOBAL GROWTH

Lifecycle target date: 2040 (probably in their thirties with 30 years or less to retirement)

Global equity bias

No bonds at all

OVERWEIGHT Emerging Markets

International bias vs UK

OVERWEIGHT EQUITIES REST, i.e. equities, infrastructure and REITs

BIAS towards size bias within equities, i.e. focus on small caps – Size Bias in UK

	Glob Grwth
Bonds vs equities vs Alt Assets	90/10
Equities : Mainstream vs Rest ratio	1:4
Equities : UK vs International ratio	1:3
Int Equity : Dev vs EM	1:1 Size Bias SC in UK
UK Equity : ALL vs Size bias	No Bonds
Bonds : Govt vs Corp	
Gilts : Conv vs Index L	No Bonds
Alt Assets : Commodit vs Other Alts	2:1
Bonds : Int vs UK	No Bonds
Equities : Value Bias	No

More detailed look at assumptions for the Global Growth Portfolio

GLOBAL GROWTH ANALYSIS

1. 90% equities, 10% alternative assets

Equities	90%
Alt assets	10%

2. Within Alt assets use 2:1 commodities over other assets

Commodities

Others

3. Within equities		
Mainstream	80%	
The Rest	20%	including REITs and Infrastructure
of which : REITS	50%	
Utilities and Infra	50%	
4. Within mainstream equities		
UK	25%	
International	75%	
5. Within international		
Emerging Markets	50%	
Global Developed	50%	
6. Within UK		
FTSE 100	50%	
FTSE 250	25%	
FTSE Small Cap	25%	

One final point: this portfolio is above all else a strongly equity-biased one and there are absolutely no bonds. If an investor has chosen this approach they are probably looking exclusively for higher-risk, higher-potential returns via equities and not for the safer and potentially boring qualities on offer from bonds.

James Norton's view on the Global Growth Portfolio

> 'It is a matter of buying into global capitalism and letting the markets do the work. Sit back and watch (not too often) and consider occasional rebalancing to realign the asset allocation. Anyone with a spare five minutes to check the websites of a few of the main providers of index funds could put this portfolio together. Some of my preferred funds would be the Lyxor FTSE 100 and 250 funds, the DBX Emerging Markets fund and iShares Infrastructure and REITs funds. For global developed market exposure I would consider either the iShares or Lyxor fund.'

2 The Low Risk Portfolio

This next portfolio is a complete contrast to its cosmopolitan sibling. It avoids much riskier equity-based assets, focusing instead on developed world equities, involving markets such as the FTSE All Share Index (which represents getting on for 98 percent of the entire market capitalisation of the London Stock Exchange) or the much broader global benchmark index (again easily tracked by any number of funds and ETFs), the MSCI World excluding UK index. The beauty of a huge, global composite index like the MSCI World index is that it captures the vast majority of the total developed world large-cap companies, including those in the US and Japanese markets.

Target date:		2020
		Low
Devel Equity: UK (FTSE 100)	FTSE 100	0
Devel Equity: UK (FTSE ALL)	FTSE ALL	16
Devel Equity: World exc UK	MSCI WORLD exc Uk	8
Devel Equity: Value Stocks UK	FTSE Div Plus or equity income fund	0
Devel Equity: Value Stocks Global	DJ Global Select Divid	0
Devel Equity: Mid Caps	FTSE 250	0
Devel Equity: Small Cap	FTSE Small Cap	0
Emerging Markets	MSCI EM	0
Global Infrastructure and Utilities	FTSE Util/S&P Glob Infra	5
REITS	EPRA/NAREIT Global	4.5
Corporate Bonds: Sterling	iBoxx Sterlign Corporates	5
Government Bonds: Conventional	FTSE All Stocks Gilt	30
Government Bonds: Index Linked	Barclays UK Index Linked	25
Alts: Commodities	DJ-AIG Composite	4
Other Alts	Credit Suisse Tremont Hedge	2.5
Total		100

Portfolio name: LOW RISK

Lifecycle target date: 2020 (closing in on retirement, probably in their fifties)

Bond bias

Capital preservation

UK FTSE All Bias – avoid unnecessary currency risk from international diversification

Bias towards equity rest, i.e. utilities and infrastructure

Reliability of returns from government bonds versus heightened risk from corporate bonds

Some income

	Low
Bonds vs equities vis Alt Assets	60/33.5/6.5
Equities: Mainstream vs Rest ratio	72/28
Equities: UK vs Global Developeds ratio	66/33
Int Equity: Dev vs EM	ALL DEV, NO EM
UK Equity: ALL vs Size bias	FTSE ALL only
Bonds: Corps vs Govt	10/90
Gilts: Conv vs Index L	60/40
Alt Assets: Commodit vs Other Alts	66/33
Bonds: Int vs UK	UK only
Equities: Value Bias	No
Other alts (exc commodities) as %	2.5

What this portfolio avoids is any investment in emerging markets – these are much riskier than developed world markets, although potentially much more rewarding. We considered this deliberate omission very carefully and some experts may argue that emerging markets (EM) do have some small place even in low-risk portfolios (maybe 2–5 percent) to spruce up potential returns, but recent evidence suggests that the risk of really big drawdowns (more than 50–60 percent losses in one year) is just too great.

Stepping back from the equities component, this portfolio is heavily biased towards more cautious bonds, and in particular government bonds, although many experts would challenge our heavy bias against corporate bonds. At the time of writing – late 2011 – many analysts reckon that corporate bonds are a great investment, especially with the most conservative companies called investment grade. This may be true, but there is no denying that corporate bonds are much more vulnerable when equity markets are distressed; in fact, the main reason that corporate bonds may be such good value in 2011 is partly because they have fallen so much in the collapses of 2008 as equities have sold off. Investors need to remember that the outfits paying the coupons on these bonds are listed, quoted companies with ordinary shares and if the market thinks these companies will go bust, it will also punish the corporate bonds. The correlation (positive and above 0.4) between corporate bonds and equities is just too high for cautious investors, although the yields on offer are, not unnaturally given the higher risk, much higher. If you want to secure a higher income then you might want to consider increasing your corporate bond holding from 5 percent to maybe 10 percent or even 15 percent, but only at investment-grade level of risk.

Within government bonds or gilts the holdings are weighted towards what are called conventional gilts, as opposed to index-linked gilts that protect investors against inflation. If you think that inflation over the very long term of more than 2–3 percent per annum is a real likelihood, you might want to consider buying more index-linked gilts (also called linkers). These portfolios are not meant as exercises in market timing – they are meant for long-term buy-and-hold investors – although if inflation was to shoot up, the composition of the portfolios might well be altered in the *Investors Chronicle* regular updates. One last point on bonds: as we have already noted, sophisticated investors may want to consider some exposure to global gilts or bonds partly to protect sterling-based assets against any sudden FX changes, but there are very few ETFs that offer this exposure – if you can find such a fund or ETF, you might consider a 60 percent UK bias and 40 percent in global gilts or bonds overall.

Last but by no means least, you may notice that category called alternative assets – these could be everything from forex and hedge funds through to commodities. We have included some commodity exposure, through the DJ AIG composite index, partly because over the long term commodities are fairly uncorrelated with equities and bonds (they move in different ways at different times) and partly because commodities are usually a good store of value in inflationary times. Some hedge fund exposure (very small at 2.5 percent) has also been included, mainly because the general commitment to what are called absolute returns in the sector is a valuable exercise for cautious investors. It is worth noting that most hedge fund indices have fallen sharply over the last year, but not by as much as most equity and commodity indices. The key is to try lots of different assets in moderation.

Stephen Barber's take on the Low Risk Portfolio

'Low risk does not mean "no risk". Investors who are prepared to accept some risk in their portfolios can expect longer-term returns to be better than deposits or cash-based products. This portfolio reflects the trade-off between accepting sufficient risk to deliver desired returns but not so much that low-risk investors will have trouble sleeping at night. When thinking about this sort of strategy, our approach should be one of planning for the longer term, riding out short-term volatility and perhaps drip-feeding funds into the market to take advantage of pound/cost averaging.

This low-risk portfolio has been built to achieve relatively safe, dependable returns and that leads to a bias towards capital protection. Here it hits the nail firmly on the head by being overweight in fixed interest, primarily government bonds. And when selecting equities, it does so from the more reliable sectors such as the defensive utilities and dependable infrastructure. This sector, in particular, offers relatively safe and consistent returns from both capital and income over the longer term as $20 trillion is spent on building roads, rail, hospitals and the like around the world over the next decade. This being said, the portfolio is careful to select assets which avoid the volatility associated with currency risk. So the objective is to minimise the potential downside while seeking good capital growth and yield. All portfolios should be diversified as this is a prime method of managing risk, but it also means that a list can have a spread of asset classes, some of which can be more adventurous. Such portfolios might also consider gaining equity exposure from using capital-protected products which give exposure to market growth but preserve capital or even cautious managed funds where fund managers select the best lower-risk multi-asset returns by mixing bonds, equities, commodities and the like.'

3 The Income Portfolio

The first decade of the twenty-first century was not very kind to income investors. Those who chose to focus on equities via their dividend payouts had an awful few years around 2007 and 2008 as the global stock markets wilted, virtually all the major UK banks stopped paying dividends and the recession cut into companies' ability to afford to make dividend payouts.

Lifecycle target date for retirement:		2010
INVESTMENT SPACE	INDEX	Income
Devel Equity: UK (FTSE 100)	FTSE 100	0
Devel Equity: UK (FTSE ALL)	FTSE ALL	5
Devel Equity: World exc UK	MSCI WORLD exc Uk	2
Devel Equity: Value Stocks UK	FTSE Div Plus or equity income fund	6.5
Devel Equity: Value Stocks Global	DJ Global Select Divid	6
Devel Equity: Mid Caps	FTSE 250	0
Devel Equity: Small Cap	FTSE Small Cap	0
Emerging Markets	MSCI EM	0
Global Infrastructure and Utilities	FTSE Util/S&P Glob Infra	12.5
REITS	EPRA/NAREIT Global	3

Corporate Bonds: Sterling	iBoxx Sterling Corporates	5
Government Bonds: Conventional	FTSE All Stocks Gilt	40
Government Bonds: Index Linked	Barclays UK Index Linked	20
Alts : Commodities	DJ-AIG Composite	0
Other Alts	Credit Suisse Tremont Hedge	0
Total		100

Portfolio name: INCOME

Lifecycle target date: 2010 (close to retirement)

Could also be used for those already in retirement

Income and bond bias

Capital preservation

UK bias – avoid unnecessary currency risk

Equity income and value bias to generate income with blue chip focus

Reliability of returns from government bonds versus heightened risk from corporate bonds

	Income
Bonds vs equities vis Alt Assets	65/35
Equities: Mainstream vs Rest ratio	60/40
Equities: UK vs Global Developeds ratio	50/50
Int Equity: Dev vs EM	ALL DEV/NO EM
UK Equity: ALL vs Size bias	FTSE ALL only
Bonds: Corps vs Govt	10/90
Gilts: Conv vs Index L	66/33
Alt Assets: Commodit vs Other Alts	Only commod
Bonds: Int vs UK	UK only
Equities: Value Bias	yes
Other alts (exc commodities) as %	0%

For bond investors those terrible few years were a great deal less choppy – nominal capital prices shot up as investors fled risk – but yields crashed, especially as inflation plummeted, forcing radical cuts in interest rates. If you had to depend on safe government bonds or gilts as a source of income, your woes would have increased in almost every month of 2008 and 2009.

The flat yield on the benchmark FTSE All Stocks Gilts index, for instance, was still paying around 4.3 percent in the middle of 2009, but that was only something called a flat yield – the actual payout versus the current index level. If a different measure was used, namely the 'gross yield to redemption' – the income payout as a percentage of the value of the gilts on redemption, i.e. what you will get back when the gilt is redeemed – that return on UK gilts dropped to 2.95 percent. For many US Treasury bills' short-term yields, the equivalent yields collapsed below 1 percent on a redemption basis, while in the UK inflation-linked gilts (their payout is linked to inflation rates) were paying out just over 1 percent.

These declining yields forced income investors to rethink everything. Although a focus on bonds – gilts or corporate bonds – is probably still the safest bet for a reliable yield, some exposure to other asset classes is also probably a good idea. Many 'alternative' equity assets, for instance, such as infrastructure shares – utilities and public–private partnership funds – pay out chunky, well-backed yields.

In this model we have tried to reflect these cross currents and very different views on risk. Overall the portfolio is weighted 65 percent towards safer bonds and 35 percent towards riskier assets. If you were to invest in ETFs – index tracking funds – that followed the main indices used in our model portfolio, you would be receiving a total portfolio return of 5.27 percent at March 2009, with much the largest component of income coming from the biggest holding in the main conventional gilts index, the FTSE All Stock Gilt. Another 20 percent of the portfolio is invested in those index-linked gilts we mentioned earlier, as a safety policy – if inflation were to start shooting up towards 4 percent per annum, investors might want to consider switching around the 40 percent conventional gilts/20 percent index-linked ratio. The allocation of just 5 percent to corporate bonds is probably the most controversial idea – many, many advisers think that corporate bonds with their current high yields are the best place to derive an income. One major benchmark index, the iBoxx Sterling Liquid Corporate Long-Dated Bond index, yields a very high 8 percent flat yield and 9.5 percent yield to redemption, as of March 2009. These are indeed very high rates and if the economy was bottoming out, they would be an obvious buy. But – and this is the really big but – if your view is still bearish and you believe the world is only beginning to work its way through a severe recession or even a depression, corporate defaults will shoot up and the yield will go even higher.

In the equity portion of the portfolio the holdings are deliberately weighted towards infrastructure assets, which are producing historically high and relatively safe yields, plus high-yielding equity indices. Tracking an index like the Dow Jones Global Select Dividend may well be a good idea – it follows the world's largest companies which pay out an above-average dividend yield.

Perhaps the most contentious idea in this portfolio is the 6.5 percent in high-yielding UK stocks, either via an index like the UK Dividend Plus or through an established equity income fund. These kind of stocks suffered badly in the bear markets of 2008 and 2009, and the UK Dividend Plus index (a major dividend-based index) turned in some dreadful results, but if markets do recover some of their poise these cautious, value-based assets may stage a rally.

The other master portfolios

Lifecycle target date for retirement:		2030	2040 Absolute returns (medium risk)	Adventurous
INVESTMENT SPACE	INDEX			
Devel Equity: UK (FTSE 100)	FTSE 100		0	12.5
Devel Equity: UK (FTSE ALL)	FTSE ALL		25.38	0
Devel Equity: World exc UK	MSCI WORLD exc UK		19	8
Devel Equity: Value Stocks UK	FTSE Div Plus or equity income fund		0	15.5
Devel Equity: Value Stocks Global	DJ Global Select Divid		0	8
Devel Equity: Mid Caps	FTSE 250		0	2
Devel Equity: Small Cap	FTSE Small Cap		0	1.5
Emerging Markets	MSCI EM		6.38	5
Global Infrastructure and Utilities	FTSE Util/S&P Glob Infra		5	8.75
REITS	EPRA/NAREIT Global		4.25	8.75
Corporate Bonds: Sterling	iBoxx Sterling Corporates		10.83	4
Government Bonds: Conventional	FTSE All Stocks Gilt		10.83	8
Government Bonds: Index Linked	Barclays UK Index Linked		10.83	8
Alts: Commodities	DJ-AIG Composite		5	6.5
Other Alts	Credit Suisse Tremont Hedge		2.5	3.5
Total			100	100

4 The Mid Risk Portfolio

Portfolio name: MIDDLE OF THE ROAD MID RISK PORTFOLIO

Lifecycle target date: 2030 (probably in their forties with 20 years or less to retirement)

Overall equity bias

Mainstream equity bias, i.e. underweight utilities and infrastructure

Balance between growth and capital preservation

Balance between conventional gilts and index-linked gilts, i.e. probably OVERWEIGHT index-linked gilts because of long-term inflation risk

OVERWEIGHT corporate bonds

UNDERWEIGHT emerging markets vs international equity markets

	Mid Risk
Bonds vs equities vis Alt Assets	32.5/60/7.5
Equities: Mainstream vs Rest ratio	85/15
Equities: UK vs Global Developeds ratio	50/50
Int Equity: Dev vs EM	75/25
UK Equity: ALL vs Size bias	FTSE ALL only
Bonds: Corps vs Govt	33/66
Gilts: Conv vs Index L	50/50
Alt Assets: Commodit vs Other Alts	66/33
Bonds: Int vs UK	UK
Equities: Value Bias	No
Other alts (exc commodities) as %	2.5

It is almost impossible to design a one-size-fits-all portfolio – each and every one of us has our own attitude to risk, our own financial goals, our own passions and hates. Yet the reality is that most investors tend to sit, like most things in life, somewhere in the middle of any range of attitudes and sensibilities. We nearly all want some element of risk in order to gain greater rewards, but we do not want 'too much risk'. When pushed, most would probably opt for some exposure to safer gilts and bonds, but they have probably also heard that the 'future' is in something like emerging market equities. The trade-off in potential for high returns and the desire to protect a portfolio from large absolute losses is at the heart of any financial adviser's approach to constructing a portfolio.

But how do you translate these contrasting forces into a single portfolio? One example of an attempt to build the elusive middle-of-the-road, mid-risk portfolio comes in the shape of a revolutionary series of funds launched in the US by iShares. In 2008 the fund manager launched a set of target risk and target date 'all-in-one' funds that combined a number of different index tracking funds in one listed entity, giving investors access to everything from real estate to corporate bonds.

Perhaps the most popular of the 'risk'-based funds was an ETF called 'Moderate' – the composition of the index is in Table 11.1. What is immediately striking about this multi-ETF fund is that over 62 percent of the total holdings were in US fixed-income securities, mostly government bonds (also known as T-bills). If you were to run the same exercise with most wealth-based advisers for instance in the UK – and the *FT Money* section does exactly this every year – you would get a very different answer, namely a 50–60 percent allocation not to bonds but to 'riskier' equities. What is even more extraordinary about this US-based multi ETF is that it is overwhelmingly US focused – less than 11 percent of the total funds are used to buy anything international, whereas most UK-based planners and advisers would probably consider foreign exposure of at least twice this level, if not closer to 50 percent for equities.

Table 11.1 iShares' Moderate Target Risk fund

iShares' asset class breakdown as of 13/2/2009

Asset class	% of fund
Domestic Fixed Income	**62.55**
Barclays Aggregate Bond Fund	26.25
Barclays Short Treasury Bond Fund	24.07
Barclays TIPS Bond Fund	12.24
Domestic Equity	**22.86**
S&P 500 Index Fund	17.87
S&P MidCap 400 Index Fund	3.02
S&P SmallCap 600 Index Fund	1.98
International Equity	**11.93**

Table 11.1 Continued

iShares' asset class breakdown as of 13/2/2009

Asset class	% of fund
MSCI EAFE Index Fund	10.86
MSCI Emerging Markets Index Fund	1.07
Domestic Real Estate	**2.56**
Cohen & Steers Realty Majors Index Fund	2.56
Individual Securities	**0.11**

Source: Based on data from iShares

Our own take on this challenge of trying to build a middle-of-the-road portfolio is outlined in Table 11.2. We have sided with most UK-based advisers and favoured a much more equity-based and internationally oriented portfolio. We have allocated only one third of the total portfolio to bonds – many academics might even suggest that this percentage is perhaps too low. Studies by the likes of Elroy Dimson and Paul Marsh at the LBS suggest that long-term returns from equities tend to average between 6 percent and 8 percent, with a 3–4 percent risk premium, as it is called, over risk-free cash deposits, i.e. equities provide higher long-term returns albeit at the cost of greater volatility. That bias towards equities needs to be put in proper perspective however – over the last decade bonds have probably been a better investment idea and there are many periods in history where bonds have consistently beaten equities.

Table 11.2 Building a portfolio

Portfolio compositions: suggested

		2030 Medium
Devel Equity: UK (FTSE 100)	FTSE 100	0
Devel Equity: UK (FTSE ALL)	FTSE ALL	25.38
Devel Equity: World exc UK	MSCI WORLD exc UK	19
Devel Equity: Value Stocks UK	FTSE Div Plus or equity income fund	0
Devel Equity: Value Stocks Global	DJ Global Select Dividend	0
Devel Equity: Mid Caps	FTSE 250	0

Table 11.2 Continued

Devel Equity: Small Cap	FTSE Small Cap	0
Emerging Markets	MSCI EM	6.38
Global Infrastructure and Utilities	FTSE Util/S&P Glob Infra	5
REITS	EPRA/NAREIT Global	4.25
Corporate Bonds: Sterling	iBoxx Sterling Corporate	10.83
Government Bonds: Conventional	FTSE All Stocks Gilt	10.83
Government Bonds: Index Linked	Barclays UK Index Linked	10.83
Alts: Commodities	DJ-AIG Composite	5
Other Alts	Credit Suisse Tremont Hedge	2.5
Total		100

Source: based on data from iShares

Our other core focus is on international diversification – of the total 50 percent plus exposure to equities, we have suggested a fairly even split between international and UK shares, with a particular focus on the equities of other developed world markets including the US and Europe. Emerging markets shares comprise just 6 percent of the total value of the portfolio. This international diversification is in effect an insurance policy – we are not entirely convinced that the UK economy will be a very happy affair over the next few years and we would suggest that buying some US, Japanese and European investments might be a wise move.

There are also some deliberate omissions. We do not think it is appropriate for a mid-risk or middle-of-the-road investor to bias their portfolio for or against small caps or large mid caps. We have chosen the FTSE All Share index as our default index in part because it covers 98 percent of the entire UK market capitalisation and includes both mid- and small-cap stocks (although it is still very large-cap heavy). We also think that any attempt to capture the 'value premium' is probably too risky for this portfolio – this term applies to the extensive research which suggests that 'cheaper', 'better-value' shares with decent balance sheets and higher yields provide better long-term returns. By and large we think the evidence does 'stack up' over the long term, but recent experience – where value stocks have underperformed the market – suggests that it is a risky and volatile strategy. We have also allocated just 5 percent of the portfolio to real estate – we would suggest that exposure be to global real estate, not just UK assets – and we have suggested 5 percent for commodities. One last thought: if the overall exposure to mainstream equities strikes you as too risky, you might want to consider upping the holdings of slightly less volatile utility and infrastructure shares. This fast-growing 'alternative equity' category tends to consist of companies with strong, regulated, asset-backed balance sheets, predictable cash flow profiles and decent yields – more cautious types might want to think about doubling their exposure to this category and cutting their FTSE All Share exposure.

5 The Adventurous Portfolio

Portfolio name: ADVENTUROUS

Lifecycle target date: 2040 (probably in their thirties with 30 years or less to retirement)

Alternative assets bias

UK bias versus International

OVERWEIGHT – EQUITIES REST, i.e. equities, infrastructure and REITs

Low level of bonds – UNDERWEIGHT BONDS

BIAS towards size bias within equities, i.e. focus on small caps

Value bias – 50%/50% within UK and developed world equities

Adventurous

Bonds vs equities vis Alt Assets	70/20/10
Equities: Mainstream vs Rest ratio	3:1
Equities: UK vs International ratio	1.5:1
Int Equity: Dev vs EM	3:1
UK Equity: ALL vs Size bias	Size Bias: SC
Bonds: Govt vs Corp	4:1
Gilts: Conv vs Index L	1:1
Alt Assets: Commodit vs Other Alts	2:1
Bonds: Int vs UK	NO
Equities: Value Bias	Yes 50%/50%
Other alts (exc commodities) as %	10

Imagine that you are 30 years old. You have got between 35 and 40 years before you retire and you are suddenly starting to earn enough money to start a retirement fund. But you are faced with a huge question: how do you build a portfolio that will give you long-term growth without taking on too much risk? The core to building any portfolio is to balance risk and reward, even for younger investors. The riskiest assets tend to produce the biggest long-term gains, although over that long term the resulting volatility will be huge. Investors have become used to the idea that over the very long term equities are a great investment – the average over the past 100 years has been more than 6 percent per annum in most major developed world markets. But no one actually saves for 100 years. Most investors face a more limited timeframe of between 20 and 40 years. That matters because over this time period volatility can make a huge difference.

US analyst and adviser John Mauldin looked at this in a paper called 'While Rome burns'.[1] He examined the frequency of returns and the impact of volatility. He found that 'in the 103 years from 1900 through 2002, the annual change for the Dow Jones Industrial Average reflects a simple average gain of 7.2 percent per year. During that time, 63 percent of the years reflect positive returns, and 37 percent were negative. Only five of the years ended with changes between +5 percent and +10 percent – that's less than 5 percent of the time'. Mauldin reminds his readers that most of the years were far from average. Almost 70 percent of the years were double-digit years, when the stock market either rose or fell by more than 10 percent. He then goes on to examine actual returns in 88 20-year periods. According to Mauldin: 'Though most periods generated positive returns before dividends and transaction costs, half produced compounded returns of less than 4 percent. Less than 10 percent generated gains of more than 10 percent.' He warns that 'the stock market rarely gives you an average year. The wild ride makes for those emotional investment experiences which are a primary cause of investment pain'.[2]

Dividends smooth returns

However, Mauldin's overall message is that equities will deliver substantial compounded returns, especially if you focus on a number of variables, including dividends. A number of realities emerge from this long-term financial analysis. The first is that if you are consistent and have a long enough timeframe, then equities stand a very high chance of yielding greater long-term returns.

The next is that income and dividends matter. Accumulating returns from dividends comprise a large part of total returns, but there is also some evidence that over the long term the market misprices more value-orientated companies that tend to produce a decent yield. Work from economists such as Ken French and Eugene Fama at the University of Chicago suggests that smaller companies produce higher returns – called the scale premium – and you may be able to boost long-term returns by anything between 1 percent and 3 percent per annum.

All these concepts sit behind our latest portfolio, our Adventurous Portfolio. It is targeted at younger investors, but it could work for anyone willing to take on more risk. Crucially, though, it is very different from our equally ambitious and risky Global Growth Portfolio. It is not exclusively focused on equities (it contains some alternative assets as well as bonds) and it has a strong UK focus (see Figure 11.1). This portfolio is aimed at investors who want some diversification away from equities but not too much diversification away from the UK – when you retire you will probably have to live off sterling-based assets. Its small bias towards caution is reflected in some bonds exposure and in a bias towards slightly safer equity assets such as utilities and infrastructure companies.

Figure 11.1 The Adventurous Portfolio

There is one last key issue: the portfolio features plenty of value stocks. Within the bit of the portfolio that is equity based we have split our holding 50/50 between a strategy that simply tracks the major indices and a strategy that focuses on equity-income strategies.

Adventurous Portfolio breakdown

Developed market equities	Suggested index	% of portfolio
UK (FTSE 100)	FTSE 100	12.5
UK (FTSE ALL)	FTSE ALL	0
World exc UK	MSCI WORLD exc Uk	8
Value stocks UK	FTSE Div Plus or equity income fund	15.5
Value stocks global	DJ Global Select Dividend	8
Mid caps	FTSE 250	2
Small cap	FTSE Small Cap	1.5
Other equities		
Emerging markets	MSCI EM	5
Global infrastructure and utilities	FTSE Util/S&P Glob Infra	8.75
Real estate investment trusts	EPRA/NAREIT Global	8.75
Bonds		
Corporate bonds: sterling	iBoxx Sterling Corporates	4
Government bonds: conventional	FTSE All Stocks Gilt	8
Government bonds: index linked	Barclays UK Index Linked	8
Alternative assets		
Alts: commodities	DJ-AIG Composite	6.5
Other alts	Credit Suisse Tremont Hedge	3.5

Sources for portfolios

> FolioFN Model portfolios
> Seven Investment Management portfolios
> Marlborough iFunds active multi ETF funds
> US-based Lazy Portfolios from *The Lazy's Person's Guide to Investing*[2]
> S&P Target Risk Index series
> iShares US-based Allocation funds
> TDX Independence Target Date funds
> Opportunistic Rebalancing

What do I do next? Where do the Essential 25 fit in?

In Table 11.3 you will see the list of all our master portfolios, with their core holdings. In the first two columns you will see the investment space and the underlying index, followed by five different model portfolios. If you sense that one of these model portfolios 'fits' your profile, start your own research.

The first step is to look at the index you are tracking. We feature all the indices below in our Essential 25 in the Appendix. Look at what comprises the index (its main holdings) and the risks and potential rewards involved. Be certain that this is what you would like to track – as we have already said, all the big indices have their vulnerabilities and they are all liable to heavy holdings in the most popular sectors and companies. That is no bad thing – equity investing is, after all, a giant weighing machine that simply rewards the most successful companies. But remember that equity indices are volatile – some more than others – and that many big developed market indices are very closely correlated with each other. In our opinion it is no good putting all your money in a simple three-way split that involves a UK FTSE 100 index tracker, followed by an S&P 500 index tracker and a European index tracker – remember that good diversification is not just about national markets but also asset classes. Alternative assets like commodities have their value, as do bonds and gilts.

Once you have researched your index and looked at your suggested percentage allocation – and remember it is only a suggested allocation – start to think about which actual fund to invest in. We are not going to tell you this vital bit in this book (that would involve favouring one fund over another), but we do

Table 11.3 *Investors Chronicle master portfolios*

Lifecycle target date for retirement:		2010 Income	2020 Low	2030 Medium	2040 Adv	2045 Global growth
INVESTMENT SPACE	INDEX					
Devel Equity: UK (FTSE 100)	FTSE 100	0	0	0	12.5	9
Devel Equity: UK (FTSE ALL)	FTSE ALL	5	16	25.38	0	0
Devel Equity: World exc UK	MSCI WORLD exc UK	2	8	19	8	27
Devel Equity: Value Stocks UK	FTSE Div Plus or equity income fund	6.5	0	0	15.5	0
Devel Equity: Value Stocks Global	DJ Global Select Divid	6	0	0	8	0
Devel Equity: Mid Caps	FTSE 250	0	0	0	2	4.5
Devel Equity: Small Cap	FTSE Small Cap	0	0	0	1.5	4.5
Emerging Markets	MSCI EM	0	0	6.38	5	27
Global Infrastructure and Utilities	FTSE Macquarie Global 100 or S&P Glob Infrastructure Index	12.5	5	5	8.75	9
REITS	EPRA/NAREIT Global Plus Index	3	4.5	4.25	8.75	9
Corporate Bonds: Sterling	iBoxx Sterling Corporate Bond Index	5	5	10.83	4	0
Government Bonds: Conventional	FTSE All Stocks Gilt	40	30	10.83	8	0
Government Bonds: Index Linked	Barclays UK Index Linked	20	25	10.83	8	0
Alts: Commodities	DJ-AIG Commodities Composite	0	4	5	6.5	6.5
Other Alts	Credit Suisse Tremont Hedge	0	2.5	2.5	3.5	3.5
Total		100	100	100	100	100

Source: based on data from iShares

suggest which ETFs and index funds are on the market, their relative costs and their success at tracking the index (where data exists). You then have to make your own decisions – look at the fund in detail, using many of the ideas discussed in this book. In particular we would recommend focusing on:

- Cost – anything above 1 percent is simply unacceptable.
- Tracking error – anything more than 1 percent per annum is a worry and more than 2.5 percent is unacceptable.
- The asset manager and examine whether you are happy with the structure of the fund: are there any counterparty risks?
- The index structure once more to see what risks you are taking using this fund. Are you buying into a small number of very big companies?
- How easy the index fund is to trade in and examine the bid–offer spread offered by a broker – do not accept any bid–offer spread much above 1 percent. Also be aware that some smaller ETFs in the US are very poorly traded and more than a few have shut up shop.

Once you have worked out your portfolio composition, go off and start buying your shares either in a lump sum or on a regular savings scheme on a monthly basis (the preferable option).

Once you are up and running we would suggest four simple portfolio management rules:

1 Do not check the portfolio more than once a week. Too much attention encourages overtrading.
2 We would recommend some form of rebalancing applied either on an annual basis or via some form of tolerance band system using the 20 percent rule.
3 If you feel confident about your knowledge of the markets, think about using a simple market-timing system – we like the simple 200-day moving average systems. If you do use a system, stick to it, through thick and thin, and do not overtrade. Only use your system for big signals that suggest a move out of all equities into cash and vice versa; likewise for other asset classes.
4 Diversify, diversify, diversify. Just focusing on equities may be a brilliant long-term strategy but it is really very risky. Be aware of that risk and contemplate some diversification away from equities, even if it is into commodities or even hedge funds. Equally within that broad category known as 'mainstream equities' seek out markets and niche markets that offer some form of diversification, i.e. utility stocks or infrastructure companies have some diversification benefits compared with mainstream equities.

Simple, lazy portfolios from *PortfolioReview*

More adventurous, sophisticated investors might want to look beyond our model portfolios and consider an alternative way of assembling a mixture of index tracking funds. The author of this book edits a free, online publication called *PortfolioReview* where every month we outline a new simple, lazy portfolio. These portfolios and the articles that go with them can be found at **www.portfolioreviewonline.com**. The idea behind these portfolios is obvious – keep it simple and do not try to over-complicate the task of building a diversified portfolio. For this book we have highlighted five lazy portfolios that can be easily constructed using ETFs and index tracking funds.

1 A No-Brainer Portfolio for the UK

Our first portfolio attempts to repeat a lazy portfolio outlined earlier in this book – it was devised by American investment thinker William Bernstein and was called the Basic No-Brainer Portfolio. We have already looked at this portfolio but here it is again – notice how all the funds are American and run by Vanguard.

William Bernstein's Basic No-Brainer Portfolio

25% in the main S & P 500 index (Vanguard 500 Index (VFINX))

25% in the main US Small Cap index (Vanguard Small Cap (NAESX) or (VTMSX))

25% in a diversified international index (Vanguard Total International (VGTSX) or (VTMGX))

25% in a US bond fund (Vanguard Total Bond (VBMFX) or (VBISX))

What might a simple No-Brainer Portfolio look like here in the UK? Rather than suggest just one fund manager (Vanguard) and its range of funds, it is possible to build your own lazy portfolio, giving the private investor a similar four-asset class structure but with a choice of alternative index tracking options. In the portfolio below we have given two choices for each asset class:

1. The physical tracker actually buys the stocks within an index and holds them in the fund. These are usually offered by the likes of iShares, Vanguard and HSBC.
2. Synthetic trackers also track an index but use derivatives within the structure (swaps) to lower the cost and reduce the tracking error. These are offered by the likes of Deutsche DBX and Lyxor.

In each case, we have only chosen the two cheapest funds (with their ticker and total expense ratio in brackets) available on the mass market through a stockbroker or IFA platform.

A UK-based No-Brainer index tracking portfolio

Asset class	Index to track
UK equities – 25%	FTSE 100 Index
UK small caps – 25%	RBS Hoare Govett Small Cap Index or MSCI UK Small Cap Index
World equities excluding the UK – 25%	MSCI World exc. UK
UK bonds – 12.5% in government gilts and 12.5% in corporate bonds	Gilts – FTSE UK All Stocks Gilt Index Corporate Bonds

2 A Lazy Investor's Fixed Income Portfolio

Our next simple, lazy portfolio is aimed at more adventurous investors who prefer to dabble in the world of fixed income securities. In the past few years both BlackRock iShares and Vanguard have greatly extended their range of index tracking funds, available either as unit trust OEICs (Vanguard) or ETFs (iShares).

Other fund providers – notably Deutsche DBX – do offer a limited variety of money market or total return bond funds, but it is only really Vanguard and iShares that offer enough choice for a bonds-only portfolio. Vanguard has even gone one better – it has also introduced multi-asset wrappers which combine different index tracking funds in one relatively simple solution and nearly all of them include a substantial fixed income component. None of these life strategy funds is entirely comprised of bonds, but Vanguard does offer a 20 percent equity fund which is overwhelmingly dominated by bond funds.

New Vanguard 20% Equity LifeStrategy Fund

Index/asset class	% of 20% Vanguard Equity Fund
UK Government Bond index	37.3
UK Investment Grade Bond index	26.5
UK Inflation-linked Gilt index	16.1
UK Equity index	7
FTSE Developed World ex. UK Index Equity	11.2
Emerging Markets Stock Index Equity	1.8

It is possible to use this Vanguard portfolio as a template for a more individual, lazy creation. In order to build this portfolio there are five initial, important decisions:

1 Should the investor only use funds provided by one fund manager? Despite the provenance of both the major issuers, if you are very cautious it is probably unwise to shackle yourself to one issuer, especially as you can so easily mix and match fund managers.

2 Are you happy with fixed income indices? Remember that bond indices, especially in the corporate space, track issuance based on market capitalisation which by default means that you are weighting your portfolio towards the largest issuers of debt. As long as these bonds are conservatively rated that may not necessarily be a challenge but investors do need to tread with care in all attempt to control risk. That makes a strong argument for investing in actively managed funds in the corporate bond space, although the charges on these funds can be high and many managers still run big risks with your funds. We would err on the side of caution and make sure that exposure to corporate debt is kept at reasonable levels within any portfolio.

3 Should you focus exclusively on sterling bonds or embrace global funds as well? On balance it probably is important that investors have some exposure to the global issuance of debt, especially in the government bond space.

4 What yield level do you want on your portfolio of bonds? The obvious truth is that the greater the yield, the higher the risk. If you are willing to invest in sub-investment grade junk bonds or in local currency emerging market bonds then you could achieve a yield well in excess of 6 or even 7 percent, but the risks increase greatly.

5 Last but by no means least, consider your attitude towards inflation risk in the future. Do you believe that we are about to enter an inflationary era when prices will increase by more than the 2.5 percent p.a. suggested by current break-even rates? If you do think this could be the case you should probably weight your assets towards inflation-linked products and funds. But be aware that the real yield on inflation linkers, for instance, is at very low levels and even if inflation rates rise, you may still lose out in total returns terms!

Obviously every investor's reactions to these questions will vary but in the table below there is an outline of what could be a potential lazy portfolio for a more adventurous investor looking to access global markets and still have some inflation protection via government linkers. One caveat: the yield on this lazy portfolio will be higher than a portfolio orientated towards more cautious index-linked gilts but on balance that extra risk is probably worth the extra yield. There has also been a deliberate decision to pick some global government and corporate bond funds to control for any risk in holding sterling-only assets. By our calculations the blended average flat yield on this portfolio is just under 4.2 percent p.a. – although the yield to maturity would be substantially lower given the relatively high price of bonds in the current market.

Suggested allocation by fixed income asset class

Index or bond asset class	% of lazy portfolio	% potential flat yield Spring 2011
UK All Stocks Gilt index – conventional government	35	4.1
UK Inflation Linked Bond index	15	0.95
UK Corporate Bonds index	20	5.77
Global Government Bonds	10	2.59
Global Government Inflation Linked	5	1.63
Emerging Markets Local Currency Debt	10	7.60
Euro High Yield Index	5	7.00

3 Lazy Portfolios for Inflation Hawks

How should investors focused on the long term construct a balanced and diversified portfolio of funds? The conventional wisdom is that inflation hawks should probably behave fairly conventionally, mixing and matching equities with bonds. Yet this thinking has come under sustained attack in recent years by academics, many of whom have started to question whether equities, for instance, actually hedge against inflation over the short to medium term.

The most powerful analysis we have encountered so far comes in a 2009 IMF paper called 'Inflation hedging for long-term investors' by Attié and Roache.[3] As you would expect from professional economists there is lots and lots of number crunching and regression analysis, but two important conclusions emerge. The first is that not all inflationary episodes are the same. Some inflationary scares are caused by sudden spikes in commodity prices while others are prompted by (excessive) monetary intervention and currency crises. The exact cause of the inflation matters hugely – if we are experiencing a commodity induced crunch, then we would expect commodities to be a great hedge, whereas in a monetary induced inflationary scare gold can be a better bet.

Crucially the IMF academics also suggest that what works over the short term – 12 months – does not always work over the very long term. Equities, for instance, can be a great long-term hedge but only if you are willing to hold them for many decades. Commodities, by contrast, tend to be a great short-term hedge but that power fades over time.

The table below summarises what seems to work over the short, 12-month period, based on the IMF analysis. It looks at inflation sensitivity for a whole bunch of assets – a positive coefficient suggests that the asset increases in value as inflation ticks up, whereas negative coefficients tend to suggest that the asset will lag behind.

Asset class sensitivity to inflation over a 12-month horizon

Asset class	Coefficients on CPI inflation	
	Level	12-month change
Cash: US 3-month T-bills	0.39	–0.24
Cash: SDR 3-month interest rate	0.27	–0.65
Bonds: US Treasuries all maturities	–0.10	–1.33
Bonds: US corporate	–0.74	–1.81
Equities: US large-cap equities	0.07	–0.03
Property: FTSE NAREIT index	–0.16	–3.84
Commodities: CRB Index	0.42	3.41
Commodities: GSCI index	7.71	9.87

Continued

Asset class	Coefficients on CPI inflation	
	Level	*12-month change*
Gold Spot	2.78	6.36
Portfolio: Dollar 60/40 Equity Bond Portfolio	0	−0.16

Source: http:www.imf.org/external/pubs/ft/wp/2009/wp0990.pdf (Table 2)

Looking at the short term, commodities and especially gold seem to be the best bet as a hedge against inflation. But as we move out to the long term, these relationships break down and the IMF academics suggest a more troubling message: that as the power of commodities fades, cash becomes more important and bonds begin to seem useful again. The table below summarises the academics' long-term conclusions.

Asset class	Short term (1–18 months)	Intermediate term (18 months to 5 years)	Long term (5 years+)	Historical long-run performance[1]
Cash	Interest rates respond gradually, leading to real losses.	Interest rates begin to climb, recovering some of the early losses.	Partial inflation hedge, elasticity of 0.8.	Modestly positive real returns.
Nominal bonds	Bond yields rise, causing price declines and real return losses.	Higher current yields begin to offset price declines, leading to some recovery.	Real losses, with elasticity of 0.1.	Real returns in excess of cash, but lower than equities.
Equities	Real return losses, but less than for bonds.	Stabilising real returns, but no meaningful recovery.	Real losses, with elasticity of −0.2.	Real returns in excess of bonds.
Commodities	Spot price increases, almost matching inflation.	Spot prices begin to gradually decline.	Real spot price losses, with elasticity of −0.2.	Insufficient total return data for commodity futures.[2]

[1] Total returns over the long run and over all phases of the inflation cycle.
[2] Spot price data were used in the long-run analysis of inflation surprises. However, this provides only a partial picture of total returns.

Source: http://www.imf.org/external/pubs/ft/wp/2009/wp0990.pdf (Table 4)

Our take on this analysis can be summed up as follows:

- If you are worried by long-term inflationary trends, you have to accept that the causes of inflation can vary enormously and that the dynamics of change can switch in a matter of months. In these uncertain circumstances a reserve of cash probably makes sense, with an allocation varying between 5 percent and 20 percent.
- Equities can make sense over the long term but you will probably have to weight your holdings towards companies with a greater sensitivity towards inflation. This probably means large blue chip companies, with strong cash flows and a generous dividend yield or companies in the utility and infrastructure space where earnings are frequently tied to RPI.
- Bonds are an essential component of any sensibly diversified portfolio, and especially so if you are worried by inflation in the future. In particular it probably makes a lot of sense to focus on inflation-linked bonds, mainly issued by the government – although some index-linked corporate bond exposure probably does make sense if you can sensibly access it.
- Last but by no means least, consider holding gold as the ultimate long-term inflation hedge, but be aware that gold prices are volatile and could fall back quickly if growth picks up.

With these simple principles in mind, our Lazy Inflation Portfolio is thus more than a little radical! We would suggest a 40/40/20 split in overall terms – 40 percent in bonds (index-linked government ones), 40 percent in commodities (with a skew towards precious metals and gold) and 20 percent in equities.

Our Lazy Inflation Portfolio

Asset class or index	*% of portfolio*	*Possible funds or trackers*
Gold	20%	ETFS Physical Gold – PHGP
Inflation-linked government securities	30% (or 40% if you cannot access index-linked corporate)	Vanguard UK Inflation-Linked Gilt Index iShares Barclays Capital £ Index-Linked Gilts (INXG)
Inflation-linked corporate securities	10% (otherwise government linkers)	M&G UK Inflation Linked Corporate Bond Fund
High yielding large caps	10%	Deutsche db-X Stoxx Global Select Dividend 100 ETF (XGSD)

Continued

Asset class or index	% of portfolio	Possible funds or trackers
Utilities – STOXX 600 Utilities, FTSE MacQuarie Global Infrastructure Index or world water indices	10%	Lyxor ETF World Water (LWAT) iShares FTSE Macquarie Global Infrastructure 100 (INFR)
Commodities – DJ UBS All Commodities Composite	20%	ETFS All Commodities £ DJ-UBSCI (AGCP)

4 Lazy Portfolios ... a Risk On Risk Off Index Portfolio

In 2011–12 a deceptively simple idea started to generate a massive amount of attention within the investing community – the risk on risk off trade. The simple concept behind this idea is that in times of stress all risky financial markets tend to move as one – downwards, except for a few safe harbour assets which start rising in value!

In bearish markets the best investment idea is to invest all your cash into what are regarded as safe harbour assets or risk off assets by which we mean short duration US government bonds, cash or gold. These are apparently risk-free assets, although we doubt that anyone experiencing a recent and sudden 10 percent loss in the value of their gold holdings would regard that holding as risk-less. We would also argue that lending money to the US government is far from risk-less, although to be fair it is also extraordinarily unlikely that the US government would default within say a typical one-year bond duration (though not impossible). Nevertheless the idea is simple – take risk off the table and invest in rock solid assets.

The risk on trade is also elegantly simple. As market confidence is rebuilt, all risky markets tend to rally as one, with only a small amount of differentiation in returns – in these circumstances the best bet for participating in the upside is simply to invest in a basket of developed world large-cap stocks. Many commentators and experts (the author of this book included) have their own significant doubts about the long-term value of the risk on risk off trade as a practical idea – many believe that it oversimplifies a complex world of varying outcomes and panders to market timing. Nevertheless even the most hardened cynic has to accept that this supposedly 'simple' trade has recently been fairly useful if only because so many markets are now moving in a predictably correlated fashion. It is also true that this trade can be relatively easily implemented by using a simple bundle of index trackers – in our lazy portfolios below we have tried to have no more than five simple markets for each approach.

Crucially in the risk off portfolio we have also stuck with ETFs provided by fund management companies that only physically track indices. The idea here is that if markets are fearful and worried about risk, you will probably want to minimise your exposure to investment banks that could sustain massive losses in a market rout which in turn probably rules out ETF providers that offer collateral as part of their synthetic index tracking range. In this worst case scenario (which we do not actually believe is a substantive risk) you will probably want your collateral to be the actual bonds or stocks you are supposedly tracking, thus leaving physical trackers as the only sensible way of passively tracking a market. We have also ruled out mutual unit trust funds – these only set their net asset values on a daily (end of day) basis which might not give investors enough time to trade in and out of.

With the risk on portfolio these worries are banished as investors are basically betting that risky financials – be they investment banks themselves or equity markets equities – are only likely to head upwards, so any worries about collateral are less pronounced, which thus puts synthetic ETFs and unit trusts back in the game.

The obvious last question is perhaps the most important: how does one decide to move between these two portfolios? Frankly the only reliable way of managing such a switch is to use your own common sense and gumption. You might also want to test the temperature of the market by looking for risk measures that start flashing red – look at the Investor Dashboard featured online at **www.portfolioreviewonline.com** every month.

> One last final caution – be aware that this trade is a risky one in that it lulls you into thinking that the world is a simpler place than it really is and that correlations always remain static. We would also wager that a focus on long-term buy and hold investing, using sensible principles, will always beat this style of speculative based investing, if only because all this switching back and forth incurs huge trading costs.

The Risk Off Portfolio

- **Developed world government bonds with a focus on the US, Japan and the UK – short-duration government bonds.** In a world fearful of risk and volatility, government bonds from the US, Japan and the UK with a duration of less than a year are probably perceived as the safest assets – just do not worry about the pitifully low yield on offer!

- **Physical gold** – in a fearful world you would probably want access to your own allocated amount of physical bullion held in a safe vault.
- **Investment grade corporate bonds** – many investors now regard huge multinationals and their bonds as safer than those issued by our national governments.
- **Inflation-linked government bonds** – a global economy flirting with a recession is unlikely to be one terrifically bothered by inflationary surges. Yet there is also plenty of evidence to suggest that low-growth countries such as the UK are still suffering from abnormally high levels of (imported) inflation, i.e. stagflation. In these circumstances an inflation-proof asset such as government inflation-linked bonds might make sense.

Risk Off Portfolio

Asset class and index	% of portfolio	Possible ETFs or index funds
Developed world government bonds	50	Vanguard Global Bond index fund or iShares Global Citigroup Global Government Bond (IGLO)
Physical Gold or NYSE Arca Gold Bugs Index	20	ETFS Physical Gold (PHGP)
Investment grade corporate bonds	10	Vanguard Investment Grade Bond index
Global inflation-linked government bonds	20	Vanguard Inflation Linked Gilt index or iShares Barclays Capital Global Inflation Linked Bond index (IGIL)

The Risk On Portfolio

- **MSCI World index** – as the world becomes more optimistic we might reasonably expect money to flood into global developed world equities and especially the very largest companies by market capitalisation. The MSCI World Equities index is dominated by the US, Japanese and UK large caps and is a simple way to access global equities.
- **MSCI Emerging Markets index** – with risk off the table we would reasonably expect the highest-growth economies to perform the best, i.e. the fast-growing emerging markets. Think BRICs – Brazil, Russia, India and China.

- **Leveraged debt** – surging confidence in the economy will eventually feed through to strong demand from lower-rated corporate bonds, especially as the number of defaults starts to decline.
- **Infrastructure** – this is the one fairly defensive idea in the portfolio in that this gives access to the world's largest companies in the infrastructure investment and utilities space.

Risk On Portfolio

Asset class and index	% of portfolio	Possible ETFs or index funds
Global developed world equities – MSCI World	50	Vanguard FTSE Developed World ex UK Equity index, iShares MSCI World (IWRD) or Lyxor ETF MSCI World (LWOR)
Emerging Markets – MSCI EM Index	20	iShares MSCI EM (IEEM) or Lyxor MSCI EM (LEME)
Leveraged corporate debt	15	iShares Markit iBoxx $ High Yield Capped Bond (SHYU) and iShares Markit iBoxx Euro High Yield Bond (IHYG)
Infrastructure	15	iShares FTSE Macquarie Global Infrastructure 100 (INFR) or Lyxor ETF World Water (LWAT)

5 Lazy Portfolios for Believers in Growth

Our last lazy portfolio is aimed at the investor hoping to capture that most elusive and fragile creature – growth! As of the end of 2011, bullish investors are in a definite minority at the moment and it has to be said that most of the major 'growth' themes look fairly beaten up and unwanted. Emerging markets have been bashed, cyclical mining stocks look thoroughly unwanted and themes such as renewable energy look positively ostracised – even the technology sector looks unloved. That caution is not unwarranted: in fragile markets we would be cautious about the idea of investing in anything that looks like it's commanding a growth premium. We would also caution that over the very long term boring themes like the importance of dividends or buying cheap stocks have in the past tended to win out in the battle between growth and value. Yet growth ideas and themes will eventually come back into favour as the global economy recovery looks more secure, sparking bullish sentiment once again. With a sustained recovery, we might reasonably expect (based on past form) for cyclical and then growth stocks to outperform their siblings. At this point growth will be back in favour and a wide range of key themes and sectors will be fashionable again.

As confidence in the global economy rebuilds, what could a diversified portfolio of cheap, simple funds look like? In the table below we have identified how one might structure a simple, lazy growth portfolio of low-cost index tracking funds. Most of the main ideas are fairly mainstream, and probably do not need much explaining – we would reasonably expect mining and oil stocks to perform strongly in the first phase of recovery. This should then benefit the main emerging market economies, with growth then fanning out into the core developed world markets. Crucially we would argue that a growth portfolio should contain some limited exposure to fixed income securities but based on distinct themes which echo those equity ideas, i.e. emerging markets bonds and junk bonds. The key is to keep costs to the minimum and attempt to diversify your exposure to growth as widely as possible.

Investment theme	*Possible % of portfolio*	*Possible index to track*
Emerging markets equities	20	MSCI EM or MSCI EM Small Cap
Frontier markets	10	MSCI Frontier
Major European resource companies	5	DJ STOXX 600 Sector – Basic Materials
Major European energy and oil companies	5	DJ STOXX 600 Sector – Energy
US technology	10	Dow Jones US technology index
Growth sectors – the Cloud	5	ISE Cloud Computing index
Growth sectors – biotech	5	NASDAQ US Biotech index
US growth stocks	10	S&P 500 Value Index
US junk bonds	10	iBoxx $ Liquid High Yield index
Emerging markets bonds	10	JP Morgan EM Bonds index or Barclays Capital Local Currency Emerging Markets Bond index
European small caps	5	MSCI Europe Small Cap or FTSE Small Cap
US small caps	5	Russell 2000 index

Appendix: The Essential 25

FTSE 100 – UK Equities

Weight of largest holding – at end December 2011	Royal Dutch Shell 9%
Weight of top 10 largest holdings	46%
Yield:	3.27% at end of December 2011

Returns

Index	2011	2010	2009	2008	2007
FTSE 100	−5.5%	7.3%	20.6%	−29%	−1.7%

Region: Europe (not Eurozone)

ANALYSIS	
Likely risk (high/medium/low)	Medium
Likely volatility	Medium
Suitable for 'simple' investors, i.e. small ISA investors	Yes
Diversification risk with top holdings, i.e. top three more than 20% of fund	Yes
Likely to be a core holding?	Yes
Market Cap based (MC)/Screened (S)	MC
Appeal to income investors?	Yes
Country breakdown: top three – December 2011	100% London listed but 60% of value of earnings sourced outside the UK
Sector breakdown: top three – December 2011	Oil and gas 21% Basic resources (mining) 12% Banks 11%

Comments

The FTSE 100 covers the largest companies by market cap, with the FTSE 250 covering the next 250 largest (i.e. those that do not make it into the FTSE 100). The composition of these indices changes regularly as companies move up and down between the relevant indices. According to the index owners, the FTSE Group, 'This index comprises the 100 most highly capitalised blue chip companies, representing approximately 81 percent of the UK market. The FTSE 100 Index also accounts for around 8 percent of the world's equity market capitalisation (based on the FTSE All World Index as at 31 December 2011). FTSE 100 constituents are all traded on the London Stock Exchange's SETS trading system.' The index is reviewed quarterly.

The weighting of shares in the index is a relatively simple exercise – the index is built around the market capitalisation of the constituent companies (all 100) so that the larger companies have a disproportionate impact on the value of the index, compared with a smaller (by market cap) company. So if HSBC, for instance, comprises 10 percent of the index and its shares rise by 10 percent, all things being equal with the other constituent companies, the index should rise by 1 percent. This 'methodology' is called the free-float methodology for constructing an index and the basic formula for any index is, Index level = $\sum$(Price of stock × Number of shares) × free-float factor/ index divisor. The **free-float adjustment factor** represents the proportion of shares floated as a percentage of issued shares and then rounded up to the nearest multiple of 5 percent for calculation purposes. To find the free-float capitalisation of a company, first find its market cap (number of outstanding shares × share price), then multiply its free-float factor. The free-float method, therefore, does not include restricted stocks, such as those held by company insiders.

The UK Blue Chip Index

The FTSE 100 is the big daddy of all UK-based indices. There are, it goes without saying, 100 stocks in the list and they comprise the largest quoted companies on the London Stock Exchange. It is also the main index for large, blue chip companies. Other key facts include:

1 There are, it goes without saying, 100 stocks in the list.
2 These are valued at a total of £1.54 trillion – that is £1,540,000 million.
3 The top five stocks are valued at a total of £486 billion.
4 The top 10 stocks are valued at £714 billion.
5 The bottom 50 stocks are valued at £189 billion.
6 Some companies in this list rose in value by more than 40 percent in a very volatile 2011; others dropped by more than 79 percent in the same year.
7 The top stock Royal Dutch Shell comprises 9.73 percent of the entire market cap while the bottom stock, financial services group Hargreaves Lansdown, comprises just over 0.13 percent of the entire market cap of the FTSE 100.

Should you track it? If you want to track the main market, with the largest, most liquid companies in the UK market, this is the index to use. But be aware that it is by its very nature heavily concentrated on the biggest companies, and many of those companies have a very strong foreign business presence. It is estimated that up to 60 percent of the turnover of FTSE 100 companies is earned in either dollars or euros. Already you can see how certain distortions could affect your use of the index – it is clearly a mega-large-cap index where big companies dominate (think BP and HSBC, for instance) and foreign earnings are important. But if you aim to capture the bulk of the value of the UK market – and in particular its daily transaction value – nothing beats the FTSE 100. Crucially, you have also got a huge range of funds to invest in, mostly at very low cost.

Investors who want to access the FTSE 100 index face two main choices in terms of index tracking funds. The most popular and well-established route is to pick an index tracking unit trust. In the table below we have listed some of the main unit trust FTSE 100 trackers.

Fund	*TER or annual management charge*
F&C FTSE 100 Tracker 1	1%
Gartmore UK Index Ret Inc	1%
Halifax UK FTSE 100 Idx Tracking C	1.52%
HSBC FTSE 100 Index Ret Inc	1%
L&G UK 100 Index	0.84%
Marks & Spencer UK 100 Cos Inc	1%
Norwich Blue Chip Tracking 1	0.90%
RBS FTSE 100 Tracker ST	1%
Santander Stkmkt 100 Trk Gth	0.35%
Smith & Williamson Munro A Inc	0.75%
HSBC FTSE 250 Index Ret Inc	0.75%
Pru UK Index Tracker A Acc	1.64%

The other big alternative are the exchange traded funds – there are a number of alternatives including ETFs from iShares, Lyxor and Deutsche DBX. In our experience, both DBX and Lyxor funds tend to be a little cheaper in TER terms – we have broken out costs in the tables below – while iShares tends to run bigger, more established funds. By and large all the ETFs are cheaper than their unit trust siblings although the cheapest ETF by far is from a little known ETF firm called Comstage (owned by the German banking group Commerzbank) with a TER of just 0.25 percent.

Featured ETFs

Name of fund	Index	TER basis points pa %	Physical or synthetic	ISIN or EPIC (italics and bold)
CS ETF IE on FTSE 100	FTSE 100	0.33	Physical	CUKX
DB FTSE 100 ETF	FTSE 100	0.30	Synthetic	***LU0292097234***
HSBC FTSE 100 ETF	FTSE 100	0.35	Physical	***IE00B42TW061***
iShares FTSE 100	FTSE 100	0.40	Physical	ISF
Lyxor ETF FTSE 100 – GBP	FTSE 100	0.35	Synthetic	LYUK
SG FTSE 100	FTSE 100	NA	Synthetic	S591
Source FTSE® 100 ETF	FTSE 100	0.25	Synthetic	S100
Lyxor ETF FTSE 100 – NTR GBP	FTSE 100	0.30	Synthetic	L100
AMUNDI ETF FTSE 100 – EUR	FTSE 100	0.45	Synthetic	AC1UG

Featured unit trusts

Name of fund	TER basis points pa %	Additional costs	Product domicile
Vanguard FTSE U.K. Equity Index	0.15%	0.50% (Stamp Duty)	UK
HSBC FTSE 100	0.27	0	UK
L & G UK 100 Index	0.65	0.16	UK

Funds to watch: You can also track the FTSE 100 using an inverse or bear tracker from Deutsche db-X trackers, called XUKS, with a total expense ratio of 0.50 percent. This is a simple tracker – for every 1 percent move down in the index, you get a 1 percent gain and vice versa, e.g. it makes money from a downwards move in the market. This is a potentially brilliant fund if you do not want the leverage of a covered warrant to make money on falling markets but still want to make money on the broad (downwards) directional move of the FTSE 100.

Investors might also be interested in a small UK unit trust tracker fund called The Munro Fund, run by a contributor to this book, Rob Davies. This tracks the constituents of the FTSE 100 but weights the shares in the portfolio by their total dividend payout, thus buying more shares in those paying out the most in dividends.

The FTSE 100 – some handy facts

- The FTSE 100 is a market capitalisation-weighted index representing the performance of the 100 largest UK-listed large-cap or blue chip companies.
- All companies in the FTSE 100 must pass a test that looks at size in terms of market capitalisation and the availability or liquidity of their shares, i.e. only easy-to-purchase shares or investable shares are included. Constituents also need to have a full listing on the London Stock Exchange with a sterling- or euro-denominated price on the SETS electronic trading system. Most constituents must by law include the abbreviation 'plc' at the end of their name, indicating their status as a publicly limited corporation.
- The index represents just over 80 percent of the entire market value of the various London-based stock exchanges.
- The index began on 3 January 1984 with a base level of 1000; the highest value reached to date is 6950.6, on 30 December 1999.
- The FTSE 100 is calculated in real time and the level of the index is published every 15 seconds. Trading lasts from 08.00–16.29 (when the closing auction starts), and closing values are taken at 16.35.
- The constituents of the index are determined quarterly. The larger companies in the adjacent index, the FTSE 250, are pushed up or promoted to the FTSE 100 index if they pass the tests above and their market cap goes above a certain level, usually between £1.5 billion and £2 billion.

FTSE All Share

Weight of largest holding	Royal Dutch Shell 9%
Weight of top 10 largest holdings	40%
Yield	2.96% as of end December 2011

Returns

Index	2011	2010	2009	2008	2007
FTSE All Share	–6.7%	9.1%	23.4%	30.4%	0.1%

The index – our analysis

ANALYSIS	
Likely risk (high/medium/low)	Medium
Likely volatility	Medium
Suitable for 'simple' investors, i.e. small ISA investors	Yes
Diversification risk with top holdings, i.e. top three more than 20% of fund	No although top three companies comprise around 20% of the total index
Likely to be a core holding?	Yes
Market Cap based (MC)/Screened (S)	MC
Appeal to income investors?	Yes
Risk factors?	Not enormously diversified and still blue chip focused High level of foreign earnings

Continued

ANALYSIS	
Top three holding as percentage of total fund end December 2011	20%
Country breakdown: top three – December 2011	100% UK listed but large foreign earnings for many companies in index
Sector breakdown: top three – December 2011	Oil and gas 18.7% Basic resources 11% Banks 9.5%

Top 10 constituents of the index

Vodafone	5.34
HSBC	5.22
Royal Dutch	5.09
BP	5.06
GlaxoSmithKline	4.45
Royal Dutch Shell B	3.89
Brit.Amer.Tobacco	3.55
Rio Tinto	2.72
BG Group	2.69
BHP Billiton	2.37

Featured ETF funds

UK All Share ETF trackers	*TER %*	*Trading currency*
Lyxor ETF FTSE All Share	0.35	Sterling GBP
Lyxor ETF FTSE All Share (Lux)	0.4	Sterling GBP
ComStage ETF FTSE All Share TR	0.35	Sterling GBP
db X-trackers FTSE All Share	0.4	Sterling GBP

Featured unit trust tracker funds

Unit trust	Total expense ratio or annual management charge
Allianz RCM UK Index A	0.50%
AXA UK Tracker Ret Inc	1.00%
F&C FTSE All Share Tracker 1 Inc	0.39%
Fidelity Moneybuilder UK Index	0.28%
Gartmore UK Index I	0.50%
Halifax UK FTSE All Share Idx Trk C	1.50%
HSBC FTSE All Share Index A I Inc	0.64%
L&G (N) Tracker	1.00%
L&G UK Idx Tr Index	0.51%
M&G Index Tracker A Inc	0.46%
Norwich UK Index Tracking 1	0.90%
Threadneedle Navigator UK Index Trk	1.14%
Virgin UK Index Tracking	1.00%

Comments

The FTSE All Share is perhaps the most important UK-based index. It is a market capitalisation-weighted index representing the performance of all eligible companies listed on the London Stock Exchange's main market, which pass a screening for size and liquidity. In total, the FTSE All Share index covers 689 companies – approximately 98 percent of the UK's market capitalisation. The FTSE All Share is also the aggregation of the FTSE 100, FTSE 250 and FTSE Small Cap indices. According to index developers FTSE Group, 'The FTSE All Share Index also accounts for 8.11 percent of the world's equity market capitalisation.'

Many investors are confused by the FTSE 100 and the FTSE All Share index. They presume that the best way to track the broad market is via the FTSE 100 (the better-known index) whereas in fact the FTSE 100 index tracks the large caps in the UK market. Which is not to say that the FTSE All Share index does not capture those large caps as well – its composition is still weighted by the size of the market cap and the top 10 companies in the FTSE All Share comprise 43 percent of the index as opposed to 52.4 percent with the FTSE 100. So although the FTSE All Share casts a wider net, it is still very focused on mega-cap blue chips.

That said, the FTSE All Share index does capture a much broader range of companies and comprises the FTSE 100, the FTSE 250 and the members of the FTSE Small Cap index, but all weighted by market cap (which means that it is still dominated by the biggest FTSE 100 companies).

But there is another crucial point – the FTSE All Share is not actually *all* the market as the title implies. It does not include some really tiny companies that comprise the 'fag end' of the market, namely micro-caps in the FTSE Fledgling index, i.e. really tiny companies valued at less than £10 million. There are many, many of these very small companies, but they do not really amount to much in 'economic size' or footprint so they are not covered by the FTSE All Share. So when you buy this index, do not think you are buying *all* the UK market – no one index captures that!

So FTSE 100 or FTSE All Share – which one should you invest in? If you want a broader market use the FTSE All Share, whereas if you want a more focused large-cap index go for the FTSE 100, but be aware that even the FTSE All Share is still, in reality, a large-cap index. Also, whatever you do *do not buy both* – you will be effectively duplicating a lot of the holdings and the FTSE All Share index tends to move in the same direction as the FTSE 100, so you will not get much diversification benefit.

As for the funds that track the index, they tend to split into two broad categories – a wide range of unit trust trackers and a smaller range of exchange traded funds. By and large, the ETFs tend to be cheaper and more effective at tracking the index, although the cheapest fund by far that tracks the FTSE All Share is a unit trust index tracker from Fidelity, charging just 0.28 percent per annum.

FTSE 250 – UK Mid Caps

Weight of largest holding	Babcock International 1.23%
Weight of top 10 largest holdings	10.74%
Yield % December 2011	2.39%

Returns

Index	2011	2010	2009	2008	2007
FTSE 250	–10%	6.6%	24.4%	–47%	–15%

Appendix: The Essential 25

The index – our analysis

ANALYSIS

Likely risk (high/medium/low)	Medium
Likely volatility	Medium
Suitable for 'simple' investors, i.e. small ISA investors	Yes
Diversification risk with top holdings, i.e. top three more than 20% of fund	No – very well diversified
Likely to be a core holding?	Yes
Market Cap based (MC)/Screened (S)	MC
Appeal to income investors?	Yes
Risk factors?	Very focused on the UK economy
Top three holding as % of total fund December 2011	3.6%
Country breakdown: top three – December 2011	100% UK listed
Sector breakdown: top three – December 2011	Financial services 26% Industrials 20% Travel and leisure 7.56%

Top 10 constituents of the index

Company	% of index
Babcock International Group	1.23
Pennon Group	1.22
Croda International	1.17
Wood Group (John) Plc ORD GBP 0.0428571	1.14
Aberdeen Asset Mgmt.	1.13
Informa	1.02
Alliance Tr.	0.98
LONMIN	0.95
Drax Group	0.95
Investec	0.95

Featured ETFs

Name of fund	Index	TER basis points pa %	Physical or synthetic	ISIN or EPIC (italics and bold)
AMUNDI ETF FTSE 250	FTSE 250	0.25	Synthetic	F25A
DB FTSE 250 ETF	FTSE 250	0.35	Synthetic	***LU0292097317***
HSBC FTSE 250 ETF	FTSE 250	0.35	Physical	***IE00B64PTF05***
iShares FTSE 250	FTSE 250	0.40	Physical	MIDD
Lyxor ETF FTSE 250 – NTR GBP	FTSE 250 – NTR	0.35	Synthetic	L250
Lyxor ETF FTSE 250 – GBP	FTSE 250 –	0.35	Synthetic	250F
Source FTSE® 250 ETF	FTSE 250 –	0.65	Synthetic	S250
CS ETF IE on MSCI UK Small Cap	MSCI UK Small Cap	0.58	Physical	CUKS
RBS HGSC Tracker	RBS HGSC	0.60	Synthetic	RS64

Featured unit trust tracker

Fund	Annual management charge
HSBC FTSE 250 Index Ret Inc	0.27%

Comments

The FTSE 250 index is another of the big market capitalisation-weighted indices, this time covering the 'mid-capitalised companies' traded on the London Stock Exchange. According to its developers, the FTSE Group, 'the Index is designed to measure the performance of the mid-cap capital and industry segments of the UK market not covered by the large-cap FTSE 100 Index, which pass screening for size and liquidity' and represents approximately 15 percent of the UK stock market capitalisation.

What are you buying when you invest in a FTSE 250 index fund? This hugely underrated and arguably under-reported index offers investors three big plays – the UK as an economy, growth companies and enormous diversification. It is also worth noting that over much of the first decade of the twenty-first century the index has also offered better returns with lower volatility. The FTSE 250 index is a crucial index in our view because it is very much focused on UK plc as an economy, with companies that will genuinely capture the future growth potential of the British economy, with sterling earnings. Obviously in a recession, that UK focus is something of a weakness and the larger-cap indices with their globally diversified components seem like a safer play, but many investors are unsure about what exactly it is they are buying with something like the FTSE 100. Is this large-cap index really capturing any broad trend except globalisation?

The FTSE 250 also tends to be jam packed with faster growing companies, many of them having risen from the FTSE Small Cap index, with more than a few on their way up into the FTSE 100. Again that growth profile is also a weakness in bear markets as growth companies can find themselves going ex growth, with the inevitable consequences for the share price. We are also strongly attracted by the diversification on offer in this index – those 250 companies (actually many index trackers have 252 funds) include a huge range of companies and the top holdings comprise much less than 5 percent of the total index value.

Should you buy it? Our feeling is that the FTSE 250 is one for more risk-friendly investors who do not mind taking on the potential for greater rewards. It tends to rise faster and fall faster than its bigger siblings (the FTSE 100 and the All Share). As for funds, there is one major unit trust tracker from HSBC plus three cheaper ETFs from iShares, Lyxor and Deutsche, all with TERs of less than 0.5 percent.

FTSE All Stocks Gilt

Weight of largest holding	4.2%
Weight of top 10 largest holdings	35%
Yield at end December 2011 (flat yield)	4%

Returns

Index	*2011*	*2010*	*2009*	*2008*	*2007*
FTSE British Government All Stocks	12%	3.2%	–4.6%	7%	1.2%

The index – our analysis

ANALYSIS	
Likely risk (high/medium/low)	Low
Likely volatility	Low
Suitable for 'simple' investors, i.e. small ISA investors	Yes
Diversification risk with top holdings, i.e. top three more than 20% of fund	No
Likely to be a core holding?	Yes
Market Cap based (MC)/Screened (S)	MC
Appeal to income investors?	Yes
Risk factors?	Very, very low risk of government default
Top three holding as % of total fund end December 2011	11%
Country breakdown: top three – December 2011	100% UK listed
Sector breakdown: top three – December 2011	100% UK conventional gilts

Top 10 constituents of the index

Top 10 holdings – 29/12/2011

Currency: GBP

Security	Coupon	Maturity	% weight
UK CONV GILT 5 09/07/2014	5	07/09/2014	4.2
UK CONV GILT 4.75 09/07/2015	4.75	07/09/2015	3.79
UK CONV GILT 4.75 03/07/2020	4.75	07/03/2020	3.76
UK CONV GILT 4.5 03/07/2013	4.5	07/03/2013	3.63
UK CONV GILT 2.25 03/07/2014	2.25	07/03/2014	3.51
UK CONV GILT 5 03/07/2018	5	07/03/2018	3.48
UK CONV GILT 4 09/07/2016	4	07/09/2016	3.44
UK CONV GILT 8 06/07/2021	8	07/06/2021	3.33
UK CONV GILT 4.25 06/07/2032	4.25	07/06/1932	3.32
UK CONV GILT 4.25 12/07/2027	4.25	07/12/2027	3

Main UK government bond ETFs

Name of fund	Index	TER basis points pa %	Physical or synthetic	ISIN or EPIC (italics and bold)
DB IBOXX® £ GILTS TOTAL RETURN INDEX ETF	iBoxx GILTS TOTAL RETURN	0.20	Synthetic	*__LU0321464066__*
iShares FTSE UK All Stocks Gilt	FTSE UK All Stocks Gilt	0.20	Physical	IGLT
Lyxor ETF iBoxx £ Gilts – GBP	iBoxx Gilts –	0.18	Synthetic	GILS
DB BOXX® UK GILT INFLATION-LINKED TR INDEX ETF	BOXX UK GILT INFLATION-LINKED TR	0.20	Synthetic	*__LU0321464223__*
iShares Barclays Capital £ Index-Linked Gilts	Barclays Capital -Linked Gilts	0.25	Physical	INXG
Lyxor ETF iBoxx UK Gilt Inflation-Linked – GBP	iBoxx UK Gilt Inflation-Linked –	0.22	Synthetic	GILI
iShares FTSE Gilts UK 0–5	FTSE Gilts UK 0–5	0.20	Physical	IGLS

Featured unit trust trackers

Name of fund	TER basis points pa %	Additional costs
Vanguard UK Government Bond Index	0.15%	0.10% (Dilution Levy)
Vanguard UK Long Duration Gilt Index	0.15%	0.10% (Dilution Levy)
HSBC UK Gilt (FTSE All Stocks TR) Index	0.27	0

Index constituents (bonds) by maturity/year

0–3 years	16.79%
3–5 years	14.63%
5–7 years	6.28%
7–10 years	18.51%
10–15 years	6.04%
15–20 years	8.77%
20+ years	28.98%

Comments

This index's full title is actually the FTSE Actuaries Government Securities UK Gilts All Stock index. It gives exposure to a diversified basket of UK government bonds, across all maturities, all in the conventional space, i.e. there are no index-linked holdings within this exclusively sterling-denominated fund. That makes this index a brilliant tool for buying into a diversified basket of what are called conventional government securities, otherwise known as gilts.

The index is not well known for sure and there are currently only a few ETFs that track this index, but we view this as an absolutely core holding for all but the most adventurous investor. Why? If you want bonds exposure, your safest bet is probably gilts and if you want the best basket of sterling gilts this index gives you that in spades. What's even better is that the ETFs that track this index are all incredibly cheap, with not one fund charging more than 30 basis points! One note of caution though – you probably shouldn't buy into this index if you think inflation is about to shoot up as the UK index-linked variant is probably a better idea.

The wider iShares bond family

It is worth noting that iShares boasts a much wider range of bond/fixed-income security index tracking funds or ETFs, offering investors access to everything from global government inflation bonds to UK corporate bonds. In the first box below we have listed all the main sterling-based bond funds available at December 2011 – the second box looks at the range of global bond funds.

Main iShares bond ETFs

Name of fund	Index	TER basis points pa %	ISIN or EPIC (italics and bold)
iShares Barclays Capital Euro Corporate Bond	Barclays Capital Euro Corporate Bond	0.20	***IEAC***
iShares Barclays Capital Euro Corporate Bond 1–5	Barclays Capital Euro Corporate Bond 1–5	0.20	***SE15***
iShares Barclays Capital Euro Corporate Bond ex-Financials	Barclays Capital Euro Corporate Bond ex-Financials	0.20	***EEXF***
iShares Barclays Capital Euro Corporate Bond ex-Financials 1–5	Barclays Capital Euro Corporate Bond ex-Financials 1–5	0.20	***EEX5***
iShares Markit iBoxx $ Corporate Bond	Markit iBoxx $ Corporate Bond	0.20	***LQDE***
iShares Markit iBoxx $ High Yield Capped Bond	Markit iBoxx $ High Yield Capped Bond	0.50	***SHYU***
iShares Markit iBoxx £ Corporate Bond	Markit iBoxx Corporate Bond	0.20	***SLXX***
iShares Markit iBoxx £ Corporate Bond 1–5	Markit iBoxx Corporate Bond 1–5	0.20	***IS15***
iShares Markit iBoxx £ Corporate Bond ex-Financials	Markit iBoxx Corporate Bond ex-Financials	0.20	***ISXF***
iShares Markit iBoxx Euro Corporate Bond	Markit iBoxx Euro Corporate Bond	0.20	***IBCX***
iShares Markit iBoxx Euro Covered Bond	Markit iBoxx Euro Covered Bond	0.20	***ICOV***
iShares Markit iBoxx Euro High Yield Bond	Markit iBoxx Euro High Yield Bond	0.50	***IHYG***
iShares Barclays Capital Emerging Market Local Govt Bond	Barclays Capital Emerging Market Local Govt Bond	0.50	***SEMI***
iShares JPMorgan $ Emerging Markets Bond Fund	JPMorgan $ Emerging Markets Bond	0.45	***SEMB***
iShares Barclays Capital Euro Aggregate Bond	Barclays Capital Euro Aggregate Bond	0.25	***IEAG***

Name of fund	Index	TER basis points pa %	ISIN or EPIC (italics and bold)
iShares Barclays Capital Euro Government Bond 10–15	Barclays Capital Euro Government Bond 10–15	0.20	IEGZ
iShares Barclays Capital Euro Government Bond 1–3	Barclays Capital Euro Government Bond 1–3	0.20	IBGS
iShares Barclays Capital Euro Government Bond 15–30	Barclays Capital Euro Government Bond 15–30	0.20	IBGL
iShares Barclays Capital Euro Government Bond 3–5	Barclays Capital Euro Government Bond 3–5	0.20	IBGX
iShares Barclays Capital Euro Government Bond 5–7	Barclays Capital Euro Government Bond 5–7	0.20	IEGY
iShares Barclays Capital Euro Government Bond 7–10	Barclays Capital Euro Government Bond 7–10	0.20	IBGM
iShares Barclays Capital Euro Inflation Linked Bond	Barclays Capital Euro Inflation Linked Bond	0.25	IBCI
iShares Citigroup Global Government Bond	Citigroup Global Government Bond	0.20	IGLO
iShares Barclays Capital Global Inflation-Linked Bond	Barclays Capital Global Inflation-Linked Bond	0.25	IGIL
iShares FTSE UK All Stocks Gilt	FTSE UK All Stocks Gilt	0.20	IGLT
iShares Barclays Capital £ Index-Linked Gilts	Barclays Capital -Linked Gilts	0.25	INXG
iShares FTSE Gilts UK 0–5	FTSE Gilts UK 0-5	0.20	IGLS
iShares Barclays Capital US Aggregate Bond	Barclays Capital US Aggregate Bond	0.25	SUAG
iShares Barclays Capital $ Treasury Bond 1–3	Barclays Capital $ Treasury Bond 1-3	0.20	IBTS
iShares Barclays Capital $ Treasury Bond 7–10	Barclays Capital $ Treasury Bond 7-10	0.20	IBTM
iShares Barclays Capital Euro Treasury Bond	Barclays Capital Euro Treasury Bond	0.20	SEGA
iShares Barclays Capital Euro Treasury Bond 0–1	Barclays Capital Euro Treasury Bond 0-1	0.20	IEGE
iShares Barclays Capital $ TIPS	Barclays Capital $ TIPS	0.25	ITPS

The indices used in the wider iShares bond range – definitions

> The **JPMorgan EMBI Global Core index** represents debt obligations issued in US dollars (USD) by sovereign and quasi-sovereign entities of emerging market countries. The US dollar-denominated index is a highly recognised benchmark for sovereign and quasi-sovereign emerging market bonds including both fixed- and floating-rate instruments. The methodology of the index is designed to distribute the weights of each country within the index by limiting the weights of countries with higher debt outstanding and reallocating this excess to countries with lower debt outstanding.
>
> The **Barclays US Government Inflation-linked Bond index** (US TIPS) measures the performance of the TIPS market. It is the largest market in the Barclays Global Inflation-Linked Bond index. Inflation-linked indices include only capital indexed bonds with a remaining maturity of one year or more. Bonds must be capital indexed and linked to an eligible inflation index. They should be denominated in US dollars and pay coupon and principal in US dollars.
>
> **Barclays Euro Government Inflation Linked Bond index** measures the performance of the EuroZone government index-linked bond market with securities from Germany, France, Italy and Greece.
>
> The **Barclays World Government Inflation-Linked Bond index** measures the performance of the major government inflation-linked bond markets. The index is designed to include only those markets in which a global government linker fund is likely to invest. To be included, a market must have aggregate issuance of $4 billion or more and have minimum rating of A3/A– for G7 and EuroZone issuers, Aa3/AA– otherwise. Markets included in the index, in the order of inclusion, are the UK, Australia, Canada, Sweden, the US, France, Italy, Japan, Germany and Greece.
>
> The **iBoxx USD Liquid Investment Grade Top 30 index** is a basket of 30 bonds, rebalanced quarterly following the close of the market on the last business day of February, May, August and November each year. It is designed to provide balanced representation of the US dollar investment-grade corporate market by the means of the most liquid corporate bonds available.

This range of corporate and government bond from iShares is market leading and hugely innovative – many if not most of them deserve to sit at the heart of any portfolio. Their biggest strength is their sheer range, taking in everything from index-linked government bonds through to sterling corporate bonds from the most reputable issuers. In particular, different funds will recommend themselves to different kinds of investors.

- As we have already noted, every investor should at least consider investing something in the FTSE All Stocks Gilts fund. It is an absolutely core holding in any mixed bonds/equity portfolio.

- Bearish investors worried by the growth of inflation in the future should opt for the index-linked funds, with most investors recommended to focus on either the UK variant or the global fund, which is also a great investment idea.
- Investors looking for a superior yield should look at the range of corporate bond funds and most probably the sterling variant. Be aware though that corporate bonds can move in sympathy with equities and if corporate defaults gather pace this fund could be in for a hard time as capital values fall – it is not a great hiding place in a recession, unlike most traditional gilts.
- Investors looking for a slightly riskier bet may want to look at the emerging markets bond fund. Emerging market bonds have shot up in value for prime low-risk countries in recent years and there is every chance that as the credit reputation of countries like Brazil and Russia improves, capital prices could go back up again.

This range of glitz bond funds is also great value in our opinion – all but a tiny handful of the funds charge less than 0.30 percent. One of the few funds to charge above that level is the emerging markets fund, which is a tad expensive with a TER of 0.45 percent, but even that is good value considering its range of investments in emerging markets bonds.

Risks? Of course there is no free lunch in modern investment and although these funds should by and large do well in bearish equity markets (with the exception maybe of corporate bond funds), they will all probably lag if shares start booming. Also be aware that if inflation does evaporate and turn into deflation, index-linked bonds may suffer.

FTSE Small Cap

Returns from FTSE Small Cap index

Index	2011	2010	2009	2008	2007
FTSE Small Cap index	14%	16%	50%	–45%	–12%

The index – our analysis

ANALYSIS	
Likely risk (high/medium/low)	High
Likely volatility	High
Suitable for 'simple' investors, i.e. small ISA investors	Yes
Diversification risk with top holdings, i.e. top three more than 20% of fund	No
Likely to be a core holding?	Yes
Market Cap based (MC)/Screened (S)	MC
Appeal to income investors?	No
Top three holding as % of total fund end December 2011	Under 3%
Country breakdown: top three – end December 2011	100% UK listed

Comments

The main UK based small-cap index is called the FTSE UK Small Cap index and it consists of companies outside the FTSE 350 index – smaller companies – and represents approximately 2–3 percent of the UK market capitalisation with an aggregate value of anything between £25 billion and £50 billion.

In the US, small-cap indices like the Russell 2000 are big business – dozens of funds (tracker or otherwise) follow the small-cap segment of the US market. In the UK, by contrast, small-cap investing is exclusively the preserve of actively managed funds – there are very few small-cap index trackers in the UK and not one ETF or unit trust tracker follows the all-important FTSE Small Cap index. This relative paucity of small-cap tracker funds in the UK is a huge pity because small-cap investing works – as we'll see a little later in this section there's a large amount of academic evidence that points to small-cap investing delivering vastly superior returns over the long term despite the increased risks.

There are currently two small-cap trackers available on the UK market – one tracks the well-regarded RBS HGSC index of smaller companies while the other (an ETF from Credit Suisse) tracks the MSCI UK Smaller Companies index. Both trackers are featured in the table below, and both possess fairly reasonable charges of 0.60 percent per annum or less. We've also featured the top holdings in the Credit Suisse ETF in another table. Note that the RBS Tracker is actually a certificate and not an ETF – it also doesn't pay a dividend as it's a total return index. Be aware that there are specific counterparty risks with any certificate as it is in effect an IOU issued against RBS debt.

Name of fund	Asset class	Index	TER basis points pa %	Physical or synthetic	ISIN or EPIC (italics and bold)
CS ETF IE on MSCI UK Small Cap	UK Small Cap	MSCI UK Small Cap	0.58	Physical	CUKS
RBS HGSC Tracker	UK Small Cap	RBS HGSC	0.60	Synthetic	RS64

The top five holdings in the Credit Suisse ETF fund

Company	Weighting
PENNON GROUP	1.55%
IMI	1.50%
CRODA INTERNATIONAL	1.46%
INFORMA GROUP	1.26%
WOOD GROUP (JOHN)	1.25%

There is one other niche fund worth examining in addition to these two conventional trackers – the Henderson Fledgling Trust Ltd. This is an unusual creature. It is a listed investment trust that largely tracks the constituents of the FTSE Fledgling Index of tiny micro-cap stocks. This little-known index tracks any company that does not make it into the FTSE All Share because it is too small – companies in the index make up some £10 billion by value of listed securities on the London Stock Exchange's main market and constitute 22 percent by number of listed UK stocks. The Henderson investment trust follows this index but then adds it own special twist – an actively managed overlay. At least 65 percent of the portfolio is managed on an indexed basis while an active overlay is then applied to up to 35 percent of the portfolio, including a maximum of 20 percent invested in AIM stocks that meet the Fledgling market capitalisation criteria and were formerly traded on the main market. According to the fund managers, the active 'overlay overweights fledgling and AIM companies favoured by Henderson's active investment process, as well as firms where directors have recently bought their own shares. Conversely, any Fledgling constituents that appear insolvent on a one-year view are not held'. This is a very unusual strategy and means that you are, in effect, buying into a hybrid passive index tracking/active small-cap fund, all with a relatively low expense ratio of just 0.8 percent.

Why small-cap investing works

> The most potent piece of evidence comes in the shape of a joint London Business School/ABN Amro study, run by Professors Elroy Dimson and Paul Marsh a few years back, on a rival small-cap index, called the HGSC index – the Hoare Govett small-cap – and its sister HG1000 index. The HGSC index (it represents the bottom 10 percent by market cap) and the HG1000 (the bottom 2 percent by market cap) have been 'live' for over 18 years, but Dimson and Marsh have pushed their analysis way back to 1955. Their conclusions are startling. Both the HGSC and the HG1000 have outperformed the FTSE All Share by 3.5 percent and 5.7 percent per annum

respectively on an annualised return basis for more than 40 years. In simple terms that outperformance means that £1000 invested in the HGSC in 1955 would today be worth £1.8 million, vs £400,000 with the FTSE All Share (with dividends reinvested in both cases). If you had opted for the HG1000 index your returns would be even greater – £4.6 million.

What seems to work in the UK also seems to work globally. James O'Shaughnessy in his research for 'What works on Wall Street' found that really tiny stocks, measured by market value and called micro-stocks, deliver by far the biggest returns. In the 45 years between 1951 and 1996 these micro-caps delivered a compounded annual return of 35 percent.

December 31 1996 value of $10,000 invested on December 31 1951 excl microcaps in millions		*Compounded annual returns*	*Sharpe adjusted risk return index by market cap* 1951–1996 (higher is better)
All stocks	2.7	14.97%	49
Large stocks	1.6	13.11%	48
Small stocks	3.8	16.30%	50
S&P 500	1.7	13.39%	48
> $1bn	1.6	13.18%	48
500m to 1bn	1.9	14.04%	47
250–500m	3.4	15.90%	50
100m to 250m	3.4	16.51%	46
25m to 100m	7.8	19.75%	48
Microcap	NA	35.93%	64

Source: What works on Wall Street, James O'Shaughnessy

Even after adjusting this return for the much greater risk taken on board (he uses a measure called the sharpe adjusted risk return) microcaps delivered the biggest return by far.

Small caps grow faster

What is behind this consistent outperformance? The best answer is probably the simplest – it is much easier for a small company to grow really fast than a huge company. Call it the investing equivalent of gravity. The hard evidence comes in the table below from the CompanyREFs guide. It shows the average earnings growth rates of companies in different indices, ranging from the microcaps of the FTSE Fledgling through to the FTSE 100.

What is interesting is that small-cap shares consistently outperform both the FTSE 100 and FTSE 250 sectors both in projected earnings growth for the coming year and over the last three and five years. But the Fledgling index – the one that contains really very small companies – has produced much lower returns. These classic micro-caps have turned in some decent five-year EPS growth rates, but over the last five years, average EPS growth has been *negative*.

All figures are median figures

Measure	Market	FTSE 100	Mid 250	Small cap	Fledgling
Prospective EPS growth rate % current year	8.62	9.02	10.6	11.3	5.31
Three-year EPS growth rate	14.7	11	8.68	12.9	11.3
Five-year EPS growth rate	7.91	5.54	7.29	7.35	−1.33

Source: CompanyREFS – Hemmington Scott

It's all about risk ... and containing it

The huge variation in earnings growth between the small-caps index and those from the micro-caps is easily answered – risk. Micro-caps tend not to have an enormously proven business trading record and many fail completely – they simply vanish without trace.

Returns can also be hugely variable. Since the HGSC index went live there have been negative returns in five years and positive returns in thirteen. There are also some other less obvious problems with investing in small caps. Small caps suffer from a distinct sector bias. Because small caps are by definition valued at no more than £500 million in the UK there are no banks or tobacco companies. There are also remarkably few utility stocks and life assurers and there is even a paucity of oil and gas stocks. More importantly O'Shaughnessy himself has noted that the small-cap returns he obtained in his analysis can be 'chimera' because the only way to achieve those returns was 'to invest a few million dollars in over 2000 stocks'.

That practical issue of capturing the small-cap effect suggests one reason why no one has yet to launch a UK small-cap ETF – it is simply too difficult and expensive to do.

FTSE World exc UK

Weight of largest holding	1.85% (Exxon)
Weight of top 10 largest holdings	11%
Yield	1.9%

Returns

Index	2011	2010	2009	2008	2007
FTSE World exc UK	−11%	10%	32%	−42%	10.8%

The index – our analysis

ANALYSIS	
Likely risk (high/medium/low)	Low to medium
Likely volatility	Low
Suitable for 'simple' investors, i.e. small ISA investors	Yes
Diversification risk with top holdings, i.e. top three more than 20% of fund	No
Likely to be a core holding?	Yes
Market Cap based (MC)/Screened (S)	MC
Appeal to income investors?	Yes
Risk factors?	It invests in global equities and has no bond component
	Underlying currency risk
Top three holding as % of total fund end December 2011	4.6%

Continued

ANALYSIS	
Country breakdown: top three – December 2011	US 56%, Japan 9.5%, Canada 5%
Sector breakdown: top three – end December 2011	Financials 18%, Industrials 12%, Consumer Goods 12%

Comments

Here is a simple idea – rather than buy lots of different developed world markets (the US, Europe and Japan, for instance), why not buy into one fund that tracks a big, well-known index of nearly all the developed world's stock markets? That's the idea behind a small band of ETFs that is a compelling proposition for private investors – you can buy the world developed markets outside of the UK and then add to that vast diversity of companies by investing in one of the UK main market trackers (FTSE 100 or FTSE All). With just two funds you would have access to the vast majority of the world's stock markets.

These global equity indices come in two guises. The most common is based around an index called the MSCI World Index, which includes the UK market (about 10 percent of total holdings) and is focused on the world's developed exchanges. Its potentially more compelling rival is the FTSE World exc UK Index. This index excludes the UK, which is useful for investors looking to add diversity to their portfolios, although the net effect on the composition of the two indices is not that great. Note also that these indices track only equities – not bonds – and are focused on developed world markets and blue chips in particular.

Global equity funds

Name of fund	Asset class	Index	TER basis points pa %	Physical or synthetic	ISIN or EPIC (italics and bold)
AMUNDI ETF MSCI WORLD – USD	**Global Developed**	MSCI WORLD	0.45	Synthetic	CW8U
CS ETF (IE) PLC CS ETF (IE) ON MSCI WORLD GBP	**Global Developed**	MSCI WORLD	0.40	Synthetic	CWD1

Continued

Name of fund	Asset class	Index	TER basis points pa %	Physical or synthetic	ISIN or EPIC (italics and bold)
DB FTSE ALL-WORLD EX UK ETF	**Global Developed**	FTSE ALL-WORLD EX UK	0.40	Synthetic	***LU0322254383***
HSBC MSCI WORLD ETF	**Global Developed**	MSCI WORLD	0.35	Physical	***IE00B4X9L533***
iShares FTSE Developed World ex-UK	**Global Developed**	FTSE Developed World ex-UK	0.50	Physical	IWXU
iShares MSCI ACWI	**Global Developed**	MSCI ACWI	0.60	Physical	SSAC
iShares MSCI World	**Global Developed**	MSCI World	0.50	Physical	IWRD
iShares MSCI World (Acc)	**Global Developed**	MSCI World	0.50	Physical	SWDA
iShares MSCI World Monthly EUR Hedged	**Global Developed**	MSCI World Monthly EUR Hedged	0.55	Physical	IWDE
iShares MSCI World Monthly GBP Hedged	**Global Developed**	MSCI World Monthly Hedged	0.55	Physical	IGWD
SPDR MSCI ACWI ETF	**Global Developed**	MSCI ACWI	0.50	Physical	ACWI
SPDR MSCI ACWI IMI ETF	**Global Developed**	MSCI ACWI IMI	0.55	Physical	ACIM
Lyxor ETF MSCI World (GBP) – NTR	**Global Developed**	MSCI World NTR	0.40	Synthetic	LWOR
Lyxor ETF MSCI World (GBP) – NTR	**Global Developed**	MSCI World NTR	0.45	Synthetic	LWOU

So, which of these global equities ETFs should you consider buying? As we have already noted above, our preference is to buy an ETF that invests globally but avoids the UK, which is why we like the FTSE exc UK funds – both iShares and Deutsche DBX offer trackers for this index with a TER of 0.50 percent and 0.40 percent respectively. We think that most investors are already rather too biased towards UK stocks and so one of these funds should fit the bill. It's also worth noting that Vanguard has a unit trust that tracks this index with a TER of just 0.30 percent which is the cheapest tracker in this class. What is even better in our view is that all of these ETFs and unit trusts are very diversified – in both cases (the MSCI World and FTSE All World) you are buying into a portfolio of companies where the top three companies comprise only between 4 percent and 9 percent of the total holdings. There is one downside though – you are buying a heavy mix of US stocks which comprise between 40 percent and 50 percent of total holdings. This may worry some UK investors concerned about exposure to the US, although we would say it is simply a reflection of what happens on the global equity markets. If you want to buy exposure in a slightly more balanced way, you could assemble an ETF portfolio that included a FTSE All UK tracker, a Eurozone tracker (the DJ EuroStoxx 50) and the MSCI USA fund – all in equal portions.

Alternatively we think it is possible to build a very simple, four-fund portfolio using either of these global funds, a FTSE All Share tracker, an MSCI Emerging Markets index fund and a global government bonds fund. Bundle up these four funds and you would have a diversified multi-asset, international portfolio on the cheap – the combined expense should not be more than 0.4 percent per annum.

FTSE World exc UK – Top 10 holdings – end December 2011

Top 10: Currency USD % 31 December 2011

Company	Country	%
EXXON MOBIL CORP	United States	1.85
APPLE INC	United States	1.75
MICROSOFT CORP	United States	1.07
NESTLE	Switzerland	1.02
CHEVRON CORP	United States	1
IBM	United States	0.99

Continued

Top 10: Currency USD % 31 December 2011

Company	Country	%
GENERAL ELECTRIC	United States	0.93
JOHNSON & JOHNSON	United States	0.87
PROCTER & GAMBLE	United States	0.87
AT&T INC	United States	0.85

MSCI – Top 10 world holdings – End December 2011

Top 10: Currency USD % 31 December 2011

Company	Country	%
EXXON MOBIL CORP	United States	1.87
APPLE INC	United States	1.67
IBM	United States	1.04
CHEVRON CORP	United States	0.95
NESTLE SA	Switzerland	0.9
MICROSOFT CORP	United States	0.89
GENERAL ELECTRIC	United States	0.86
AT&T INC	United States	0.83
PROCTER & GAMBLE	United States	0.81
JOHNSON & JOHNSON	United States	0.8

DJ EuroStoxx 50 – European Shares

All data from end December 2011

Weight of largest holding	6.5% (total)
Weight of top 10 largest holdings	39%
Yield	4.56% as of end December 2011

Returns

Index	2011	2010	2009	2008	2007
DJ EuroStoxx 50	−20%	−9%	12%	−26%	16%

The index – our analysis

ANALYSIS	
Likely risk (high/medium/low)	High
Likely volatility	Medium to high
Suitable for 'simple' investors, i.e. small ISA investors with small portfolios	Yes
Diversification risk with top holdings, i.e. top three more than 20% of fund	No
Likely to be a core holding?	Yes
Market Cap based (MC)/Screened (S)	MC
Appeal to income investors?	Yes

Continued

ANALYSIS	
Risk factors?	Eurozone markets, so some currency risk
	Underlying companies have strong export bias
Top three holding as % of total end December 2011	16%
Country breakdown: top three – end December 2011	France 36%
	Germany 31%
	Spain 14%
Sector breakdown: top three – end December 2011	Banks 13%
	Chemicals 8%
	Oil and Gas 11%

Highlighted DJ EuroStoxx 50 Europe (ETF) funds

Name of fund	Index	TER basis points pa %	Physical or synthetic	ISIN or EPIC (italics and bold)
CS ETF IE on EURO STOXX 50	EURO STOXX 50	0.20	Physical	CS51
DB EURO STOXX® 50 ETF	EURO STOXX 50	0.00	Synthetic	*LU0274211217*
DB EURO STOXX® 50 ETF	EURO STOXX 50	0.00	Synthetic	*LU0380865021*
iShares EURO STOXX 50	EURO STOXX 50	0.35	Physical	EUE
iShares EURO STOXX 50 (Acc)	EURO STOXX 50	0.35	Physical	SEUA
iShares STOXX Europe 50	EURO STOXX 50	0.35	Physical	EUN
Lyxor ETF EURO STOXX 50 TR – Net EUR	EURO STOXX 50	0.25	Synthetic	MSEG

Continued

Name of fund	Index	TER basis points pa %	Physical or synthetic	ISIN or EPIC (italics and bold)
Lyxor ETF EURO STOXX 50 TR – Net EUR	EURO STOXX 50	0.25	Synthetic	MSET
HSBC EURO STOXX 50 ETF	EURO STOXX 50	0.15	Physical	*IE00B4K6B022*
AMUNDI ETF MSCI EMU	MSCI EMU	0.38	Synthetic	CMU

Comments

The DJ EuroStoxx 50 has an ever so slightly snazzy-sounding ring to it, conjuring up images of smoky 1970s' Euro Disco, but the reality of this bellwether index is rather different. The DJ EuroStoxx 50 is the biggest and probably the most tracked European index for Eurozone blue chip outfits like Total or Siemens. According to index developer Dow Jones, 'it captures approximately 60 percent of the free-float market capitalisation of the Dow Jones Euro Stoxx Total Market Index (TMI), which in turn covers approximately 95 percent of the free-float market capitalisation of [Eurozone] countries'. It aims 'to provide a blue-chip representation of … leaders in the Eurozone' and includes companies from Austria, Belgium, Finland, France, Germany, Greece, Ireland, Italy, Luxembourg, the Netherlands, Portugal and Spain.

Before working out whether you should buy (or short) this index as part of your portfolio, it is important to understand that the DJ EuroStoxx 50 is one of many popular blue chip indices on offer, with rival indices (and accompanying index tracking funds) from both the FTSE Group and MSCI.

The first key distinction is between those such as the MSCI Europe index and the FTSEurofirst 100 index that include countries such as the UK and Switzerland which sit outside the Eurozone – this is also true for the broad MSCI Europe index. The DJ EuroStoxx 50 (alongside the FTSEurofirst 80 index) by contrast includes only companies from inside the Eurozone and excludes all UK and Swiss stocks (as well as nearly all Nordic companies) – there's also a smaller, less widely used MSCI index that does a similar job called the MSCI EMU. Just to confuse matters, the MSCI Europe excluding the UK index, used by ETF provider iShares, excludes the UK but includes all other European markets, including those outside the Eurozone. Our advice for most UK-based investors is to avoid any fund that is European by title but still invests in UK companies – you will probably already have a bias towards UK stocks in your portfolio and indices such as the FTSEurofirst 100 or MSCI Europe will simply increase that bias if only because 36 percent of the stocks in a European-wide index are British.

DJ EuroStoxx 50 composition as at end December 2011

Company	Country	%
TOTAL	France	6.49
SANOFI	France	5.16
SIEMENS	Germany	4.76
TELEFONICA	Spain	3.97
BANCO SANTANDER	Spain	3.73
BASF	Germany	3.7
ENI	Italy	3.13
UNILEVER	Netherlands	3.07
BAYER	Germany	3.07
SAP	Germany	2.81

Sector allocation

Sector	%
Financials	22.99
Consumer Goods	17.44
Oil & Gas	11.06
Basic Materials	9.79
Industrials	9.53
Utilities	8.51
Telecommunications	8.33
Health Care	5.16
Technology	3.88
Consumer Services	3.33

Composition of related European indices as at end December 2011

FTSEurofirst 100

Company	Country	%
VODAFONE GROUP	United Kingdom	3.61
HSBC HOLDINGS PLC	United Kingdom	3.49
BP PLC	United Kingdom	3.47
ROYAL DUTCH SHELL	United Kingdom	3.35
GLAXOSMITHKLINE	United Kingdom	2.99
TOTAL	France	2.98
ROYAL DUTCH SHELL PLC-B	United Kingdom	2.63
SANOFI	France	2.5
BRITISH AMERICAN TOBACCO	United Kingdom	2.4
SIEMENS	Germany	2.3

FTSEurofirst 80

Company	Country	%
TOTAL SA	France	5.18
SANOFI	France	4.33
SIEMENS	Germany	4
TELEFONICA	Spain	3.63
BASF	Germany	2.95
BANCO SANTANDER	Spain	2.92
ENI	Italy	2.55
UNILEVER	Netherlands	2.43
BAYER	Germany	2.43
LVMH MOET	France	2.37

MSCI Europe

Company	Country	% Weight
NESTLE	Switzerland	3.08
VODAFONE GROUP	United Kingdom	2.28
HSBC HOLDINGS	United Kingdom	2.2
BP PLC	United Kingdom	2.19
NOVARTIS	Switzerland	2.17
ROYAL DUTCH SHELL PLC-A	United Kingdom	2.16
ROCHE HOLDING	Switzerland	1.93
GLAXOSMITHKLINE	United Kingdom	1.87
TOTAL SA	France	1.78
ROYAL DUTCH SHELL PLC-B	United Kingdom	1.65

The next key distinction is in number of shares listed – the DJ EuroStoxx 50 is by definition focused on just the top 50 companies, the FTSEurofirst 80 on the top 80 and the FTSEurofirst 100 on the top 100. That concentration on top companies matters because the top three stocks in the DJ EuroStoxx index account for just under 17 percent of the fund whereas in the MSCI Europe Index they account for less than 8 percent.

So, if you are after an index that tracks only Eurozone blue chips – and only the biggest – the DJ EuroStoxx 50 is probably the index for you. Luckily there's a great deal of choice with most ETFs charging a very low rate to track the main indices – the cheapest is from Deutsche DB with a TER of 0.00 percent or zero. This low fee is accomplished by some clever financial engineering using everything from dividend optimisation through to stock lending. Market leader iShares seems expensive by comparison for its physical tracker at 0.35 percent although it's worth noting that Vanguard has an equivalent physical tracker fund with a TER of just 0.25 percent (that unit trust tracks something called the FTSE Developed Europe ex-UK Equity Index). Overall, these DJ EuroStoxx ETFs are a bargain compared with virtually any active fund manager who will probably own roughly the same set of companies and charge you at least an extra 1 percent per annum for the privilege. It is also worth adding that if you want to stay focused on the Eurozone countries but with a slightly wider basket of shares that includes the 80 largest companies, you might want to consider looking at the iShares FTSEurofirst 80 ETF with a TER of just 0.4 percent.

Money Market Funds

The index – our analysis

ANALYSIS	
Likely risk (high/medium/low)	Low
Likely volatility	Low
Suitable for 'simple' investors, i.e. small ISA investors	Yes
Diversification risk with top holdings, i.e. top three more than 20% of fund	No
Likely to be a core holding?	Yes
Market Cap based (MC)/Screened (S)	MC
Total return (TR) or pays income (Inc)?	TR – rolls up into index and the ETF
Appeal to income investors?	No – does not make a payout

Comments

It is very unlikely that many private investors will have heard of an index called SONIA, which is a pity because it is a supremely important index if you happen to be in the banking game. The SONIA index is absolutely critical to the working of the UK financial system because it tells investors – and banks – what interest they can expect from overnight holdings of sterling cash. In essence, it is a proxy for the return on cash – or as the academics might say, it is the risk-free rate of return because it is the return from offering your cash overnight to the banks (though that may not strike all readers as an absolutely risk-free exercise, given the recent banking collapse). In technical terms the SONIA Total Return Index 'reflects a daily rolled deposit earning the SONIA rate (the Sterling Overnight Index Average), which is the short-term money market reference in the UK', according to ETF provider Deutsche db X-trackers. 'The Sterling Overnight Index Average is the weighted average rate of all unsecured sterling overnight cash transactions brokered in London ... with all counter parties in a minimum deal size of £25 million. SONIA is sponsored by the Wholesale Markets Brokers' Association (WMBA).'

You may also have noticed two key extra words in the index title – total returns. This index of returns from overnight sterling cash does not pay an income – the sterling deposits tracked by this index are compounded (reinvested) daily and the compounding is done every day during the year. So, do not buy into any vehicle that tracks this index expecting to receive an income – you will receive that income, but that return will come from capital gains rolled up over the period of your holding.

Why invest in a product that tracks this index? In simple terms, this is an alternative to holding cash in your portfolio. You do not have to rely on your investment provider working out what laughable rate they will pay you – you get the market return they would get if they invested their money on the markets. Banks borrow from each other if they do not have the exact funds and they use the SONIA index as their reference point. It also moves up and down with interest rates – when interest rates are low, this index will offer a low return and vice versa.

Currently there are only a few money market trackers, focused on the UK and US money markets – details of the DB and Credit Suisse ETFs are in the table below.

Name of fund	TER basis points pa %	Physical or synthetic	ISIN or EPIC (italics and bold)
CS ETF (IE) PLC CS ETF (IE) ON EONIA GBP	0.14	Synthetic	CEO1
CS ETF (IE) PLC CS ETF (IE) ON FED FUNDS EFFECTIVE RATE GBP	0.14	Physical	CFF1
DB FED FUNDS EFFECTIVE RATE TR INDEX ETF	0.15	Synthetic	*LU0321465469*
DB STERLING CASH ETF	0.15	Synthetic	*LU0321464652*
DB STERLING MONEY MARKET ETF	0.15	Synthetic	*LU0356592187*
DB US DOLLAR MONEY MARKET ETF	0.15	Synthetic	*LU0356591882*
Alternative?			
Source PIMCO Sterling Short Maturity ETF	0.35	Synthetic	QUID

As ETFs go, these money market trackers are a great idea, but with one big proviso – they cannot be used in an ISA. On the plus side, we really like the idea of money market ETFs because of their simplicity – Deutsche for instance uses derivatives and options to mimic the underlying action of buying into a basket of short-term deposit accounts (money market accounts) and then pays out the return to holders of the ETF.

Obviously there are two big provisos worth repeating. The first is that point about total returns – the interest is paid out as part of the total market value of the fund (which goes up every day in value because of that accrued interest), not as a dividend cheque. The second key point to consider is that this cannot be used in a maxi ISA – it can be used only in a mini-cash ISA because of the tax rules, which is a real shame in our humble opinion. Nevertheless, if you are looking for a cash alternative to hold some reserves, or an alternative vehicle to gilts funds, this is definitely one to consider. It is also worth noting that there is an equivalent US dollar money market ETF. According to Deutsche this separate index reflects a daily rolled deposit earning the federal funds effective rate, which is the short-term money market reference in the US. The federal funds rate is decided at Federal Open Market Committee (FOMC) meetings. Again the interest paid is compounded – according to DB the deposits are compounded (reinvested) daily and the compounding is done on a 360-day-per-year convention.

One final thought – there is an alternative way of accessing 'cash' or money market rates through an ETF from provider Source in collaboration with bonds giant Pimco. Their MINT PIMCO Sterling Short Maturity ETF tracks the major short duration (less than a year) bonds in issue in the UK and is very close to being as liquid as you can get in the world of bonds.

MSCI Emerging Markets

Weight of largest holding	3.26% (Korean electronics company Samsung)
Weight of top 10 largest holdings	17.5%
Yield	1.23%

Returns

Index	2011	2010	2009	2008	2007
MSCI Emerging Markets	–20.5%	2%	54%	–34%	34%

The graph below is for the iShares ETF and not the index.

The index – our analysis

ANALYSIS	
Likely risk (high/medium/low)	High
Likely volatility	High
Suitable for 'simple' investors, i.e. small ISA investors	Yes
Diversification risk with top holdings, i.e. top three more than 20% of fund	No
Likely to be a core holding?	Yes
Market Cap based (MC)/Screened (S)	MC
Appeal to income investors?	Yes
Risk factors?	Political risk, volatile markets
Top three holding as % of total fund end December 2011	7.2%
Country breakdown: top three – end December 2011	China 17% South Korea 15% Brazil 15%
Sector breakdown: top three – end December 2011	Financials 23% Energy 14% IT 13.5%

Comments

Investors have always harboured a strange dichotomy in their minds, involving a stark contrast between value and growth. Value is all about cheap stuff. It is boring, it is sensible, it is safe and it is the kind of stuff you would buy at a Morrisons or Asda if they sold shares, and it sort of does what it says on the tin, i.e. provide good value. Ranged against this is something called growth – faster-growing, sexier stuff that is a bit more expensive but worth the extra cost because it predicts a great future, provided the managers can deliver on the hope and the market position.

This hugely simplified dichotomy has usually been applied to developed world equities – there are even indices in the UK and US dedicated to only value or growth stocks. But this division can also be applied on a much grander level to all assets and investment ideas – increasingly large stock markets like ours in the UK and the US are, in effect, value markets, full of boring utilities, overweight oil mega-corporations and tobacco companies puffing out cash profits. The growth 'bits' of the globalised markets tend increasingly to belong to emerging markets in the developing world – places like India or China or even Russia (on a good day) are seen as much more exciting, much faster growing, more 'with it' in the new order of things.

The big problem for most ordinary mortals is one of accessibility – how on earth can investors hope to buy into the dozens of markets that comprise this fast-growing new investment universe (emerging markets as an asset class only really emerged in the 1980s)? Luckily there is an answer – the well-established MSCI Emerging Markets Index or MSCI EM for short. It is widely used by the institutions as a benchmark index and comprises all the world's main emerging stock markets in one composite index, although it's worth adding that you can also buy into the various different components (regional or national) on an individual basis if you so choose.

Over the past 20 or so years, returns from this index have been spectacular, even after the mauling of 2007, 2008 and 2011!

% returns from MSCI EM index

Index level:	*Price*
Currency:	*USD*
Date	*EM (EMERGING MARKETS) % change*
1988	34.9
1989	59.2
1990	−13.8
1991	56.0
1992	9.0
1993	71.3
1994	−8.7
1995	−6.9
1996	3.9
1997	−13.4
1998	−27.5

Continued

Index level:	Price
Currency:	USD
Date	EM (EMERGING MARKETS) % change
1999	63.7
2000	−31.8
2001	−4.9
2002	−8.0
2003	51.6
2004	22.4
2005	30.3
2006	29.2
2007	36.5
2008	−34.5
2009	54
2010	2
2011	−20

Before we look at the various funds that track this investment space, let's look at the index in a little more detail. According to index builders MSCI Barra, the 'MSCI Emerging Markets Index is a free-float-adjusted market-capitalisation index that is designed to measure equity market performance of emerging markets. As of June 2007 the MSCI Emerging Markets Index consisted of the following 25 emerging market country indices: Argentina, Brazil, Chile, China, Colombia, Czech Republic, Egypt, Hungary, India, Indonesia, Israel, Jordan, Korea, Malaysia, Mexico, Morocco, Pakistan, Peru, Philippines, Poland, Russia, South Africa, Taiwan, Thailand, and Turkey'. The top 10 companies within the index are in the table below – it is a smattering of Chinese and Taiwanese technology giants, Russian and Brazilian oil companies and the odd Israeli drugs company.

Top holdings of MSCI EM index

Top 10 holdings in MSCI EM US$

Company	Country	%
SAMSUNG ELECTRONICS	Korea (South)	3.26
TAIWAN SEMICONDUCTOR	Taiwan	2.01
CHINA MOBILE	China	1.97
GAZPROM	Russian Federation	1.75
AMERICA MOVIL	Mexico	1.61
PETROBRAS - PETROLEO BRAZ	Brazil	1.56
BANCO ITAU HOLD	Brazil	1.55
CIA VALE DO RIO	Brazil	1.43
BANCO BRADESCO	Brazil	1.24
PETROBRAS - PETROLEO BRAS ORD	Brazil	1.18

The MSCI EM index comprises a number of smaller, more specific regional and national indices, nearly all of which are tracked by separate ETFs. There are also a number of related smaller indices that do not quite fit inside the MSCI Emerging Markets mother ship but overlap. Chief among them is the MSCI AC (All Country) Far East ex Japan Index, which is a free-float-adjusted market-capitalisation weighted index that is 'designed to measure the equity market performance of the Far East, excluding Japan and comprises China, Hong Kong, Indonesia, Korea, Malaysia, Philippines, Singapore, Taiwan, and Thailand', i.e. emerging Asia. You may also notice MSCI AC Far East Ex-Japan Small Cap which is a variation of the emerging Asia index and tracks small-cap stocks.

The featured emerging markets (EM) ETF funds

Name of fund	TER basis points pa %	Physical or synthetic	ISIN or EPIC (italics and bold)
AMUNDI ETF MSCI EMERGING MARKETS – EUR	0.25	Synthetic	AEEM
AMUNDI ETF MSCI EMERGING MARKETS – USD	0.45	Synthetic	AUEM

Continued

Name of fund	TER basis points pa %	Physical or synthetic	ISIN or EPIC (italics and bold)
CS ETF Lux on MSCI Emerging Markets	0.68	Physical	CM1
DB MSCI EMERGING MARKETS TRN INDEX ETF	0.65	Synthetic	LU0292107645
HSBC MSCI EMERGING MARKETS ETF	0.60	Physical	IE00B5SSQT16
iShares MSCI Emerging Markets	0.75	Physical	IEEM
iShares MSCI Emerging Markets (Acc)	0.75	Physical	SEMA
Lyxor ETF MSCI Emerging Markets (GBP) – NTR	0.65	Synthetic	LEME
Lyxor ETF MSCI Emerging Markets (GBP) – NTR	0.65	Synthetic	LEMU
SPDR MSCI Emerging Markets ETF	0.65	Physical	EMRG
Source MSCI Emerging Markets ETF	0.40	Synthetic	MXFS

The most obvious choice for mainstream investors looking to buy into the emerging markets investment space is to start with the mother-ship index, namely the MSCI EM index, tracked by Lyxor, DBX and iShares among others. All these global EM ETFs are cheap, fairly diversified across different countries (although resources do tend to figure heavily) and biased towards the biggest and best companies in the global emerging markets space. We would recommend these global funds over any of the more country- or region-specific funds – ETFs that concentrate on just Russia or China, for example, are too risky and volatile for most simple, basic investors.

Returns from emerging markets

MSCI EM data to 1 January 2012 US$

Regional performance

MSCI index	1 Yr	3 Yr	5 Yr	10 Yr
BRIC	−24.6%	13.2%	−1.4%	13.6%
EM (EMERGING MARKETS)	−20.4%	16.4%	−0.2%	11.0%
EM ASIA	−19.3%	16.3%	0.0%	9.5%
EM EASTERN EUROPE	−23.0%	15.7%	−10.1%	11.4%
EM EUROPE	−25.0%	15.3%	−9.1%	10.7%
EM EUROPE & MIDDLE EAST	−25.0%	14.2%	−7.0%	8.7%
EM FAR EAST	−16.4%	16.8%	0.4%	9.1%
EM LATIN AMERICA	−21.4%	18.0%	3.6%	15.1%

Country performance

	1 Yr	3 Yr	5 Yr	10 Yr
CHINA	−20.3%	7.3%	−0.2%	12.2%
INDIA	−37.8%	12.8%	−2.5%	14.4%
INDONESIA	3.7%	44.3%	13.5%	29.3%
KOREA	−12.6%	23.4%	1.1%	11.5%
TAIWAN	−24.6%	16.1%	−3.7%	1.2%
BRAZIL	−24.1%	17.3%	4.9%	16.8%
RUSSIA	−21.0%	22.0%	−10.1%	12.0%
SOUTH AFRICA	−17.3%	18.6%	2.1%	15.0%

Source: MSCI Barra

The big question – index or passive?

Our broader concern with global EM index funds is whether a passive fund is necessarily the best approach to investing. One particularly trenchant critic of the index route is Dr Slim Feriani, veteran manager of Advance Developing Markets (ADD), one of the most successful emerging markets investment trusts. 'Particularly in the case of emerging markets,' says Dr Feriani, 'you do not want to invest in ETFs because they are structurally biased towards larger markets and larger companies. Therefore, you'd be missing out on some of the best investment opportunities in this asset class, which are often in smaller countries and the small and mid-cap space. These are best exploited by good, specialist and active stock pickers. We strongly believe that investing in emerging markets is for specialists, because of the complexity of investing in 25–40 different countries. You certainly should not go with single-country funds. Indeed, trying to play the "emerging markets" theme through a single-country ETF is like putting all your eggs in one basket. If you did invest in an Indian ETF early this year (XNIF), you'd have lost a third of your money by now.'

Supporters of index tracking emerging markets funds point out that specialist, active fund managers may be able to provide market-timing and risk-management skills, but that their expertise comes at a cost. Most actively managed, diversified emerging markets funds charge at least 1.5–2 percent a year in management fees plus an initial charge that can amount to 5 percent. ETFs from the likes of iShares, Lyxor and DBX charge between 0.5 percent and 0.8 percent a year, giving investors an automatic 1 percent or more extra return a year.

ETF supporters also argue that index funds are simpler and cleaner. They claim that most active fund managers fail to hit their benchmark returns whereas with an ETF you are simply buying the market. But Dr Feriani begs to differ. 'Even if you were to try to go for a more diversified ETF like a global emerging markets ETF, then it's no guarantee that it's actually going to track its index. Indeed, the iShares emerging markets ETF (EEM) was 6 percent behind the MSCI emerging markets index in 2007. That's a huge tracking error. Many good active managers did a lot better than that last year.'

The numbers tell a slightly more balanced story. Over some periods active fund managers such as Dr Feriani and Dr Mark Mobius at Templeton Emerging Markets Investment Trust have beaten the benchmark index. But in the first half of 2008, for example, Templeton's flagship fund was down 11 percent (compared with a 12 percent loss on the benchmark), whereas the iShares fund was down only 8.9 percent.

Investing in small caps

By and large we would accept that there is a strong case to be made for tracking emerging markets cheaply and effectively at a global level, although investors may want to top up their holdings with a more specialised actively managed fund from the likes of Progressive or Templeton. We cannot – by contrast – see any rationale for investing in specific national markets, bar perhaps in the major BRIC markets (Brazil, Russia, India and China). We believe that country-specific index tracking funds in the developing world are just too risky and specialised for the ordinary investor. Your best bet with specific countries is to either use a specialised active fund manager who can take those judgement calls for you or stick with a global EM index fund.

The one big exception to this rule of staying out of specialist markets comes with small caps. iShares offers two very specialist EM funds that we think are compelling for more adventurous types. The first is called the iShares Asia ex Japan Small Cap Fund. It is hugely diversified on a number of levels, with a great variety of nations and different sectors (Taiwan 22 percent, South Korea 21 percent, China 17 percent and Hong Kong 12 percent; financials, industrials, technology all fairly evenly represented). Crucially the focus on smaller caps is very welcome, especially when you consider that the average PE ratio of the 900-plus companies held in the portfolio is relatively low.

Clearly this is not a fund for risk-averse, inexperienced investors, but if you are willing to live with the likely increased volatility, this could be a great investment idea. We also like the idea of the iShares MSCI Emerging Markets Small Cap fund. The index providers define this segment of their wider EM index as any company in a 'country's equity universe whose total market capitalisation lies between $200 million and $1.5 billion'. This little-known index started in 1998 and by its peak in 2007 had quadrupled in value, but in the bear market of 2009 and 2011, the index crashed back in value, although it is still well ahead of its starting levels in 1998. The top 10 holdings are in the table below.

Top 10 holdings of iShares' MSCI EM SC

Company	Country	%
HOME PRODUCT CENTER	Thailand	1.88
MAHANAGAR TELEPHONE	India	1.64
HELBOR EMPREENDIMENTOS	Brazil	1.24
SUMMARECON AGUNG	Indonesia	1.18
HEMARAJ LAND DEVELOPMENT	Thailand	1.17
MARCOPOLO	Brazil	1.05
DIALOG GROUP	Malaysia	1.04
THAI UNION FROZEN	Thailand	0.95
MR PRICE GROUP LTD	South Africa	0.95
A.F.P. PROVIDA	Chile	0.93

What about BRIC funds?

There is one last emerging markets investment idea worth considering - why not invest in an emerging markets index that focuses on the top companies in Brazil, Russia, India and China, otherwise known as the BRIC countries? A number of providers offer tracker funds that track indices from all the major index - details are in the table below. These indices track the top 50 or 40 largest companies in the developing world and nearly all the funds include outfits like Petrobas from Brazil and Gazprom from Russia - companies that some analysts call the mega-caps of tomorrow. It is a potentially brilliant idea for an investor looking for a very focused investment, but there are some potentially big flaws.

Name of fund	Index	TER pa %	Physical or synthetic	ISIN or EPIC (italics and bold)
DB MSCI BRIC TRN INDEX ETF	MSCI BRIC TRN	0.65	Synthetic	***LU0589685956***
HSBC S&P BRIC 40 ETF	S&P BRIC 40	0.60	Physical	***IE00B5YLK706***
iShares FTSE BRIC 50	FTSE BRIC 50	0.74	Physical	BRIC
Market Access Daxglobal BRIC	Daxglobal Bric	0.65	Synthetic	BRDX

Perhaps the biggest potential flaw is that in some of the indices - the FTSE BRIC one for instance - well over 75 percent of the fund's investment is accounted for by big Chinese and Brazilian companies, with India and Russia comprising a rather measly 25 percent between them. To be fair to iShares and the FTSE, this index does precisely what it claims to, namely track the world's top 50 largest quoted companies based in the developing world, and it just so happens that these are mainly Chinese and Brazilian mega caps.

This makes us nervous. What we think you may be capturing here is not the emerging markets story you think you are catching - you are actually buying into a very small number of hugely successful Russian, Chinese and Brazilian oil companies (Gazprom, Lukoil, Vale and Petrobas), plus a smattering of successful Brazilian conglomerates.

You are also buying into funds where the top three holdings typically account for just over 20 percent of the fund - the top 10 account is usually well over 50 percent of the total holdings. That makes BRIC trackers highly concentrated (not unexpected in a mega-cap fund, to be fair) and not necessarily the most diversified we have seen.

All in all this is another great idea that might make rather a good investment if a) oil starts rising in price sharply, b) Brazil carries on growing fast and c) China avoids an economic hard landing. All of these eventualities could come to pass, but we wouldn't count on it – in our humble opinion the iShares BRIC 50 fund is just too risky for our main Essential 25 list.

Japan – TOPIX, MSCI Japan and Nikkei 225

Weight of largest holding	MSCI Japan (4% Toyota), Nikkei (6.8% Fast Retailing), Topix (Toyota 3%)
Weight of top 10 largest holdings	Varies
Yield %	Varies

Returns

Index	2011	2010	2009	2008	2007
Nikkei 225	–17%	–3%	19%	–42%	–11%
TOPIX	–19%	–1%	5.6%		
MSCI Japan	–16%	16%	–7%	–2%	–8.1%

Featured ETFs

Name of fund	Index	TER basis points pa %	Physical or synthetic	ISIN or EPIC (italics and bold)
AMUNDI ETF MSCI JAPAN – EUR	MSCI JAPAN	0.23	Synthetic	CJ1
ComStage ETF Nikkei 225®	Nikkei 225	0.45	Synthetic	ETF020
ComStage ETF TOPIX®	TOPIX	0.45	Synthetic	ETF021
CS ETF IE on MSCI Japan	MSCI Japan	0.38	Physical	CSJP

Continued

Name of fund	Index	TER basis points pa %	Physical or synthetic	ISIN or EPIC (italics and bold)
CS ETF IE on Nikkei 225	Nikkei 225	0.48	Physical	CNKY
DB MSCI JAPAN TRN INDEX ETF	MSCI JAPAN TRN	0.50	Synthetic	*LU0274209740*
HSBC MSCI JAPAN ETF	MSCI JAPAN	0.40	Physical	*IE00B5VX7566*
iShares MSCI Japan	MSCI Japan	0.59	Physical	IJPN
iShares MSCI Japan (Acc)	MSCI Japan	0.59	Physical	SJPA
iShares MSCI Japan Monthly EUR Hedged	MSCI Japan	0.64	Physical	IJPE
Lyxor ETF Japan (Topix®) (GBP) – GRT	Topix	0.50	Synthetic	LTPU
SG MSCI Japan (Quanto)	MSCI Japan	NA	Synthetic	JAPG
SG Nikkei 225	Nikkei 225	NA	Synthetic	S594
CS ETF IE on MSCI Japan Large Cap	MSCI Japan Large Cap	0.38	Physical	CJPL
iShares MSCI Japan SmallCap	MSCI Japan SmallCap	0.59	Physical	ISJP
CS ETF IE on MSCI Japan Small Cap	MSCI Japan Small Cap	0.48	Physical	CJPS

Comments

When most investors hear about Japan they usually hear about the price movements in something called the Nikkei 225 index. It is the most widely used measure of Japanese stock markets by the global media but most institutions prefer to use other indices as their benchmark. The most widely used index is a subset of the MSCI World index, called the MSCI Japan index, although Lyxor also uses a locally developed index, operated by the Tokyo Stock Exchange, called the TOPIX. This latter index is also known as the Tokyo Stock Price Index, and it is a fairly conventional capitalisation-weighted index of all companies listed on the First Section of the Tokyo Stock Exchange. The index is supplemented by the sub-indices of the 33 industry sectors. The MSCI index is also a market-capitalisation basis index comprising 85 percent of the constituents of the Tokyo Stock Exchange. The small-cap variation of the MSCI index comprises the smallest 40 percent of that index group, with market cap in the range of $200–$1,500 million.

This index is widely used by institutional investors and is also popular with structured product providers. It covers much the same kind of companies as the Nikkei but with a wider spread of companies and sectors, i.e. it is slightly less concentrated than the Nikkei. The MSCI index does not track an actual market by the same name as such – it is an institutional construct based on the widely used MSCI index series and includes virtually all the companies found on the TOPIX index.

As to which index or fund to use if you want to track Japan, the truth is that there is not a huge difference. The table below contains the top holdings in each of two main index structures covering Japan, MSCI Japan and the Nikkei. More adventurous types may also want to take a closer look at a specialist Japanese small-cap fund from iShares based on that MSCI index – small caps have had a torrid time in recent years, but the potential for a value-induced recovery is huge. We also like the fact that you are not paying an awful lot in terms of expenses for this specialised fund – its TER is a very reasonable 0.59 percent per annum.

MSCI Japan		**Nikkei 225**	
Company	*%*	*Company*	*%*
TOYOTA MOTOR	4.49	FAST RETAILING CO	6.88%
MITSUBISHI UFJ	2.64	FANUC	5.87%
CANON	2.45	SOFTBANK CORP	3.20%
HONDA MOTOR	2.43	KYOCERA CORP	2.88%
SUMITOMO MITSUI FINANCIAL	1.83	CANON INC	2.44%
TAKEDA PHARMACEUTICAL	1.69	KDDI	2.32%
MIZUHO FINANCIAL GROUP	1.5	HONDA MOTOR CO	2.18%
FANUC CORP	1.43	TOKYO ELECTRON	1.82%
MITSUBISHI CORP	1.39	SHIN-ETSU CHEMICAL CO	1.76%
NTT DOCOMO	1.37	TERUMO CORP	1.70%
		SECOM CO	1.66%
		TDK CORP	1.59%

DJ-UBS Agriculture

Returns

Index	*2011*	*2010*	*2009*	*2008*
DJ UBS Agri	–14%	40%	5%	–5.1%

The index – our analysis

ANALYSIS	
Likely risk (high/medium/low)	Medium to high
Likely volatility	Medium to high
Suitable for 'simple' investors, i.e. small ISA investors	No
Large/mid/small-cap bias?	NR
Diversification risk with top holdings, i.e. top three more than 20% of fund	NR
Likely to be a core holding?	Yes
Market Cap based (MC)/Screened (S)	MC
Appeal to income investors?	No
Risk factors?	Very specific sector Risk of falling agriculture prices
Appeal to investors looking to short main markets?	No

Featured ETFs

Name of fund	*Index*	*TER basis points pa %*	*ISIN or EPIC (italics and bold)*
Agricultural equities			
ETFX S-Net ITG Global Agri Business Fund	S-Net ITG Global Agri Business	0.65	AGRI
ETFX S-Net ITG Global Agri Business Fund £	S-Net ITG Global Agri Business	0.65	AGRP
iShares S&P Commodity Producers Agribusiness	S&P Commodity Producers Agribusiness	0.55	SPAG
PowerShares Global Agriculture NASDAQ OMX Fund	Global Agriculture NASDAQ OMX	0.75	PSGA

Continued

Name of fund	Index	TER basis points pa %	ISIN or EPIC *(italics and bold)*
Broad agricultural commodity			
ETFS Agriculture £ DJ-UBSCI SM	Agriculture DJ-CI SM	0.49	AGAP
ETFS Agriculture DJ-UBSCI SM	Agriculture DJ-UBSCI	0.49	AIGA
ETFS Forward Agriculture DJ-UBSCI-F3 SM	Forward Agriculture DJ-CI-F3 SM	0.49	FAGR
ETFS Leveraged Agriculture DJ-UBSCI SM	Agriculture DJ-UBSCI	0.98	LAGR
ETFS Leveraged Agriculture DJ-UBSCI SM	Agriculture DJ-UBSCI	0.98	LAGR
ETFS Short Agriculture DJ-UBSCI SM	Agriculture DJ-UBSCI	0.98	SAGR

Comments

If you want to capture the agriculture investment theme you have two basic choices – either track the agricultural commodities themselves (via their futures-based markets) or invest in the companies that supply the agriculture sector. In the pure commodities space that means focusing on an index called the Dow Jones UBS Agriculture sub-index. This tracks a basket of agricultural commodities and is a sub-index of the wider DJ-UBS Composite All Index. The table below lists the constituent individual agricultural commodities within this broad index.

Commodity	*% weight in DJ UBS index*
Soybeans	26
Corn	23
Wheat	15
Sugar	11
Soybean Oil	10
Coffee	8
Cotton	7

For agriculture companies there's more choice as you can see from the featured ETFs table above – S&P, S-Net and NASDAQ all track the performance of globally traded securities of the largest and most liquid companies involved in agriculture and farming-related activities. The variation of each index varies enormously, but the table below shows the current makeup of the iShares S&P ETF.

Company	*Country*	*%*
MONSANTO CO	United States	10.29
POTASH CORP OF SASKATCHEWAN	Canada	9.7
DEERE & CO	United States	8.77
SYNGENTA AG	Switzerland	7.61
KOMATSU LTD	Japan	5.63
ARCHER-DANIELS-MIDLAND	United States	5.23
MOSAIC CO	United States	4.12

Continued

Company	Country	%
BRF – BRASIL FOODS	Brazil	3.61
AGRIUM INC	Canada	2.9
URALKALI-SPON	Russian Federation	2.72

Both of these agricultural investment themes – and their accompanying ETFs – are potentially excellent ideas for investors looking to build some exposure to the global agriculture space. They access this space in two very different ways:

- The equity-based funds invest in all companies (big companies) that supply the world's farming sector. That includes companies such as fertiliser companies (Potash), biotech companies (Monsanto), tractor and plant machinery (Deere) and agricultural agents and suppliers.
- The pure commodity funds are focused on just agricultural commodities and invest in a range of futures-based contracts in everything from soybeans (the main constituent) to coffee and wheat (but no livestock, which is a separate ETC).

The attractions of both structures together is that you could pretty much buy global access to all things farming related with the exception maybe of land. The bigger question is perhaps whether you want to have any access at all to agriculture.

Bulls of 'soft commodities' – agricultural products to you and I – advance a number of key arguments, including the following:

- Agricultural commodities outperformed most other asset classes in the bear market of 2008.
- Agriculture has a relatively low level of correlation to the business cycle and to other asset classes.
- A growing world population and rising per capita incomes are likely to fuel growing demand for certain key softs including livestock, rice and grains.
- The supply of land is obviously fairly constrained, made worse by diminishing water resources.
- According to ETF Securities investors also need to be aware that 'tight supply relative to growing demand has caused inventories of many agricultural products to fall to near 50-year lows, making prices highly sensitive to negative supply events'.

- Agricultural products are a strong hedge against inflation.
- Last but by no means least, government efforts to combat climate change and increase biofuel usage have fed through to increase pressure on grains.

The case for investing in agricultural products and companies is not a one-way street though – soft commodities are hugely volatile in price and many economists point to the long-term relative decline in real prices for most food commodities. Despite all the rhetoric about 'they ain't making enough land any more', crop yields and agricultural productivity have increased substantially over the very long term, making most farmers in the West for instance dependent on income from government subsidies, from selling valuable land and from ancillary activities including tourism.

FTSE UK Dividend Plus

Weight of largest holding	3.3% (Tui Travel)
Weight of top 10 largest holdings	27%
Yield as at end December 2011	5.53%

Returns

Index	2011	2010	2009	2008	2007
UK Dividend Plus Index	–10%	7.7%	26%	–49%	–15%

The index – our analysis

ANALYSIS	
Likely risk (high/medium/low)	High
Likely volatility	High
Suitable for 'simple' investors, i.e. small ISA investors	Yes
Diversification risk with top holdings, i.e. top three more than 20% of fund	No
Likely to be a core holding?	Yes
Market Cap based (MC)/Screened (S)	Screened for yield
Appeal to income investors?	Yes
Risk factors?	Mid- and small-cap biased – also has been too reliant on financial services companies Very volatile
Top three holding as % of total fund end December 2011	9%
Country breakdown: top three – end December 2011	100% UK listed
Sector breakdown: top three – end December 2011	Financials 30% Consumer services 20.50% Utilities 13%

Top holdings in index

Company	%
TUI TRAVEL PLC	3.32
RESOLUTION LTD	2.96
AVIVA PLC	2.89
LEGAL & GENERAL GROUP PLC	2.83
CATLIN GROUP LTD	2.78
HALFORDS GROUP	2.7
RSA INSURANCE GROUP	2.69
AMLIN PLC ORD	2.67
STANDARD LIFE PLC	2.49
BAE SYSTEMS PLC	2.34

Featured ETFs

Name of fund	Index	TER basis points pa %	Physical or synthetic	ISIN or EPIC (italics and bold)
AMUNDI ETF FTSE UK DIVIDEND PLUS	FTSE UK DIVIDEND PLUS	0.30	Synthetic	AUKD
iShares FTSE UK Dividend Plus	FTSE UK Dividend Plus	0.40	Physical	IUKD

Comments

As indices go, this is not one of the best known – it gives investors exposure to around 50 UK companies which pay out the highest forecasted dividend yields in the FTSE 350. It is designed to select high dividend-paying stocks using just one specialist index. According to the index developers, the FTSE Group, 'The FTSE UK Dividend Plus index selects the top 50 stocks by one-year forecast dividend yield. The constituents' weightings within the index are determined by their dividend yield as opposed to market capitalisation. The FTSE UK Dividend Plus index was created to allow investors to capture the long-term effect of higher compounding returns, and benefit from the lower correlations to traditional market cap weighted indices.'

Investors may want to pay attention to that last sentence in the index definition – 'the long-term effect of higher compounding returns'. The key here is that dividends matter – an awful lot – and especially if you then reinvest the dividends in shares. Sadly, capturing that dividend effect is rather trickier – lots of companies pay a juicy dividend and any investor trying to build a portfolio might find themselves inundated with shares. The FTSE UK Dividend Plus index is designed to give investors an alternative – track the highest-yielding FTSE 350 stocks based on their forecast payout.

In theory, this is a promising idea and the academic literature certainly suggests that this is potentially a brilliant long-term investment idea, but the reality in the past few years has been rather less positive – returns in bear markets from this kind of index have been utterly dreadful. Countless tens of millions of pounds of investors' money poured into the iShares ETF that tracks this index in the years after 2004 and much of that money flooded back out again in the latter part of the decade as the market savagely turned against value stocks. And that is the key point – by default most value stocks pay out a good yield, which means that any strategy that captures high-yielding stocks catches value stocks and value stocks are more volatile and much riskier in a bear market.

The reverse of this is also true – value stocks and in particular high-yielding stocks may be a bad idea in bear markets, but in bull markets returns can be spectacular. The point here is the length of the investment – invest for only a few years and time that purchase of the index poorly and you could be looking at colossal losses. By contrast, your profits could be huge if you time that purchase well and then hold over 10, 20 years or even longer periods and reinvest the yield.

Dividends really matter

The academic literature – backed up by a mountain of analysis from City strategists such as Andrew Lapthorne at SocGen – suggests that dividends benefit investors over the long term in a number of different ways.

The first and perhaps most obvious is the regular dividend payment as a contributor to what are called total shareholder returns (the capital returns plus the income yield), but the magic of dividends does not stop there. There is some evidence that a strategy of buying the right kind of dividend payers (reliable or progressive dividend payers with a decent balance sheet) will actually deliver better returns in and of itself, i.e. the market itself tends to highly rate reliable dividend payers and gives those companies' shares a higher rating. The reason for this market preference is obvious in retrospect – dividends are easy to calculate and involve simple, hard numbers made in regular payments as opposed to profits and earnings which can be overstated and hugely volatile. Dividends also tend to be much more stable over time compared with earnings (annual earnings growth has historically been 2.5 times more volatile than dividend growth according to SocGen), while the discipline of making the regular dividend payout encourages a more focused management, determined to conserve the financial resources of the firm. As Lapthorne at SocGen reminds us: 'The retention of a too high proportion of earnings can encourage unnecessary mergers and acquisition (and often wasteful) investment in the pursuit of higher earnings growth.' As an example of this discipline and focus it is worth noting that very few companies ever set their management teams a dividends target as a way of calculating their bonuses – the cynic might note how difficult it is to manipulate the dividends stats compared with earnings.

The long-term case for dividends and their importance to private investors rests on a combination of all these factors – the dividend payout itself, the rating attached to a high-yielder and growth in the dividend payout over time. But there is one last, vital element to reckon with: the reinvestment of these dividend payouts.

The hard spade work for this analysis into dividend reinvestment comes from London Business School Professors Elroy Dimson, Paul Marsh and Mike Staunton, featured regularly in their Credit Suisse Global Investment Returns Yearbooks. Like many analysts, they break down the long-term returns from equities into four components:

- the actual yield itself (usually compared to the risk-free rate of return from holding cash or index-linked gilts);
- the growth rate of real dividends (increased dividends above the inflation rate);
- the way the market rewards a company because of its dividend, i.e. the rating it will give the shares via a measure like the price to dividend ratio; and last but no means least
- the reinvestment of the dividend using schemes like the dividend reinvestment investment plans or DRIPs.

According to Dimson et al., 'the dividend yield has been the dominant factor historically' and they add that 'the longer the investment horizon, the more important is dividend income'. Dimson's point is that the long-term real dividend growth rate is actually only about 1 percent per annum and thus cannot make that big a difference while the rerating of stocks based on its multiple to dividends is also very variable over time and does not make that much of a difference – as the authors note, 'dividends and probably earnings have barely outpaced inflation'.

But the actual payout is dwarfed by the importance of reinvesting dividends. Looking at the 109 years since 1900 Dimson et al. suggest that the average real capital gain in just stocks plus the dividend payout is about 1.7 percent per annum (an initial $1,000 would have grown six fold), but over the same period dividends reinvested would have produced a total return of 6 percent per annum (or a total gain of 582 times the original $1,000).

Andrew Lapthorne and his quantitative team at SocGen have looked at the same territory over a slightly smaller, more recent time period. They decomposed the returns of equities since 1970 in the major developed world markets including the UK, and discovered a slightly different picture to the LBS study. They reckon that the actual dividend yield represented just 30 percent of the nominal returns versus 70 percent for dividend growth, with their analysis suggesting that real dividend growth has been closer to 1.2 percent over the period. Looking at the UK the SG team reckon that of total annualised equity returns since 1970 of 11.4 percent, the actual dividend yield accounted for 4.3 percent per annum, dividend growth 8 percent per annum and multiple expansion (a higher or lower share price to dividend yield) –1.1 percent, i.e. high-yielding shares were actually rated lower by the market.

Lapthorne's analysis contains a number of other hugely important insights. His team's analysis looked at the relationship between earnings – profits – and dividends, for instance. Most people commonly assume that there is a very close relationship between profits and dividends, but that relationship is not in reality that strong. The SG team looked at the volatility of earnings growth, for instance, and dividend growth – earnings were hugely more volatile. Crucially, when they used a measure called beta to look at the sensitivity of dividends to earnings, they discovered relatively low numbers (0.00 indicates no sensitivity while 1 implies absolute sensitivity) of between 0.12 and 0.50 for nearly all major equity sectors with the exception of health care, building and construction, and travel and leisure. The point here is that dividends do not change as much as earnings and that markets value that consistency.

The wider range of value/dividend funds

Most UK investors in high-yield equity funds have tended to focus only on the FTSE UK Dividend Plus index, but there is a much greater range of global high-yield equity funds available. They are listed in the table below and cover most of the major developed and emerging markets globally.

Name of fund	*Asset class*	*Index*
Lyxor ETF EURO STOXX 50 Dividends	Dividends	EURO STOXX 50 Dividends
Lyxor ETF EURO STOXX 50 Dividends – EUR	Dividends	EURO STOXX 50 Dividends
SG Eurostoxx 50 Dividends Tracker Certificate	Dividends	Eurostoxx 50 Dividends
iShares Dow Jones Emerging Markets Select Dividend	**EM : Dividends**	Dow Jones Emerging Markets Select Dividend
SPDR S&P Emerging Markets Dividend ETF EUR	**EM : Dividends**	S&P Emerging Markets Dividend
ComStage ETF DivDAX® TR	**Europe Dividends**	DivDAX TR

Continued

Name of fund	Asset class	Index
DB STOXX® GLOBAL SELECT DIVIDEND 100 ETF	**Europe Dividends**	STOXX GLOBAL SELECT DIVIDEND 100
iShares EURO STOXX Select Dividend 30	**Europe Dividends**	EURO STOXX Select Dividend 30
DB EURO STOXX® SELECT DIVIDEND 30 ETF	**Eurozone Large Cap Dividends**	EURO STOXX SELECT DIVIDEND 30
ETFX Dow Jones Global Select Dividend Fund	**Global Developed: Dividend**	Dow Jones Global Select Dividend
SPDR S&P US Dividend Aristocrats ETF EUR	**US Dividends**	S&P US Dividend Aristocrats

Name of fund	TER basis points pa %	Physical or synthetic	ISIN or EPIC (italics and bold)
Lyxor ETF EURO STOXX 50 Dividends	0.70	Synthetic	**LDIV**
Lyxor ETF EURO STOXX 50 Dividends – EUR	0.70	Synthetic	**DIV**
SG Eurostoxx 50 Dividends Tracker Certificate	NA	Synthetic	**ST04**
iShares Dow Jones Emerging Markets Select Dividend	0.65	Physical	SEDY
SPDR S&P Emerging Markets Dividend ETF EUR	0.65	Physical	EMDV
ComStage ETF DivDAX® TR	0.25	Synthetic	ETF003
DB STOXX® GLOBAL SELECT DIVIDEND 100 ETF	0.50	Synthetic	***LU0292096186***
iShares EURO STOXX Select Dividend 30	0.40	Physical	IDVY
DB EURO STOXX® SELECT DIVIDEND 30 ETF	0.30	Synthetic	***LU0292095535***
ETFX Dow Jones Global Select Dividend Fund	0.50	Synthetic	GDIV
SPDR S&P US Dividend Aristocrats ETF EUR	0.35	Physical	UDDV

This long list of dividend tracking funds essentially falls into three main groupings:

1 Most of the ETFs in this list follow the methodology of the UK FTSE Dividend Plus index and track the highest yielding stocks on offer in a regional or global market.
2 The S&P Dividend trackers (issued by State Street) take a slightly different approach and look for companies where the dividend has been maintained for many years – the idea here is to target only those companies committed to a generous and growing dividend.
3 Last but by no means least there's a small but growing number of funds that track the combined payouts of all the companies in a major index such as the DJ EuroStoxx 50 or FTSE 100. The key idea here is to strip away the change in the share price of the companies in an index and instead add up all the dividends paid out. This aggregate dividend payout is itself tracked both as a spot price and via futures contracts through to the end of the decade. Why track these dividend futures? The concept here is that dividends are less volatile than profits and, over time, dividends tend to increase at a relatively steady rate above inflation.

The wider range of dividend indices – definitions

> The Dow Jones regional indices – Asia, Europe and Global – are all based on dividends. According to the provider each index includes a fixed number of components, ranging from 20 to 100 depending on the size of the market. To be eligible for selection to the indices, stocks must pass screens for dividend quality and for liquidity in most markets. Stocks are then selected to the indices based on dividend yield. For the Dow Jones STOXX regional indices, a stock's dividend performance is evaluated relative to its home market. Index constituents are dividend weighted rather than market capitalisation weighted. The weights of individual securities are capped to prevent one or several components from dominating the indices. The composition of each index is reviewed on an annual basis.

S&P Global Water

Weight of largest holding	Geberit 10.3%
Weight of top 10 largest holdings	61%
Yield %	1.88%

Returns

Index	2011	2010	2009	2008
S&P Global Water 50 Index	–8%	16%	14%	–17%

The index – our analysis

ANALYSIS	
Likely risk (high/medium/low)	Medium
Likely volatility	Medium
Suitable for 'simple' investors, i.e. small ISA investors	Yes
Diversification risk with top holdings, i.e. top three more than 20% of fund	Yes
Likely to be a core holding?	Yes
Market Cap based (MC)/Screened (S)	MC
Appeal to income investors?	No
Risk factors?	Highly volatile and specialised equity sector
Appeal to investors looking to short main markets	No
Top three holding as % of total fund End December 2011	21%
Country breakdown: top three – end December 2011	US 38%, UK 21%, Switzerland 10%
Sector breakdown: top three – end December 2011	Utilities 47% Industrials 47% IT 2%

Featured ETFs

Name of fund	Index	TER basis points pa %	Physical or synthetic	ISIN or EPIC (italics and bold)
ETFX S-Network Global Water Fund	S-Network Global Water	0.65	Synthetic	WATE
ETFX S-Network Global Water Fund £	S-Network Global Water	0.65	Synthetic	WATP
iShares S&P Global Water	S&P Global Water	0.65	Physical	IH2O
Lyxor ETF World Water (GBP) – NTR	World Water NTR	0.60	Synthetic	LWAT
Lyxor ETF World Water (GBP) – NTR	World Water NTR	0.60	Synthetic	LWAU
PowerShares Palisades Global Water Fund	Palisades Global Water	0.75	Physical	PSHO

iShares S&P Global Water & FTSE 100 ETF

www.sharescope.co.uk Chart (c) **Share**Scope

Comments

We believe an investment in the global water sector is possibly one of the best niche ideas we have ever heard of. In fact, we prefer the idea of global water over, say, clean energy or even global infrastructure because it is much more targeted and precise – you are buying companies that will benefit from the huge global wave of investment in water as a sector. Here is a range of compelling facts supporting the case for the water industry.

- Less than 1 percent of the world's fresh water (about 0.007 percent of all water on earth) is readily accessible for human use.
- 884 million people, around 13 percent of the world's population, lack access to safe drinking water, while 2.5 billion people worldwide lack access to basic sanitation.
- Global consumption of water is doubling every 20 years – more than twice the rate of human population growth.
- By 2025 two-thirds of the world's population will be living with serious water shortages or water scarcity.
- 88 percent of all diseases are caused by unsafe drinking water, inadequate sanitation and poor hygiene.

A recent report from fund management group Henderson's, one of the best SRI teams in the business, drew attention to the huge business potential of this sector:

- The global water market addressing municipal and industrial water/ wastewater equipment and services is estimated to be $425 billion.
- Wastewater use and recycling is increasingly seen as the fastest and lowest-cost way of procuring more water.
- 60 percent of all water main pipes in the US will be classified as substandard by 2020. Estimates for water infrastructure replacement and upgrades range from $300 billion to $1 trillion.
- Agriculture accounts for 70 percent of world fresh water usage and an estimated 31 percent of this is wasted.

All in all we agree with Henderson's assessment of the potential here but we would add one other crucial strength – steady cash flow. By and large, the companies in this sector operate in fairly regulated markets (the utilities certainly do) and that means that they will never grow at a phenomenal rate, but they will grow sustainably with strong profits. It is in the interest of regulators to let these companies invest in new capacity and improve the service and that means more profits in the long term. Add this all up and we think you have the perfect investment case, even for cautious investors with a suspicion of equity markets. Crucially, these investment pluses have not gone unnoticed in recent years – the table below shows returns from holding the main indices on offer via ETFs. The bottom line: water has been a great investment space – until 2008, of course, when water utilities like everything else went into freefall.

The problems start when you try to work out which index or fund to invest in. There are four main options, detailed in the table below.

iShares S&P

Company	% Weight
GEBERIT	10.31
UNITED UTILITIES	8.16
SEVERN TRENT	7.06
AMERICAN WATER WORKS	6.95
XYLEM INC	6.21
DANAHER CORP	5.61
PENNON GROUP	5.04
ALFA LAVAL	4.28
CIA SANEAMENTO BASICO	3.98
VEOLIA	3.9

Lyxor Global Water

Company	% Weight
United Utilities	10.58
Severn Trent	10.04
Geberit	9.93
American Waterworks	9.7
Nalco	9.61
Veolia	8.38
Pentair	6.38
ITT Corp	5.2
Aqua America	5.4
Kurita	5.19
Cia Saneamento	5.09

Palisades Global Water

Company	% Weight
Hyflux	5.55
Kurita Water Inds	4.91
Grontmij N.V.	4.89
Organo Corp.	4.88
Memira	4.88
KSB AG	4.52
Geberit AG	4.3
Uponor Oyj	4.25
Pentair Inc	4.24
ARCADIS N.V.	4.22

S- Network Global Water

Company	% Weight
Veolia	5.4
ITT Corp	5.2
Geberit	5.1
United Utilities	4.7
Severn Trent	4
American Waterworks	3.7
Pall Corp	3.3
Nalco	3.2
Suez Environmental	2.9
Pennon	2.7

All invest in companies that have a substantial investment in water, but some (the Palisades index, for instance) are much more biased towards companies that make equipment for the water sector. Others, like the SocGen index (followed by Lyxor) and the S&P Index, are weighted more heavily towards water utilities. You also need to be aware that the funds have a bias towards US stocks and that, by and large, they are all more volatile than holding a basket of ordinary stocks like the S&P 500. More cautious investors may tend to favour the Lyxor/SocGen fund with its heavy utility bias, while more adventurous investors may gravitate towards the Powershares/Palisades fund and the iShares fund. Overall, on balance we like the look of the S&P Global Water index as the best way of capturing both utility firms and water specialists.

Global Property – FTSE NAREIT Developed Markets (Global) Property Index Series

(Note that all figures are from December 2011.)

ANALYSIS	
Likely risk (high/medium/low)	Medium to low
Likely volatility	Medium to low
Suitable for 'simple' investors, i.e. small ISA investors	Yes
Diversification risk with top holdings, i.e. top three more than 20% of fund	No
Likely to be a core holding?	Yes
Market Cap based (MC)/Screened (S)	MC
Appeal to income investors?	Yes
Risk factors?	Sector risk Very American and Anglo Saxon markets biased (55% of index including USA, UK and Australia)

Returns from iShares Property ETFs

Name of iShares ETF	EPIC	2011	2010	2009	2008	2007
			% change			
iShares FTSE EPRA Euro Property	IPRP	–18.17	14.5	23	–19.8	–15
iShares FTSE EPRA NAREIT UK Property Fund	IUKP	–10.76	1.1	9.5	–48	
iShares FTSE EPRA/NAREIT Asia Property Yield Fund	IASP	–20.32	20	31.4	–40.3	25.3
iShares FTSE EPRA/NAREIT Global Property Yield Fund	IWDP	–4.65	21.1	20.5	–30.8	–9.9
iShares FTSE EPRA/NAREIT US Property Yield	IUSP	8.51	25.1	15	–25.4	–22.6

Featured Property ETFs

Name of fund	Index	TER basis points pa %
AMUNDI ETF REAL ESTATE REIT IEIF	REAL ESTATE REIT IEIF	0.25
DB FTSE EPRA/NAREIT DEVELOPED EUROPE REAL ESTATE ETF	FTSE EPRA/NAREIT DEVELOPED EUROPE REAL ESTATE	0.40
DB FTSE EPRA/NAREIT EUROZONE REAL ESTATE ETF	FTSE EPRA/NAREIT EUROZONE REAL ESTATE	0.35
DB FTSE EPRA/NAREIT GLOBAL REAL ESTATE ETF	FTSE EPRA/NAREIT GLOBAL REAL ESTATE	0.60
HSBC FTSE EPRA/NAREIT DEVELOPED ETF	FTSE EPRA/NAREIT DEVELOPED	0.40
iShares FTSE EPRA/NAREIT Asia Property Yield Fund	FTSE EPRA/NAREIT Asia Property Yield	0.59

iShares FTSE EPRA/NAREIT Developed Markets Property Yield Fund	FTSE EPRA/NAREIT Developed Markets Property Yield	0.59
iShares FTSE EPRA/NAREIT UK Property Fund	FTSE EPRA/NAREIT UK Property	0.40
iShares FTSE EPRA/NAREIT US Property Yield Fund	FTSE EPRA/NAREIT US Property Yield	0.40
iShares FTSE/EPRA European Property Index Fund	FTSE/EPRA European Property	0.40

Name of fund	*Physical or synthetic*	*ISIN or EPIC (italics/bold)*
AMUNDI ETF REAL ESTATE REIT IEIF	Synthetic	C8R
DB FTSE EPRA/NAREIT DEVELOPED EUROPE REAL ESTATE ETF	Synthetic	***LU0489337690***
DB FTSE EPRA/NAREIT EUROZONE REAL ESTATE ETF	Synthetic	***LU0489336965***
DB FTSE EPRA/NAREIT GLOBAL REAL ESTATE ETF	Synthetic	***LU0489337005***
HSBC FTSE EPRA/NAREIT DEVELOPED ETF	Physical	***IE00B5L01S80***
iShares FTSE EPRA/NAREIT Asia Property Yield Fund	Physical	IASP
iShares FTSE EPRA/NAREIT Developed Markets Property Yield Fund	Physical	IWDP
iShares FTSE EPRA/NAREIT UK Property Fund	Physical	IUKP
iShares FTSE EPRA/NAREIT US Property Yield Fund	Physical	IUSP
iShares FTSE/EPRA European Property Index Fund	Physical	IPRP

Comments

Property, and especially commercial property, has emerged over the last decade as perhaps the single most important alternative asset class, helped in part by the boom (until recently) in capital prices and the increasing number of specialist, tax-efficient real estate investment trusts (REITs). That growth has opened the space for a multitude of funds that takes an active approach to accessing the sector, but in recent years a number of international indices have emerged that give investors more 'passive exposure'. The most important comes via the FTSE Group in alliance with a trade group called NAREIT.

Their FTSE EPRA/NAREIT Global Real Estate Index Series is designed to track the performance of listed real estate companies and REITs worldwide. According to the FTSE Group they launched the FTSE EPRA/NAREIT Global Dividend Plus index as a 'market cap-weighted index designed to measure the performance of global higher yielding stocks within the developed universe of the EPRA/NAREIT Global index, excluding Greece'. The yield bias of the index refers to the requirement for stocks to have a one-year forecast dividend yield of 2 percent or greater. The index is then weighted by market capitalisation in line with the free float-adjusted EPRA/NAREIT

Global index. The Developed Markets version of the fund covers most of the world, including Japan, the UK, the US and Europe, but excludes emerging markets property companies. The index series is then broken down into regional sub-indices including one for the UK, for Europe and for the US – each of these sub-indices is tracked by an ETF from iShares with Deutsche db X-trackers also offering access to the range alongside single fund offerings from HSBC and Amundi.

On paper we would recommend any of these funds as a core investment for all investors. Property trackers offer investors a number of not insubstantial advantages:

- They allow you to diversify across national and regional markets.
- They also allow access to global commercial property markets, from offices through to industrial estates.
- The funds are usually invested in core REIT holdings which are tax efficient – REITs must pay most of their income stream as a dividend to investors (free of tax).
- They produce a useful dividend yield.
- They also offer investors a way of diversifying risk against core equity holdings.

The biggest advantage, of course, is that this asset class has stormed ahead over the last decade – the average annual gain for the Global version is a fantastic 25 percent per annum up until 2008. But those stunning annual gains need to be put into perspective – prices collapsed in 2007, 2008 and 2011. The main UK Markets index, for instance, was yet another 10 percent in 2011 – the Asian ETF fell by an even bigger 20 percent in the same year!

Beyond these short-term price weakness issues, we are slightly concerned by a number of other factors:

1 Dangerous concentrations. The iShares funds look highly diversified across national markets but once you dig a bit deeper you discover that you are betting on just six key national property markets. In the Asia fund, Australia and Hong Kong account for a huge percentage of the total holdings, while in Europe, France and Holland account for over 60 percent. Turning to the Global fund, the US accounts for the largest share followed by Australia and Hong Kong.
2 There is potential for the tracking error to be fairly noticeable with all of these funds. Tracking errors on the longer lasting iShares funds have ranged from a minuscule 0.1 percent through to a whopping 1.6 percent per annum (in 2007).

3   The TER for two of the iShares funds – Asia and Global – looks rather high at 0.59 percent. That's not expensive compared with actively managed property funds but it is not exactly cheap for such a liquid range of underlying holdings – the HSBC fund by contrast charges just 0.40 percent while the Amundi fund is very cheap, with a TER of just 0.25 percent.

The bottom line? We do have some concerns with these property funds but we think they really do deserve a place in most long-term portfolios. They are still a cheap and easy way of buying access to the best commercial real estate companies and they also pay out an above-average yield. Funds that track the global index are less interesting in our view because of the strong US bias – we would favour picking up, say, the US and the UK fund as a starter.

China – HSCEI and MSCI

Weight of largest holding for MSCI China	9.8% China Mobile
Weight of largest holding for HSCEI	10.5% China Construction
Weight of top 10 largest holdings	49% in MSCi and 70% HSCEI
Yield % (as at end December 2011)	2.19% for MSCI

Returns

Name	EPIC	2011	2010	2009	2008	2007
				% change		
db X-trackers MSCI China TRN Index ETF	XCS6	–18.83				
iShares FTSE Xinhua China 25	FXC	–18.6	4.6	34.8	–31.5	49.1
Lyxor China Enterprise (HSCEI)	LCHN	–20.1	4	44.3	–30.1	

Note that the following chart is not for the index but for the Lyxor fund which tracks that index.

The index – our analysis

ANALYSIS	
Likely risk (high/medium/low)	High
Likely volatility	High

Continued

ANALYSIS

Suitable for 'simple' investors, i.e. small ISA investors	No
Diversification risk with top holdings, i.e. top three more than 20% of fund	Yes
Likely to be a core holding?	No
Market Cap based (MC)/Screened (S)	MC
Appeal to income investors?	No
Risk factors?	Political risk – it's a communist state with high levels of political interference. A very volatile market

Comments

The idea of investing in individual national emerging markets is a tricky subject. Many adventurous types love focusing on a specific nation and then going aggressively long, but we think the risks are just too great and that investors do not realise just how volatile these individual national markets really are. But even we accept that a case can be made for investing in China as an individual market over the long term – unlike other BRIC countries, such as Russia and Brazil, it is not an obvious resources play and its private sector is growing much faster than rival India. More importantly China is already a huge economy, a growing part of the global trade and financial system and its size alone makes it equivalent to most emerging markets regions.

The big issue is which index to focus on. There are a number of different ways of buying into big Chinese mega caps plus the odd few small-cap options. Our preference is for an index called the Hang Seng China Enterprises index, which is, according to its developers, 'a free float capitalisation-weighted index comprised of H-Shares listed on the Hong Kong Stock Exchange and included in the Hang Seng Mainland Composite index. As of 15 January 2008, the constituents comprised 43 H-shares'.

Chinese share classes

> **A shares** – these are companies incorporated in mainland China and traded on the mainland A-share markets. The prices of A shares are quoted in Renminbi (the Chinese currency) and currently available only to mainlanders, although selected foreign institutional investors are allowed to trade A shares.
>
> **B shares** – these are companies incorporated in mainland China and are traded in the mainland B-share markets (Shanghai and Shenzhen). B shares are quoted in foreign currencies. In the past, only foreigners were allowed to trade B shares. Since March 2001, mainlanders can also trade B shares, although they must trade with legal foreign currency accounts.
>
> **H shares** – these are companies incorporated in mainland China and listed on the Hong Kong Stock Exchange and other foreign stock exchanges.

All this jargon about H shares needs some explaining. The key principle to grasp is that China is not really like other countries. On paper it is a capitalist's paradise but in reality most of the very big companies are largely owned – and certainly controlled through their management – by the state, aka the Chinese Communist Party. One of the ways that the state/the CPC exercises control is via different classes of equity, with some available only for local Chinese nationals and quoted on the local Chinese exchanges (Shanghai principally), alongside other classes (H shares) that are available to foreigners through well-established exchanges such as the Hong Kong market. This Hong Kong dimension adds another complication – there are some very successful Chinese companies that are based on the Hong Kong exchange, which have nearly all their operations in China, but are not in reality properly Chinese companies. Confused? So are most institutional investors. To make matters even worse, you will also encounter some rival indices, chief among them the FTSE/Xinhua China 25 index, which tracks shares of the most widely followed 25 mainland enterprises available to offshore investors, which are traded on the Stock Exchange of Hong Kong Limited (SEHK). On paper it is very similar to the HSCEI but it tracks a smaller number of companies and is much less diversified. There's also the MSCI China index which is hugely popular with major institutions – this is perhaps the most comprehensive of the indices on offer. This index includes H, B, Red Chip and P Chip shares but no domestic shares.

This variety of indices – and we are not including the main Hong Kong index, the Hang Seng, in this quick overview – is duplicated in a number of competing exchange traded funds on the London market.

The highlighted funds

Name of fund	*Index*	*TER basis points pa %*	*Physical or synthetic*	*ISIN or EPIC (italics and bold)*
AMUNDI ETF MSCI CHINA – EUR	MSCI CHINA	0.55	Synthetic	CC1
AMUNDI ETF MSCI CHINA – USD	MSCI CHINA –	0.55	Synthetic	CC1U
ComStage ETF HSCEI	HSCEI	0.55	Synthetic	ETF023
DB FTSE CHINA 25 ETF	FTSE CHINA 25	0.60	Synthetic	***LU0292109856***
DB MSCI CHINA TRN INDEX ETF	MSCI CHINA TRN	0.65	Synthetic	***LU0514695690***
HSBC MSCI CHINA ETF	MSCI CHINA	0.60	Physical	***IE00B44T3H88***
iShares FTSE China 25	FTSE China 25	0.74	Physical	FXC
Lyxor ETF China (HSCEI)	China Enterprise (HSCEI) GTR	0.65	Synthetic	LCHN
Source MSCI China ETF	MSCI China	0.45	Synthetic	MXCS

All three indices offered are a potentially excellent way of buying into the big Chinese growth story, although our preference is for the HSCEI index tracked by the Lyxor ETF. All three funds buy into huge Chinese mega caps that list certain classes of their shares on the main Hong Kong market, the Hang Seng. Most of these companies are ultimately state owned with major holdings in the oil/gas sector, mobile telecoms and banking – you will not see that many purely privately owned companies in any of these ETFs. If you are after smaller-cap Chinese shares you are better off looking to the US ETF market and the China small-cap ETF HAO offered by Alphashares.

Investors also need to be aware that the underlying shares owned by these three large-cap funds are usually classes exclusively for foreigners and do not grant ultimate power or control over the companies concerned. Also, it is worth noting that all three indices concentrate on a small number of very big companies – 43 for the China Enterprises index and 25 for the FTSE index.

The only really big difference – and it is not even that big – is in cost. The cheapest China tracker is from Source at 45 basis points while the most expensive is from iShares at 74 basis points (although the iShares fund is a physical tracker where the admin and trading costs are substantially higher).

Private investors looking to invest in any of these funds also need to be aware of the much broader risks of investing in China. Apart from the political control we mentioned above, Chinese equities are enormously volatile and liable to fluctuate madly, with many frequent busts.

Infrastructure – S&P Global Infrastructure Index

Weight of largest holding	5.6% (GDF Suez)
Weight of top 10 largest holdings	37%
Yield (end December 2011)	4.7%

Returns

Index	2011	2010	2009	2008	2007
S&P Global Infrastructure Index	–1.3%	5%	24%	–39%	N/A

Note that the following chart is for the DBX ETF of the index and not the actual index.

The index – our analysis

ANALYSIS	
Likely risk (high/medium/low)	Medium
Likely volatility	Medium
Suitable for 'simple' investors, i.e. small ISA investors	Yes
Diversification risk with top holdings, i.e. top three more than 20% of fund	No
Likely to be a core holding?	Yes
Market Cap based (MC)/Screened (S)	MC
Appeal to income investors?	Yes
Risk factors?	Many companies subject to regulatory oversight and thus vulnerable to political pressure Deflation could be a risk to margin structures
Top three holding as % of total fund End December 2011	14%

The highlighted funds – infrastructure funds

Name of fund	Index	TER basis points pa %	ISIN or EPIC (italics and bold)
DB S&P GLOBAL INFRASTRUCTURE ETF	S&P GLOBAL INFRASTRUCTURE	0.60	***LU0322253229***
ETFX Dow Jones Brookfield Emerging Markets Infra	Dow Jones Brookfield Emerging Markets Infrastructure	0.65	BIEM
ETFX Dow Jones Brookfield Global Infra	Dow Jones Brookfield Global Infrastructure	0.65	BGIT
iShares FTSE/Macquarie Global Infra 100	FTSE/Macquarie Global Infrastructure 100	0.65	INFR
iShares S&P Emerging Market Infra	S&P Emerging Market Infrastructure	0.74	IEMI

The infrastructure space has been one of the fastest growing bits of the investment universe over the last decade, fuelled in part by the growth of a number of competing global and regional indices. The two main indices come courtesy of the S&P Group and FTSE, although Dow Jones also works with an outfit called Brookfield to produce both a global and emerging markets infra index (tracked by ETF Securities).

The S&P Global Infrastructure Index series includes 75 large, liquid infrastructure stocks from around the world, with one-fifth of the constituents emerging market stocks with a liquid, developed market listing (NYSE ADRs, LSE GDRs or Hong Kong listings of Chinese stocks). To ensure diversified exposure across different infrastructure clusters, S&P makes sure that the 75 constituents are distributed at each rebalancing as follows:

- energy 15–20 percent
- transportation 30–40 percent
- utilities 30–40 percent.

Constituent weights are driven by size, with no single stock having a weight of more than 5 percent in the index at rebalancing.

S&P Global Infrastructure Index	
Transurban Group	5.26
TransCanada Corporation	4.75
Enbridge	4.45
Abertis Infraestructuras	3.63
Autostrade	3.40
El Paso	3.28
E.ON	3.26
Spectra Energy	3.09
Williams Cos	3.03
GdF Suez	2.95

Sector weighting	
Utilities	38.69%
Transportation	38.50%
Energy	22.81%

Country weighting	
United States	28.21%
Canada	11.24%
Australia	7.65%
France	7.08%
United Kingdom	6.61%
Germany	6.37%
Italy	6.16%
Spain	5.56%
China	4.79%
Others	16.34%

The other main index comes from rival outfit FTSE, namely the FTSE Macquarie. The Macquarie Global Infrastructure Index (MGII) series is calculated by FTSE and is designed to 'reflect the stock performance of companies worldwide within the infrastructure industry, principally those engaged in management, ownership and operation of infrastructure and utility assets'. The main index in the series is the Macquarie Global Infrastructure 100 Index, which includes the top 100 constituents from developed and advanced emerging countries of the main Global Infrastructure Index series. In practice, this index focuses on utilities-based businesses, with 86 percent of the holdings and the remaining 10 percent in oil and gas companies and industrials.

Top 10 companies Macquarie 100 Infrastructure Index	Country	%
GDF SUEZ	France	4
E.ON	Germany	3.7
SOUTHERN CO	US	3.44
NATIONAL GRID PLC	UK	3.01
TRANSCANADA CORP	Canada	2.68
DOMINION RESOURCES INC/VA	US	2.64
ENBRIDGE INC	Canada	2.57
DUKE ENERGY	US	2.55
ENEL SPA	Italy	2.47
EXELON CORP	US	2.43
Sector weightings		% weight
Utilities		86.51
Oil & Gas		10.29
Industrials		3.13
Electricity		0.07

There is one last index worth noting. It is called the S&P Emerging Markets Infrastructure index and it provides liquid and tradable exposure to 30 of the largest publicly listed emerging market companies in the global infrastructure industry. The index follows a modified market capitalisation-weighted scheme that reduces single-stock concentration and balances exposure across the three clusters. At rebalancing, the transportation, energy and utilities clusters have weights of 20 percent, 40 percent and 40 percent, respectively.

The investment case for infrastructure assets

> According to the FTSE Group, infrastructure and utility assets are essential for all investors. They cite the following positives for the investment space:
>
> - Essential and irreplaceable services with inelastic demand means exposure to infrastructure provides adequate gearing for growth in portfolio.
> - Global trend towards PPPs and privatisation of traditionally public-funded assets is driving rapid growth of infrastructure with expectations for continued development in the three diverse areas of roads, airports and telecommunications.
> - Strong cash flows characterised by low volatility and average correlation with other asset classes make infrastructure an excellent tool for properly diversifying a portfolio.
> - Strong record of market index outperformance.

All three of the main global indices and accompanying funds are hugely innovative and potentially very useful for investors – they give you access to the world's leading utility and public infrastructure companies. Thankfully they are all rather different in emphasis. The iShares Emerging Markets fund does what it says on the tin and focuses on less developed markets, although it is still rather focused on Hong Kong/China alongside South America, while the sibling iShares FTSE/Macquarie 100 fund is much more focused on first-world utility companies, with a particular emphasis on electricity companies.

Deutsche db X-trackers focuses on the S&P Global Infrastructure index. The resulting db X ETF is the cheaper of the two global index tracking trackers and it is less concentrated in its holdings than the two iShares funds.

MSCI Latin America

Weight of largest holding	8.8% (Petrobas)
Weight of top 10 largest holdings	45%
Yield	2.81%

Returns

Index	2011	2010	2009	2008	2007
MSCI Latin America Index	–14%	12%	98%	–45%	N/A

Note that the following chart is from iShares ETF and not the index.

The index – our analysis

ANALYSIS	
Likely risk (high/medium/low)	High
Likely volatility	High
Suitable for 'simple' investors, i.e. small ISA investors	No
Diversification risk with top holdings, i.e. top three more than 20% of fund	Yes – 22%
Likely to be a core holding?	No
Market Cap based (MC)/Screened (S)	MC
Risk factors?	Political risk and national dependence on commodities Volatile market

Continued

ANALYSIS	
Top three holding as % of total end December 2011	22%
Country breakdown: top three – end December 2011	64% Brazil
21% Mexico
7.3% Chile
Sector breakdown: top three – end December 2011	Financials 22%
Mining 21%
Consumer Staples 15%

Comments

Our general advice is to stay clear of specific countries and regions within the fast-expanding emerging markets investment universe – we feel that the risks are just too great even though some countries like India or even Russia do present enormous opportunity. Our view is that your exposure to these growth markets is best achieved through a general MSCI Emerging Markets index tracker. But there are two notable exceptions to this rule – China and Latin America.

The sudden emergence of Latin America and especially Brazil on to the investment landscape in this century is nothing short of extraordinary. Growth in countries like Brazil and Mexico and even Chile and Peru has been translated into some astonishing stock market gains and a number of world-beating mega-corporations have emerged – names like Petrobas from Brazil (a massive oil company) and America Movil (a Mexican mobile phone giant) are increasingly forces to be reckoned with.

We think adventurous investors should seriously consider some sort of investment in this region, although we would caution that its heightened volatility and bias towards the resource sector will probably put off more conservative investors who are risk averse. Also we would recommend exposure to the whole region and not just to Brazil – most Latin American funds tend to have massive exposure to Brazil anyway, but you also get the benefit of some diversification into interesting economies like Mexico and Chile.

Top holdings of iShares MSCI Latin America ETF at end of January 2012

Company	Country	%
PETROBAS	Brazil	8.8
AMERICA MOVIL	Mexico	6.43
BANCO ITAU	Brazil	6.04
BANCO BRADESCO	Brazil	4.9
CIA VALE DO RIO DOCE	Brazil	4.16
CIA DE BEBIDAS DAS AME	Brazil	3.92
VALE SA	Brazil	3.89
WALMART DE MEXICO	Mexico	2.59
BANCOLOMBIA	Colombia	2.42

The funds

Until just a few years ago, any investors wanting to invest in Latin America as a specific region would have had very few choices – basically only a few specialist investment trusts operated in this new investment space. Now we have three ETFs all tracking the same regional index, which includes massive outfits like Petrobas as well as minnows from countries like Colombia and Peru plus the odd outfit from once mighty markets including Argentina. What is even better is that these funds are all fairly cheap, charging between 0.45 percent (Amundi) and 0.74 percent (iShares).

Selected Latin American funds

Name of fund	Index	TER basis points pa %	Physical or synthetic	ISIN or EPIC (italics and bold)
AMUNDI ETF MSCI EM LATIN AMERICA – EUR	MSCI EM LATIN AMERICA	0.45	Synthetic	ALAT
AMUNDI ETF MSCI EM LATIN AMERICA – USD	MSCI EM LATIN AMERICA –	0.45	Synthetic	ALAU

Name of fund	Index	TER basis points pa %	Physical or synthetic	ISIN or EPIC (italics and bold)
CS ETF IE on MSCI EM Latin America	MSCI EM Latin America	0.65	Synthetic	CML1
DB MSCI EM LATAM TRN INDEX ETF	MSCI EM LATAM TRN	0.65	Synthetic	***LU0292108619***
HSBC MSCI EM LATIN AMERICA ETF	MSCI EM LATIN AMERICA	0.60	Physical	***IE00B4TS3815***
iShares MSCI EM Latin America	MSCI EM Latin America	0.74	Physical	LTAM
Lyxor ETF MSCI EM Latin America (GBP) – NTR	MSCI EM Latin America NTR	0.65	Synthetic	LLAT
Lyxor ETF MSCI EM Latin America (GBP) – NTR	MSCI EM Latin America NTR	0.65	Synthetic	LLAU
SPDR MSCI EM Latin America ETF	MSCI EM Latin America	0.65	Physical	EMLA

Brazilian funds

You could, of course, just go straight to the source of much of the biggest returns of recent years and invest directly in a Brazilian index tracking fund. There are two main indices worth following in Brazil. The most common comes from the ubiquitous MSCI Barra which tracks nearly all the most liquid stocks on the Brazilian market and is a subset of the wider MSCI EM Latin American index. The other main choice is based on the main local market and is called the Bovespa Index, which is an index of about 50 stocks traded on the São Paulo Stock Exchange (Bolsa de Valores do Estado de São Paulo). According to the index developers, 'the index is composed by a theoretical portfolio with the stocks that accounted for 80 percent of the volume traded in the last 12 months [on the São Paulo Stock Exchange] ... comprises 70 percent of all the stock value traded' on the exchange. In sum, it is the local, smaller equivalent of our FTSE 100.

Brazilian ETFs

Name of fund	Index	TER basis points pa %	Physical or synthetic	ISIN or EPIC (italics and bold)
AMUNDI ETF MSCI BRAZIL	MSCI BRAZIL	0.45	Synthetic	BRZ
CS ETF IE on MSCI Brazil	MSCI Brazil	0.65	Physical	CBR1
DB MSCI BRAZIL TRN INDEX ETF	MSCI BRAZIL TRN	0.65	Synthetic	*LU0292109344*
HSBC MSCI BRAZIL ETF	MSCI BRAZIL	0.60	Physical	*IE00B5W34K94*
iShares MSCI Brazil	MSCI Brazil	0.74	Physical	IBZL
Lyxor ETF Brazil (IBOVESPA) (GBP) – NTR	IBOVESPA NTR	0.65	Synthetic	LBRU
Lyxor ETF Brazil (IBOVESPA) (GBP) – NTR	IBOVESPA NTR	0.65	Synthetic	LBRZ
Source MSCI Brazil ETF	MSCI Brazil	0.65	Synthetic	MXBS

Brazil is obviously a resource play first and foremost and investors need to understand that bias – holdings in this broad sector account for between 40 percent and 60 percent of these fund holdings. In particular ETFs that track the MSCI Brazil index are a big bet on the giant Brazilian private oil company Petrobas (10 percent), alongside a gamble on the Brazilian iron ore company (Vale 8.44 percent) plus the odd huge bank like Bradesco – all the other sectors on the Brazilian market are dwarfs by comparison.

MSCI World Islamic Index

Volatility (GLOBAL index)	
Weight of largest holding	EXXON MOBIL at 4%
Weight of top 10 largest holdings	20%
Yield %	1.7%

Returns

Short-term returns in 2008 and 2009

Index	2011	2010	2009	2008	2007
MSCI World Islamic Index	−2%	11%	28%	−33%	N/A

iShares MSCI World Islamic & FTSE 100 ETF

ANALYSIS	
Likely risk (high/medium/low)	Medium to low
Likely volatility	Medium to low
Suitable for 'simple' investors, i.e. small ISA investors	Yes
Diversification risk with top holdings, i.e. top three more than 20% of fund	No
Likely to be a core holding?	Yes
Market Cap based (MC)/Screened (S)	MC but ethically screened
Appeal to income investors?	No

Continued

ANALYSIS

Risk factors?	Still very biased towards energy and materials
	Biased to US markets
Appeal to investors looking to short main markets	No
Top three holding as % of total fund end December 2011	8%
Country breakdown: top three – end December 2011	US 52%, UK 12, Japan 7%
Sector breakdown: top three – end December 2011	Energy 25%
	Health Care 15%
	Mining 14%

Featured ETFs

Name of fund	Index	TER basis points pa %	Physical or synthetic	ISIN or EPIC *(italics and bold)*
DB DJ ISLAMIC MARKET TITANS 100 ETF	DJ ISLAMIC MARKET TITANS 100	0.50	Synthetic	*LU0328475529*
DB S&P 500 SHARIAH ETF	S&P 500 SHARIAH	0.50	Synthetic	*LU0328475362*
DB S&P EUROPE 350 SHARIAH INDEX ETF	S&P EUROPE 350 SHARIAH	0.50	Synthetic	*LU0328475107*
DB S&P JAPAN 500 SHARIAH ETF	S&P JAPAN 500 SHARIAH	0.50	Synthetic	*LU0328475289*
iShares MSCI Emerging Markets Islamic	MSCI Emerging Markets Islamic	0.85	Physical	ISEM
iShares MSCI Emerging Markets SmallCap	MSCI Emerging Markets SmallCap	0.74	Physical	IEMS

Continued

Name of fund	Index	TER basis points pa %	Physical or synthetic	ISIN or EPIC (italics and bold)
iShares MSCI USA Islamic	MSCI USA Islamic	0.50	Physical	ISUS
iShares MSCI World Islamic	MSCI World Islamic	0.60	Physical	ISWD

Top holdings in MSCI Islamic World Index

Company	Country	%
Exxon Mobil	United States	4.1
IBM	United States	2.2
Chevron	United States	2.09
Nestlé	Switzerland	1.89
Procter and Gamble	United States	1.81
Johnson & Johnson	United States	1.74
AT&T	United States	1.72
Pfizer	United States	1.66
Coca-Cola	United States	1.43
Vodafone	United Kingdom	1.39

Comments

The MSCI Islamic Index Series (the 'Islamic Indices') follows something called Sharia investment principles. This 'screened' index is based on an MSCI equity index (or any combination of MSCI equity indices), but excludes all the non-'compliant' securities. Following the Sharia investment principles, MSCI excludes securities using two types of criteria: business activity and financial ratios. The first category means that the index provider must exclude any company that derives more than 5 percent of its revenue (cumulatively) from any of the following activities:

- alcohol: distillers, vintners and producers of alcoholic beverages, including producers of beer and malt liquors, owners and operators of bars and pubs;

- tobacco: cigarettes and other tobacco products' manufacturers and retailers;
- pork-related products: companies involved in the manufacture and retail of pork products;
- financial services: commercial banks involved in retail banking, corporate lending, investment banking; companies involved in mortgage and mortgage-related services; providers of financial services, including insurance, capital markets and specialised finance; credit agencies; stock exchanges;
- gambling/casino: owners and operators of casinos and gaming facilities, including companies providing lottery and betting services;
- music: producers and distributors of music, owners and operators of radio broadcasting systems;
- hotels: owners and operators of hotels;
- cinema: companies engaged in the production, distribution and screening of movies and television shows, owners and operators of television broadcasting systems and providers of cable or satellite television services;
- adult entertainment: owners and operators of adult entertainment products and activities.

Sharia investment principles also do not allow investment in companies deriving significant income from interest or companies that have excessive leverage. MSCI uses the following three financial ratios to screen for these companies:

- total debt over total assets;
- sum of a company's cash and interest-bearing securities over total assets;
- accounts receivables over total assets.

While the two first financial ratios may not exceed 33.33 percent, the third ratio may not exceed 70 percent.

The Islamic sector has been growing at an astonishing rate in recent years. Part of that is down to strong demand from a large number of immigrant and non-immigrant Muslims for Sharia-compliant financial services and transactions. But that is not the whole picture – another key factor has been growing oil wealth, with demand for suitable investments soaring in the Gulf GCC region. Crucially these demand-led factors have been helped by the growth of new financial structures that let Islamic investors mix belief with profit. The fact that Islamic laws prohibit paying and receiving interest does not imply that they frown on making money or encourage reverting to an all-cash or barter economy. Received religious opinion simply demands that all parties in a financial transaction share the risk and profit or loss of the venture. Depositors in Islamic banking are closer in form to shareholders, for instance, who can earn dividends when the bank makes a profit or lose part of their savings if the bank posts a loss. The idea is to link the return in an Islamic contract to productivity and the quality of the project, thereby ensuring a more equitable distribution of wealth. Looking at the legal framework, Islamic financial instruments take the form of contracts between providers and users of funds to manage risk. On the asset side, Islamic banks engage in investment and trading activities according to the various contracts available while deposits, for instance, are usually based on a *Mudaraba* contract or an interest-free loan contract (*Qard Al Hasan*).

With Islamic banking growing fast, it was inevitable that the asset management boys would follow. In fact, the concept of stock indices compliant with the beliefs of Islam is not new. The first Shariah-compliant indices from a major index provider were launched by Dow Jones Indexes in 1999, and FTSE followed suit with its own family in 2000. The iShares ETF platform is based in turn on a relatively new entrant to the market (2007), MSCI. A report released by S&P last year put estimates of current Shariah-compliant assets at $400 billion, and estimated the potential market for Islamic financial services to be in the area of $4 trillion. Like rival index provider S&P, MSCI works with a consulting firm, Kuwait-based Ratings Intelligence Partners, to ensure that the indices are Shariah-compliant. Crucially, it is important that investors understand that not all Islamic indices are created in the same way – the S&P index, for instance, screens out those companies that engage in the trading of gold and silver as cash on a deferred basis. MSCI screens out companies involved in the music industry (including radio broadcasting), hotels and the film and television industry (including television broadcasters, cable providers and theatres).

With these ethically strict screening techniques in place, it comes as no surprise to learn that some social (SRI) investors who are not Muslims have started taking these funds seriously. There is a real paucity of ethical index funds, after all, and these funds do a good job of removing some of the more sinful companies on the main developed markets. Many Christian investors, for instance, would probably share many if not most of the same ethical views as Islamic investors – the only key difference seems to be that these Islamic funds do not exclude weapons manufacturers, but they do exclude banks which tend to pass most SRI tests.

Looking at the funds in detail you need to be aware that the decision to exclude financials does have one major effect – you are likely to increase your exposure to energy and resource stocks. Health care also becomes important in these funds, which in bear markets may be something of a plus as most health care stocks are fairly defensive. Investors in the Emerging Markets fund will also have to contend with the moral implications of investing in Russia (its invasion of Afghanistan is hardly a bright spot in Islamic/Russian relations) and a large holding in technically communist and thus heathen China.

S&P Global Forestry and Timber

Weight of largest holding	9% (Rayonier)
Weight of top 10 largest holdings	56%
Yield	6%

Returns

Index	2011	2010	2009	2008
S&P Global Forestry and Timber	–17%	14%	38%	–48%

Note that the following chart is from iShares ETF and not the index.

The index – our analysis

ANALYSIS	
Likely risk (high/medium/low)	High
Likely volatility	High
Suitable for 'simple' investors, i.e. small ISA investors	No
Diversification risk with top holdings, i.e. top three more than 20% of fund	Yes (25%)
Likely to be a core holding?	Yes but only for adventurous investors
Market Cap based (MC)/Screened (S)	MC
Appeal to income investors?	Yes
Risk factors?	Highly volatile Very focused on US and Canadian companies
Top three holding as % of total end December 2011	25%
Country breakdown: top three – end December 2011	US 55% Japan 9% Finland 8%
Sector breakdown: top three – end December 2011	100% timber related

Featured ETF

Details	
Fund	iShares S&P Global Timber and Forestry
Ticker/EPIC	WOOD
Issuer	iShares Barclays
TER	0.65%
Currency	GBP
Underlying Index	S&P Global Timber and Forestry Index

Comments

Timber and forestry is one of the newest of the various alternative asset classes to have emerged in the last decade or so. Big-name investors like David Swensen, head of Yale's hugely successful endowment investment fund, have made substantial profits by investing in global forestry and as news of those profits has spread, investors have been keen to find some way of accessing a very specialised niche. Unsurprisingly, a large number of funds and indices have sprung up to take part in this new alternative assets land grab and one of the most successful new indices to emerge has come from Standard & Poor's. Its S&P Global Timber & Forestry index comprises 25 of the largest publicly traded companies engaged in the ownership, management or upstream supply chain of forests and timberlands. According to the index developers, 'these may be forest products companies, timber REITs, paper products companies, paper packaging companies, or agricultural product companies that are engaged in the ownership, management or the upstream supply chain of forests and timberlands'.

Index constituents exhibit the following characteristics:

- **weighting** – modified capitalisation weighted;
- **market capitalisation** – $250 million;
- **liquidity** – three-month average daily volume of at least $2 million;
- **reconstitution** – annual.

What emerges out of this index is a varied bunch of logging companies, as well as timber-based real estate investment trusts (REITs) including names like Plum Tree (a US timber REIT). Currently there is one ETF that tracks the index – from iShares – but for some strange reason, this new fund has received a rather subdued welcome from the UK market and financial press, for no good cause in our view. For more adventurous investors, this index could well be a useful alternative asset giving investors the chance to invest in a sector that is genuinely different.

Top holdings in iShares funds

Company	Country	%
Rayonier	United States	8.9
WEYERHAEUSER	United States	8.76

Continued

Price	Country	%
Plum Creek	United States	7.99
SVENSKA CELLULOSA	Sweden	4.75
Potlathc	United States	4.54
INTERNATIONAL PAPER	United States	4.52
MEADWESTVACO CORP	United States	4.41
West Fraser Timber	Canada	4.31
Sonoco Products	United States	4.08
Stora Ensa	Finland	4.06

There are some important caveats, not least that performance has been a little lackluster – **the index was down over 45 percent in 2008**, for instance. The biggest plus in our books is that this asset class is fairly uncorrelated with wider equity markets. Run any analysis of markets and you will see timber companies constantly cropping up as lowly correlated with indices like the FTSE 100. And, of course, there is a good reason for this – the mechanics of the forestry sector (like some similarly uncorrelated agricultural products) is driven more by environment, weather and tax breaks rather than globalisation or liquid capital flows. The top three companies account for a chunky 25 percent of the total holding (of only 25 companies) but there does seem to be a good mix of paper packagers, forestry products directly and specialist timberland owners, with US companies especially prominent (55 percent of total holdings).

There are, of course, some big, chunky risks. There is no getting away from the fact that this index has been very volatile in recent years and returns have been dreadful. But if you buy the long-term investment argument for paper – constrained global supply, increased global demand via industrialisation – and for established forestry land companies in well-regulated parts of the world, then those poor returns could be reversed in the coming decades. If nothing else you are buying a bunch of companies with double-digit operating margins and heavy asset backing (the US REITs are frequently land revaluation plays).

S&P Global Clean Energy

Weight of largest holding	6.43% (CEMIG)
Weight of top 10 largest holdings	54%
Yield	3.4%

Returns

Index	*2011*	*2010*	*2009*	*2008*
S&P Global Clean Energy	−43%	−28%	3.5%	−62%

Note that the following chart is not the index but the iShares ETF which tracks the index.

The index – our analysis

ANALYSIS	
Likely risk (high/medium/low)	Very high
Likely volatility	High
Suitable for 'simple' investors, i.e. small ISA investors	Yes
Diversification risk with top holdings, i.e. top three more than 20% of fund	No
Likely to be a core holding?	No
Market Cap based (MC)/Screened (S)	MC
Total return (TR) or pays income (Inc)?	Inc
Appeal to income investors?	No
Risk factors?	Technology focused and vulnerable to changes in energy prices US focused
Top three holding as % of total fund end December 2011	18%
Country breakdown: top three – end December 2011	Japan 16.6% USA 16.6% Hong Kong 13%
Sector breakdown: top three – end December 2011	Utilities 55% IT 29% Industrials 15%

The highlighted funds – Green Energy ETFs

Name of fund	Index	TER basis points pa %	Physical or synthetic	ISIN or EPIC (italics and bold)
AMUNDI ETF GREEN TECH LIVING PLANET	GREEN TECH LIVING PLANET	0.35	Synthetic	AWWF
CS ETF (IE) PLC CS ETF(IE)ON CS GBL ALTRN.ENGYGBP	GBL ALTRN.ENGY	0.65	Physical	CAE1

Continued

Name of fund	Index	TER basis points pa %	Physical or synthetic	ISIN or EPIC (italics and bold)
ETFX DAXglobal Alternative Energy Fund	DAXglobal Alternative Energy	0.65	Synthetic	ALTE
ETFX DAXglobal Alternative Energy Fund £	DAXglobal Alternative Energy	0.65	Synthetic	ALTP
ETFX WNA Global Nuclear Energy Fund	WNA Global Nuclear Energy	0.65	Synthetic	NUKE
ETFX WNA Global Nuclear Energy Fund £	WNA Global Nuclear Energy	0.65	Synthetic	NUKP
iShares S&P Global Clean Energy	S&P Global Clean Energy	0.65	Physical	INRG
PowerShares Global Clean Energy Fund		0.75	Physical	PSBW

Comments

Green investing until 2007 was the 'next big thing', the new dotcom sector for the start of a new millennium. And then it all went horribly wrong. The Global Financial Crisis took the wind out of the sails of any 'growth' stock perceived as being risky. Governments also started interfering in the green markets, sometimes for the good, sometimes for the bad – introducing special rates in one year, and then cancelling them the year after. In particular, sentiment has turned sharply against clean energy at the federal level in the USA, although local state governments continue to plough on with valuable schemes. Add it all up and you can understand why investors have turned so savagely against clean energy stocks – and punished the ETFs that specialise in this space. Investors also haven't been helped by the fact that many of the clean energy indices boast radically different constituents, making comparison between them especially difficult. At the end of 2008, for instance, the Lyxor SocGen fund had 46 percent of its total holdings in wind power companies by our calculations whereas the iShares S&P fund had just 26 percent. Hydro is a big component of the iShares and the Lyxor funds but a tiny component of the Powershares fund.

Note: all figures below from July 2008.

Comparison of holdings in clean energy ETFs

iShares		Lyxor		Powershares	
Wind	26.00%	Wind power	46%	Wind	27%
Solar	46%	Solar	33%	Solar	27%
Hydro	15%	Hydro	10.50%	Energy efficiency	20%
Biofuels	7%	Efficiency/power	7.67%	Biofuels	13%
Geothermal	2.37%	Fuel cell	1.37%	Power storage	3%
30 June 2008		31 July 2008		30 June 2008	

With this huge discrepancy in underlying holdings – what exactly is your index investing in? – many investors might begin to question whether a passive approach is the right one for the private investor. Should you be looking to invest using an active fund manager instead? Impax, for instance, has a hugely successful investment trust that tracks a lot of the themes mentioned above but holds a much more interesting and unique range of assets, yet its TER is just over 1 percent, which is not much more than 30 basis points above these passive ETF funds. Impax in particular is very knowledgeable about this sector and has been building its own index with the FTSE that tracks clean energy stocks.

Given all these caveats many investors might conclude that avoiding the Green energy space is probably a good idea altogether, especially given the immense volatility in share prices – but we'd beg to differ. We have a sense that Green energy will be hugely crucial in the next few decades and adventurous investors simply have to be patient and probably opt to invest in this sector only for the very long term using monthly savings plans. If you do decide that the passive approach is best for you, which index and which fund should you choose? All three of the big ETFs in this space will give you exposure to the sector (notwithstanding our comments about different holdings), but we would suggest that more adventurous types might look at the S&P index while more cautious types might look at the Powershares ETF, which tracks a less well-known index called WilderHill.

Different clean energy index compositions at the end of 2011

S&P Global Clean Energy – iShares

Company	Country	%
CEMIG	Brazil	6.43
HOKURIKU ELECTRIC POWER	Japan	6.27
CIA PARANAENSE	Brazil	5.82
KYUSHU ELECTRIC POWER	Japan	5.71
EMPRESA	Chile	5.65
EDP RENOVAVEIS	Portugal	5.18
CHINA LONGYUAN POWER GROUP	Hong Kong	5.12
GCL-POLY ENERGY HOLDINGS LTD	Hong Kong	4.91
VERBUND	Austria	4.75
ENEL GREEN POWER	Italy	4.74

DAX Alt Energy Index – ETF Secs

Company	Country	
Nextera	US	11
EDP Energy	Portugal	11
BG Group	UK	10
Archer Daniels	USA	10
Bunge	USA	9
First Solar	USA	8
Hokuriku	Japan	7
Iberdola	Spain	7
Meyer	Switzerland	6
Apache Corp	USA	5

WilderHill New Energy Global Innovation Index – Powershares

Company	%
LSB Industries Inc.	2.31
Contact Energy Ltd.	2.16
Ormat Technologies Inc.	2.08
Energy Development Corp.	2.07
Enel Green Power S.p.A.	2.07
Brookfield Renewable Energy Partners L.P.	1.99

Continued

Company	%
Verbund AG	1.98
GT Advanced Technologies Inc.	1.91
EDP Renovaveis S/A	1.91
Renewable Energy Corp. ASA	1.90
Meyer Burger Technology AG	1.85

S&P 500

Weight of largest holding	Exxon Mobil 3.5%
Weight of top 10 largest holdings	21.5%
Yield	2.12%

Returns

Index	2011	2010	2009	2008	2007
S&P 500	2%	13%	23%	−34%	0.85%

The index – our analysis

ANALYSIS	
Likely risk (high/medium/low)	Medium
Likely volatility	Medium
Suitable for 'simple' investors, i.e. small ISA investors	Yes
Diversification risk with top holdings, i.e. top three more than 20% of fund	No
Likely to be a core holding?	Yes
Market Cap based (MC)/Screened (S)	MC
Appeal to income investors?	No
Risk factors?	Currency risk
Top three holding as % of total fund – end December 2011	9%
Country breakdown: top three – end December 2011	100% US listed
Sector breakdown: top three – end December 2011	IT 19% Financials 13.7% Energy 12.3%

The highlighted funds – the full range of US funds

Name of fund	Asset class	Index
SPDR S&P US Dividend Aristocrats ETF EUR	**US Dividends**	S&P US Dividend Aristocrats
AMUNDI ETF MSCI USA – EUR	**US Large Cap**	MSCI USA
AMUNDI ETF MSCI USA – USD	**US Large Cap**	MSCI USA
AMUNDI ETF NASDAQ-100 – EUR	**US Large Cap**	NASDAQ-100
AMUNDI ETF NASDAQ-100 – USD	**US Large Cap**	NASDAQ-100 –
AMUNDI ETF S&P 500 – EUR	**US Large Cap**	S&P 500
AMUNDI ETF S&P 500 – USD	**US Large Cap**	S&P 500

Continued

Name of fund	Asset class	Index
ComStage ETF Dow Jones Industrial AverageTM	**US Large Cap**	Dow Jones Industrial AverageTM
ComStage ETF Nasdaq-100®	**US Large Cap**	Nasdaq-100
ComStage ETF S&P 500	**US Large Cap**	S&P 500
CS ETF IE on Dow Jones Industrial AverageSM	**US Large Cap**	Dow Jones Industrial Average
CS ETF IE on MSCI USA	**US Large Cap**	MSCI USA
CS ETF IE on MSCI USA Large Cap	**US Large Cap**	MSCI USA Large Cap
CS ETF IE on Nasdaq 100	**US Large Cap**	Nasdaq 100
CS ETF IE on S&P 500	**US Large Cap**	S&P 500
DB MSCI USA TRN INDEX ETF	**US Large Cap**	MSCI USA TRN
DB S&P 500 EQUAL WEIGHT ETF	**US Large Cap**	S&P 500 EQUAL WEIGHT
DB S&P 500 ETF	**US Large Cap**	S&P 500
ETFX Russell 1000 US Large Cap Fund	**US Large Cap**	Russell 1000 US Large Cap
ETFX Russell 1000 US Large Cap Fund £	**US Large Cap**	Russell 1000 US Large Cap
HSBC MSCI USA ETF	**US Large Cap**	MSCI USA
HSBC S&P 500 ETF	**US Large Cap**	S&P 500
iShares MSCI USA	**US Large Cap**	MSCI USA
iShares S&P 500	**US Large Cap**	S&P 500
iShares S&P 500 (Acc)	**US Large Cap**	S&P 500
iShares S&P 500 Monthly EUR Hedged – note hedge	**US Large Cap**	S&P 500
iShares S&P 500 Monthly GBP Hedged – note hedged	**US Large Cap**	S&P 500

Continued

Name of fund	Asset class	Index
Lyxor ETF Dow Jones Industrial Average (GBP) – NTR	**US Large Cap**	Dow Jones Industrial Average NTR
Lyxor ETF Dow Jones Industrial Average (GBP) – NTR	**US Large Cap**	Dow Jones Industrial Average NTR
Lyxor ETF MSCI USA (GBP) – NTR	**US Large Cap**	MSCI USA NTR
Lyxor ETF MSCI USA (GBP) – NTR	**US Large Cap**	MSCI USA NTR
Lyxor ETF S&P 500 – NTR D USD	**US Large Cap**	S&P 500
Lyxor ETF S&P 500 – NTR D USD	**US Large Cap**	S&P 500
SG Dow Jones	**US Large Cap**	Dow Jones
SG S&P 500 Index (Quanto)	**US Large Cap**	S&P 500
Source S&P 500 ETF	**US Large Cap**	S&P 500
Source US Consumer Discretionary Sector ETF	**US Large Cap: Sectors**	US Consumer Discretionary Sector
Source US Consumer Staples Sector ETF	**US Large Cap: Sectors**	US Consumer Staples Sector
Source US Energy Sector ETF	**US Large Cap: Sectors**	US Energy Sector
Source US Financials Sector ETF	**US Large Cap: Sectors**	US Financials Sector
Source US Health Care Sector ETF	**US Large Cap: Sectors**	US Health Care Sector
Source US Industrials Sector ETF	**US Large Cap: Sectors**	US Industrials Sector
Source US Materials Sector ETF	**US Large Cap: Sectors**	US Materials Sector

Continued

Name of fund	Asset class	Index
Source US Technology Sector ETF	**US Large Cap: Sectors**	US Technology Sector
Source US Utilities Sector ETF	**US Large Cap: Sectors**	US Utilities Sector
PowerShares Dynamic US Market Fund	**US Large Cap Fundamental**	Dynamic US Market
PowerShares EQQQ Fund	**US Large Cap**	EQQQ
PowerShares FTSE RAFI US 1000 Fund	**US Large Cap Fundamental**	FTSE RAFI US 1000
DB RUSSELL MIDCAP INDEX ETF	**US Mid Cap**	RUSSELL MIDCAP
CS ETF IE on MSCI USA Small Cap	**US Small Cap**	MSCI USA Small Cap
DB RUSSELL 2000 ETF	**US Small Cap**	RUSSELL 2000
ETFX Russell 2000 US Small Cap Fund	**US Small Cap**	Russell 2000 US Small Cap
ETFX Russell 2000 US Small Cap Fund £	**US Small Cap**	Russell 2000 US Small Cap
iShares S&P SmallCap 600	**US Small Cap**	S&P SmallCap 600

Name of fund	TER basis points pa %	Physical or synthetic	ISIN or EPIC (*italics and bold*)
SPDR S&P US Dividend Aristocrats ETF EUR	0.35	Physical	UDDV
AMUNDI ETF MSCI USA – EUR	0.15	Synthetic	CU2
AMUNDI ETF MSCI USA – USD	0.28	Synthetic	CU2U
AMUNDI ETF NASDAQ-100 – EUR	0.28	Synthetic	ANX
AMUNDI ETF NASDAQ-100 – USD	0.23	Synthetic	ANXU

Continued

Name of fund	TER basis points pa %	Physical or synthetic	ISIN or EPIC (italics and bold)
AMUNDI ETF S&P 500 – EUR	0.25	Synthetic	500
AMUNDI ETF S&P 500 – USD	0.15	Synthetic	500U
ComStage ETF Dow Jones Industrial AverageTM	0.45	Synthetic	ETF010
ComStage ETF Nasdaq-100®	0.25	Synthetic	ETF011
ComStage ETF S&P 500	0.18	Synthetic	ETF012
CS ETF IE on Dow Jones Industrial AverageSM	0.33	Physical	CID1
CS ETF IE on MSCI USA	0.33	Physical	CU1
CS ETF IE on MSCI USA Large Cap	0.33	Physical	CUL1
CS ETF IE on Nasdaq 100	0.33	Physical	CNX1
CS ETF IE on S&P 500	0.20	Physical	CSP1
DB MSCI USA TRN INDEX ETF	0.30	Synthetic	*LU0274210672*
DB S&P 500 EQUAL WEIGHT ETF	0.30	Synthetic	*LU0659579493*
DB S&P 500 ETF	0.20	Synthetic	*LU0490618542*
ETFX Russell 1000 US Large Cap Fund	0.35	Synthetic	RONE
ETFX Russell 1000 US Large Cap Fund £	0.35	Synthetic	RONP
HSBC MSCI USA ETF	0.30	Physical	*IE00B5WFQ436*
HSBC S&P 500 ETF	0.09	Physical	*IE00B5KQNG97*
iShares MSCI USA	0.40	Physical	SSAM
iShares S&P 500	0.40	Physical	IUSA

Continued

Name of fund	TER basis points pa %	Physical or synthetic	ISIN or EPIC (italics and bold)
iShares S&P 500 (Acc)	0.40	Physical	SACC
iShares S&P 500 Monthly EUR Hedged – note hedge	0.45	Physical	IUSE
iShares S&P 500 Monthly GBP Hedged – note hedged	0.45	Physical	IGUS
Lyxor ETF Dow Jones Industrial Average (GBP) – NTR	0.50	Synthetic	LIND
Lyxor ETF Dow Jones Industrial Average (GBP) – NTR	0.50	Synthetic	LINU
Lyxor ETF MSCI USA (GBP) – NTR	0.50	Synthetic	LMUS
Lyxor ETF MSCI USA (GBP) – NTR	0.35	Synthetic	LMUU
Lyxor ETF S&P 500 – NTR D USD	0.20	Synthetic	LSPU
Lyxor ETF S&P 500 – NTR D USD	0.20	Synthetic	LSPX
SG Dow Jones	NA	Synthetic	S593
SG S&P 500 Index (Quanto)	NA	Synthetic	SP5G
Source S&P 500 ETF	0.35	Synthetic	SPXS
Source US Consumer Discretionary Sector ETF	0.30	Synthetic	XLYS
Source US Consumer Staples Sector ETF	0.30	Synthetic	XLPS
Source US Energy Sector ETF	0.30	Synthetic	XLES
Source US Financials Sector ETF	0.30	Synthetic	XLFS

Continued

Name of fund	TER basis points pa %	Physical or synthetic	ISIN or EPIC (*italics and bold*)
Source US Health Care Sector ETF	0.30	Synthetic	XLVS
Source US Industrials Sector ETF	0.30	Synthetic	XLIS
Source US Materials Sector ETF	0.30	Synthetic	XLBS
Source US Technology Sector ETF	0.30	Synthetic	XLKS
Source US Utilities Sector ETF	0.30	Synthetic	XLUS
PowerShares Dynamic US Market Fund	0.75	Physical	PSWC
PowerShares EQQQ Fund	0.30	Physical	EQQQ
PowerShares FTSE RAFI US 1000 Fund	0.39	Physical	PSRF
DB RUSSELL MIDCAP INDEX ETF	0.35	Synthetic	***LU0592217953***
CS ETF IE on MSCI USA Small Cap	0.43	Physical	CUS1
DB RUSSELL 2000 ETF	0.45	Synthetic	***LU0322248658***
ETFX Russell 2000 US Small Cap Fund	0.45	Synthetic	RTWO
ETFX Russell 2000 US Small Cap Fund £	0.45	Synthetic	RTWP
iShares S&P SmallCap 600	0.40	Physical	ISP6

Comments

We would suggest that any internationally diversified portfolio should have some exposure, no matter how small, to the US – that could be done indirectly through a world developed markets index, which would have a heavy US weighting, or directly through a fund that tracks a major US index.

If you decide to track a major US index you will be spoilt for choice. There is an almost bewildering array of ETFs based on major US indices, both large cap and small cap. These include the following:

- The major one – and our preferred index – the S&P 500, which is a value-weighted index published since 1957 of the prices of 500 large-cap liquid stocks actively traded in the US. The stocks included in the S&P 500 are those of large publicly held companies that trade on either of the two largest American stock markets, the New York Stock Exchange and NASDAQ. Almost all of the stocks included in the index are among the 500 American stocks with the largest market values or capitalisations.

- The Dow Jones Industrial Average, which is a price-weighted average of blue-chip stocks and the oldest index by far. The index covers all industries with the exception of Transportation and Utilities. The index has been a widely followed indicator of the stock market since 1 October 1928.

- The Russell 1000® index, which measures the performance of the large-cap segment of the US equity universe. It is a subset of the Russell 3000® index and includes approximately 1,000 of the largest US securities. According to ETF Securities, 'The Russell 1000® represents approximately 92 percent of the US equity market vs. only 66 percent for the S&P 500. Russell Indexes are used by more US institutional investors than all other index providers combined.'

- THE MSCI USA index. This is based around the hugely popular MSCI World Developed Markets index and covers almost 98 percent of all the stocks – large and small – listed on the US stock markets (including the NASDAQ and the NYSE).

- The iShares S&P SmallCap 600 reflects the total return performance of the S&P SmallCap 600 index. The index comprises 600 small-capitalisation companies in the US and covers approximately 3–4 percent of the US equity market. S&P generally defines the small-cap segment of a country's equity universe as being securities whose total market capitalisation lies between $300 million and $2 billion.

- The Russell 2000® index measures the performance of the small-cap segment of the US equity universe. The Russell 2000® index measures the performance of the 2,000 smallest companies in the Russell 3000® index, which represents approximately 8 percent of the total market capitalisation of the US equity market vs. 3–4 percent for the S&P 600.

Which index to use? Given this huge range we would stick with perhaps the best known of the large-cap indices, namely the S&P 500 index, which is tracked in turn by a huge range of ETFs including ones from iShares, Deutsche

DBX (the Deutsche fund is slightly cheaper with a TER of just 0.3 percent) and Lyxor. It is also worth noting that Deutsche DBX offers a short S&P 500 fund – its ticker is SPXTS and it pays 1:1 on the downside. If you are looking for a slightly more comprehensive index that includes small caps, we would suggest looking at the MSCI USA index, while the Russell 2000 is our preferred index for capturing the vibrant small-cap segment in the US markets.

S&P Select Frontier Markets

Weight of largest holding in S&P Select Frontier index	8%
Weight of top 10 largest holdings	58%
Yield	4.3%

Returns

Index	2011	2010	2009	2008
	−21%	22%	23%	−67%

Note that the chart below is of the db X-tracker fund and not the index.

The index – our analysis

ANALYSIS	
Likely risk (high/medium/low)	High
Likely volatility	High
Suitable for 'simple' investors, i.e. small ISA investors	No
Diversification risk with top holdings, i.e. top three more than 20% of fund	Yes
Likely to be a core holding?	Yes for adventurous investors
Market cap based (MC)/screened (S)	MC
Appeal to income investors?	No
Risk factors?	Political risk Volatile national markets
Top three holding as % of total fund end December 2011	22%
Country breakdown: top three – end December 2011	Kuwait 22% Qatar 21% Colombia 15.5%

Top 10 Holdings in DB Select Frontiers index tracker

Company	% of fund
Mobile Telecommunications	7.93
Ecopetrol	7.28
Industries Qatar	6.73
Qatar National Bank	6.52
Kuwait Finance House	5.91
National Bank of Kuwait	5.89
Kazakhmys	5.21
Masraf al Rayan	4.69
Eurasian Natural Resources Corporation	4.10
Mercadolibre	4.09

Comments

Frontier markets comprise roughly 1 billion people and well over $2 trillion of global capital, with $111 billion of that pot represented by the S&P Select Frontiers index. Defined loosely by international bodies like the World Bank, frontier markets are high-risk, low-income countries. They typically:

- are difficult to access for outside investors;
- are fairly risky on the political (and economic) front;
- have the potential for huge returns and even bigger declines.

According to a report by analysts at S&P back in 2009, frontier market economies have been growing at a 'brisk pace since 2000'. Over this time, frontier markets' GDP has grown at an annualised rate of 5.6 percent, outpacing the growth of both emerging and developed markets. According to S&P, 'frontier market GDP growth has been higher than that of emerging and developed markets for every year since 2001'.

To be fair, this huge growth is primarily because the countries concerned started from a much lower base – the GDP per capita of much of the developed world is roughly $37,500 compared with just $1,845 for frontier markets (and $2,390 for emerging markets). That relative economic under-achievement is also marked in their financial services sector – most frontier markets do have stock markets (there is the odd exception such as Cambodia) but they are typically fairly difficult to invest in if you are a foreigner, heavily protected, over-regulated and subject to massive volatility. Still, the potential is obvious – obvious enough, in fact, for economists at Goldman Sachs to speculate on the countries most likely to follow in the path of the mighty BRIC economies of today. Their top candidates – called the Next 11 – included Egypt, Pakistan, Vietnam, Turkey and even Iran (which is notoriously difficult to access for foreigners).

Are frontier markets a good investment?

The big problem with all of these grand-sounding global investment narratives is that frequently they are precisely just that, broad stories and huge global narratives with little actual investment logic. Economies like Pakistan or Cambodia may be growing like gang-busters, but will any of that rapid economic growth actually a) trickle down to local stock markets, and b) ever make it out of the country into the investment portfolios of investors who have financed this growth?

The risks here are fairly obvious. The biggest and nastiest risk is of national economic meltdown – think Zimbabwe. You will be familiar with terms like 'bread basket of Africa' and 'economic powerhouse of southern Africa', but prior to the meltdown inspired by its leader Robert Mugabe, Zimbabwe had a fairly robust stock market, open to foreign investors since 1993. In the last decade this market slumped, as economic paralysis infected all parts of the economy – national GDP is half of what it was in 2000, and is declining for the eighth consecutive year. Ever since President Mugabe's disastrous land-reform campaign, the country's farming, tourism, and gold sectors have collapsed.

On a more general global level, frontier markets are perceived as being highly risky by many investors and it's fair to say that over the four years since 2008, frontier markets have tended to lag behind both emerging and developed world markets – in 2008 frontier markets fell by over 65 percent in one year. That poor recent performance has helped push down relative valuations of frontier market companies to levels some contrarian investors regard as attractive, especially as these markets tend to provide diversified, relatively lowly correlated returns when compared to mainstream equity indices.

How to invest

Investing in frontier markets directly is very difficult for private investors in the UK. There are a few companies listed on the London exchange that do give you some exposure to markets like Cambodia and Nigeria, but they are few and far between. The more sensible alternative is to invest across the board in a wide range of countries, so that you can balance out the potential risks.

Many emerging markets fund managers are beginning to enter this space in a small way. Emerging markets guru Mark Mobius, for instance, has started buying into frontier markets through his various small-cap Templeton funds. There is also a specialist frontiers market investment trust run out of London called the Advance Frontiers market fund and it takes a very active fund-of-fund approach.

The other alternative is to invest in one of the few ETFs that invest in this space – one from Deutsche db X-trackers, and the other from RBS Markets, although it's worth noting that there are also some African-focused trackers available on the market.

The DB fund tracks the Select Frontier index from S&P. This index is actually a subset of something called the S&P/IFCG Extended Frontier 150, and comprises 40 of the largest and most liquid stocks from countries that have smaller economies or less developed capital markets than traditional emerging markets and are, therefore, excluded from most emerging market benchmarks and investment funds.

To be eligible for the index a stock must have a minimum free-float market capitalisation of $100 million, an average daily value traded over six months greater than $2 million, and a minimum of 15 days traded over each of the previous six months. The top 30 stocks are then ranked by market capitalisation and those that meet these inclusion criteria are chosen for the index, subject to the constraint that a maximum of five stocks from any particular country can be included. The index is free-float market cap weighted with adjustments to ensure that no country has a weight over 30 percent, no stock has a weight over 10 percent and a minimum daily basket trade based on average trading history over the last six months of $200 million assuming 100 percent participation. The index is rebalanced on a semi-annual basis in January and July of each year. Countries in the index include Bahrain, Bulgaria, Colombia, Croatia, Jordan, Oman, Pakistan, Romania, Sri Lanka, UAE and Vietnam.

Featured range of Frontier, Africa and GCC trackers

Name of fund	Index	TER basis points p.a. %	ISIN or EPIC *(italics and bold)*
RBS Market Access MSCI Frontier Markets Index ETF	MSCI Frontier Markets	0.9	***LU0667622202***
DB S&P SELECT FRONTIER ETF	S&P SELECT FRONTIER	0.95	***LU0328476410***
RBS Market Access MSCI GCC Countries ex Saudi Arabia Top 50	MSCI GCC Countries ex Saudi Arabia Top 50 Capped	0.7	***LU0667622111***
RBS Market Access South-East Europe Index ETF	South-East Europe	0.6	***LU0259329869***

Continued

Name of fund	Index	TER basis points p.a. %	ISIN or EPIC *(italics and bold)*
AFRICA Frontier			
DB MSCI EFM AFRICA TOP 50 CAPPED TRN INDEX ETF	MSCI EFM AFRICA TOP 50 CAPPED TRN	0.65	***LU0592217524***
RBS Market Access FTSE/JSE Africa Top 40 Index ETF	FTSE/JSE Africa Top 40	0.65	***LU0270000028***
RBS Market Access MSCI Emerging and Frontier Africa ex South Africa Index	MSCI Emerging and Frontier Africa ex South Africa	0.85	***LU0667622384***
GULF STATES (GCC) Frontier			
iShares MSCI GCC Countries ex-Saudi Arabia (physical replication)	MSCI GCC Countries ex-Saudi Arabia	0.80	***IGCC***
Lyxor ETF Kuwait (FTSE Coast Kuwait 40) -USD	FTSE Coast Kuwait 40	0.65	***LKUU***
Lyxor ETF Kuwait (FTSE Coast Kuwait 40) -USD	FTSE Coast Kuwait 40	0.65	***LKUW***

DB doesn't have the frontier markets entirely to itself – there's also a range of global frontier trackers available from RBS Markets. The RBS offering includes a global tracker based on the MSCI index – this is slightly cheaper than the DB ETF at 0.90 percent TER vs 0.90 percent for the DB tracker. The RBS range also includes an African tracker plus funds that focus on the Gulf state markets and South Eastern Europe. iShares also offers its own GCC (Gulf states) physically replicating tracker – all the other ETFs in the frontier space use synthetic replication. Investors need to be aware that the frontier space requires a huge amount of caution and risk control – skills that may favour a more active fund management approach. ETFs may be efficient and cheap, but if they operate in intrinsically inefficient markets that are busily going nowhere, your investment could suffer. You need to know what you are investing in with such a fund – a strong Gulf States bias (plus Colombia) and a strong focus on banks and telecom companies plus the odd property giant.

Appendix: The Essential 25

Brent Oil

Returns

Index	2011	2010	2009
Brent Oil Spot $	19.35%	20.3%	85.6%
West Texas Intermediate	15%	15%	104%

The index – our analysis

ANALYSIS	
Likely Risk (High/Medium/Low)	High
Likely Volatility	High
Suitable for 'Simple' Investors, i.e. small ISA investors	No
Diversification Risk with Top Holdings, i.e. top three more than 20% of fund	No
Likely to be a core holding?	Possibly for Adventurous Investors

Comments

Oil seems to have become everyone's favourite commodity after gold – barely a day goes by without a national newspaper or specialist magazine making a bold prediction on the future direction of oil prices. We have absolutely no idea if oil is likely to shoot up through $100 a barrel again or crash below $50.

What we do understand is that many investors are tempted by the defensive qualities of oil – it is almost like gold, a backup commodity in case of financial meltdown. The global economy may grind to a halt with expensive oil, but investors in long oil funds are likely to be richly rewarded. There are also the long-term oil bulls with their peak oil theories to contend with – many maintain that we have already gone past the point at which extra demand for oil is increasing at a faster rate than the growth in supply.

Again we have no idea if this is the case – what does slightly alarm us is that oil and oil-based funds have become so popular that there is some evidence (hotly contested to be sure) that financial speculation is beginning to overwhelm some markets. Big US oil ETFs based on futures prices have begun to heavily influence the direction of futures-based markets as fund managers have to buy up positions to maintain the fund's exposure.

Our sense is that if you really must buy access to an individual commodity in your portfolio, you are probably best off focusing on just two – oil and gold. The trickier question is how to buy that access – do you invest in a fund that tracks something called WTI or Brent? In the box below we have outlined the differences between these two types of oil – the basic difference is that Brent is slightly heavier than its West Texas cousin (WTI) and tends to trade at a different price, on different markets.

But this distinction between Brent and WTI is just the start of the process of working out how to invest – your next challenge is to decide whether you want to invest in a broad crude oil index, a specific Brent/WTI fund and whether you want to track futures prices. Just to add to the confusion you can also make money on price falls in oil – by investing in an inverse short ETC – or gear up your exposure to oil increases by investing in a leveraged oil ETC. The full list of oil-based options from ETF Securities is in the table below.

If we had a preference we would suggest the Brent Oil 1 month futures ETC – sterling based – which, as the name suggests, invests in one-month futures-based contracts based on spot Brent oil prices.

Featured oil and energy trackers

Name of fund	Index	TER basis points p.a. %	ISIN or EPIC (italics and bold)
OIL Trackers			
ETFS Brent 1mth	Brent 1mth	0.49	OILB
ETFS Brent 1mth £	Brent 1mth	0.49	OLBP
ETFS Brent 1yr	Brent 1yr	0.49	OSB1
ETFS Brent 2yr	Brent 2yr	0.49	OSB2
ETFS Brent 3yr	Brent 3yr	0.49	OSB3
ETFS Crude Oil	Crude Oil	0.49	CRUD
ETFS Forward Crude Oil	Forward Crude Oil	0.49	FCRU
ETFS Energy DJ-UBSCISM	Energy DJ-UBSCI	0.49	AIGE
UBS Brent Crude Oil	Brent Crude Oil	0.30	LCOU
UBS Crude Oil	Crude Oil	0.30	OILD
UBS Crude Oil	Crude Oil	0.80	OILL
SPGS Crude Oil ER	Crude Oil ER	0.40	CRDU
SPGS Crude Oil ER (Quanto)	Crude Oil ER	N/A	CRDG
SPGS Crude Oil ER (Quanto)	Crude Oil ER	N/A	CRDE
ETFS WTI 1yr	WTI 1yr	0.49	OSW1
ETFS WTI 2mth	WTI 2mth	0.49	OILW
ETFS WTI 2mth £	WTI 2mth	0.49	OLWP
ETFS WTI 2yr	WTI 2yr	0.49	OSW2
ETFS WTI 3yr	WTI 3yr	0.49	OSW3
ETFS Leveraged Crude Oil	Crude Oil	0.98	LOIL
ETFS Short Crude Oil	Crude Oil	0.98	SOIL
Energy Trackers			
ETFS Forward Energy DJ-UBSCI-F3 SM	Forward Energy DJ-CI-F3 SM	0.49	ENEF
ETFS Forward Heating Oil	Forward Heating Oil	0.49	HEAF
ETFS Forward Natural Gas	Forward Natural Gas	0.49	NGAF

Continued

Name of fund	Index	TER basis points pa %	ISIN or EPIC (italics and bold)
Energy Trackers			
ETFS Forward Petroleum DJ-UBSCI-F3 SM	Forward Petroleum DJ-CI-F3 SM	0.49	FPET
ETFS Gasoline	Gasoline	0.49	UGAS
ETFS Heating Oil	Heating Oil	0.49	HEAT
ETFS Leveraged Energy DJ-UBSCISM	Energy DJ-UBSCI	0.98	LNRG
ETFS Leveraged Gasoline	Gasoline	0.98	LGAS
ETFS Leveraged Heating Oil	Heating Oil	0.98	LHEA
ETFS Leveraged Natural Gas	Natural Gas	0.98	LNGA
ETFS Leveraged Petroleum DJ-UBSCISM	Petroleum DJ-UBSCI	0.98	LPET
ETFS Natural Gas	Natural Gas	0.49	NGAS
ETFS Natural Gas £	Natural Gas	0.49	NGSP
ETFS Petroleum DJ-UBSCISM	Petroleum DJ-UBSCI	0.49	AIGO
ETFS Short Energy DJ-UBSCISM	Energy DJ-UBSCI	0.98	SNRG
ETFS Short Gasoline	Gasoline	0.98	SGAS
ETFS Short Heating Oil	Heating Oil	0.98	SHEA
ETFS Short Natural Gas	Natural Gas	0.98	SNGA
ETFS Short Petroleum DJ-UBSCISM	Petroleum DJ-UBSCI	0.98	SPET
iPath S&P GSCI Energy Index TR (DE) ETN	S&P GSCI Energy TR	0.75	***DE000BC1DBH9***
SPGS Natural Gas ER	Natural Gas ER	0.50	GASU
SPGS Natural Gas ER (Quanto)	Natural Gas ER	NA	GASG
SPGS Natural Gas ER (Quanto)	Natural Gas ER	NA	GASE
UBS Energy	Energy	0.90	ENRG
UBS Natural Gas	Natural Gas	0.90	NATG
UBS Natural Gas	Natural Gas	0.40	NATU

Definitions of different types of oil from the Energy Information Administration in the US

> **West Texas Intermediate**
>
> West Texas Intermediate (WTI) crude oil is of very high quality and is excellent for refining a larger portion of gasoline. Its API gravity is 39.6 degrees (making it a 'light' crude oil), and it contains only about 0.24 percent of sulphur (making a 'sweet' crude oil). This combination of characteristics, combined with its location, makes it an ideal crude oil to be refined in the US, the largest gasoline-consuming country in the world. Most WTI crude oil gets refined in the Midwest region of the country, with some more refined within the Gulf Coast region. Although the production of WTI crude oil is on the decline, it still is the major benchmark of crude oil in the Americas. WTI is generally priced at about a $5–6 per-barrel premium to the OPEC Basket price and between $1 and $15 per-barrel premium to Brent, although on a daily basis the pricing relationships between these can vary greatly.
>
> **Brent**
>
> Brent blend is actually a combination of crude oil from 15 different oil fields in the Brent and Ninian systems located in the North Sea. Its API gravity is 38.3 degrees (making it a 'light' crude oil, but not quite as 'light' as WTI), while it contains about 0.37 percent of sulphur (making it a 'sweet' crude oil, but again slightly less 'sweet' than WTI). Brent blend is ideal for making gasoline and middle distillates, both of which are consumed in large quantities in Northwest Europe, where Brent blend crude oil is typically refined. However, if the arbitrage between Brent and other crude oils, including WTI, is favourable for export, Brent has been known to be refined in the US (typically the East Coast or the Gulf Coast) or the Mediterranean region. Brent blend, like WTI, production is also on the decline, but it remains the major benchmark for other crude oils in Europe or Africa. For example, prices for other crude oils in these two continents are often priced as a differential to Brent, i.e. Brent minus $0.50. Brent blend is generally priced at about a $4 per-barrel premium to the OPEC Basket price or about a $1 to $15 per-barrel discount to WTI, although on a daily basis the pricing relationships can vary greatly.

Gold

Returns

Index	2011	2010	2009	2008	2007
Gold Bullion (LBM) £	18.52%	33.7%	15.2%	40.4%	32.3%

The index – our analysis

ANALYSIS	
Likely risk (high/medium/low)	Medium to low
Likely volatility	Medium

Continued

ANALYSIS	
Suitable for 'simple' investors, i.e. small ISA investors	Yes
Diversification risk with top holdings, i.e. top three more than 20% of fund	No – not relevant
Likely to be a core holding?	Yes

Chart: Gold (LBM) $ & FTSE 100, 5/6/02 – 13/4/12. www.sharescope.co.uk, Chart (c) ShareScope

The highlighted funds including precious metals trackers

Name of fund	Index	TER basis points p.a. %	ISIN or EPIC *(italics and bold)*
Precious Metals including Gold			
ETFS Leveraged Precious Metals DJ-UBSCISM	Precious Metals DJ-UBSCI	0.98	LPMT
ETFS Precious Metals DJ-UBSCISM	Precious Metals DJ-UBSCI	0.49	AIGP

Continued

Name of fund	Index	TER basis points p.a. %	ISIN or EPIC (italics and bold)
Precious Metals including Gold			
ETFS Short Precious Metals DJ-UBSCISM	Precious Metals DJ-UBSCI	0.98	SPMT
iPath S&P GSCI Prec Mtls Idx TR (DE) ETN	S&P GSCI Prec Mtls Idx TR	0.75	DE000BC1C7L7
UBS Precious Metals	Precious Metals	0.49	PREC
ETFS Physical PM Basket	Physical PM Basket	0.43	PHPM
ETFS Physical PM Basket £	Physical PM Basket	0.43	PHPP
Gold specific			
ETFS Gold	Gold	0.49	BULL
ETFS Gold £	Gold	0.49	BULP
ETFS Leveraged Gold	Gold	0.98	LBUL
ETFS Short Gold	Gold	0.98	SBUL
Gold Bullion Securities	Gold Bullion Securities	0.40	GBS
Gold Bullion Securities £	Gold Bullion Securities	0.40	GBSS
SG Gold	Gold	N/A	S940
SG Gold (Quanto)	Gold	N/A	GOLE
SG Gold (Quanto)	Gold	N/A	GOLG
Source Gold P-ETC	Gold P-ETC	0.39	SGLD
SPGS Gold	Gold	0.40	LTNG
UBS Gold	Gold	0.26	GLDD
UBS Gold	Gold	0.76	GLDG
Physical Gold			
ETFS Physical Gold	Physical Gold	0.39	PHAU
ETFS Physical Gold £	Physical Gold	0.39	PHGP

Continued

Name of fund	Index	TER basis points p.a. %	ISIN or EPIC *(italics and bold)*
ETFS Physical Swiss Gold	Physical Swiss Gold	0.39	SGBS
iShares Physical Gold ETC	Physical Gold	0.25	SG

Comments

Gold is a peculiar investment class – even those investors with absolutely no interest in commodities generally will tend to have more than a passing interest in the shiny stuff, if only because of its safe haven status and redoubtable qualities against inflation and financial Armageddon.

We do not tend to favour investing in individual commodities but we can understand why investors might want to gain access to gold in times of distress. To be honest, we are not convinced of the investment benefits of gold beyond this distressed imperative – although there are users of gold in industry and especially jewellery, as a commodity its only real value is as a store of ... value!

Nevertheless, our skepticism with gold is not shared by the millions of investors who have pumped countless tens of billions into US and UK-based gold funds and especially ETCs. Flows into ETCs have continued to build even during periods when the gold price was falling, indicating that strategic investors are increasingly using ETCs to build long-term positions in gold.

Part of that increased interest is a function of easier access via various ETC and ETF-based platforms – investors now have the choice to invest in gold both short and long and as part of a wider basket of precious metals. They can also invest in futures-based forward prices and in spot prices. Crucially, they can also invest in actual physical holdings of gold, not futures-based rolling contracts – these physical-backed ETCs have proved hugely popular. If we had to express a preference we'd suggest that a physical-based gold fund like PHGP (a sterling-based tracker) would probably be the safest bet for ultra-cautious investors looking to profit from any increase in financial volatility.

Appendix: The Essential 25

iBoxx Sterling Corporate Bonds

Weight of largest holding	4.1% Vattenfall
Weight of top 10 largest holdings	33%
Yield	Distribution yield 5.03%
	Yield to maturity 4.61%

Returns

Index	2011	2010	2009	2008	2007
iBoxx £ Liquid Corporates Long Dated Index	9%	5%	12.6%	−9.6%	−1%

The index – our analysis

ANALYSIS	
Likely risk (high/medium/low)	Low to medium
Likely volatility	Low to medium

Continued

ANALYSIS

Suitable for 'simple' investors, i.e. small ISA investors	Yes
Diversification risk with top holdings, i.e. top three more than 20% of fund	No
Likely to be a core holding?	Yes
Market cap based (MC)/screened (S)	MC
Appeal to income investors?	Yes

The featured ETF

Details

Fund	iShares £ Corporate Bond
Ticker/EPIC	SLXX
Issuer	iShares
TER	0.2%
Underlying index	iBoxx £ Liquid Corporates Long Dated index
Launch Date	26/03/04

Details of index

Fixed Income Information

No. of Holdings 57

Weighted Avg. Maturity (years) 14.05%

Inclusion criteria for index

Bond types: fixed coupon, step-ups, rating-driven bonds and callable hybrid capital

Min. time to maturity: 1.5 years at the rebalancing date

Minimum rating: BBB- from Fitch or S&P or Baa3 from Moody's (the lowest available rating is taken)

Amount outstanding: £250m

Maximum age since issuance: 2 years

Max # bonds per issuer: 1

Top holdings in iShares ETF

Coupon	Coupon %	Maturity	Country	%
VATTENFALL AB MTN 6.875 04/15/2039	6.88	15/04/1939	Sweden	4.14
STATOILHYDRO ASA MTN 6.875 03/11/2031	6.88	11/03/1931	Norway	3.89
BARCLAYS BANK PLC MTN 10 05/21/2021	10	21/05/2021	United Kingdom	3.72
IMPERIAL TOBACCO FINANCE PLC 9 02/17/2022	9	17/02/2022	United Kingdom	3.46
TESCO PLC MTN 6.125 02/24/2022	6.12	24/02/2022	United Kingdom	3.22
LLOYDS TSB BANK PL MTN 6.5 09/17/2040	6.5	17/09/1940	United Kingdom	3.15
KONINKLIJKE KPN NV MTN 5.75 09/17/2029	5.75	17/09/2029	Netherlands	3.13
ANHEUSER-BUSCH INB MTN 6.5 06/23/2017	6.5	23/06/2017	Belgium	3.09
SKANDINAVISKA ENSK MTN 6.625 07/09/2014	6.62	09/07/2014	Sweden	3.04
BG ENERGY CAPITAL MTN 5.125 12/01/2025	5.12	01/12/2025	United Kingdom	2.81

Comments

Virtually every major listed company issues some form of fixed income debt – the most popular form is something called a corporate bond. Like government bonds or gilts, this promises to pay the holder a fixed income coupon regularly until the bond is redeemed.

Unlike most Western governments, though, there is a major default risk – no major OECD country has ever defaulted on its debt (yet!) but plenty of corporations have. That risk, an extra risk, is quantifiable and is expressed in the yield – the riskier the company, the higher the yield. Crucially, it is important to understand that not every high-yielding, high-risk bond-issuing company goes bust – the vast majority carries on paying their interest coupons. But it is also true that the highest quality, most blue-chip companies – especially those given the term investment grade, for the very lowest potential risk – are the least likely to go bankrupt and stop paying their debts.

In recent years that investment grade status has been taken to bizarre lengths – in 2009, for instance, corporations like McDonald's possessed better-rated debt than some Western countries. Italy may be forced out of the euro but global hamburger specialists will probably continue paying their interest coupons.

All of these relatively simple challenges and debates – plus many more – form the background to why so many investors like investing in corporate bonds. They like the higher yield (bar McDonald's) as compared to government debt – they also appreciate the fact that most of these big debt issues are very liquid and easy to trade in.

Sadly, though, there is a big problem facing most ordinary private investors – big corporations issue most of their bonds in big bundles requiring an initial outlay of £50,000 or more. Direct ownership of corporate bonds by private investors is, unsurprisingly, very low as a consequence.

Step forward corporate bond funds and indices. These aggregate the most liquid, most popular bond issues into one structure – in this case an index produced by a specialist markets firm called MarkIt. Only the most liquid bonds get into this fund – although it is important to say that not all the bonds in the fund are of the highest 'risk grade'. Investors use ratings firms to assess the potential risk of default and the safest companies tend to get the coveted AAA rating with the lowest rating (outside junk bonds) getting BBB ratings.

This index, and the accompanying iShares ETF, invests only in these popular, liquid, BBB and above-rated bonds – and it produces a yield which is substantially in excess of any government bond. But there is a real risk – corporate bonds are issued mostly by quoted, listed companies and when these companies are in distress, their bonds tend to fall in value as investors fret about bankruptcy and default. And they are right to worry about that risk – the financial meltdown of the once mighty Detroit car firms involved bondholders taking a massive hit on their investments. If you believe that corporate failure is likely to increase as a result of economic distress, you should avoid corporate bonds like the plague – their prices will fall as investors demand a higher risk premium via the yield which will, in turn, increase. If, on the other hand, you believe that corporate financial health is about to substantially improve, then corporate bonds could be the perfect place to receive a decent yield plus some capital uplift.

Two final observations on the iShares ETF and corporate bonds in general – we'll start with a warning! Investors need to bear in mind that corporate bond trackers follow an index which is market capitalisation weighted – this means that the biggest holdings in the index are those companies issuing the most bonds. This doesn't necessarily mean that these are the most successful companies or even the highest rated in terms of credit quality – it just means that they issue a lot of debt. Many professional investors are fearful of corporate bond indices where the quality of the underlying company and its balance sheet isn't the main 'filter' – there are very few indices by contrast that use a fundamental approach to bond issuance and none available to track in the UK at present. That means that investors need to be aware that with the major corporate bond indices they are taking on a very specific risk, i.e they might be weighting their holdings in the tracker to the riskier, more indebted companies.

Our last observation is that there are more tracker funds available than the iShares corporate bond ETF featured in this section, most of which boast a more specialised focus. The table below shows the full range of corporate bond trackers available on the UK market – some track non-sterling denominated bonds while others only buy into high-yield bonds (riskier though higher-yielding paper) or non-financial corporate bonds.

Full range of UK listed corporate bond trackers

Name of fund	Index	Total return
DB iBOXX® € LIQUID CORPORATE 100 FINANCIALS SUB-INDEX TR ETF	iBoxx € LIQUID CORPORATE 100 FINANCIALS	Total Return
DB IBOXX® € LIQUID CORPORATE 100 NON-FINANCIALS SUB-INDEX TR ETF	iBoxx € LIQUID CORPORATE 100 NON-FINANCIALS	Total Return
iShares Barclays Capital Euro Corporate Bond	Barclays Capital Euro Corporate Bond	Distributing
iShares Barclays Capital Euro Corporate Bond 1-5	Barclays Capital Euro Corporate Bond 1-5	Distributing
iShares Barclays Capital Euro Corporate Bond ex-Financials	Barclays Capital Euro Corporate Bond ex-Financials	Distributing

Continued

Name of fund	Index	Total return
iShares Barclays Capital Euro Corporate Bond ex-Financials 1–5	Barclays Capital Euro Corporate Bond ex-Financials 1–5	Distributing
iShares Markit iBoxx $ Corporate Bond	Markit iBoxx $ Corporate Bond	Distributing
iShares Markit iBoxx $ High Yield Capped Bond	Markit iBoxx $ High Yield Capped Bond	Distributing
iShares Markit iBoxx £ Corporate Bond	Markit iBoxx Corporate Bond	Distributing
iShares Markit iBoxx £ Corporate Bond 1–5	Markit iBoxx Corporate Bond 1–5	Distributing
iShares Markit iBoxx £ Corporate Bond ex-Financials	Markit iBoxx Corporate Bond ex-Financials	Distributing
iShares Markit iBoxx Euro Corporate Bond	Markit iBoxx Euro Corporate Bond	Distributing
iShares Markit iBoxx Euro Covered Bond	Markit iBoxx Euro Covered Bond	Distributing
iShares Markit iBoxx Euro High Yield Bond	Markit iBoxx Euro High Yield Bond	Distributing
Lyxor ETF iBoxx £ Liquid Corporates Long Dated – GBP	iBoxx Liquid Corporates Long Dated	Total Return
Lyxor ETF iBoxx EUR Liquid High Yield 30 – EUR	iBoxx EUR Liquid High Yield 30 – EUR	Total Return

Name of fund	ISIN or EPIC (italics/bold)	TER basis points p.a. %
DB iBOXX® € LIQUID CORPORATE 100 FINANCIALS SUB-INDEX TR ETF	*LU0484968812*	0.20
DB IBOXX® € LIQUID CORPORATE 100 NON-FINANCIALS SUB-INDEX TR ETF	*LU0484968655*	0.20

Continued

Name of fund	Index	Total return
iShares Barclays Capital Euro Corporate Bond	IEAC	0.20
iShares Barclays Capital Euro Corporate Bond 1–5	SE15	0.20
iShares Barclays Capital Euro Corporate Bond ex-Financials	EEXF	0.20
iShares Barclays Capital Euro Corporate Bond ex-Financials 1–5	EEX5	0.20
iShares Markit iBoxx $ Corporate Bond	LQDE	0.20
iShares Markit iBoxx $ High Yield Capped Bond	SHYU	0.50
iShares Markit iBoxx £ Corporate Bond	SLXX	0.20
iShares Markit iBoxx £ Corporate Bond 1–5	IS15	0.20
iShares Markit iBoxx £ Corporate Bond ex-Financials	ISXF	0.20
iShares Markit iBoxx Euro Corporate Bond	IBCX	0.20
iShares Markit iBoxx Euro Covered Bond	ICOV	0.20
iShares Markit iBoxx Euro High Yield Bond	IHYG	0.50
Lyxor ETF iBoxx £ Liquid Corporates Long Dated – GBP	COUK	0.20
Lyxor ETF iBoxx EUR Liquid High Yield 30 – EUR	YIEL	0.45

References

Chapter 1

[1] Jensen, M. (1968) 'The performance of mutual funds in the period 1945–1964', *Journal of Finance*, Vol. 23, May.

[2] Gruber, M.J. (1996) 'Another puzzle: the growth in actively managed mutual funds', *Journal of Finance*, Vol. 51, pp. 783–810.

[3] Carhart, M.M. (1997) 'On persistence in mutual fund performance', *Journal of Finance*, Vol. 52, pp. 57–82.

[4] Elton, E., Gruber, M.J., Das, S. and Hlavka, M. (1993) 'Efficiency with costly information: a reinterpretation of evidence from managed portfolios', *The Review of Financial Studies*, http://ideas.repec.org/a/oup/rfinst/v6y1993i1p1-22.html.

[5] Elton, E., Gruber, M. and Blake, C. (1995) 'Fundamental economic variables, expected returns, and bond fund performance', *Journal of Finance*, Vol. 50.

[6] Clements, J. (1999) 'Stock funds just don't measure up', *The Wall Street Journal*, 5 October.

[7] Fletcher, J. (1997) 'An examination of UK unit trust performance within the Arbitrage Pricing Theory framework', *Review of Quantitative Finance and Accounting*, pp. 91–107.

[8] Ibid.

[9] See note 4.

[10] Cuthbertson, K., Nitzsche, D. and O'Sullivan, N. (2008) 'False discoveries: winners and losers in mutual fund performance', *European Financial Management*.

[11] Booth, D. (2001) 'Index and enhanced index funds', www.dfaus.com/library/articles/index_enhanced_funds/.

[12] French, K.R. (2008) 'The cost of active investing', http://ssrn.com/abstract=1105775.

[13] Ibid.

[14] Ibid.

[15] http://johncbogle.com/speeches/JCB_FAJ2005.pdf.

[16] Ibid

[17] Ibid.

[18] Ibid.

Chapter 2

[1] Fama, E. (1965) 'Random walks in stock market prices', *Financial Analysts Journal*, September–October.

[2] Lo, A.W. and MacKinlay, A.C. (1999) *A Non-Random Walk Down Wall Street*, Princeton University Press, New Jersey, N.J.

[3] Dimson, E. and Mussavian, M. (1998) 'A brief history of market efficiency', *European Financial Management*, Vol. 4, No. 1, pp. 91–193.

[4] Quoted in Dimson and Mussavian (1998).

[5] Malkiel, B. (1973) *A Random Walk Down Wall Street*, W. W. Norton & Co., London.

[6] Samuelson, P. (1965) 'Proof that properly anticipated prices fluctuate randomly', *Industrial Management Review*, Vol. 6, No. 2.

[7] See note 1.

[8] Fama, E. (1970) 'Efficient capital markets: a review of theory and empirical work', *The Journal of Finance*, Vol. 25, No. 2.

[9] Fama, E. (2003) 'The Efficient Market Hypothesis and its critics', *Journal of Economic Perspectives*, Vol. 17, No. 1.

[10] Fama, E., Fisher, L., Jensen, M. and Roll, R. (1969) 'The adjustment of stock prices to new information', *International Economic Review*, Vol. 10, pp. 1–21.

[11] Jensen, M. (1968) 'The performance of mutual funds in the period 1955–1964', *Journal of Finance*, Vol. 23, pp. 389–416.

[12] See note 3.

[13] See note 2.

[14] Malkiel, B. (2003) 'The Efficient Market Hypothesis and its critics', CEPS Working Paper No. 91, Princeton University, New Jersey, NJ.

[15] Shiller, R.J. (2000) *Irrational Exuberance*, Princeton University Press, New Jersey, NJ.

[16] Vanguard (2003) 'Sources of portfolio performance: the enduring importance of asset allocation', July, https://institutional.vanguard.com/iip/pdf/icr_asset_allocation.pdf.

[17] See note 14.

[18] Fama, E.F. and French, K.R. (1992) 'The cross-section of expected stock returns', *Journal of Finance*, Vol. 47, No. 2, pp. 427–465.

[19] www.dfaus.com/philosophy/dimensions/.

[20] DeBondt, W.F.M. and Thaler, R. (1995) 'Financial decision-making in markets and firms: a behavioural perspective', in Jarrow, R.A., Maksimovic, V. and Ziemba, W.T. (eds) *Handbooks in Operations Research and Management Science: Finance*, Elsevier, Amsterdam, pp. 385–410.

[21] Quoted in Malkiel, B. (2003) 'The Efficient Market Hypothesis and its critics', *Journal of Economic Perspectives*, Vol. 17, No. 1, pp. 59–82.

[22] Ibid.

[23] Fama, E. (2000) 'The new indexing', at www.dfaus.com/library/articles/new_indexing/.

[24] See note 14.

[25] Fluck, Z. Malkiel, B. and Quandt, R. (1997) 'The predictability of stock returns: a cross-sectional simulation', *Review of Economics and Statistics*, Vol. 79, No. 2, pp. 176–183.

[26] Schwert, G.W. (2001) 'Anomalies and market efficiency', University of Rochester Simon School Working Paper No. FR 02-13.

[27] Roll, R. and Shiller, R. (1992) 'Comments: Symposium on Volatility in U.S. and Japanese Stock Markets', *Journal of Applied Corporate Finance*, Vol. 5, No. 1, pp. 25–29.

[28] See note 14.

[29] Lummer, S. and Riepe, M. (1994) 'The role of asset allocation in modern portfolio management', in Lederman, J. and Klein, R.A. (eds) *Global Asset Allocation: Techniques for Optimizing Portfolio Management*, John Wiley and Sons, Chichester.

[30] Brinson, G.P., Singer, B.D. and Beebower, G.L. (1991) Determinants of portfolio performance II: an update', *The Financial Analysts Journal*, Vol. 47, No. 3, p. 40.

Chapter 3

[1] Abstract—The Case for Indexing: European- and Offshore-Domiciled Funds, Vanguard Investment Counseling & Research, https://advisors.vanguard.com/iwe/pdf/ICRICIS.pdf.

[2] Malkiel, B. (1973) *A Random Walk Down Wall Street*, W. W. Norton & Co., London.

[3] Hebner, M.T. (2006) *Index Funds: The 12 step program for active investors*, IFA Publishing, Newport Beach, CA.

[4] Quoted at www.ifa.com/book/book_pdf/02_nobel_laureates.pdf.

[5] Fama, E. (2000) 'The new indexing', http://www.dfaus.com/library/articles/new_indexing/.

[6] Burgess, G., 'Are equal weighted indexes better than market cap weighted indexes?' at http://www.dfaus.com/library/articles/new_indexing/.

[7] Choueifaty, Y. and Coignard, Y. (2008) 'Towards maximum diversification', *Journal of Portfolio Management*, Vol. 35, No. 1, pp. 40–51.

[8] Richards, A. (2002) *All About Exchange Traded Funds*, McGraw-Hill.

[9] Ibid.

[10] www.amex.com.

[11] State Street Advisors (2011) 'ETF trading and execution in the European markets', research paper.

[12] Costandinides, C. (2011) *Deutsche Bank Global Index Research*, July.

[13] Ibid.

[14] See note 1.

Chapter 4

[1] Rogers, J. (2004) *Hot Commodities*, Random House.

[2] Gorton, G.B. and Rouwenhorst, K.G. (2005) 'Facts and Fantasies about Commodity Futures', Yale ICF Working Paper No. 04-20.

[3] Ibid.

[4] Bernstein, W. (2002) *The Four Pillars of Investing: lessons for building a winning portfolio,* McGraw-Hill Professional.

Chapter 5

[1] Costandinides, C. (2011) 'In the EFT labyrinth where does the thread begin?', *EFT Research – Industry Perspective,* 7 July.

Chapter 6

[1] Fama, E. and French, K. (1992) 'The cross-section of expected stock returns', *The Journal of Finance,* Vol. 48, No. 2.

[2] Bernstein, W. from his website http://www.efficientfrontier.com/ef/702/3FM-10.htm.

[3] Arnott, R. and Hsu., J. (2005) 'Fundamental indexation', *Financial Analysts Journal*, Vol. 67, No. 2, pp. 83–99.

[4] Ibid.

[5] Ibid.

[6] Ibid.

[7] Siegel, J. (2009) 'The stock market's little shop of horrors: and you thought the aftermath of 1929 was grim', *The Journal of Investing*, Vol. 18, No. 2, pp. 6–12.

[8] Smith, T. (1996) *Accounting for Growth: Stripping the Camouflage from Company Accounts*, Century Business.

[9] Siegel, J. (1994) *Stocks for the Long Run, The Definitive Guide to Financial Market Returns and Long-term Investment Strategies*, Irwin Professional Publishing, Burr Ridge, IL.

[10] Arnott, R.D., Hsu, J.C. and West, J.M. (2008) *The Fundamental Index: A Better Way to Invest*, Wiley.

Chapter 8

[1] Keynes, J.M. (1936) *The General Theory of Employment, Interest and Money*, Harcourt Brace and Co., New York.

Chapter 10

[1] Merriman, P. and Buck, R., available online at www.fundadvice.com/articles/market-timing/one-portfolio-for-life.html.

[2] Ibid.

[3] Ibid.

[4] Smith Barney, 'The art of rebalancing: How to tell when your portfolio needs a tune-up', available online at www.asaecenter.org/files/ArtofRebalancing.pdf.

[5] Vanguard, 'Portfolio rebalancing in theory and practice', available online at https://institutional.vanguard.com/iip/pdf/ICRRebalancing.pdf.

[6] Ibid.

[7] www.seekingalpha.com.

[8] DeMuth, P. and Stein, B. (2009) *Yes, You Can Supercharge Your Portfolio!*, Hay House.

[9] Ibid.

[10] Ibid.

[11] Daryanani, G. (2008) 'Opportunistic rebalancing: a new paradigm for wealth managers', *Journal of Financial Planning*, January.

[12] Ibid.

[13] Schwab Center for Investment Research (2000) 'The costs and benefits of waiting to invest', Vol. 3, No. 1.

[14] Graham, J.R. and Harvey, C.R. (1995) 'Market timing ability and volatility implied in investment newsletters' asset allocation recommendations', available at http://ssrn.com/abstract=6006.

[15] Morningstar article available at www.ifa.com/archives/articles/staff_20020315_morningstar_study_confirms_virtues_of_buy_and_hold_in_bearmarket.asp.

[16] Graham, B. (1986) *The Intelligent Investor: A Book of Practical Counsel*, Harper & Row.

[17] Pesaran, H. and Timmermann, A. (2000) 'A recursive modelling approach to predicting UK stock returns', *The Economic Journal, January*.

[18] Hendry, H. (2008), available at http://uk.reuters.com/article/idUKLNE4AK05B20081121.

[19] Mauldin, J., 'While Rome Burns', available online at www.investorsinsight.com/blogs/thoughts_from_the_frontline/archive/2009/02/20/while-rome-burns.aspx.

[20] Faber, M. (2007) 'A quantitative approach to tactical asset allocation', *Journal of Wealth Management*, Spring.

[21] Bond, T. (2008) Barclays Equity Gilt Study.

[22] Britton, J., quoted in *Investors Chronicle*. [still searching for this one]

[23] Ibid.

[24] See www.share.com.

[25] FTSE data are available through Sharescope.

[26] Available at https://advisors.vanguard.com/iwe/pdf/ICRIBM.pdf.

[27] Ibid.

[28] Farrell, P. (2004) *The Lazy Person's Guide to Investing*, Warner Business Books.

[29] Bernstein, W. (2002) *The Four Pillars of Investing: Lessons for Building a Winning Portfolio*, McGraw-Hill.

[30] Lowell, J. (2006) *What Every Fidelity Investor Needs to Know*, Wiley.

[31] Schultheis, B. (2005) *The Coffeehouse Investor*, Palouse Press.

[32] https://institutional.vanguard.com/iam/pdf/IAM_Lifecycle_funds.pdf.

[33] www.cpmkts.com/.

[34] Ibid.

[35] www.mscibarra.com/products/indices/us/index.jsp.

[36] BlackRock (2011) ETF Landscape: Global Handbook – Q1 2011, http://www.blackrockinternational.com

[37] See http://www.fsa.gov.uk/pubs/cp/cp09_18.pdf.

[38] Brinson, G. P. Hood, l. R. and Beebower, G. L. (1986) 'Determinants of Portfolio Performance', *The Financial Analysts Journal*, July/Aug; and (1991) 'Determinants of Portfolio Performance II – and update', *The Financial Analysts Journal*, Vol. 47, No. 3.

[39] Ibbotson, R. G. and Kaplan, P. D. (2000) 'Does Asset Allocation Policy Explain 40%, 90%, or 100% of Performance?', *The Financial Analysts Journal*, Jan/Feb.

[40] Markowitz, H. M. (1959) 'Portfolio Selection: Efficient Diversification of Investments', *Journal of Finance*.

[41] Published in Bergstresser, D. and Poterba, J. (2000) 'Do After-Tax Returns Affect Mutual Fund Inflows?', Working Paper 7595, National Bureau of Economic Research, http://www.nber.org/papers/w7595.pdf

[42] IMA (2010) *Asset Management in the UK 2009–10*, annual survey, July.

[43] http://www.investmentfunds.org.uk/

Chapter 11

[1] Mauldin, J. (2009) 'While Rome burns', available online at www.investorsinsight.com/blogs/thoughts_from_the_frontline/archive/2009/02/20/while-rome-burns.aspx.

[2] Ibid.

[3] Attié, A.P. and Roache, S.K. (2009) 'Inflation hedging for long-term investors', IMF Working Paper No. 09/90, April.

Index

absolute return funds 285
accounts 173
active ETFs 89
active funds 5-12, 141-2, 193
   absolute return 285
   average fund lag 12
   bear market performance 257-8
   below-average managers 254
   bonds 7
   comparing 142
   costs 9-12, 24, 141, 187, 240
   emerging markets 370-1
   fund-of-fund managers 254, 258-9
   hot funds 206
   marketing 208
   multi-asset 285
   performance to benchmarks 6-8, 24, 142-3, 257-8
   star managers 2, 29, 286
   style drift 280
   survivorship bias 142
   turnover ratio 9, 247
administrators 63
Advance Developing Markets (ADD) 370
advantages of tracker funds 15
Adventurous Portfolio 306-9
advisers 4
Africa 437-43
agency businesses 170
agriculture
   commodities 129

DJ-UBS Agriculture index 377-82
   farmland 217-18
AIG 136
All Share index 330-4
All Stocks Gilt index 338-41
all-in-one fund 274-6
allocation of resources 23
alpha return 41, 179
alternative assets 42-3, 222, 297
American Stock Exchange (AMEX) 61
anti-benchmarking 59-60
Arbitrage Pricing Theory 7
arbitraging 68
Arnott, R. 156, 158, 168, 172
Asia Pacific Select Dividend 181
asset allocation 194, 197-200, 278, 280-1
asset class investing 2-4, 29
   number of asset classes 286, 289
attitudes to risk 241, 287, 302
authorised participants 63, 66
average fund lag 12

Bachelier, L. 20-1
backwardation 121, 129, 145
bandwagon effect 27
banking sector 256
Barber, S. 209, 297-8
Barclays 55
   Equity Gilt Study 190-1
baskets of commodities 101
bear ETFs 89-101, 145, 329
   commodities 119, 128

bear markets
  and active funds 257–8
  and index investing 254, 255–6, 259
  and momentum strategies 214
  safe harbour assets 320
  value stocks 385
beating the market 38
behavioural bias 238–40
below-average managers 254
benchmarks 115, 144
  active fund performance 6–8, 24, 142–3, 257–8
Bernstein, W. 135, 155, 261, 313
beta plus ETFs 89
beta return 41, 42, 179
bid-offer spreads 66, 106–7
big theme investing 209–22
  alternative assets 42–3, 222
  biofuels 218
  brand trends 169, 221
  bubbles 212–13
  business cycle 201–11
  climate change 218
  consumer goods 211
  decoupling 215
  fads 215
  farmland 217–18
  globalisation 215–16
  green investing 220, 423–8
  infrastructure 218–19, 300–1, 323, 403–8
  market cycle 201–11
  nuclear power 220–1
  renewable energy 220, 423–8
  sector rotation 210–11
  security 221
  technology companies 212
  urbanisation 218
  water 219, 389–94
biofuels 218
BlackRock 13, 78, 81
blended indices 172–3

Blue Sky Asset Management 133
BNP Paribas 120
Bogle, J. 10–11, 54–5, 58, 205
bombed-out shares 30, 31–2
bonds *see* fixed interest
book value indices 169–70
Booth, D. 55
BP 162
brand names 169, 221
Brazil 373–4, 408–13
breadth indicators 227, 229
Brent oil 117, 128, 443–7
BRIC funds 373–4
Britton, J. 254–5
Brooks, N. 135
bubbles 212–13
Buck, R. 242, 267
Buffett, W. 28–9, 38, 162
Burgess, G. 58–9
Burns, S. 265
business cycle 201–11
buy-and-hold strategy 246, 277–8
buying and selling ETFs 283

capital asset pricing model (CAPM) 34, 36–7, 277
Capital Markets Index 274–5
capturing the index 54–60
carbon emissions 220
Carhart, M.M. 6, 7
cash 291, 319
  money market funds 361–4
cash flow-based indices 171
charts *see* technical analysis
China 216, 218, 219
  funds 399–403
choosing an index 110
Cisco 256
Claymore 101, 275
clean energy 220, 423–8
climate change 218
Close 120

closing a fund 112
Coe, T. 214
Coffeehouse Portfolio 265–6
commodities super-cycle 137
commodity companies 169, 170
commodity-based index funds 42–3, 101, 103–4, 116–37, 221–2
    agricultural 129, 377–82
    basket funds 101
    composite return 127
    concentration of ownership 134
    concentration rules 144
    correlations 118, 133
    custodians 146
    diversification 118, 133, 216
    futures ETCs 119, 120–4, 129, 136, 144–5
    gold 10–1, 117, 131, 134, 319, 320, 447–50
    growth 117, 135
    indices 124–5, 144–5
    inflation proofing 119, 133
    inverse ETCs 119, 128
    leveraged ETCs 119, 128
    oil 117, 128, 211, 443–7
    physical ETCs 119, 129, 136, 144
    and private investors 136
    production-weighted benchmark 124
    returns 118, 122, 130–2
        calculating 145
    risks 118, 119, 129
    roll yield 121–4, 135, 145
    silver 131
    spot prices 120, 129, 131
    structures 119–20, 128–9, 135
    sub-groups 128
    technical analysis 236
    volatility 118, 119, 129
composite return 127
compound effect of costs 11
concentration of ownership 134
concentration rules 144

Considine, G. 11–12, 41, 43
consumer goods 211
contango 121, 129, 145
contrarian approach 34
core-satellite strategy 252, 254, 279
corporate bonds *see* fixed interest
correlations 118, 133, 216
costs
    active funds 9–12, 24, 141, 187, 240
    dealing costs 53, 141, 152
    ETFs 106, 108, 111–14, 143, 146–7, 151–2
    hedge funds 9–10
    index investing 53, 58, 112–14
    and returns 11, 192
    stamp duty 143, 144
Cottee, J. 101, 138
Couch Potato Portfolio 265
counterparty risk 74, 105, 139, 140, 147–52
Coward's Portfolio 261
CRB Commodity Index 125
creation and redemption of ETF shares 67
credit risk 144, 199
currencies 236
custodians 63, 146
cyclical shares 211

Daryanani, G. 245
data providers 63
Davies, R. 153, 154, 155, 165
day trading 212
dealing costs 53, 141, 152
    see also costs
DeBondt, W. 31–2
debt 191, 213
decoupling 215
DeMuth, P. 243–4
depositary trusts 61–2, 63
Deutsche Bank 81, 86
    Liquid Commodity Index 125

Di Teresa, P. 247
DIAMONDS 64
diffusion of information 27
Dillow, C. 269
Dimensional Fund Advisors 175
Dimson, E. 21, 24
discipline 193, 207
discounts and premiums 67
distress risk 30, 31
diversification 2, 12, 29, 41–3, 214–15, 266–7, 312
　anti-benchmarking 59–60
　and commodities 118, 133, 216
　correlation 118, 133, 216
　equity diversification 201–3
　international 201–2, 216–17, 267, 290, 305
　number of asset classes 286, 289
Dividend Plus ETF 159, 161, 180, 382–7
dividend-weighted indexes 159–60, 161, 162, 171–2, 177–81
dividends 32–3, 307–8, 384–7
　ETFs 109, 112
　high-yielding stocks 32–3, 385
　reinvestment 171, 386–7
　see also income funds
DJ EuroStoxx 50 funds 180, 355–61
DJ-UBS Agriculture index 377–82
DJ-UBS Commodity Index 124–5
Dogs of the Dow Strategy 33
Dorchester Fund Management 274
Dow Jones Industrial Average 46, 436
　1929 Crash 250
duration 200

Eclectica 249
efficient frontier 259, 260
Efficient Markets Hypothesis (EMH) 16, 19, 22–40, 165, 277
　bandwagon effect 27
　criticisms 27–9
　diffusion of information 27
　emerging markets 26
　Grossman-Stiglitz paradox 28
　high-yielding stocks 32–3
　insider trading 24
　key attributes 23–4
　and market outperformance 28–9
　overreaction to information 28
　post-event continuation 28
　price-cash flow multiples 33
　price-earnings multiples 33
　private equity 26
　rational market participants 25–6, 28, 38–9
　semistrong efficiency 25
　smaller companies 29–31
　strong form efficiency 24, 25
　underreaction to information 27, 28
　value premium 30–1
　weak efficient markets 24, 25
ELEMENTS ETN 119
emerging markets 26, 216, 290, 296, 322
　active funds 370–1
　bonds 315
　BRIC funds 373–4
　China 399–403
　Far East ex Japan 368
　frontier markets 437–43
　income funds 181, 182–3, 387–9
　infrastructure funds 407
　Latin America 408–13
　MSCI Emerging Markets index 364–71
　returns 370
　single-country funds 371, 372
　smaller company funds 371–2
energy trackers
　clean energy 220, 423–8
　oil 117, 128, 211, 443–7
equal weighted indexes 58–9
equity asset allocation 194–6
equity diversification 201–3

Equity Gilt Study 190–1
equity income *see* income funds
equity returns *see* returns
equity risk premium 192
ETF Securities 117, 129
ethanol 218
EURO STOXX 180, 355–61
European ETF market 85–7
European funds 355–61
  income 387–9
event studies 24
Evolve Financial Planning 186
exchange traded commodities (ETCs)
    see commodity-based index funds
exchange traded funds (ETFs)
  active funds 89
  arbitraging 68
  bear funds 89–101, 145
  benchmarks 115
  beta plus funds 89
  bid-offer spreads 66, 106–7
  buying and selling 283
  choosing 312
  closing a fund 112
  compared to mutual funds 69–70, 103, 104, 143–5
  costs 106, 108, 111–14, 143, 146–7, 151–2
  creation and redemption of shares 67
  definition 64–5
  depositary trusts 61–2, 63
  DIAMONDS 64
  dividend payments 109, 112
  European market 85–7
  exotic beta funds 87
  history 60–4
  index participation shares 64
  leveraged funds 89–101, 145
  liquidity 106–7
  market growth 81–5, 139, 284
  multi ETF portfolio funds 101

  net asset value (NAV) 66
  OTC (over-the-counter) markets 107
  parties involved 63
  physical replication 67, 70, 102, 104–5
  premiums and discounts 67
  profits for providers 110–12, 139
  reference basket 148–52
  regulation and reporting 114–15, 140, 145–6
  semi-active funds 89
  short-selling 63
  SPIDER 61–4
  stock lending 78–81, 102, 106, 143, 147–8
  structures 88
  SuperTrusts 62
  synthetic replication 71–5, 85–6, 102–5, 139–40, 148–52
    see also counterparty risk
  taxation 107–8, 143–4, 280, 281
  TIPs 64
  total return structure 112, 281
  transparency 114
  undivided interest 62
  workings 65–70
  World Equity Benchmark Shares (WEBS) 64
  see also tracking error
exchange traded notes (ETNs) 103–4, 139, 146
exchange traded products (ETPs) 103–4, 139–40, 145–6
exotic beta ETFs 87

Faber, M. 251
fads 215
Fama, E. 19, 23, 24–5, 30, 33, 58, 155, 175, 259
Far East ex Japan 368
farmland 217–18
  see also agriculture

Farrell, P. 260
fashionable sectors 166-7
fat tail events 22
Feriani, S. 370-1
Fibonacci extensions 235
financial compensation service (FCS) 105, 282
financial independence 187
financial planning 187-90, 281
First Index Investment Trust 54-5
fixed interest
   active bond funds 7, 315
   asset allocation 194, 196
   bond indices 144, 160-1, 315, 338-41, 344
   corporate bonds 290, 296-7, 300, 322
      iShares bond funds 341-5, 451-7
   emerging market bonds 315
   government bonds 296-7, 299-300, 321-2
      main ETFs 338-41
   index-linked 297, 300, 319, 322, 340
   international 291, 315
   junk bonds 315
   Lazy Portfolio 314-16
   managed funds 7, 315
   technical analysis 236
Fledgling index 334, 348
Fletcher, J. 7
forecast data 172-3
forestry 420-2
free float adjustment 47, 327
French, K. 9, 30, 155, 175
Fresnillo 154, 166
frontier markets 437-43
FTSE 100 index 45-51, 325-30
   changes over time 154, 255-6, 326
   choice of funds 328-9
   constituents 48-51, 162
   entry tests 46
   ETF 75-8, 79, 80
   free float adjustment 47, 327
   inverse trackers 329
   key facts 46-8, 325-30
   rebalancing 154, 326
   suitability for tracking 327-8
   weighting of shares 326-7
FTSE 250 index 334-8
FTSE All Share index 330-4
FTSE All Stocks Gilt index 338-41
FTSE Fledgling index 334
FTSE Group 46
FTSE Small Cap index 345-50
FTSE World exc UK index 350-5
fund-of-fund managers 254, 258-9
fundadvice.com 263
fundamental analysis 23
fundamental indexing 33, 153-85, 290
   blended indices 172-3
   book value indices 169-70
   cash flow-based indices 171
   Dimensional Fund Advisors 175
   dividend indexes 159-60, 161, 162, 171-2, 177-81
   forecast data 172-3
   historic data 172-3
   Munro fund 159, 161, 163, 164, 177-8, 181-2, 329-30
   performance 184-5
   profit-based indices 170-1
   RAFI indices 156-9, 163, 182
   Research Affiliates 176-7
   revenue-based indices 170
   value bias 161-2
   Wisdom Tree 159, 175-6
Fundamental Tracker Investment Management 153, 177-8
funded swap structure 73
futures ETCs 119, 120-4, 129, 136, 144-5

geared funds 89-101, 145
   commodities 119, 128
gifts 190

gilts *see* fixed interest
global bonds 291, 315
global funds 64, 350-5, 352
   Clean Energy 423-8
   Growth Portfolio 291-4
   Select Dividend 181
globalisation 215-16
Glowrey, M. 214
goals 191
gold 10-1, 117, 131, 134, 319, 320, 447-50
government bonds 296-7, 299-300, 321-2
   gilt index 338-41
Graham, B. 14, 34, 248
Grantham, J. 162
greater fool theory 213
green investing 220, 423-8
Grossman-Stiglitz paradox 28
growth portfolios 291-4, 306-9, 323-4
growth stocks 30, 155, 167, 365-6
Gruber, M.J. 6

Hang Seng 401-2
HardAssetsInvestor.com 121-3
hedge funds 134, 140, 218, 249, 297
   costs 9-10
Henderson Fledgling Trust 348
Hendry, H. 249
high-yielding stocks 32-3, 385
   see also dividends
Hince, J. 276-84
historic data 172-3
history of ETFs 60-4
Hong Kong 401-2
hot funds 206
Hsu, J. 156

Ibbotson Associates 42, 117-18, 278
iBoxx Sterling Corporate Bond 451-7
IFAs (Independent Financial Advisers) 276-84, 285

income funds 290, 387-9
   Asia Pacific Select Dividend 181
   Dividend Aristocrat 160, 162, 183
   dividend-weighted indexes 159-60, 161, 162, 171-2, 177-81
   Emerging Markets Dividend Index 182-3
   Equity Income index 159, 161, 163, 164, 179-80
   Global Select Dividend 181
   Income Portfolio 298-301
   UK Dividend Plus 159, 161, 180, 382-7
index investing 30-3, 52-60
   anti-benchmarking 59-60
   bear markets 254, 255-6, 259
   bond indices 144, 160-1, 315, 338-41, 344
   capturing the index 54-60
   choosing an index 110
   commodity indices 124-5, 144-5
   costs 53, 58, 112-14
   equal weights 58-9
   fashionable sectors 166-7
   index providers 63
   market capitalisation 39-40, 53, 165-8, 257, 277
   momentum bias 154
   perfect index 40-1, 54
   rules-based indices 166, 175
   sampling 58
   subjective indices 166
   value judgements 154
   volatility weighting 59
   see also tracking error
index participation shares 64
index-linked gilts 297, 300, 319, 322, 340
industry analysis 228-32
inflation 269, 290, 297, 316
   and commodities 119, 133
   Lazy Portfolio 316-20

infrastructure funds 218–19, 300–1, 323, 403–8
insider trading 24
interest rate changes 27
international bonds 291, 315
international diversification 201–2, 216–17, 267, 290, 305
  European funds 355–61, 387–9
  global funds 64, 350–5, 352
  Japanese funds 374–7
  United States 46, 54–7, 428–37
  see also emerging markets
inverse funds 89–101, 145, 329
  commodities 119, 128
Investing 2.0 1–3
Investment Management Association (IMA) 284
investment managers 63
Investors Intelligence 227
iRebal 245
iShares 13, 78, 80, 87, 101, 148
  bond funds 341–5, 451–7
  target risk portfolios 271–3, 303–4
  UK Dividend Plus 159, 161, 180, 382–7
Islamic index 413–19

Jackman, D. 243
January Effect 35
Japanese funds 374–7
Jensen, M. 6, 24
Jones, R. 168
junk bonds 315

Kaplan, P. 278
Kendall, M. 21–2
Keynes, John Maynard 212, 251
Kinnel, R. 205
Kiplinger 266
Kirk, C. 264
Kirk Report 263

Latin America 408–13
Lazy Portfolios 260–6, 313–24
leveraged funds 89–101, 145
  commodities 119, 128
lifecycle approach 187–90, 268–74, 287
LifeStrategy 273
liquidity 106–7
Lo, A. 19, 27
Low Risk Portfolio 294–8
Lyxor 86, 125

MacKinlay, C. 19, 27
McQuown 55
Malkiel, B. 19, 22, 23, 27, 29, 35, 54
management of portfolios 312
market capitalisation weights 39–40, 53, 165–8, 257, 277
market cycle 201–11
market growth 81–5, 139, 284
market risk 112
market timing 42, 203–7, 240, 246–51, 312
marketing active funds 208
MarketWatch 260
Markowitz, H. 42, 259, 278
Mauldin, J. 250, 307
mean reversion 34–5, 167, 239
measure rule 235
Merriman, P. 242, 263, 267
Mid Risk Portfolio 302–6
Miller, Bill 2, 254
mind of the market 39–40
minimum variance concept 59
Minsky, H. 213
MINT PIMCO ETF 364
modern portfolio theory 41, 259, 278, 287
momentum bias 154
momentum investing 20, 27, 28, 162, 213–14
  bear markets 214
  technical indicators 226

money market trackers 361–4
money-weighted returns 204–5
Montier, J. 27, 32, 37, 238–9
Morningstar 205, 247
moving averages 227, 251, 312
MSCI Emerging Markets index 364–71
MSCI Japan index 374–7
MSCI World Index 352–3
MSCI World Islamic index 413–19
multi ETF portfolio 101
multi-asset funds 285
Munro fund 159, 161, 163, 164, 177–8, 181–2, 329–30
Mussavian, M. 21, 24
mutual funds, compared to ETFs 69–70, 103, 104, 143–5

NASDAQ 61
NEST pension scheme 156
net asset value (NAV) 66
new energy 220
New York Stock Exchange (NYSE) 61
news 21
Nikkei 225 index 374–7
No-Brainer Portfolio 261, 313–14
Norman, D. 101, 138
Norton, J. 186, 239, 294
nuclear power 220–1
number of asset classes 286, 289

objectives of portfolios 191, 193, 208
oil 117, 128, 211, 443–7
optimised portfolios 259, 279, 287
Osborne, M.F.M. 22
O'Shaughnessy, J. 349
OTC (over-the-counter) markets 107
overbought/oversold indicators 226
overreaction to information 28
overtrading 9, 239–40

past price movements 19
path dependent returns 145

pensions 189
perfect index 40–1, 54
performance *see* returns
Pesaran, H. 248
pharmaceutical companies 169
Philips, C. 257
physical ETCs 119, 129, 136, 144
physical replication 67, 70, 102, 104–5
Pimco 117, 364
portfolios 186–208
　all-in-one fund 274–6
　asset allocation 194, 197–9, 199–200, 278, 280–1
　behavioural bias 238–40
　core-satellite strategy 252, 254, 279
　discipline 193, 207
　equities 194–6, 201–3
　fixed interest 194, 196
　goals 191
　lifecycle approach 187–90, 268–74, 287
　management rules 312
　market timing 203–7, 240, 246–51, 312
　objectives 191, 193, 208
　optimised portfolios 259, 279, 287
　overtrading 239–40
　reason for investing 190–1
　rebalancing 207–8, 240, 241–6, 312
　risk 194–7
　simple approach 259–66
　standard deviation 198
　switching rules 251
　target date funds 269–70, 271
　target risk funds 270, 271
post-event continuation 28
Powershares 119, 157, 161
premiums and discounts 67
price targets 235
price-cash flow multiples 33
price-earnings multiples 33
price-reversal strategies 34

private equity 26
production-weighted benchmark 124
profit-based indices 170–1
profits for ETF providers 110–12, 139
property trackers 305–6, 394–9
public-private partnerships 218

RAFI indices 156–9, 163, 182
Random Walk theory 19, 20–4
range of ETFs 13–14
rational market participants 25–6, 28, 38–9
RBS 92
Reaganomics 212
real estate 305–6, 394–9
reason for investing 190–1
rebalancing 207–8, 240, 241–6, 312
redemption of ETF shares 67
reference basket 148–52
registrars 63
regulation and reporting 109, 114–15, 140, 145–6
reinvestment of dividends 171
relative charts 232–4
Relative Strength Index (RSI) 226
renewable energy 220, 423–8
Research Affiliates 156, 176–7
resistance levels 224–5
resource allocation 23
retirement 264, 269
returns
    active funds 6–8, 24, 142–3
    asset-weighted 11
    commodities 118, 122, 130–2, 145
    and costs 11, 192
    emerging markets 370
    from equities 191, 195, 197–8
    fundamental indexing 184–5
    money-weighted 204–5
    reinvestment of dividends 171
    and risk 29–30, 35, 36–7, 194, 252, 278
    time-weighted 204–5

revenue-based indices 170
Richards, A. 62
risk
    attitudes to 241, 287, 302
    commodities 118, 119, 129
    counterparty risk 74, 105, 139, 140, 147–52
    credit risk 144, 199
    distress risk 30, 31
    fat tail events 22
    Low Risk Portfolio 294–8
    market risk 112
    Mid Risk Portfolio 302–6
    portfolio construction 194–7
    and reward 29–30, 35, 36–7, 194, 252, 278
    size risk 29–30
    stock specific risk 279–80
Risk On Risk Off Portfolios 320–3
risk premium 192
risk-free return 41, 192
    SONIA rate 362
Rogers International Commodity Index 125
Rogers, J. 116, 137, 221–2
Roll, R. 35
roll yield 121–4, 135, 145
rules-based indices 166, 175
Russell 2000 index 347, 436

S&P 500 index 46, 54–7, 428–37
S&P Dividend Aristocrat 160, 162, 183
S&P Global Clean Energy 423–8
S&P Goldman Sachs Commodity Index 124
S&P Select Frontier Markets 437–43
safe harbour assets 320
sampling 58, 109
Samuelson, P. 22–3
scale effect 30
Schmalenberger, W. 275
Schneider, L. 205

Schultheis, W. 265-6
Schwarz, J. 175
Schwert, G. 35
sector rotation 210-11, 229-32
security 221
selling ETFs 283
semi-active ETFs 89
semistrong efficiency 25
Sharia investing 413-19
Sharpe, W. 259
Shiller, R. 27, 35, 39
short-selling ETFs 63
Shoven, J. 280
Siegel, J. 32, 159, 168, 172, 176
silver 131
Sinquefield, R. 6, 55
size risk 29-30
smaller companies 29-31, 155, 202-3, 308
  advantages 348-50
  emerging markets 371-2
  FTSE 250 index 334-8
  FTSE Fledgling index 334
  FTSE Small Cap index 345-50
  Henderson Fledgling Trust 348
  MSCI UK Smaller Companies tracker 347
  RBS HGSC tracker 347
  risk factors 58, 350
  United States 347, 436
Smart Beta 179
Smith, Terry 173
SONIA index 362
Sower's Growth Portfolio 265
SPIDER 61-4
spot prices 120, 129, 131
stamp duty 143, 144
standard deviation 198
star fund managers 2, 29, 286
State Street 62, 148, 161, 284
Stein, B. 243-4, 264
Steinberg, J. 176

Steinberg, M. 176
Stiglitz paradox 28
stock lending 78-81, 102, 106, 143, 147-8
stock selection 2
stock specific risk 279-80
stop losses 234-5
strategic market timing 248
strategy 1-2
strong form efficiency 24, 25
structures
  commodity funds 119-20, 128-9, 135
  ETFs 88
style drift 280
subjective indices 166
SuperTrusts 62
support levels 224-5
survivorship bias 142
swap-based ETFs *see* synthetic replication
Swenson, D. 42, 208, 262
switching rules 251
synthetic replication 71-5, 85-6, 102-5, 139-40, 148-52
  counterparty risk 74, 105, 139, 140, 147-52

tactical market timing 248
target date funds 269-70, 271
target risk portfolios 270, 271-3, 303-4
Tate and Lyle 154, 166
taxation 107-8, 143-4, 171, 280, 281
TCF Investment 138, 140-1
TD Waterhouse 274
technical analysis 23, 27, 223-37
  breadth indicators 227, 229
  commodities 236
  currencies 236
  Fibonacci extensions 235
  fixed interest 236
  golden rules 237

technical analysis (*continued*)
  industry analysis 228–32
  measure rule 235
  momentum indicators 225
  moving averages 227, 251, 312
  overbought/oversold indicators 226
  price targets 235
  relative charts 232–4
  Relative Strength Index (RSI) 226
  resistance levels 224–5
  stop losses 234–5
  support levels 224–5
technology companies 212
TER (total expense ratio) *see* costs
Thaler, R. 31–2
Thatcherism 212
timber 420–2
time-weighted returns 204–5
timing the market 42, 203–7, 240, 246–51, 312
Timmermann, A. 248
TIPs 64
TOBAM 59–60
tolerance-based rebalancing 243–5
Topix index 374–7
Toronto Stock Exchange 64
total return structure 112, 281
total swap return (TSR) *see* synthetic replication
tracking error 58, 70–1, 74, 76, 146–7, 152
  causes 108–10
  limits 312
transfer agents 63
transparency 114
Treasury Bills 196
Treynor, J. 36
turnover ratio 9, 247

UCITS rules 145–6, 150
UK Dividend Plus ETF 159, 161, 180, 382–7

UK Equity Income index 159, 161, 163, 164, 179–80
underreaction to information 27, 28
undivided interest 62
unit investment trusts 62
unit trusts, compared to ETFs 69–70, 103, 104, 143–5
United States 46, 54–7, 428–37
urbanisation 218
US dollar money market ETF 363

value stocks 14, 30–1, 58, 154, 161–2, 167, 202–3, 365–6
  in bear markets 385
Vanguard 54–7, 61, 114, 257
  LifeStrategy 273
  rebalancing portfolios 242–3
  UK Equity Income index 159, 161, 163, 164, 179–80
Virgin Money 254–5
volatility
  commodities 118, 119, 129
  standard deviation 198
  weightings 59

water sector 219, 389–94
weak efficient markets 24, 25
wealth managers 140
Webvan 212
Wells Fargo 55
Wisdom Tree 159, 175–6
withholding tax 108
Woodford, Neil 2
World Equity Benchmark Shares (WEBS) 64
World Index 350–5, 352
  Islamic indices 413–19
WTI (West Texas Intermediate) 444, 447

zero-sum game theory 277